Revolution on My Mind

Revolution on My Mind

WRITING A DIARY UNDER STALIN

Jochen Hellbeck

HARVARD UNIVERSITY PRESS
Cambridge, Massachusetts
London, England
2006

Printed in the United States of America

Library of Congress Cataloging-in-Publication Data

Hellbeck, Jochen.
Revolution on my mind : writing a diary under Stalin / Jochen Hellbeck.
p. cm.
Includes bibliographical references and index.
ISBN 0-674-02174-6 (alk. paper)
1. Soviet Union—Biography. 2. Soviet Union—Politics and government—1936–1953.
3. Russian diaries. 4. Soviet Union—Social conditions.
5. Political persecution—Soviet Union. I. Title.
DK268.A1H45 2006
947.084'2092247—dc22
[B] 2005056708

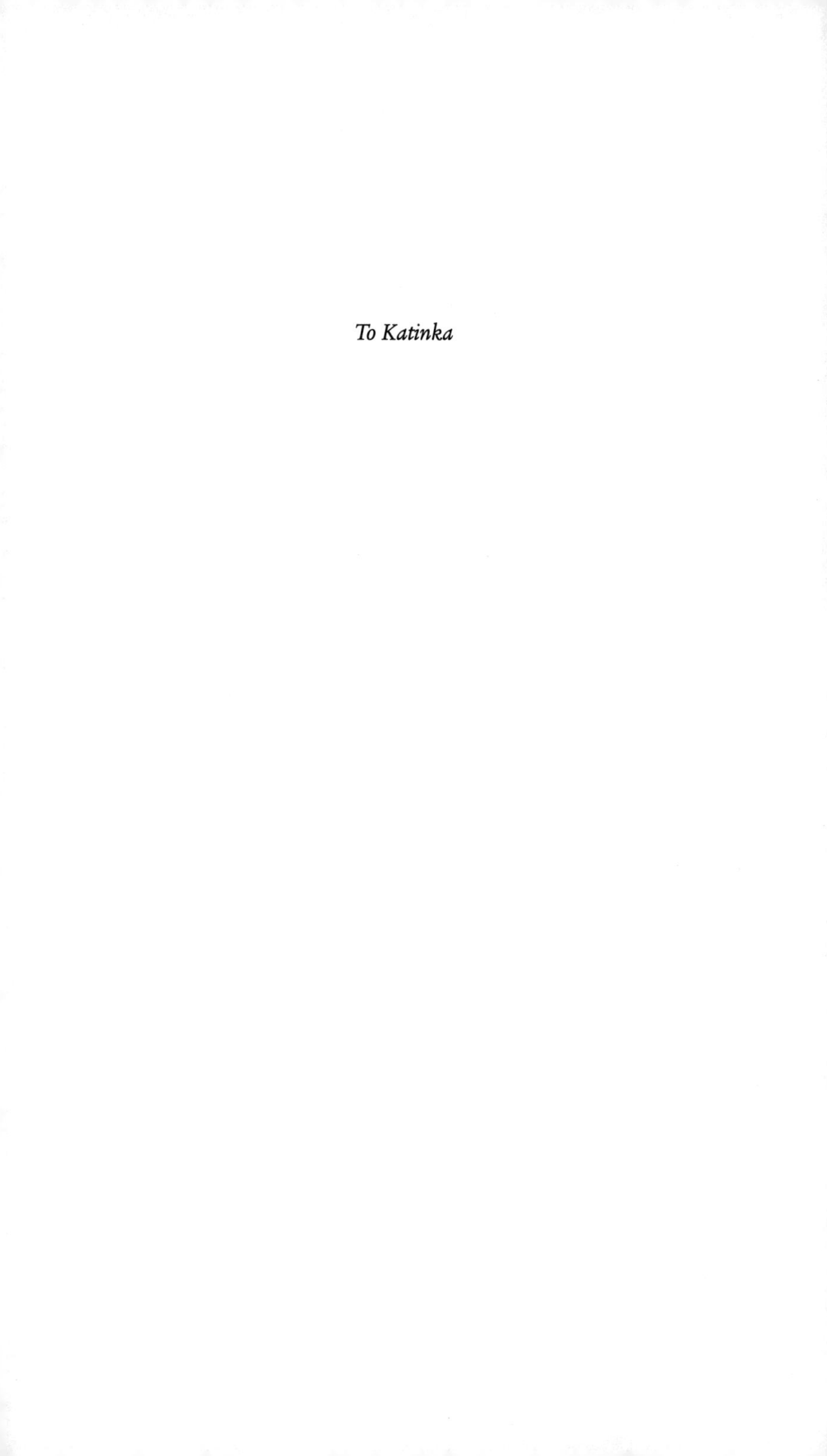

To Katinka

Contents

Preface

I first entered the inner world of Stalin's Russia on a hot August day in 1990. This was during the turning point of perestroika, when Mikhail Gorbachev's liberal reforms began to unravel the Soviet order. For historians, perestroika marked the beginning of an archival revolution: a massive declassification of Communist party records would continue through much of the 1990s, prompting new interpretations of the Soviet past. I had just spent several weeks in Moscow's libraries collecting material for a research project on the fate of Russia's peasants under Stalin. My stay was coming to an end—in a couple of days I would fly back to New York. After the morning steam bath my Russian friends had assured me would counteract the heat of the day, I walked through the streets of the city center in a vaguely energetic mood. A sign on a building caught my eye: People's Archive. After a moment's hesitation, I walked in.

At first I wondered whether I'd made a mistake: I found myself in a seedy shop crammed with cheap transistor radios and pop music tapes. But when I inquired about the archive a shopkeeper directed me to a back room facing a courtyard. Like most archives, it was dark and cool; small barred windows provided the feeblest illumination. Ranks of metal shelves held rows of large gray boxes. The improvised reading room and its battered furniture signaled that enthusiasm rather than generous funding kept this archive open. It turned out that the director was away; his young assistants excitedly told me about their commitment to collecting and preserving the voices of ordinary citizens, which they believed could challenge the oppressive Soviet state and its sway over personal and collective memory.

Soon enough our conversation touched on Stalin's rule. When I talked about my research, one of the archivists pulled from the shelves a box filled with yellowed, dusty notebooks. I opened the notebook lying on top and read the following title: "Work Diary of the '9th-Komsomol-Congress' Brigade and Daily Notes of the Brigadier and Student Stepan Filipovich Podlubny." I read on and was soon absorbed by the story of a young man persecuted by the Soviet regime because his father was a "class enemy." When Podlubny escaped his village and reached Moscow, he managed to conceal his shameful past and passed himself off as a model worker and Communist. The diary revealed a double life fraught with tension and danger; but most remarkably it documented this man's attempts to remake himself—he seemed to yearn to become the person he impersonated.

Some hours later, dazed, I left the archive and reentered the music store, now crowded with customers hungry for goods and experiences long unavailable under Soviet rule. They all appeared to be oblivious to the historical house of memories behind the shop. The insistent beat of Russian pop that filled the store followed me through the screeching door, burst onto the street, and billowed toward the Kremlin a short distance away.

An entirely new perspective on Stalin's time had opened up to me, and though I could not prolong my stay in Moscow that summer, I returned for further visits in the years that followed. In the beginning I believed that Stepan Podlubny's diary had to be an exceptional case. But on each trip I found more and more diaries, written by men and women who were old and young, rich and poor, artists and intellectuals, students and housewives. I found diaries in archives in and around

Moscow. Others came from private sources, offered by the diarists or their descendants. Several of these diarists invited me to their homes to discuss the records of their lives. While the KGB archives, which contain the single largest collection of Stalin-era diaries, remained closed to me, I was able to read published versions of some of those diaries, as well as many other published diaries, letters, and memoirs from the period.

Some diaries could be read in an afternoon; others were thousands of pages long. Some were dreary and bland; others brimmed with confessions both heartrending and chilling. And while some diarists never examined their inner worlds, the ones I found myself reading with mounting interest often asked themselves who they were and how they could change. These introspective and self-interrogating voices lie at the center of this book, where I explore what is meant by writing the word *I* in an age of a larger *We*.

Many scholars have used social and political theories to explain how totalitarian regimes work. I have taken a different approach. The historical actors who parade across the pages of this book wrote in rich and often startling language: many revelations take place at the surface, but others call for careful attention. In reconstructing the hopes, dilemmas, and choices of these diarists, I found, time after time, an astounding depth of individual involvement in the revolutionary age. These actors do not speak for the whole of Soviet society, but the language of self that they share helps explain what life was like under Stalin's rule. Their voices resonate with utopian fervor; they introduce us to a time at once fascinating and disturbing, when many ordinary people felt impelled to inscribe their lives into the revolution and into world history.

Prologue

FORGING THE REVOLUTIONARY SELF

In the early morning hours of July 8, 1937, the secret police arrested Osip Piatnitsky. One of the highest-ranking Communist officials in Stalin's Russia, Piatnitsky was charged with plotting terrorist acts against the Soviet state. Ten days later his wife began to keep a diary. In moving detail, Julia Piatnitskaya's journal recounts the circumstances of her husband's arrest and the hardship and grief that cut, suddenly and deeply, into her own life as a member of the Communist elite. Neighbors and former friends shunned her as the wife of an "enemy of the people"; she lost her job as an engineer, and she and her two young children were left to their fate, with neither income nor assets. In her despair, a question about her husband revolved in her mind and came to preoccupy her. "Who is he?" she wrote in the diary. Was Piatnitsky really the devoted Communist he had claimed to be? Her first inclination was to trust him; after all, they had been married for seventeen years. But this would mean that the party was at fault. Piatnitskaya cut her reflections short: "Obviously I don't think that. Obviously Piatnitsa was never a professional revolutionary, but a professional scoundrel—a spy or provocateur . . . And that's why he lived the way he did, and was always so reserved and stern. Obviously, his soul was not at peace and he did not see any other way out, except to wait to be exposed or grab an opportunity and run, escape punishment."[1]

Piatnitsky was Osip's pseudonym. Born Iosif Tarshis, he had been renamed after joining the underground Bolshevik organization. Derived from *piatnitsa,* the Russian word for Friday, the name was given to him by his comrades, who likened his dedication to the revolutionary cause to Friday's devotion to his master Robinson Crusoe. Yet in spite of these credentials, Julia felt unable in the wake of Osip's arrest to state with full certainty who her husband was. She wanted to believe his assurances that his Bolshevik conscience was "as white as freshly fallen snow," yet to believe this was to think "black" and "evil" thoughts. The logic of these thoughts, which contradicted the official charges, led her to question the direction in which the country was going under Stalin's rule. Ultimately, it undermined her own identity as a Soviet citizen and a member of the fighting community of fellow Communists. This identity, grounded in the commitment to march with the collective and build the glorious future, was for Julia Piatnitskaya the essence of her life.

The pages of Piatnitskaya's diary document the struggle between her spontaneous views and the reflective labor she applied to restore her worldview as a committed Communist. The diary served as a tool by which she could release her poisonous thoughts and thereby regain the assured and unified voice of a devoted revolutionary. Her task was to "prove, not for others, but for yourself . . . that you stand higher than a wife, and higher than a mother. You will prove with this that you are a citizen of the Great Soviet Union. And if you don't have the strength to do this, then to the devil with you."[2]

Personal documents such as Julia Piatnitskaya's diary, made available to scholars only recently, challenge the Western notion of totalitarian societies and particularly of the Stalinist regime, which stands out as totalitarianism's paradigmatic case. When thinking about self-expression in Stalin's Russia we think that the state denied its citizens the ability to express themselves, and that individuals' true thoughts and aspirations were voiced only in private realms, shielded from the intrusive gaze of the state. We think that in their private core Soviet citizens differed qualitatively from the way they presented themselves "officially." We see these people as liberal subjects: individuals in pursuit of autonomy who cherished privacy as a sphere of free self-determination. In this view, Soviet citizens surely stood in opposition to the Soviet state, given its determination to destroy their autonomy and privacy.[3]

In its ideal form the diary is imagined as a receptacle for private convictions expressed in spontaneous and uncoerced fashion. Given the omnipresence of state repression in totalitarian systems, only exceptional persons risk keeping secret diaries, impelled by conscience or a concern for posterity. In George Orwell's novel *1984*, Winston Smith begins to keep a diary for the purpose of expressing his self in defiance of the Big Brother state. Keeping a diary is an infraction that, if detected, is "reasonably certain" to be "punished by death, or at least by twenty-five years in a forced-labor camp." Orwell's Big Brother state actively strives to abolish any notion of an individual self. Enforced collective forms of life deprive individuals of time, space, and even the necessary tools—paper and pencil—to articulate any personal thought. Winston Smith's diary is "a peculiarly beautiful book," with "smooth creamy paper, a little yellowed by age . . . of a kind that had not been manufactured for at least forty years past." He had bought it in a "frowsy little junk shop in a slummy quarter of the town." The message is clear: a personal diary—a fact of daily life in the bygone liberal age—has no place in a totalitarian state.[4]

Diaries, which thrived in prerevolutionary Russian culture, were presumed to have become extinct in the postrevolutionary climate of terror and distrust. Those who kept their journals through the revolution and the early Soviet years were thought to have ceased to do so in the Stalin era, when possession of a personal text could easily become self-incriminating.[5] The writer Mikhail Bulgakov had his diary confiscated by the secret police in 1926. After it was returned (no charges were brought against him), he destroyed it.[6] Surviving members of the intelligentsia concur that the diary was an anachronism in the Stalin period. It was impossible to "even conceive of keeping a real diary in those days," Lydia Chukovskaya remarks in the preface to her conversations with the poet Anna Akhmatova, recorded in diary form in 1938–1941. Chukovskaya adds that she always "omitted or veiled" the "main content" of her conversations with the poet. In a memoir produced in 1967, Veniamin Kaverin remembered visiting his fellow writer Yuri Tynianov in Leningrad in the late 1930s. His host, pointing out the window where the air was filled with fine ash, said: "They are burning memory, they have been doing it for a long time, every night . . . I lose my mind when I think that every night thousands of people throw their diaries into the fire."[7]

Yet the notion of pervasive and uniform repression of personal narratives is countered now by a flood of personal documents from the first decades of Soviet power—diaries, letters, autobiographies, poems—which have emerged from the recently opened Soviet archives. Diaries in fact appear to have been a popular genre of the period, especially during Stalin's reign. Diarists included writers and artists as well as engineers and scientists, teachers, university professors and students, workers, peasants, state administration employees, party workers and Komsomol activists, soldiers, schoolchildren, and housewives. Among them were party members of various ranks as well as non-Communists, including people convicted as political counterrevolutionaries.

Their personal chronicles map an existential terrain marked by self-reflection and struggle. Many Soviet diaries were distinctly introspective, but introspection was not linked to individualist purposes. In contrast to Winston Smith, whose diaristic "I" turns against the goals and values propagated by the state, these Soviet diarists revealed an urge to write themselves into their social and political order. They sought to realize themselves as historical subjects defined by their active adherence to a revolutionary common cause. Their personal narratives were so filled with the values and categories of the Soviet revolution that they seemed to obliterate any distinction between a private and a public domain. Many Stalin-era diarists were preoccupied with finding out who they were in essence and how they could transform themselves. They put pen to paper because they had pressing problems about themselves and they sought answers in diaristic self-interrogation. Their diaries were active tools, deployed to intervene into their selves and align them on the axis of revolutionary time.

The concern with self-transformation, shared by the Communist regime and these Soviet diarists, was rooted in the revolution of 1917, which promoted a new thinking about the self as a political project. All political actors who sided with the revolution, whatever their ideological differences, linked it to the goal of remaking the life of society as well as of each individual according to revolutionary standards of rationality, transparency, and purity. The long-anticipated overthrow of the tsarist system was to inaugurate an enlightened political order that would deliver Russia from the "darkness" and sluggish acquiescence that characterized its peasant masses and lay at the core of the country's cursed backwardness. The revolution marked the threshold separating the old from the new life. It pointed toward a perfect future dictated by the "laws of history," a future that appeared within reach through the application of rationalist science and modern technology. This future was widely imagined as the habitat of a perfect human being, the "new man," whom revolutionary actors described as a human machine, an untiring worker, or an unfettered, integrated "personality."[8]

To create an "improved edition of mankind" (Trotsky) was a stated goal of the Bolshevik regime that came to power in October 1917. To reforge humanity and create an earthly paradise was the raison d'être of the Communist movement. While preaching these goals to the Soviet population at large, each Communist personally lived under a mandate to transform his or her own life in the image of the new man. The Communist attempt to usher in the new world proceeded in great measure as a violent struggle against the "remnants" of feudal and capitalist society, which bred selfish and exploitative attitudes. At the same time, the Bolsheviks sought to transform the population into politically conscious citizens who would embrace historical necessity and become engaged in building socialism out of understanding and personal conviction. Through a multitude of political-education campaigns the Soviet regime prodded individuals to consciously identify with the revolution (as interpreted by the party leadership), and thereby to comprehend themselves as active participants in the drama of history. They were summoned to internalize the revolution and grant it an interpretation defined not only by the objective course of history but also by the spiritual unfolding of their subjective selves.[9]

Under Stalin, the regime declared its intention to make the new socialist man a reality. The decisions in 1928–1929 by the party majority to industrialize the country at breakneck speed, to collectivize the peasantry, and to intensify the war against all class enemies, expressed a fervent desire to destroy all that was left of the "old" world and proceed with the construction of the "new" world. Stalin's regime believed that the revolution had come of age and produced a new consciousness among its followers which would allow for this assault. Industrialization would create the rich material habitat of the new man. A panoply of Stalin-era heroes—from polar aviators to record-setting coal workers and milkmaids—was represented as embodying the socialist personality. Their heroic deeds demonstrated what all Soviet citizens could, and in fact should, aspire to, in order to justify their human potential. The Stalin era promoted a Soviet dream, the contours of which the party ideologist Nikolai Bukharin delineated in implicit rivalry with the individualist American dream. In the Soviet dream, socialism turned soulless workers, oppressed by capitalist exploitation, "into persons, into collective creators and organizers, into people who work on themselves, into conscious producers of their own 'fate,' into real architects of their own future."[10] Under these revolutionary imperatives, Soviet citizens were judged upon the trajectories of their subjective lives. In the double context of potent revolutionary narratives of self-transformation and a regime of political surveillance that monitored self-expression for what it revealed about individuals' subjective essence, people could not but be aware of their duty to possess a distinct "biography," to present it publicly, and to work toward self-perfection. Talking and writing about oneself had become intensely politicized activities. One's "biography" had become an artifact of considerable political weight.

The increased thinking about and acting on the self occasioned a veritable explosion of Russian autobiographical literature. It was not just that many more individuals began writing and talking about themselves but that the autobiographical domain reached entirely new layers of the population. This process led to authors groping for a language of self-expression at the same time as they learned to read and write.[11] And yet, while the Communist regime was heavily invested in the production of autobiographical testimony, these voices were not solely adapting to the regime's interests. The language of self did not originate in a preformulated ideological litany. It thrived, rather, in a larger revolutionary ecosystem of which the Communist regime was as much a producer as a product. The commitment to self-improvement, social activism, and self-expression in concert with history predated the Russian revolution by many decades; it was rooted in the tradition of the Russian intelligentsia. In fact, to be worthy of the ascription *intelligent* was to show a disposition as a critically thinking subject of history. This nineteenth-century legacy shaped the self-understanding of revolutionary actors in 1917, and it provided the frame in which the politics of social identity and individual self-definition were pursued.[12]

Some Soviet revolutionaries considered the diary, along with other forms of autobiographical practice, as a medium of self-reflection and transformation. Others, however, viewed it with unease and suspicion, believing diary-keeping to be an inherently "bourgeois" activity. It was a matter of dispute whether a diary befitted a Communist. It was legitimate as long as it helped develop a socialized consciousness and a will to action, but there was also the possibility that it could breed empty talk or, even worse, "Hamletism"—brooding thought instead of revolutionary action. Diarists writing on their own, outside their comrades' gaze, risked cutting themselves off from the nurturing collective. Unchecked, the diary of a steadfast comrade could turn into a seedbed of counterrevolutionary sentiment. Not accidentally, diaries were among the materials most coveted by the secret police during searches of the premises of suspected "enemies of the people."

Thus the diaries of the 1930s are far more than unmediated products of Soviet state policies of fostering revolutionary consciousness. Only in a few cases did diaries originate as clear assignments prescribed in a classroom, an editorial bureau, or a construction site. For the most part, these records were kept on the initiative of their authors, who in fact often deplored the lack of guidelines according to which they could pattern their lives: there existed no official formula for how to purge oneself of an "old" essence and how to retain faith in an emerging new one. As an ongoing engagement with oneself through time, the diary showed tensions and fissures that other personal narratives glossed over or repressed. For this reason diaries yield unsurpassed insights into the forms, possibilities, and limits of self-expression under Stalin. To be sure, not every diary of this period served introspective purposes or revealed a rich language of self. But a great number of diarists, from a variety of social, generational, and occupational backgrounds, grappled with the same questions of who they were and how they could change. They held in common a striving to inscribe their life into a larger narrative of the revolutionary cause. Their records show shared forms of self-expression and ideals of self-realization, which point beyond the individual cases and suggest a wider cultural significance.

The authors of these diaries conceived of themselves in distinctly modern ways. "To be modern," Michel Foucault writes, "is not to accept oneself as one is in the flux of the passing moments; it is to take oneself as object of a complex and difficult elaboration."[13] It means to understand oneself as a subject over one's own life—as opposed to comprehending oneself as, say, an object of higher fate. Modern subjects cease to recognize social roles predetermined for them; they seek to create their individual biographies. Subjectivity thus subsumes a degree of individuals' conscious participation in the making of their lives.[14] More specifically, the Soviet diaries I have consulted provide insights into the making of an illiberal, socialist subjectivity. From its inception as a political movement in the nineteenth century, socialism was defined by its adherents in opposition to liberal capitalism. When Soviet revolutionaries proceeded to build a socialist society, they competed with a standard of industrial modernity established by the capitalist West. They shared with the latter a dedication to technology, rationality, and science, but they believed that socialism would win out, economically, morally, and historically, because of its reliance on conscious planning and the power of the organized collective.[15] In this context, self-narratives flesh out the meaning and appeal of socialism as an anticapitalist form of self-realization. Diarists conceived of an ideal form of existence in opposition to the capitalist West, which they perceived as individualist, selfish, narrow-minded, in a word, bourgeois. They worked toward what one diarist called a "second stage" of understanding—an ability to escape one's atomized existence and comprehend oneself as a particle of a collective movement.

The enlarged life of the collective was seen as the source of true subjecthood. It promised vitality, historical meaning, and moral value, and it was intensely desired. By contrast, a life lived outside the collective or the flow of history carried a danger of personal regression stemming from the inability to participate in the forward-thrusting life of the Soviet people. Julia Piatnitskaya was aware of this dynamic, and her diary resonated with a desperate insistence to rejoin the collective. Having lost her job as an engineer after her husband's arrest, she spent her days at the public library, leafing through technical journals: "I looked through the March issue of *Mechanical Engineering.* Every day that I live pushes me further back. New machines are being built: lathes, agricultural tools, machines for the Metro, for bridges, etc . . . Engineers are raising in new ways questions of organization and the technology of tool production. In general, there is no doubt that life is moving forward, regardless of any 'spokes in the wheel.' The wonderful Palace of Culture for the ZIS [car] factory. I'm downright envious: why aren't I in their collective?"[16]

To belong to the collective and be aligned with history was a condition predicated on work and struggle, complete with lapses, failings, and renewed commitments. Against a background of incessant calls for "vigilance," diarists like Julia Piatnitskaya described their inability to live up to the standards of thought and behavior required of them. They had pronounced questions and doubts about how to square glossy official representations of the emerging socialist society with the gray and dismal realities of their personal lives. But they turned against their own observations, which they believed to be born of a "weak will," and vowed to struggle on. To an extent, hesitations and doubts were indispensable for the work on the self and produced a renewed dynamic of struggle and forward movement, the very dynamic through which diarists could experience the unfolding of their will.

A division between inner striving and outward compliance no longer suffices to understand the self-transformative and self-awakening power of Soviet revolutionary ideology. Many personal narratives from the Stalin era suggest that ideology was a living tissue of meaning that was seriously reflected upon. Ideology created tensions, as it often stood in marked contrast to an author's observational truth. The point, however, is not to focus on the points of tension themselves but to see how individuals worked through them: how intolerable they found a condition of a "dual soul," how little appeal a retreat into private life had to them, and how they applied mechanisms of rationalization in attempts to restore harmonious notions of themselves as part of socialist society. Much of the ideological tension in the early Soviet system did not exist between the state on the one hand and its citizens (as fully constituted selves) on the other, but in the ways citizens engaged their own selves.

Against a widespread proclivity to read Stalin-era subjectivity between the lines and focus on cracks and silences, reading should begin with the very lines of autobiographical statements. Hannah Arendt, who studied the testimony of totalitarian subjects for many years, came to the conclusion that "true understanding has hardly any choice" but to accept statements as what they seem to express: "The sources talk and what they reveal is the self-understanding as well as the self-interpretation of people who act and who believe they know what they are doing. If we deny them this capacity and pretend that we know better and can tell them what their real 'motives' are or which real 'trends' they objectively represent—no matter what they themselves think—we have robbed them of the very faculty of speech, insofar as speech makes sense." With the exception of those rare and easily detectable cases where people consciously tell lies, Arendt concludes, "self-understanding and self-interpretation are the very foundation of all analysis and understanding."[17]

With its emphasis on the shaping power of ideology over the lives of Stalin-era subjects, this book might appear to hark back to theorists of totalitarianism, including Arendt and Orwell. Adherents of the totalitarian paradigm conceive of ideology in the Communist realm as a corpus of official truths which issued from central state institutions and served the interests of the regime. Ideology indoctrinated individuals, suggesting to them participation in a great "movement," while in fact deluding them about their true condition of unfreedom. Though in many ways compelling, this interpretation reduced Soviet citizens to mere victims of the regime's aspirations. More recently, a generation of social historians revealed the active participation of large segments of the population in the Bolshevik enterprise. In the process the Soviet order was strangely de-ideologized and its workings were explained in terms of the "self-interests" of the groups in society that were identified as its beneficiaries. Yet these historians made no attempt to critically examine the forms self-interest could take in a socialist society.[18] A synthesis of these positions would rehabilitate ideology and at the same time maintain a sense of individual agency, agency that is not autonomous in nature but is produced by, and dynamically interacts with, ideology. Such attention to ideology and subjectivity as intertwined and interacting entities provides a better sense of the existential stakes of the times, something that, with the exception of Arendt, neither totalitarian theorists nor revisionists were interested in.[19]

Rather than a given, fixed, and monologic textual corpus, in the sense of "Communist party ideology," ideology may be better understood as a ferment working in individuals and producing a great deal of variation as it interacts with the subjective life of a particular person. The individual operates like a clearing house where ideology is unpacked and personalized, and in the process the individual remakes himself into a subject with distinct and meaningful biographical features. And in activating the individual, ideology itself comes to life. Ideology should therefore be seen as a living and adaptive force; it has power only to the extent that it operates in living persons who engage their selves and the world as ideological subjects. Much of the logic of the revolutionary master narratives of transformation (transformation of social space and of the self), collectivization (collectivization of individualist producers and of the self), and purification (political purge campaigns and acts of personal self-improvement) was provided and reproduced by Soviet citizens who kept rationalizing unfathomable state policies and thus were ideological agents on a par with the leaders of party and state.

Stalin-era diarists' desire for a purposeful and significant life reflected a widespread urge to ideologize one's life, to turn it into the expression of a firm, internally consistent, totalizing *Weltanschauung.* This orientation toward meaning and social inclusion intersected with the Bolsheviks' endeavor to remake mankind. The regime was thus able to channel strivings for self-validation and transcendence that emerged outside the ideological boundaries of Bolshevism. In this light, the Soviet project emerges as a variant of a larger European phenomenon of the interwar period that can be described as a twofold obligation, for a personal worldview and for the individual's integration into a community. This ideal form of being was called an "aligned life"; it promised authenticity and intense meaning, to be realized in collective acts fulfilling the laws of history or nature.[20]

The appeal to the self lay at the core of Communist ideology. It was its defining feature and also a great source of its strength. On a fundamental level, this ideology worked as a creator of individual experience. Anyone who wrote himself into the revolutionary narrative acquired a voice as an individual agent belonging to a larger whole. Moreover, in joining the movement individuals were encouraged to transform themselves. The power of the Communist appeal, which promised that those who had been slaves in the past could remold themselves into exemplary members of humanity, cannot be overestimated. It is poignantly expressed in the groping autobiographical narratives of semiliterate Soviet citizens who detailed their journeys from darkness to light. The universal ambition and scope of the Soviet revolution raised the participating individual to the level of a historical subject who in his daily life helped implement history's progression toward the perfect future. Many of the diaries I will discuss were produced in dialogue with the twofold, transformative and participatory, appeal of the Communist project.

1

Rearing Conscious Citizens

When the revolution broke out in February 1917, Dmitri Furmanov was working as an instructor, teaching evening classes to workers in his industrial home town of Ivanovo, northeast of Moscow. A part-time writer and former student who had quit Moscow University to join the Red Cross in the initial weeks of World War I, the 25-year-old Furmanov immediately involved himself in the sprawling network of revolutionary councils and party cells. One month into the revolution he noted in his diary: "The honorable title 'social worker' has made me ten times more powerful . . . it obligates one to be as careful, sensible, and strict as possible, it inculcates consciousness, personal judgment, and personal self-evaluation . . . In this new school principles are worked out, the will is hardened, a plan is created, a course of action . . . This great revolution has brought about a psychological turning point in me as well."[1]

As Furmanov suggested, the revolution as a harbinger of a new, rational, and just social order transformed him in its image. In entering his personal life, the revolutionary will rationalized the workings of his mind and body. Yet not all of Furmanov's diary entries of this period were so exuberant in tone. Many passages resonated with self-doubt and anxious attempts to position himself politically: in an entry for August 1917 entitled "Who am I?" he sought to define his politics: was he "a socialist-revolutionary, an internationalist, a maximalist"? Two years later—by which time he had joined the Bolshevik party and assumed a responsible post as a political commissar in a Red division fighting in the Civil War—he still complained about his inadequate training and uneven political enthusiasm, indicating that his psychological life was not fully aligned with the revolution.[2]

Furmanov was one of many teachers, writers, doctors who identified with Russia's democratic intelligentsia and embraced the revolution as the dawn of a new age. For them it signified the long-anticipated moment when scenarios of social and human transformation, sketched out by preceding generations of the intelligentsia, were to be implemented and become reality. These scenarios suggested total renewal, total possibility, and total perfectibility of humankind, and they were coined in the vision of the socialist "new man." Maxim Gorky expressed these expectations in an article in his newspaper, *New Life,* in April 1917: "The new structure of political life demands from us a new structure of the soul." Furmanov took on this imperative in strikingly literal fashion. For him the commitment to produce a new, better society, entailed in important measure a commitment to renew himself.[3]

The dedication to new forms of social and individual life, expressed in the act of revolution, united revolutionaries of all camps, from the Bolsheviks who took power in October 1917, to their fierce critic Maxim Gorky, to the politically wavering activist Dmitri Furmanov. As members of the Russian intelligentsia, they shared a moral commitment to devote their lives to a common cause, social progress, the well-being of the people, or the advancement of history. The task of the intelligentsia was to educate and enlighten, to raise Russia's "dark masses" to the stature of true "human beings" *(chelovek)* and critically thinking "personalities" *(lichnost'),* who would then rise up against their oppressors and thus move history along on its preordained emancipatory trail. By dint of his privileged education, the *intelligent* had superior insight into the laws of history. This vanguard role gave him the right to direct others toward the light, but it also imparted a moral duty to live a life of exceptional devotion and purity, in communion with history—to embody the qualities of the vaunted new man.

At the origins of this thinking about the new man was a novel by the nineteenth-century writer and critic Nikolai Chernyshevsky, entitled *What Is to Be Done?,* which provided an influential portrayal of the "new people"—young men and women distinguished by their ability to lead completely rationalist lives and wholeheartedly dedicate themselves to the revolution. Each of these "people of the new age" was a "strong personality": "bold, unwavering, relentless, capable of taking matters in hand and of holding onto them tightly so they do not slip from his fingers." One distant day these revolutionaries would become everyday types, but at present (in 1863) they were "rare specimens": "They are like theine in tea, like the bouquet of a fine wine; they are its strength and fragrance. They are the flowers of the best people, the primal sources of energy, the salt of the salt of the earth!"[4]

Chernyshevsky composed *What Is to Be Done?* as a call for action, and it was received as precisely that. Scores of radical students in late tsarist Russia molded themselves in the image of the novel; Lenin spoke of it as the single most important book in his life; as late as 1933 the Comintern head Georgi Dimitrov, accused by the Nazis of masterminding the fire at the Reichstag, consulted the book to gather spiritual strength while he awaited trial in a Berlin prison. Significantly, Chernyshevsky produced the novel in part to define a norm of behavior for his own personal life. The pursuits and issues of his novelistic heroes were also the questions of his life, and both were ultimately dedicated to history's progress.[5]

The decisive quality of the new man, and the most important quality for any critically thinking person to espouse, was consciousness. Concentrated in exemplary individuals—writers, critics, ideologues—consciousness was the ability to see the laws of history and comprehend one's own potential as a subject of historical action who would help chart the road toward a better future. This understanding grounded moral action: it fueled the will and imparted the desire to work untiringly for the realization of the ideal. The laws of history were laws of social emancipation; hence the fundamentally social orientation of consciousness, which spurred the individual to think and act on behalf of the oppressed masses and thus created an enlarged sense of individual self, filled with purpose, significance, and moral value. The rational clarity of consciousness was attained in personal struggle against dark and chaotic forces, in the social world as well as within the individual. The criterion for such order and clarity was the possession of a "harmonious social worldview" that situated the individual on the "correct and just path" and signified the beginning of his "new life." In some sense consciousness was the very measure of life. You did not fully live before developing a worldview that disclosed the light.[6]

It was in pursuit of consciousness that Dmitri Furmanov set out in his diary to trace the workings of history in his personal life. In a retrospective entry in late December 1919 he surveyed his development since the outbreak of the revolution; despite its uneven character, he noticed a distinct growth from spontaneity to consciousness, from "childhood, enthusiasm, ignorance" to "courage, calm, greater consciousness and greater knowledge." In a basic sense, he thought, the revolution had made him into a developed human being. He had led an "empty, stupid, unserious" existence prior to his political awakening: "Only during the days of revolution did the scales fall from my eyes; I was a complete infant up to then."[7] The concept of consciousness invited thinking about oneself in biographical terms. The journey from darkness to light was a journey from non-being to full humanity; it proceeded as a growing self-disclosure of an interiorized, psychological self. As Furmanov's case suggests, consciousness created autobiographical narratives of exceptional appeal, given its twofold emphasis on social activation and self-transformation on the one hand, and psychological exploration and self-monitoring on the other.

From the moment it was founded by Lenin, the Bolshevik party defined itself as the concentrated expression of revolutionary consciousness. Composed of a tightly woven circle of professional underground workers, the party combined highest commitment to the revolution with a mandate of exceptional self-discipline on the part of every member. After assuming power in October 1917, the party extended its mission to disseminate its ideology and win over ever larger segments of the population to the Communist cause. In seeking to make consciousness a universal experience, the Bolsheviks deployed a gigantic project of self-change, much along the lines of the self-transformation described by Furmanov in his diary. The challenge was to make their followers think and act as the Bolsheviks—and the radical intelligentsia as a whole—saw themselves: as historical subjects whose lives were conditioned by the revolution. Communist activists were not solely concerned with changing individuals' outward attitudes; they sought to appropriate their souls, in the sense that they wanted them to understand the historical mission of the Communist party and embrace it out of their own will. Throughout there was a voluntaristic assumption at work, which stipulated that the success or failure of the revolution hinged on the degree of consciousness animating its followers, on the extent to which they recognized their lives as historical in essence and acted on that recognition.

The Bolsheviks were verbal imperialists; they granted, with Marx, that "being determined consciousness" and that therefore the worker needed the power of the revolutionary script to fully understand his historical mission. Revolutionary language in Communist understanding had more than referential significance; it was, as Trotsky put it, the "heart of the ideas themselves . . . the very shape of consciousness." Soviet Communists sought to impart consciousness in great measure by linguistic means: through practices of reading, writing, and oral and written self-presentation.[8]

An exploration of these practices must pay particular attention to the place they occupied in the Bolsheviks' historical imagination. All along, Bolshevik policies were motivated by an acute sense of the historical stages through which the revolution was passing. Man, in Soviet Marxist understanding, was a historically evolving being. As a psychologist of the 1930s put it, "all of man, from his consciousness to every cell of his organism, is a product of historical development."[9] If consciousness was historical in nature, it unfolded in historical stages, which corresponded to distinct political phases of the Soviet regime as the executor of history. Consciousness was not ready-made and universally present; rather, it had to be disseminated by arduous political effort, and it gradually took hold of the individual, first controlling his environment and outward behavior, and then entering the recesses of his psyche. Leon Trotsky—writing in 1923—pointed to this dynamic of working from the outside in, as he charted the stages the revolution had traversed and had yet to cross to realize the socialist future:

> Man first drove the dark elements out of industry and ideology, by displacing barbarian routine by scientific technique, and religion by science. Afterwards he drove the unconscious out of politics, by overthrowing monarchy and class with democracy and rationalist parliamentarianism and then with the clear and open Soviet dictatorship. The blind elements have settled most heavily in economic relations, but man is driving them out from there also, by means of the Socialist organization of economic life . . . Finally, the nature of man himself is hidden in the deepest and darkest corner of the unconscious, of the elemental, of the subsoil. Is it not self-evident that the greatest efforts of investigative thought and of creative initiative will be in that direction?[10]

With its stress on self-mastery and the individual will, consciousness had the potential to disclose a rich culture of the individual and, indeed, the expanse of a Romantic mind. Trotsky described the socialist future as a time when "average" people would "rise to the heights of an Aristotle, a Goethe, or a Marx." Yet this scenario of self-activation could be realized only after a prolonged historical phase of mobilization and disciplinary violence which evoked the spirit of the Enlightenment much more than that of Romanticism. During the decade after the end of the civil war, Bolshevik activists cast Soviet power as an enlightened dictatorship. Even Lenin's famous slogan of "electrifying the whole state" betrayed the self-understanding of the Communist party as a bearer of light whose mission was to bring education and technology to Russia's "dark" masses. Starting in the early 1930s, the party leadership endorsed a momentous shift toward a Romantic sensibility. Electrification, it implied, had made such progress that Soviet citizens themselves were beginning to shine. Consciousness was no longer simply imposed on backward people; it had begun to unfold from within, animating Soviet citizens in ever greater numbers and deeper measure.[11]

Furmanov, who died in 1926, firmly adhered to the Enlightenment stage of the Communist project. After joining the Bolshevik party in 1918 he became a leading disseminator of Communist consciousness. Appointed political commissar, he was dispatched to a division of partisan regiments as an ideological supervisor for their legendary peasant commander, Vassily Chapaev. Furmanov, who kept his diary throughout these years, later wrote a documentary novel about his encounter with Chapaev. In both the diary and the novel the relationship is told through the binary opposition of elementary spontaneity and revolutionary consciousness. Chapaev was a spirited but undisciplined leader. His anarchistic spirit had to be channeled and organized in order to serve the revolution and be of use to history. This was the task of the political commissar, who in the novel bears the name Fedor Klychkov. Klychkov always thinks and speaks in a perfectly rationalist idiom, and his speech molds Chapaev, who is physically strong but intellectually weak, "like wax." If considered as a pair, however, Chapaev and Klychkov fuse the revolutionary qualities of activism and consciousness, popular resourcefulness and intelligentsia culture. In light of Furmanov's own flirtation with anarchist positions in 1917 and the campaigns he conducted in his diary against his own disorganized psyche, the two leading actors in the novel read as a representation of the author's personal struggle to become a conscious subject of the revolution. Furmanov wrote the novel, *Chapaev,* in Chernyshevsky's tradition, as an autobiographically inspired story of exemplary revolutionaries who were to be emulated. When *Chapaev* was published in 1923 it became an instant bestseller and set the standard for scores of later Soviet novels that would offer variations on the same tension between spontaneity and consciousness.[12]

Furmanov's civil war writings make clear how much effort the nascent Soviet regime expended on the rhetorical battlefield. The Red Army soldiers described in *Chapaev* understood that "the war had to be waged and won, not only at the point of a bayonet, but by means of wise, fresh words, a clear mind, and the ability to grasp the entire situation and convey its meaning to others as required." Furmanov took part in the recapturing of the city of Ufa from the Whites in June 1919. Within hours after the storming of the city, "a huge quantity of leaflets were distributed among the population, explaining the situation. Wall newspapers covered the walls of the houses, and from the morning of the next day on, the divisional newspaper was regularly issued every morning. Improvised meetings were held in all corners of the town."[13] "Our word is our best weapon," declared Nikolai Podvoisky, head of the Red Army's universal military training administration. Words had the power to "disintegrate" the enemy's "soul, paralyze his nerves, split him into warring camps and class factions." But words could also impart to individuals the consciousness of a larger whole and mold them into particles of a collective body. Most important, revolutionary words had an intense biographical appeal; they created personal threads in a larger narrative of class struggle, emancipation, education, and empowerment, and thereby made the revolutionary message relevant to those to whom it was preached. "They conduct unceasing agitation," a White officer said, grudgingly acknowledging the success with which the Red Army's political workers campaigned among their recruits; "[they take] advantage of every available opportunity and [exploit] even the most trivial fact to highlight the benefits that the Bolshevik regime has brought to their lives."[14]

A census carried out by the Soviet regime in 1920 established that 60 percent of the adult population could not read and write. Under these conditions, the ability to preach the power of political language depended on establishing elementary literacy. The literacy campaigns relentlessly conducted by the Soviet state were explicitly aimed at inculcating a revolutionary consciousness. The government decree on illiteracy issued in December 1919 opened with the following declaration: "For the purpose of allowing the entire population of the Republic to participate consciously in the political life of the country, the Council of People's Commissars decrees . . ." Distributed in hundreds of thousands of leaflets, the decree ordered all illiterate citizens between the ages of 8 and 50 to study. Lenin formulated the same imperative: "The illiterate person stands outside of politics. First it is necessary to teach him the alphabet. Without it there are only rumors, fairy tales, prejudices, but not politics." The struggle against illiteracy was a "precondition of politics."[15] The technical ability to read and write was inextricably linked to the agenda of creating politically literate citizens. The work of political enlightenment was to raise "active and conscious" Soviet citizens, to "awaken activity" and "instill the habit of being active."

During the "cultural crusade" of the First Five-Year Plan, Maxim Gorky, by now an ardent supporter of the socialist state, issued a plea to the Soviet public to donate money for adult education: "Help, comrades! Every ruble will give pencils and notebooks to people who want to study in order to build the new life with greater energy and a clearer consciousness."[16]

As part of the drive to raise individuals' consciousness, Soviet activists devised clear precepts on how to read and write. As they emphasized, these processes should not evolve thoughtlessly. Reading and writing were not to be done by rote; on the contrary, they were to be instances of creative self-investment. A Soviet educator, writing in the 1920s, recommended that "conscious reading" be part of the training of Red Army soldiers: "The first rule of rational reading should be its full consciousness; . . . for a conscious reader, a book ought not to be a source of ready-formed ideas, but material for one's own thoughts, only facilitating one's serious, independent work in this or that discipline." Authors stressed the importance of acquiring political literacy "independently": "In order to truly be politically literate, it is not enough to work through the theoretical and historical books in the social sciences. One must still be able to independently apply the acquired material to contemporary life. It is necessary to orient oneself in current political life." In demanding that texts be engaged individually and independently, educators argued that the notion of consciousness had to arise from within individuals and could not be enforced from outside. Similarly, the Soviet school curriculum emphasized that assignments should bring out students' independent, creative abilities. Work on a given assignment "should train and educate not only the student's intellect, but also his will."[17]

The Bolsheviks emerged victorious from the civil war, but at the cost of a country ravaged by seven years of war. The Soviet state had to cope with the loss of millions of lives due to warfare, diseases, and its own indiscriminate violence. Moreover, the country's urban and industrial centers, vital resources for the "dictatorship of the proletariat," were depleted; most of their workers had left the idle or destroyed factories to return to their home villages. In Bolshevik interpretation this indicated an alarming drop in revolutionary consciousness among the party's mainstays. In view of these losses, the regime had no choice but to grudgingly accept a private sector in the economy. The New Economic Policy (NEP) created great anxieties among party leaders and their followers, who feared that the petit-bourgeois consciousness embodied by millions of small-scale producers and traders would contaminate and fatally corrupt the young revolutionary mind of Soviet society. The powerful resurgence during the NEP of forces from the old world dampened the transformative ambitions of all but the most ardent revolutionaries. Most Bolsheviks interpreted this period of ideological compromise as a temporary retreat in order to regain momentum for the decisive assault on the capitalist system.[18]

To remain intact in the swamp of unreformed peasant Russia and the glittering world of the NEP bourgeoisie, the party closed its ranks, conceiving of itself as an embattled bastion of consciousness. A series of purges, beginning in 1921, just when the Soviet state had adopted the NEP, were to test the ideological purity of each party member. Besides "outright enemies of the proletariat," "agents and provocateurs" hired by counterrevolutionary parties, the purges targeted those "petit-bourgeois" self-seekers who had joined the party out of concern for "their personal well-being [rather] than the interests of proletarian struggle and revolution." The vigilant Communist could recognize these types by seeing through their at best superficial adherence to the collective cause. "Weak" and "unprincipled" in character, they lacked the willpower to master their instinctual craving for self-gratification and were unable to discern the ploys of enemies who manipulated them at will. While eliminating these unfit elements, the party honored and validated those who withstood its scrutiny and demonstrated "dedication, endurance, political maturity, and readiness to sacrifice [themselves]," as a party resolution defined the essence of Communist consciousness. The purge was to serve as an impetus for Communists to "stage their own 'October' [Revolution]." They were called upon to use the test of their purity to "look into themselves and, with the help of a good Bolshevik broom, to sweep out the petit-bourgeois within . . . To learn to understand the will, the interests of the collective, and to define one's own will and interests by them—this is a first step to creating a new life."[19]

The Communist's subjective essence, the strength or weakness of his character, came to the fore in his "autobiography," which he recited to his party comrades in the climactic dramatic moment of the purge process. The autobiography emerged in the Communist party milieu, but in the course of the 1920s it spread to the Komsomol and nonparty institutions. Every Soviet citizen who applied to become a university student or to work in a government agency had to compose an autobiography. Moreover, citizens were required to resubmit their autobiographies at recurrent intervals throughout their lives. It is therefore safe to assume that most adult Soviet citizens were familiar, not only with this genre of self-presentation and its attendant rules, but also with the underlying assumption that their biographies were subject to rewriting, in accordance with the progression of the revolution and the development of their own, subjective political consciousness.

A short account in prose of a given Communist's life, the autobiography listed educational and professional achievements, but at its core it focused on the formation of its author's personality as an unfolding subject of revolutionary consciousness. While the themes and emphases in this act of public self-presentation followed established guidelines, the autobiography retained an important subjective dimension, because individuals had to convincingly lay out the paths of their journeys toward the Communist light. Often these self-narratives took their point of departure in an abyss of subjective tenebrosity, to better highlight both the ensuing conversion toward the Soviet cause and the distance of the route traveled. The degree to which an individual could convey to the audience that he was a socialist citizen at heart ultimately decided his admission to the Communist party.[20]

The Communist autobiography of the 1920s was a gesture of self-expression in the form of self-abnegation. The ideal Communist—witness Furmanov/Klychkov—was a loudspeaker of the revolution and resembled a machine more than a Romantic subject with an expressive soul. Indeed, revolutionary activists of the 1920s frequently cast the ideal type of humanity in the form of a machine man. The filmmaker Dziga Vertov dreamed of a "perfect electric man"—one whose soul was no longer subject to chaotic psychological impulses but functioned with the directed energy and precision of machinery: "The New Man, free of unwieldiness and clumsiness, will have the light, precise movements of machines." If revolutionary consciousness was defined as utter discipline and the ability to tirelessly function as part of a larger whole, the machine was the measure of such consciousness.[21]

Another biographical medium actively solicited during the 1920s was the memoir of the October Revolution. From the vantage point of the ideologically polluted NEP period, the revolutionary spirit appeared to have been at its purest in October 1917. A newly founded history section of the Communist party invited veterans of 1917 to produce memoirs about how they had participated in, and made, the Bolshevik revolution. This initiative sparked a spontaneous influx of other personal reminiscences about 1917, many of them "illiterate and poorly written." It was through these narratives that participants came to *own* the revolution—almost regardless of their actual roles in 1917: some autobiographical accounts of that October were sent in from regions that had not witnessed a Bolshevik uprising in 1917. No matter how truthful or fictitious, these instances convey the appeal of inscribing oneself into the revolutionary narrative.[22]

Yet the appeal of both the Communist autobiography and the revolutionary memoir was limited by a fixation on 1917 as the decisive threshold of revolutionary consciousness. In the late 1920s, when the Soviet regime under Stalin's leadership launched a second revolution and set out to build the new socialist world, this fixation was overcome. Soviet activists now proclaimed that in the years since October 1917 the revolution had come of age—it had produced a sufficient degree of consciousness among its followers to will the future into being. The Soviet system was deemed sufficiently strong for the government to proceed with the breakup of class society and the creation of a classless socialist order. This meant that a fully conscious subject had appeared, who was to inhabit the classless society, and the energy provided by this fully formed individual was to fuel the drive for industrialization. The ideal of the Stalinist state was voluntarist; it privileged the individual rather than the collective as the defining basic entity of human behavior; it also rehabilitated the individual soul as the basis of the conscious will. The Stalinist ideological apparatus cultivated individual biographies, emphasizing the making of exceptional personalities rather than the exceptional deeds of inanimate machines.

Maxim Gorky played an instrumental role in creating the new man of the Stalinist regime. A writer with strong Nietzschean leanings, Gorky hoped that the revolution would inaugurate a social order that would release man's inborn heroic essence and allow him to live a new, rich, vital, and beautiful life. Gorky, who had left Russia in the early 1920s, returned to the Soviet Union for two widely publicized visits, in 1928 and 1929, before settling there for good in 1931. He wrote of being amazed by the psychic changes he observed in the Soviet population. The people were saturating themselves with political ideas, and "political consciousness" was becoming "an everyday phenomenon." "Everybody had become younger in essence." Gorky placed this image in deliberate contrast to the sentiment he recalled from journeys to the same places before the revolution: "Russian feebleness and spiritual mourning" and the "specifically Russian bent for sadness."[23]

The new man was a product of history, more specifically the "world historical" campaign unleashed by the Stalinist leadership to bring a socialist society into being. In calling on Soviet citizens to involve themselves in the collective building of the new world, the leadership appealed to their heroic disposition. That disposition fueled their rationalist zeal, optimistic self-confidence, and creative energy—all central characteristics of the Stalinist new man, in explicit contrast to the "old man" of the bourgeois West, who was self-seeking, atomized, and antiprogressive.

Yet, as Gorky maintained, the workers on Stalin-era construction sites were as yet not fully aware of the greatness of their age and the human implications it held. The task of literature was to provide a "magnifying mirror," in which they could comprehend themselves as active participants in a heroic reality.[24] With Stalin's support, Gorky redirected the entire Soviet writing profession toward the goal of instilling a socialist consciousness into the new man, of "engineering his soul." Invoking a tradition that went back to Chernyshevsky, Gorky and the Communist leadership called on Soviet writers to create exemplary heroic types to be emulated by the writers and their readers alike. Unlike the utopian novel of the past, however, "socialist realist" art of the Stalin period was not to evoke a future hero. Its task was instead to document the amazing deeds of the best Soviet citizens, while endowing these real heroes with the rich inner world that befitted them as "total personalities" of the socialist age. Literature was to show the new Soviet citizens what they were at essence but did not yet know they were: expressive individuals with endless creative potential.

The new attention to the heroic individual as epitome of the new man went along with a new veneration of the biographical mode. A full-fledged biography, delineating a trajectory from nothing to everything, served as the most tangible material substance of the new man. Boris Pasternak at the founding congress of the Soviet Writers' Union in 1934 called for a poetic "language that would capture the reality of the new Soviet people, "who have torn themselves from the anchors of property and who are soaring freely . . . in the space of the biographically conceivable."[25] Biography—even if stretched to its imaginable limit—was the fitting mold of socialist man; it provided the form in which a life was properly represented and understood.

Gorky actively promoted the Soviet biographical medium. After returning to the Soviet Union he initiated a series of biographical projects, most notably the "History of the Factories," a documentation of more than a hundred of the country's largest enterprises in the form of biographical and autobiographical accounts of those who were building them. His reliance on biography as a narrative of unfolding consciousness resembled the earlier project of collective remembrance of 1917, but unlike that initiative, Gorky's project sought to link political subjectivity to the unfolding of history in the present, and it appealed to every worker to become an autobiographical subject. There was a new sense that every worker in Stalinist construction, by tying his fate to a larger working collective and a transformative event of world historical proportions, enlarged himself to heroic, superhuman proportions, became, as Gorky declared, a "M-A-N with capital letters."[26]

The most outstanding biographies of the Stalinist age belonged to the record-setting coal miners, milkmaids, and polar aviators whose stories proliferated in the 1930s. Their exploits were underwritten by an ideological apparatus eager to identify acts of individual heroism that confirmed the regime's claims that a socialist society had truly come into being. In the Communist view these singular achievements were made possible by the elimination of the capitalist structures of NEP and the establishment of a socialist environment that allowed the Soviet citizen to freely develop his full potential and to experience, as Bukharin put it, "creativity, material sufficiency, cultural growth, a broadening mental horizon, heightened social activity, exposure to an ever growing amount of spiritual pleasures, the sense that his powers and his personality is ever growing. The *personality* appears for the first time as a mass phenomenon and not just as part of the slave-owning upper class in its various historical variants."[27]

Commenting in his diary on the extraordinary feats of Ivan Gudov, a Stakhanovite coal miner who exceeded his daily labor quota by forty-five times, the playwright Alexander Afinogenov—one among many literati in search of Stalin-era heroes—likened him to an artist, "a virtuoso and a talent," and went on: "Gudov is a prototype of the socialist talent which is flowering so powerfully in our land. This is a totally new quality of man, a quality that has been born of the socialist structure of society. And he is far from alone! There they are—atoms of human energy bursting into freedom. The radiation of their energy is inexhaustible. And this makes the order in which they live invincible!"[28]

The qualities ascribed to the new men and women of the Stalinist age were Romantic to the core. They were rich personalities who expressed themselves in fantastic feats and whose artistic creativity helped shape the beautiful new socialist world. Their example superseded and eclipsed the earlier revolutionary ideal of the machine man. If during the first years of Soviet power Alexei Gastev, a fervent advocate of Taylorism, had fantasized about "expressionless faces without a soul, which know no poetry or emotions and which are not moved by writing or laughter, but are measured with manometer and taxometer," the Stakhanovites wielded metal technology with the burning flame of their will. In contrast to the preceding generation of Communists, who had been reared as ascetic, self-denying beings, they had "feelings, . . . passions."[29]

The period of "high Stalinism" during the mid-1930s was the apotheosis of the Soviet revolutionary appeal to the self. From an earlier insistence on molding and enlightening the "broad masses," the emphasis had shifted toward a more powerful and complex idiom of the individual soul. Communist activists of the 1930s called on Soviet citizens to express their rich essence in contributing to the collective project of building the perfect future. Stalin defined heroic expressivism as the central attribute of the Soviet system. In March 1938 he met with a delegation of polar aviators who had been spectacularly rescued following an emergency landing on drifting ice. European countries and the United States, Stalin declared in his toast to the pilots, judged every one of their citizens by his monetary worth: "Americans will say that a hero costs 100,000 dollars." The Communist government, by contrast, had introduced a new, "Soviet," "method of evaluating people, not in rubles, nor in dollars." It appraised people by their "daring talent and potential," thanks to which they accomplished unprecedented deeds. The Soviet Union, Stalin suggested, possessed the same planes and modern technology as the West, but it ranked far above the West because of the people it bred. Rich in dollars, the West lacked a currency to evaluate man's innate heroism. Only the Soviet government acknowledged the "huge capital" that man represented. This wager on man's heroism and the expressive resources of his soul unleashed an intense desire among Soviet citizens to work for the Soviet state because this activity was the measure of their life. Like the polar aviators in distress, Soviet citizens wanted to "struggle and live, struggle in all spheres of industry, agriculture, and culture; they did not want to die, but to live; to live and strike down the enemies; to live in order to prevail."[30]

Stalin's toast bespoke limitless possibilities, stemming from the confidence that Soviet citizens, under the guidance of the Communist party, had the capacity to will the Communist world into existence. This expectation resonated with the belief that man could bend the whole universe to the rhythm of his desires by an act of will. In opposition to Romantic ideology of the nineteenth century, however, Soviet Communists insisted that theirs was an ideology of *action*. Furthermore, they knew their faith to be grounded in scientific analysis, in contrast to the mystical orientation of Romanticism. Bukharin declared: "In our conditions, the Romantic is connected in particular measure to the *heroic*, and it is not at all oriented to a metaphysical heaven, but instead to the earth, with all of its aspects, to victory over the enemy and to victory over nature."[31]

Stalinist Neo-Romanticism differed from the nineteenth-century Romantic spirit in another significant respect. The powerful spirit ascribed to the heroes of the Soviet age was never absolute or self-induced; it was nurtured by the Communist party and owed its expressive power to Stalin himself, who described himself as rearing "every capable and understanding worker" like a "gardener, who rears his beloved fruit tree."[32] As expressive beings Soviet citizens, unlike Chapaev in Furmanov's novel, were no longer unconscious and soft like wax—they grew and blossomed, but in a garden landscape controlled by Stalin. Stalin fostered the fruit-carrying trees, he trimmed their stems and branches, and he excised parts deemed harmful for the ordered garden environment. While the historical progression of this gardening project mandated an ever greater investment in self-expression and individual growth, its primary emphasis remained on enlightened urges to shape, direct, and intervene in individuals' lives.

Like the call to self-expression, Stalinist repression also had an individuating thrust. In a developed socialist order individuals could no longer point to an imperfect social environment as a source of their deformation; this had been the assumption on which Soviet law of the 1920s was built. By contrast, legal specialists of the Stalin era asserted that "divergences from the moral norm in a socialist society are the manifestations of the remnants of capitalism in the consciousness of man." From now on, individuals were fully responsible for their deeds and thoughts. As a popular textbook on psychology stated: "A man takes part in the shaping of his own character and he himself bears a responsibility for that character." The individual's spirit could appear in only one of two ways—either as good, with the individual growing in the image of his transformed environment, or as evil, with the individual resisting his transformation. The individual's will thus figured as either revolutionary and creative or counterrevolutionary and destructive. Even as it hailed the superhuman creative efforts of the Stakhanovites, the political language of the time engaged in grueling descriptions of the will's destructive power, manifested in "wreckers," whose actions were equally beyond human imagination. The evil will of the "enemies of the people" was such that they had to be removed from Soviet society.[33]

The fear among party leaders that their ranks were filled with hidden enemies dated back to the early revolutionary period. But this fear became much more acute once the Soviet leadership decided to construct utopia, to abolish class society and to proceed with the building of socialism. With the disappearance of non-Soviet classes, the environment lost its original significance as a polluting influence. From now on all instances of impurity could only emanate from individual souls. Impurity, previously discernible through the markers of class identification, had retracted into the depths of the human psyche. The exploding political paranoia of the 1930s, the massive increase in suspicion against supposed enemies of the people, also expressed a crisis induced by the breakdown of the traditional Marxist tool of class analysis in evaluating the individual. Where there were no more alien classes to point to, the proclivity to demonize existing obstacles on the road to socialism became overwhelming.[34]

The Great Purges of the 1930s stood at the apex of an enormous project to classify souls according to purity. In exterminating all individuals deemed harmful to the new, socialist order, the terror was the flip side of the Stalinist humanist program of creating a social body defined in terms of absolute purity of spirit. By the same token, the purge was another powerful individualizing technique of the Soviet state, and to this extent it furthered the Stalinist policies of subjectivization. Throughout the purge period, even at its very height, when thousands of sentences were being passed daily, defendants were tried not in summary fashion, but individually, with the state organs relying on an enormous array of prosecutorial material, again organized by individuals. The amount of resources and effort that the state invested in this process—for instance, staffing NKVD interrogation cells with secretaries, available around the clock, who typed and copied version after version of countless individual confessions—cannot but appear grotesque if viewed as a mere cover-up for a campaign of arbitrary state terror. The purges appear less grotesque, though, when seen as a large-scale project of classification conceived for the pursuit of irrefutable truth regarding the state of individuals' souls.[35] Throughout the purges, the party leaders repeatedly stressed their individualizing emphasis, specifically the degree of individual care they applied to the investigation. Time and again, the Moscow Center issued reprimands to "overzealous" local prosecutors whom it charged with expelling party members in summary fashion. "Honest Communists" were portrayed as receiving "insufficient individual study." The party, embodied above all by Josef Stalin, cast itself as a final judge, weighing each soul individually and carefully.[36]

2

Bolshevik Views of the Diary

The Soviet revolutionary project of self-change had features of a "Soviet Reformation."[1] Indeed, the Bolsheviks' double emphasis on spreading consciousness throughout the realm and on making this consciousness a matter of individual experience recalls the efforts of the Reformation church to create an individualized faith. Both the sixteenth-century Reformation and the Soviet revolution had a subjectivizing thrust—they called for the creation of self-reliant subjects, who in the case of the Reformation were to monitor their spiritual health, and who in the Soviet case were to comprehend themselves as political subjects with a historical mission.

The Reformation led to a dissemination of the diary as an account book of the reformed Christian's soul. As an individual and social practice, the diary gained particular prominence in the fervent religious climate of Puritan New England. Puritan ministers adopted the technique of diary-keeping as a way to work on the self in the service of salvation and as a means of disseminating their faith. Their autobiographical literature was personal and prescriptive at the same time. It was personal, in that the themes of pilgrimage and conflict, of trouble and grace, were reflections of the diarist's experience and products of his self-consciousness. But it was also prescriptive, in that the genre was accepted as a model frame within which the "basic patterns of the godly life" were to be inscribed and take shape, and "within which [an individual's] experience was to be understood."[2] The Puritan diary was not conceived of primarily as an intimate record to be scrutinized by the author alone. The diary functioned as an instrument of its author's own salvation and to this extent supported notions of personal individuality, but Puritan saints always kept a public audience in mind while producing their confessions. For the Puritans, personal and national regeneration took place in a shared pilgrimage toward salvation. This alignment of the subjective, individual self with the collective in the pursuit of salvation is strongly reminiscent of the Soviet conception of the raising of individuals' subjective consciousness to the level of objective truth through their joining of the revolution. Did Soviet Communists likewise deploy the diary as a means of totalizing and individualizing their ideology?

Judging by the "Red Army notebook" of the civil war period, at least some revolutionary activists sought to make use of the diary for the purposes of political education. This was a booklet handed out to each Red Army soldier, in which he was to record the ammunition, food, and clothing distributed to him. The book contained several blank pages at the end. The first of them bore the heading "For personal notes," followed by this instruction: "If possible, keep a diary of your service in the Workers' and Peasants' Red Army."[3] Although no notebooks are known to have survived that would show to what use soldiers put the space allotted for personal notes, this prescriptive diary is in tune with other strategies pursued by the Red Army to impart political literacy and make soldiers comprehend themselves as participants in a struggle of world-historical proportions.

In the decade after 1917 the diary received attention especially from scientists and the literary avant-garde, who sought to connect the diaristic genre to the revolutionary cause. Among them were "pedologists," revolutionary-minded psychologists who devoted themselves to the study of the child. Assuming that young people had no autonomous consciousness and could be molded by a given social environment, pedologists believed that examining children yielded direct insights into the psycho-physical effects of the revolution. Psychologists valued diaries in particular because of their supposed authenticity. Since a diary was written on the diarist's own initiative, they assumed that it was sincere and provided an unmediated reflection of psychic processes. "Analyzing a diary allows one to study forms of behavior which are difficult to reveal in any other medium." To be sure, this authenticity was achieved only in a "correct diary," which was defined as the result of regular recordkeeping in a self-reflective mode.[4]

Pedologists published young people's diaries to demonstrate the determining power of the social milieu over an individual's psycho-physical development. A diary of a German girl, originally published by a Vienna-based psychoanalytical association, appeared in Russian translation in 1925, with a preface by a professor of the Military-Medical Academy. As the professor explained, the diary, which described the sexual awakening of a prepubescent girl, showed that "hypocritical" bourgeois parents and educators shunned "correct" sexual education and left their children helpless in the face of overpowering instincts. "The book should be of interest to pedologists, pedagogues, doctors, social workers, and parents in general. It will . . . force many to reflect on how not to educate children. From this point of view the content of the book can have propagandistic uses."[5]

The publication of the *Diary of Kostya Riabtsev* in 1926 was in part a Soviet response to the diary of the German girl. A fictional diary, written by Nikolai Ognev (M. G. Rozanov), it had such a lifelike appeal that it was followed by two sequels and one reviewer wondered whether Ognev had not simply compiled the material from "authentic" diaries. Kostya is a rebellious teenager, mischievous and undisciplined, and his account of topics such as child abuse, masturbation, and abortion are more tangible and shocking than the reveries of the German girl; nevertheless critics portrayed him as a positive role model for Soviet youth. Kostya is a proletarian with "Communist convictions." His sound working-class environment ensures his social and activist disposition. Though a hooligan, Kostya distinguishes between nonproletarian and "proletarian nonsense." Nowhere in the account of his life does the reader doubt that Kostya will eventually gain control over his instincts, which are responsible for his anarchistic behavior. The diary concludes with Kostya's acceptance into the Komsomol, the Communist youth organization. Kostya's diary, to which Ognev added a sequel, went through several editions and undoubtedly played a significant role in popularizing the diary medium among Soviet readers. In 1933 Leonid Potemkin, a nineteen-year-old worker, compared his diary unfavorably to that of Kostya Riabtsev, whom he envied for his practical mastery of life: "In my case there are only sick reflections. No practice, no sparkling public activities. I must master life in practice, I must live."[6]

Pedologists' ambitions went beyond using diaries to show the adverse or beneficial influences of the social environment. They sought to create a corpus of autobiographical writing that both testified and lent support to the socialist direction of the proletarian state. In 1919 Nikolai Rybnikov, director of the Moscow Pedological Museum, pressed the People's Commissariat for Enlightenment to create a biographical institute, to be devoted to the collection and analysis of diaries and other autobiographical sources by young Soviet subjects. His initiative fell through for lack of funding, but Rybnikov proceeded to collect autobiographical testimony from young Soviet citizens. By 1928 he had collected 120,000 questionnaires from grade-school students living in the provinces. His diagnosis was sobering: only a small fraction of these students knew the purpose and the history of the revolution, which had taken place ten years before. The questionnaires also revealed that the greatest number of diarists in Russia hailed not from the exploited classes, with whom the pedological profession preferred to experiment, but from the "bourgeois intelligentsia." Nevertheless pedologists expressed hope that "with the growth of psychological culture and the increase of interest in the inner world, [Soviet] diary literature can be expected to become much more widespread."[7]

There are a few indications that as early as the 1920s diary-writing was used in Soviet schools as a pedagogical tool—to train linguistic expression, but also as a medium of self-development. Diaries were assigned both on an individual level and for the class as a whole. A striking example is the diary of Lev Bernshtein, a teenager who would later become a well-known physicist and member of the Academy of Sciences. His diary of 1926, which bears traces of the teacher's correcting red pencil, describes a class excursion to the Volkhov River dam, the first in a series of grand Soviet construction projects: "The Volkhov dam workers' settlement is a wonderful achievement of Soviet workers' construction. It's a real America! Clean, large streets, with barracks on both sides: dormitories for the workers. At each intersection there is a pole with illuminated signs of the street name and the barracks numbers . . . The Volkhov dam workers' settlement is an exemplary workers' commune, it is a blueprint for Communist society of the future."[8]

Bernshtein's diary also demonstrates the mechanisms through which pupils were to acquire and internalize Soviet political and sociological taxonomy. Visiting the Old Ladoga region near the dam, they were assigned the "task" of making the acquaintance of "different types of peasants, in whom we try to detect signs of social differentiation, although the latter have not actively revealed themselves in the village." They were to distinguish between exploited, poor; middle; and exploiting, rich peasants, the ominous kulaks. Ironically it was a kulak who most fascinated the students with his accounts of life under serfdom and the advent of the revolution, "when our brothers, the worker and the peasant, governed our Mother Russia." Bernshtein's teacher left his admiring characterization of this peasant-exploiter uncommented upon—a testimony to how widely the 1920s were regarded as an ideologically contaminated age in which it was legitimate to make statements that in the historically more developed socialist environment of the 1930s were bound to be read as heretical and dangerously subversive of Communist ideology.

The significance of diary-keeping was also emphasized by the "Left Front in Art" (LEF), a group of Soviet avant-garde writers associated for the purpose of creating a proletarian culture. The particular goal of LEF was to promote a new literary style, called "literature of the fact." These activists grounded their call for a new literature in the claim that the traditional literary style, epitomized in the bourgeois novel, had become outdated. The novel was characterized chiefly by its detachment from the concerns and practices of current life; its effect was only to mystify the reader, to work on his imagination. By contrast, "Our epics are the newspapers . . . What is the good of talking about bookish novels . . . when every morning as we snatch our newspaper we turn over a new page of the most astounding novel called *Our Today*. The characters in this novel, its authors, and its readers, are we ourselves."[9]

The literature advocated by LEF was documentary, or factographic, encompassing a wide variety of sources which testified to the revolutionary agenda of the Soviet state. These were for the most part human documents: biographies, memoirs, travelogues, autobiographies, and diaries. Holding these texts together was the "fact," which acted as the "primary material cell for the construction of the edifice." In contrast to the contemplative idealism of bourgeois literature, this was a "new aesthetic . . . or rather a new science . . . The new science of art presupposes to change reality by transforming it . . . Hence the emphasis on the document, and hence literature of the fact."[10] Implicitly, LEF encouraged every proletarian to keep a daily diary that would document the epic process of transformation and self-transformation under way in all areas of Soviet life. The calendar grid of the diary lent itself to

LEF's agenda of documenting the building of the future, day by day. Yet this agenda worked only if the "facts" of Soviet life, on both social and individual psychic levels, revealed a steady development over time.

Tellingly for Communist conceptions of the diary, it was at the construction site of the Moscow metro where the most wide-ranging discussion on diary-keeping during this period took place. The Moscow metro occupied a central place in Gorky's "History of the Factories" project. As with all the other factories and construction sites that formed part of this project, an editorial board of professional writers was instituted at *Metrostroy;* their task was to direct the production of workers' memoirs and eventually publish them in lavish documentary series. The *Metrostroy* editors specifically encouraged workers to write "production diaries," the best of which were to be included in the projected volumes. The deliberations among the editors shed light on what they envisioned as the forms and goals of Soviet diary-keeping—on the construction site and beyond. For one, the diary figured as a disciplining technique in the labor process; it was to encourage the worker-author to "keep more order, to be more systematic, to reflect about what he does, in order to assimilate and reinforce his [work] experience." As one editor, Leopold Averbakh, put it, diary-keeping was to proceed like a party "purge": "You examine yourself in everything, what and how. The diary must we written so that the worker or another person asks himself what he has done of value on a given day."[11]

The editors considered the ability of the diary to induce self-reflection as a key aspect: "The diary . . . is a way of establishing the balance of one's actions, day after day; of reflecting on one's life." More than a mere work record, the worker's journal should "show the process of development of the entire person." Ultimately, the editors wanted diarists to link their lives to the construction site, and to understand that their subjective lives evolved within the frame of the construction of socialism. This process was to be both totalizing, in terms of opening the self to the collective, and self-completing, in the sense of bringing out the individual's creative faculties. On one hand, "every [individual] biography [was] to become a part of the biography of the metro." On the other, the publication devoted to the construction site was expected to contribute to the shaping of the personality of each contributor. The act of "collective creation" was to "enrich each creator's individuality."[12]

In deliberating about the Soviet production diary, the editors sought to make it unlike a "bourgeois" diary—a socially useless record filled with ineffectual talk: "Why do we often look down on the diary?" one of them, Leopold Averbakh, asked. "Because the diary connotes a girl's high school activity: a girl who sits down and writes all sorts of nonsense." By contrast, Averbakh emphasized, the Soviet production diary was firmly embedded in an environment of concentrated, collective striving which lent it direction and use: "In our case, the diary is part of a system."[13]

Beyond aligning the diarist to the Soviet project, diary-writing also had a public purpose. Diaries and memoirs were to be discussed in worker brigades and printed on wall newspapers to educate and mobilize lagging members of the collective. Hence the editors' insistence that especially "shock workers," workers who exceeded their labor norms, write diaries. Their exceptional work records pointed to their developed political consciousness and lent hope that they would produce diaries particularly suitable for inclusion in the published volumes commemorating the building of the metro. The shock workers were also to encourage other, less able workers to keep diaries and to work on themselves.[14] The Soviet production diary, as envisioned by its progenitors, was at once an intensely personal document, disclosing the individual's spiritual essence, and a public, educational text; much like the Puritan diary, it welded spiritual to propagandistic functions. The editors never conceived of the production diary—or of the diary genre as a whole—as a purely private document. Rather, it was a medium and tool of self-formation, defined in terms of the merging of the individual and the collective, the subjective and the objective.

Assuming that workers were not familiar with the diaristic genre and would not know how to keep a "creative diary," the editorial board established detailed guidelines on how to "correctly" write a production diary. They outlined a number of questions that the diarist should engage as part of his reflections: "The party, its guiding role; . . . the role of the engineer; the face of the Komsomol; international life; class struggle in the *Metrostroy;* women and the metro; culture and way of life; all of Moscow builds the metro, all of the [Soviet] Union builds the metro." These prescriptions culminated with a call for truthful representation: "The essential exigency of the diary is maximum truth, sincerity, and authenticity. No pseudo-literature . . . Write the truth!" Truth was to be attained through a faithful adherence to the stylistic and thematic guidelines provided by the editors. It was defined as a diarist's correct understanding of political life and his ability to position himself in its unfolding, be it "the class struggle in the *Metrostroy*" or "international life." Truth could be felt only as an inner experience, transcending the veneer of external appearances, and the site at which it was to be produced was the diary: "The diary is the reflection of our consciousness of the world. One must go beyond appearances, beyond what captures the eye. One has to understand events, create links between them. There must be a central theme. The criterion of the diary is truth." Truthful representation, the editors stressed, should not lead to an embellishment of reality. It was not only permissible but necessary for the diarist to record negative appearances in life. Yet he also had to explain the provenance and nature of these deficiencies.[15]

The results of the initiative proved disappointing. Only a fraction of the metro workers heeded the appeal to write diaries. Of the journals the editors received, many were barely literate, filled with orthographic errors and clumsy expressions. Others did not reach the interpretive depth the editors had sought to attain, instead confirming their initial fears that production diaries would be kept as mere "account books," detailing "how many cubic meters were done" on a given day. The narratives were "superficial" and "dry," they lacked "interiority," they did not "get to essential things." Worst of all, they operated on the "useless" level of description or contemplation, thus failing the test of the "correct" diary, which "must be conceived for action." The grand project of a collective autobiographical record of the *Metrostroy* did not bear its intended fruit.[16] Eventually the editorial commission published two volumes with memoirs and autobiographical sketches—but not diaries—related to the building of the Moscow metro.[17]

The editors had to concede that their plan to elicit production diaries, to which they had attached "very great importance," was a much longer-term endeavor than they had anticipated. Still, they had not lost faith in the significance of the diary medium. As one of the editors remarked: "Do we have to keep diaries? Without any doubt. They can give great results, but these results won't come overnight. The diary demands time, but we need material now." This final statement bespeaks a revealing hesitation. In some distant future, the editors believed, socialist citizens with developed political consciousness would write the type of diaries they had called for. At present, however, such journals could not be produced without extensive editorial supervision and intervention. Impatient to document the historical transformation carried out by the Soviet regime, the editors turned to workers' memoirs, which, compared with diaries, were more quickly produced, more easily supervised, and yielded biographical results.[18]

If Soviet workers in general still lacked sufficient political literacy to keep a "correct" diary, what about Communists like Dmitri Furmanov, whose political consciousness was beyond doubt? Furmanov, along with other members of the radical intelligentsia, was a dedicated diarist.[19] But even for him, keeping a journal was a controversial matter. He repeatedly worried that writing in the diary led him to overemphasize aspects of his personal life, thus disconnecting him from the revolution and the fate of the Soviet people. With its emphasis on personal emotions, on "love, suffering, happiness, memories, expectations," his diary made him think of the diary of Nicholas II, excerpts of which he remembered reading in a 1917 newspaper: "I ate, took a walk in the garden, lay on the grass, the dear sun was shining, I had a quarrel–etc. etc." But, Furmanov hastened to add, what distinguished him fundamentally from the last Romanov was that the bulk of his life was devoted to the great cause of "the Revolution"–a commitment that his diary failed to convey. Furmanov was convinced that the diary medium could not capture the full essence of his life.[20] This conflict between a lyrical personal realm and an epic "life" is not present in the diary of Furmanov's literary hero, Fedor Klychkov. Klychkov's diary is of one mold–it bespeaks a voice of developed reason, firmly dedicated to social use and revolutionary action. As such, Klychkov's record stood for what Furmanov imagined to be the ideal Communist diary.

Communists continued to express reservations about the diary, even as they began to evoke the "rich personal life" of the new socialist individual in the early 1930s. It remained a matter of doubt whether the diary was a suitable tool for self-training and individualization in a Soviet setting. A Komsomol activist in the mid-1930s rebuked a friend for suggesting "that a man works out the way of his own development by means of a diary, by means of organizing and studying his own self": "No, my dear, what is most valuable in man's life is his work and not his diary . . . Because knowing and loving one's work, . . . keeping in step with the multimillion-member collective, is the main thing in contemporary training and self-training. And the diary is not a method of self-training, but a method of self-rummaging. It is suitable for the 'intellectuals' (in the derogatory sense of the word) who 'study' themselves and dig in the depths of their own psychology—here am I, a mean and weak-willed man; here is the misdeed I committed."[21]

While in agreement with his correspondent that a Communist should "organize" his psychic life so as to align it with the life of the collective, the Komsomol activist criticized the diary as a useless and, indeed, harmful instrument. A purely reflective medium, it carried the risk of divorcing thought from action, the mind from the body, and the individual from the collective. The very act of individual diary-keeping could weaken the Communist's essence—his willpower, which needed the proximity of the collective and the work sphere to be replenished. Thus the diary had the uncanny ability to remake solitary, writing Communists into bourgeois subjects. The contrast between Communist strength and bourgeois weakness evoked an opposition as well between supposedly male attributes of firm, rational, and collective action and female narcissism, hysteria, and socially useless chatter. These last characteristics were sometimes identified with the diary as a literary form. Tainted by its supposed proclivity to make the Communist bourgeois, weak, feminine, the diary did not figure prominently among the many forms of "work on the self" that the Communist regime promoted throughout the 1930s.[22]

The turn from the 1920s to the 1930s entailed a transition from an age of compromise and historical impurity to the uncompromising pursuit of a final historical age of utmost purity. This transition affected the readership as well as the reading styles of diaries in the Soviet realm. The most prominent readers and analysts of diaries during the 1920s were pedologists, who traced lapses in consciousness in a journal back to the social environment of the imperfect Soviet present. The pedological profession was abolished in 1936, when all class antagonisms were decreed to have been abolished in Soviet society. Now the NKVD became the chief interpreting agency of Soviet diaries.[23]

NKVD officers analyzed diaries seized during searches of the apartments of suspected counterrevolutionaries for signs of subjective deviation from, or opposition to, the single, socialist historical formation that the Soviet regime embodied. NKVD officials were not trained as psychologists or literary experts, but they fully shared the assumption held both by pedologists and the Soviet writing profession that the diary disclosed the truth about its author—whether in direct expression of what the lines said or in its direct inversion. In the latter case the NKVD assumed that counterrevolutionary enemies were masquerading as Communists and that their loyal Communist diaries formed part of the elaborate mask.[24]

In two prominent cases, diaries of Communists accused of counterrevolutionary crimes were publicly cited to disclose their moral and political makeup. The first of them involved Boris Kozelev, a trade union leader and a supporter of Mikhail Tomsky, who was discredited in the late 1920s as a "Right Deviationist." In his diary Kozelev sarcastically commented on the way Stalin outmaneuvered his adversaries one by one and consolidated the cult of himself as political leader. The diary was discovered by a drunken colleague whom Kozelev had brought home and put up in his office to sober up. The colleague found the diary in a drawer of Kozelev's desk and passed it on to the GPU (the Soviet secret police, renamed NKVD in 1934), which forwarded it to the Politburo. Passages from the diary appeared in the Soviet press, which denounced the author for his "anti-party pranks." The diary was also discussed at the Sixteenth Party Conference in June 1930, at which the fate of the Right Opposition was sealed. Kozelev, who was expelled from the Communist party, seemed to accept at least some of the charges: in a gesture of expiation he set out to work as a metal worker in Moscow's "Hammer and Sickle" plant, and in the fall of 1930 he left for Magnitogorsk to help build the city of steel. He was arrested in 1936 and shot in 1937.[25]

Another diary intensely scrutinized by Communist leaders and the

NKVD was that of Leonid Nikolaev, the disaffected Communist who shot Sergei Kirov in December 1934 and set off Stalin's political terror campaign against his erstwhile adversaries, including Tomsky and Kozelev. When Nikolaev was arrested, his diary was found in his briefcase. The diary, prominently cited in reports of the murder investigation, served as prime evidence of the process of inner degeneration that had led a Communist to kill a comrade. In his diary Nikolaev described his despondency after being reprimanded by the Communist party in early 1934, and how his frustration turned into a conscious decision to attack the collective body from which he had been expelled.[26]

Neither in Nikolaev's nor in Kozelev's case did prosecutors argue that the very fact that the suspect wrote a diary incriminated him. Instead they focused on what the diaries revealed about their authors. While a Communist observer might have established a causal link between secretive individual diary-keeping and the state of subjective degeneration that it possibly induced, this argument was not made. This was a further indication of how inconsistently the diary fared in the Communist imagination, cast alternatively as a legitimate medium of self-perfection and as an inherently bourgeois pursuit.

In spite of the ethos of self-activation and the individuating thrust that characterized the Bolshevik revolution as well as seventeenth-century Puritanism, the two movements pursued different goals. The Puritans accorded the utmost importance to a Christian believer's relationship with his soul. By definition the soul of a fallen man was sinful, but to acknowledge and expose one's sin through vigilant self-observation was key to the believer's salvation in the afterlife. The diary's calendar grid and first-person narrative lent it power as a daily record in which the sinful Christian staged a personal court of conscience. As a daily form of self-engagement, diaristic practice was the essential component of the work of salvation; hence the central significance Puritans accorded to the diary both as a self-practice and as a propagandistic tool. The Bolshevik revolution, by contrast, was not oriented toward an afterworld; it was bent on changing *this* world. Hence Soviet Communists sought to instill a universal consciousness in order to propel citizens into conscious action. In contrast to the Puritans' concern with interiority as a goal in and of itself, Soviet culture accorded the highest value to conscious external activity. To act consciously presupposed self-knowledge and self-mastery, an ordered psycho-physical life. To this extent, interiority was important, too, but only as a stepping stone toward the act of conscious labor.

Consciousness and action as the measure of an individual's worth in the Soviet realm were also the decisive criteria against which the value of diary-keeping was judged. To keep a diary was a legitimate and valuable pursuit if the diarist used it to reinforce his mental commitment toward work within the Soviet collective. Arguably the production diary envisioned by the *Metrostroy* editors was the ideal Soviet diary: its purpose was to foster diaristic reflection on the work space and thus imbricate physical work with mental dedication. The environment of work and the laboring collective, combined with guidance by the editorial board, would make sure that the diarist's thoughts traveled safely in the direction of conscious action. Yet to operate in this fashion, the production diary required politically literate diarists, who were not to be found in significant numbers at the Moscow metro construction site. As for diaries that were written outside the work sphere and the monitoring gaze of the collective, they carried the risk of diminishing rather than enhancing their authors' Communist will. They threatened to privilege reflection at the expense of action, and were therefore looked upon with ambivalence and a degree of suspicion. These reservations help explain why diaries were not of central significance for the subjectivization policies carried out by the Bolshevik state.

Thus Soviet diarists wrote their personal records in the absence of the prescriptive culture that characterized the Puritan diary. They were unsure about the benefits of diary-keeping and of how to keep a "correct" diary. Most of them wrote diaries on their own initiative, and some in fact lamented the absence of official precepts for how to achieve the work of self-transformation. An investigation of these diaries thus highlights the extent to which individuals, acting on their own, creatively wove themselves into a loose matrix of subjectivization produced by the Soviet Revolution, and how these individuals themselves supplied some of the core categories and mechanisms of self-realization in a Soviet vein.

3

Laboratories of the Soul

In 1893 Mavriky Fabianovich Shilling, a young nobleman and aspiring diplomat living in St. Petersburg, noted in his diary that he had scoured the stores to find a thick notebook with a lock, but they were sold out and all he could do was place an order. Such diaries, elaborately crafted and equipped with lock and key, were generally unavailable in Soviet Russia. Stalin-era diarists had to make do with school exercise books, and even those were in short supply. Many diarists mentioned that for lack of paper and notebooks they had to suspend the writing of their chronicles. An article in *Pravda* bemoaned the shortages of school notebooks and their low quality: "The rough and coarse covers of indeterminate color easily absorb dirt and are therefore soiled and untidy. There are many more blots and smeared words than would be permissible even for first-graders, and the children are not to blame for this." In the absence of notebooks some diarists wrote in account books they presumably found at their workplaces.[1] Using an account book seem to have inspired Alexander Medvedkov, a trade union official, to an idiosyncratic form of diaristic bookkeeping. He recorded the events of each day of his life in several tables, with such subheadings as "date," "day of the week," "designation of performed work and rest," "content of work and rest," "wasted time," and "intimacy." In the tables he recorded the number of hours spent on a given activity each day. Another diarist wrote on loose sheets of official stationery that bore both Soviet and prerevolutionary letterheads.[2]

Stalin-era diaries thus contrast sharply in outward appearance with diaries from prerevolutionary times, which were more often kept in thick, sometimes leather-bound, volumes made of finely grained paper. This contrast is put in even sharper relief in the case of diarists who wrote across the revolutionary divide and at some point had to abandon their bound volumes for the coarse notebooks produced by the Soviet regime.[3] Emblematic of the way diarists were jolted from orderly lives into a state of impoverishment and violent upheaval, the image of the two books—leather volume and school notebook—also encapsulates another transition: from diary-keeping as a pursuit of privileged members of society to a democratic agenda of universal literacy, schooling, and recording of the self.

The paper shortages with which diarists of the 1930s had to contend only underscore the urge they felt to take pen to paper. The same sense of urgency is reflected in a set of shared themes in their diaries, which they voiced as pressing mandates and questions demanding engagement, struggle, and ultimately, resolution. Many diarists believed they were living in a historical epoch, and they strove to participate in its unfolding. The unquestioned duty and, for many, desire to become involved in the march of history took hold in equal measure of loyal supporters of the Stalinist regime and of some its vocal critics. These diarists also knew that to participate in a revolutionary politics of transformation they must first transform themselves. They used their diaries to monitor their thoughts and their performance in light of the mandate of "social use." To be aligned with history required work and struggle. While many authors failed to commune with the revolution consistently and were instead preoccupied with smaller pursuits, ranging from daily chores to matters of the heart, they blamed themselves for their "petty" concerns and insisted that their value as human beings and progressive citizens depended on their ability to serve the wider interests of society. They strove to write themselves into the experience of a larger collectivity, which they imagined as a living organism. Adherence to the collective promised them meaning and vitality beyond sheer survival in an age of intense ideological surveillance. In turn, many of those who were unable or unwilling to think in step with the marching collective felt depressed and useless, and some recorded their wish to die. A life-creating force, the revolution confronted those who opposed the revolutionary state with a question of life or death.

A Revolutionary Time

Many Soviet diaries from the 1930s bespeak a strong sense of living in an exceptional, historic period and having an obligation to record it. "When will I finally write my memoirs about the 1930s?" one diarist asked. The fact that this author posed the question in 1932, when the decade had barely begun, illustrates how much of a notion there already existed of the Stalinist industrialization campaign as a distinct epoch in the making. More than just the record of an observing chronicler, the diary frequently had the additional task of writing its author into the age: of creating a dialogue between the self and the age in historical terms, and of thus raising the self to the level of a historical subject. This double purpose of the diary, as a record both of history in the making and of the self as a historical subject in the making, defined many a Communist diary of this period, but it also extended to diarists who critically engaged the Communist regime. The more vocally these diarists criticized the political order, in fact, the more strongly did they appeal to history.[4]

Alexander Zhelezniakov, a Communist active in the collectivization campaign in the Vologda region, began to keep a diary upon hearing that he would be appointed chairman of a village soviet in another district. In the first entry he bade farewell to his fellow "activists." Detailing their "struggles" and achievements—70 percent of the peasant households collectivized; 12 kolkhozes (collective farms) successfully organized—Zhelezniakov wrote that this "victory must be registered in the history of the kolkhozes of the Likhtoshskoe village soviet." Zhelezniakov embedded the news of his reappointment in the larger narrative of a collective class struggle: "The class enemy, the kulak, did not sleep, inciting the backward masses of poor peasants and those peasants of average means against the kolkhozes . . . Thus, in a bitter skirmish with the obsolete and dying capitalist elements, our kolkhozes were born, reared, and strengthened. A lot of struggle still lies ahead, especially at the new location, the Pirogov village Soviet, where I have been transferred by the party's district committee."[5]

The same strategy is visible in the diary of Masha Scott, who expanded the ideological frame structuring the narration of her personal life to its utmost extent—the epic of international class struggle. Masha, a teacher of peasant background living in Magnitogorsk, recalled meeting John Scott, a visiting American engineer, whom she would later marry. She described her impressions upon seeing an emaciated young man, dressed in rags and covered with blast-furnace dust:

> The first American I had ever seen, he looked like a homeless boy. I saw in him the product of capitalist oppression. I saw in my mind's eye his sad childhood; I imagined the long hours of inhuman labor which he had been forced to perform in some capitalist factory while still a boy; I imagined the shamefully low wages he received, only sufficient to buy enough bread so that he could to go work the next day; I imagined his fear of losing even this pittance and being thrown on the streets unemployed in case he was unable to do his work to the satisfaction and profit of his parasitic bosses.[6]

The playwright Vsevolod Vishnevsky regarded it as his "task" to keep a diary to "preserve for history our observations, our present point of view—the point of view of the participant." In reading about the historical "mistakes and victories" of Vishnevsky and his contemporaries future generations would be strengthened in their dedication to build the perfect Communist society.[7]

Even a diary that its author conceived of strictly as a chronicle of everyday life had a historical thrust. Nikolai Zhuravlev, an archivist from Kalinin (Tver), wanted to create a serial record of "normal [days] in the life of a normal person" for the sake of a future historian of the city and of Soviet daily life. Tellingly Zhuravlev began his chronicle of ordinary life on an extraordinary day—the eight hundredth anniversary of the city's founding. That Zhuravlev attached a historical intention to his project is clear in the conclusion to his account of the day's parades and speeches: "Celebrations like this can take place only in the land of socialism! I remember these official 'festivities' under tsarism . . . But our holiday is a genuine mass holiday, a genuine holiday of the people." His was an attempt to document Soviet daily life as qualitatively different from that of previous times, changed by the revolution, commensurate with the Stalinist claim to have revolutionized everyday life.[8]

The sense that a diary should be historical in orientation in order to be a legitimate personal record is reflected in the laments of diarists that their chronicles failed to achieve such an orientation. Concluding the very first entry of his diary, which for years to come would revolve around his unhappy love for a girl called Katya, the Moscow komsomolist Anatoly Ulianov chided himself for a "stupid" inability to tie his diary to a more significant purpose in life: "Is the saying correct that keeping a diary is petit-bourgeois? Yes and no, I think. If you write only about love, about how you suffer in love, that probably is a foul petit-bourgeois trick." Realizing that he was somewhat infected by such a spirit, Ulianov vowed to stop practicing "babbology" and henceforth focus only on the "facts" of "real life." By this he meant "the life people write books about," the life of the heroes who were building the new socialist world. His life, by contrast, as exemplified by his diary, was empty, filled with brooding thoughts, void of the "essence of existence."[9]

Another diarist, the writer Alexander Peregudov, realized only from the distance of a quarter-century that his diary project had failed. In an entry of 1961 he related that in rereading his notes from the 1930s he was struck by how "petty" they were: "Where are all the great things that took place in our country, changing its face and strengthening its might? My explanation for this is that the diary was not destined for such a high purpose, but was kept for small, 'intimate and lyrical' notes which revolved only around my family life and nature and were of great interest only to myself and Maria. How I regret now that I did not keep a different, a great diary, devoted to the great events. I often tried, but I never wrote it."[10]

Similarly to Ulianov and Peregudov, the young schoolteacher Vera Pavlova regretted that her diary concerned only small and superficial episodes of her daily existence and failed to address the "big and vast" questions of life. Her diary was too "subjective," she concluded, and hence "boring and schematic in form." She admonished herself to "write more simply, create something new, so that this new style would reveal, would celebrate some turning-point . . . a new period . . . Yes, to write something objective, one must portray, must create new images . . . to condense the events, and tie them together with a single thread, into a single idea and a single tendency." To write about life "subjectively," without reflection, from the standpoint of personal observation, was to write in an old-fashioned, uncreative way. The challenge was to grasp the course of history as it progressed through her personal life. When making these observations in 1931 and 1932, Pavlova prefigured central tenets of the emerging socialist realist doctrine, which called upon Soviet writers to portray reality in its revolutionary development and to present their literary characters as concentrated expressions of the class struggle and the march toward a classless society. Pavlova reveals a distinct narrative expectation: to be a worthwhile record, her diary had to be devoted to the guiding idea of the age.[11]

In conceiving of their diaries as historical chronicles, diarists like Pavlova, Ulianov, and Vishnevsky were at pains to cast themselves as subjects of history. The calendar grid provided by the diary helped them articulate a temporal consciousness that was central for the formulation of a historical subjectivity.[12] The diary of Vladimir Biriukov, an ethnographer and librarian from the Ural region, demonstrates how calendar dates could serve as temporal markers to distinguish a new time from an old time and situate the author firmly in the Soviet realm. In his forties, Biriukov criticized his mother's elaborate preparations for the Easter holiday, "although she knows perfectly well that Lara and I don't believe in Easter and such things." The next day he remarked on the mountains of Easter cake on the table, that there would be enough left over to celebrate May Day: "Let today's holiday be mother's holiday—the next one will be ours." In a similar vein, Vasily Pedani, a Leningrad professor of engineering who began to keep a diary in 1930, on the occasion of the birth of his grandson Slava, recorded that on April 12, 1931—when Slava was not yet a year old—the family had taught the child how to respond to the pioneer greeting "Be prepared!" Slava "would raise his little hand: 'Always prepared!'" By pointing out that this exercise took place on the traditional Easter holiday, Pedani underscored the Communist direction of his grandson's upbringing. Upon reading a novel by the nineteenth-century writer Ivan Goncharov, Vera Pavlova was struck by how much the lifestyles of prerevolutionary Russia were at odds with Soviet life: "It seems as if those events took place at least several centuries ago . . . Only eighty years, but what a great leap—a historical turn."[13]

Nina Lugovskaya (born in 1919) was the daughter of a Socialist Revolutionary party veteran who kept being harassed by Communist authorities. Despite the fact that the family's apartment was repeatedly searched by the secret police, Nina's father urged his three daughters to keep diaries, telling them that the current times would be "exceedingly interesting" to look back on in later years. In her diary Nina sought to expose the "lies" of Communist propaganda by recording the reality of hunger and oppression around her. Complaining about her spineless, oblivious peers, she dreamed of a life of revolutionary action, which in the spirit of the Socialist Revolutionary party could well mean terrorist acts. At one point she jotted down her intention to kill Stalin to avenge the injustices committed against her father.[14]

The Leningrad history student Arkady Mankov also kept a diary that brimmed with acerbic political commentary. Like the Kalinin archivist Zhuravlev, Mankov conceived of his journal as raw material for a history of Stalinist everyday life that historians would write one day, but unlike Zhuravlev, he wrote the diary to discredit the political regime. The contemporary social structure in the Soviet Union, Mankov wrote, was "purely capitalist"; to refer to it as a Marxist state was blasphemous. All the while, however, Mankov called for the realization of Marx's revolutionary goals—the end of exploitation and the arrival of material plenty. In formulating his critique, he emphasized its progressive quality. He described himself as a "revolutionary activist," who "opposes contemporary reality . . . in the name of the ideal of the future. He knows that the future life will be better but that it can only be reached by mercilessly destroying the structures of the present life."[15]

The renowned biochemist Vladimir Vernadsky devoted his journal of the period of the Great Purges to chronicling the waves of arrests at his own research institute and among his friends and colleagues. Vernadsky's laconic record starkly evokes the frenzy and monstrosity of the purge campaign. Yet one of his strongest concerns was the deleterious effect of the purges on the power of the Soviet state, a state that, he asserted, fundamentally pursued "the interests of the masses in their entire real significance (except for freedom of thought and freedom of religion)." Vernadsky suspected that Stalin and the people surrounding him were gripped by a collective mental disorder, for how else could they "ruin the great cause of the new [order], which they have introduced into the history of mankind"? The "great cause" was the construction of the Soviet state, an accomplishment for which, according to Vernadsky, Stalin deserved personal credit. It was this ideal of Soviet statehood that caused Vernadsky, a former leader of the liberal Kadet party and an ardent proponent of statism, to critically engage the policies of the Bolshevik regime.[16]

Notwithstanding their different generational and occupational backgrounds, Vernadsky's and Mankov's critical perspectives on the regime were strikingly similar in structure. Both men believed in laws of historical development that would usher in a perfect future social order, both claimed for themselves an active role in the creation of the future, and neither could understand people who did not accept this vision and instead looked to the past. Among those was Mankov's uncle, a disenfranchised former merchant. Mankov castigated his uncle, an outwardly "pleasant" man, for having a negative and retrograde attitude: "Uncle Vanya is an embodiment of vile hatred toward Soviet power, toward everything that is real, on the part of an average philistine-bourgeois who, along with his income, has been deprived of all purpose for existence and every reason to live." With the same resoluteness, the writer Mikhail Prishvin opposed a possible return to the past: "The Orthodox cross . . . the monarchy . . . priests . . . funeral masses . . . village constables . . . land captains—impossible!" Even though Prishvin condemned the inhumane policies of the Soviet state, he conceived of the era as a historically necessary iron age that demanded discipline and compliance on the part of its citizens. His daily diary served to record the movements of the "wind of history."[17]

Whatever their political differences, these diarists all bespoke an intense consciousness of their time as a historical age and of themselves as historical subjects with a duty to participate in the creation of the socialist world. Against this corpus of diaries, several others stand out that eschew the revolutionary horizon of meaning. Among them is the diary of Evdokim Nikolaev, a self-educated Moscow worker born in 1872 and a former member of the Kadet party. Nikolaev's private library, numbering some ten thousand books, was confiscated following his arrest in 1920 for alleged counterrevolutionary activities. After a series of further arrests, he was executed in 1938. Throughout the Soviet period, in his diary, Nikolaev strictly observed the old Julian calendar, which lagged behind the Gregorian calendar, introduced in 1918, by thirteen days. He referred religiously to local streets and factories by their prerevolutionary names. In contrast to the ethnographer Biriukov, who denigrated Easter to invoke May Day, Nikolaev was moved by the Soviet labor holiday to reminisce about life under tsarism: "How merry and joyful everybody felt back then. What a wealth of everything existed, and how inexpensive and happy everything was . . . All this has vanished, like a dream. A disturbance occurred, and criminal people, alien to the country and the Russian people, came back from exile. They seized power over the Russian people and began to perform one experiment after another." Unlike other critics who condemned the current regime in the name of a better future, Nikolaev denounced the revolutionary enterprise as such as a "utopian and senseless system of some sort of a kolkhoz life for the people, a system that operates solely through coercion and terror."[18]

Ignat Frolov, a kolkhoz peasant from the Moscow region, also observed the Julian calendar in his Stalin-era diary. He, however, did not use his diary for political ends. His record evolved as a cyclical calendar of the natural seasons, complete with detailed daily observations on the weather and the state of the potato crop. He mentioned all the Russian religious holidays. Only occasionally was the narrative flow punctuated by remarks on the pernicious deeds of the "godless" Communists who ran the kolkhoz. Frolov's diary showed no sign of self-reflection or introspection, and it is an exemplary case of premodern consciousness—life in a universe governed by the forces of nature and religion.[19]

There were notably fewer of these last-mentioned diaries than of those clamoring for involvement in the revolutionary age. It was not just the danger of keeping such a dissenting journal that kept the numbers low; Lugovskaya's, Mankov's, and Prishvin's diaries were at least as politically explosive. At issue, rather, was the self-marginalization that ensued from writing oneself out of revolutionary time. In an age of political mobilization and public participation it was difficult to "keep quiet . . . and just stand on the sidelines," as another diarist, Andrei Arzhilovsky, a peasant from the Ural region with a "counterrevolutionary" political record, described his plight.[20] Many Soviet diarists found it even less desirable to endorse the discredited tsarist regime as an alternative to the Communist state, and yet this was precisely the direction in which Evdokim Nikolaev's total rejection of the Soviet regime led him.

The writer Prishvin recognized the problem of self-marginalization in the Communist age. Commenting on the history of the relationship between the intelligentsia and the Bolshevik party, which he interpreted as a trade of culture for political activism, he concluded: "Whereas [the Bolsheviks] thought they were in charge, we thought that eventually we would lead them. Meanwhile those who remained on the sidelines turned into spinsters." Nadezhda Mandelstam reported that her brother Evgeny used to say that much of the power wielded by the Soviet regime over the intelligentsia was carried in the word "Revolution," "which [no member of the intelligentsia] could bear to give up. It is a word to which whole nations have succumbed, and its force was such that one wonders why our rulers still needed prisons and capital punishment." Mandelstam added that the allure of "the Revolution" had taken hold of even the "most worthy" of her contemporaries, including her own husband Osip. Prishvin and Nadezhda Mandelstam addressed only the party and the intelligentsia, but as the great number of self-educated diarists from the lower classes suggests, the appeal to get involved in the revolution extended far beyond these two groups.[21]

Two diaries of the mid-1930s illustrate the extent and the limits of the historical consciousness that spurred the production of so many self-reflective diaristic records. While both were written by returning émigrés, they could not have differed more in tonality and orientation. Nikolai Ustrialov, a law professor and one-time officer in the White army who had emigrated to China after the civil war, had long envied the Soviet revolutionary project for its "historical pathos." He returned to Soviet Russia in 1935, eager to involve himself in the construction of the new world. Ustrialov used his diary to record signs of the historical dawn that he saw breaking everywhere in Moscow. The sight of a youth parade in Red Square reinforced his conviction that "our revolution" was an "upsurge, a beginning, a thesis in a new dialectical cycle." There was a strong self-reflexive component in his observations, for he believed that only through his ability to see the work of history could he "earn a Soviet biography." Ustrialov knew that his record as a former White officer would make it difficult for him to claim a place in the new order. Moreover, the sight of the parading young athletes reinforced his sense of being old and outlived by history. But he could not conceive of being a mere bystander as history marched toward completion: "It is difficult to feel like a 'superfluous person' these days, when, it would seem, everyone finds themselves with so much to do. I want to be up to my neck in activity—if only not to be superfluous in our time, at this historic hour—when the fate of our great country, our great revolution, is being decided. You want to hold your own to the fullest extent among the Soviet people, Soviet patriots, and you painfully endure your hateful isolation and the stares of cold 'vigilance' and dignified distrust that surround you on all sides." Ustrialov was arrested on conspiracy charges in the summer of 1937 and shot.[22]

The other returning emigrant was Tatiana Leshchenko-Sukhomlina, a singer and poet who had lived in Western Europe and the United States and returned to Moscow in 1935 after divorcing her American husband. Leshchenko-Sukhomlina neither took up nor rejected the self-transformative ethos of the Soviet revolution. Unlike many Soviet immigrants of the 1930s, among them scores of German Communists who had escaped from Nazi Germany, she cited no political reasons for her return to Russia. What drew her back was an overwhelming homesickness. With no previous exposure to the Soviet system, she was not conditioned to subject daily life to a political reading; her observations were shaped by an aesthetic sensibility absent in many other diaries of the period. She described her shock at the coarseness of human encounters in public, at the "streetcar, which is packed with people who fight and shout, who insult each other and smell bad." At the zoo, where she went with her young daughter, a man sitting on a bench next to her stared at her. When she smiled at him he spoke: "Forgive me, just recently I was at the Tretyakov Gallery. You are like an Italian Madonna I saw there. I haven't seen any woman like this. It's impossible to tear oneself away. I want to look at you all the time." A woman on the streetcar also praised her looks: "Well, now I can say I have seen a beautiful woman. You are obviously not Russian. I can tell from the expression on your face that you're not one of us."[23]

Leshchenko-Sukhomlina's aesthetics, centering on individual style and lacking any temporal dynamic, differed starkly from socialist realist aesthetics, which apprehended the coarse present through glimpses of the perfect future and evaluated a given fact only through its social use. As if to banish the unpleasant impressions engulfing her in Moscow, she evoked in her diary memories of three years she had spent in Spain: "the ocean, the cliffs, the glossy green of the orange trees, the roses and the sand . . . And the sun, blinding and magnificent, as if the whole world were lying below it. And it warms this entire world, it melts in its rays all ugliness, all bitterness, all disease. Oh, sun of Spain—what happiness!" In contrast to many Soviet diarists, Leshchenko-Sukhomlina found the source of her happiness in a bygone past, not in a radiant future to be constructed. She equated happiness with a peaceful existence in nature, not in an active struggle to subjugate nature. Her stance was contemplative, not activist. It is ironic that her nostalgic passage is devoted to Spain. Spain figured prominently in Soviet diaries of the period, but most diarists invoked a very different image of Spain—a nation engaged in a heroic civil war against the forces of fascism. Rather than serving as a projection for memories of a golden past, Spain was represented as an arena of bitter class struggle, in which the future was being decided.[24]

In fact, Leshchenko-Sukhomlina's thinking about Spain evolved significantly in the weeks following this diary entry. After reading in the newspapers about the fascist bombing raids on Spanish cities that were dear to her, she recognized a tension between the "stenciled" quality of her memories and the ugly reality of war. She accepted an invitation to give a speech on Spain to the Union of Sculptors and Artists and was pleased and amazed by the enthusiastic response to her presentation. It was subsequently published in the Red Army daily, *Krasnaya zvezda.* The evolution of her notions of Spain suggests the power of Soviet propagandistic imagery to shape not only individuals' self-definition but even their memories. In 1947, amid the xenophobic climate of the immediate postwar period, Leshchenko-Sukhomlina would be arrested and sentenced to eight years in a forced-labor camp.[25]

The Work of Self-Transformation

It took work and struggle to align the self with history. Diaries documented this process as much as they helped bring it about. Many diaries from the 1930s allowed the diarists to monitor their own physiological and intellectual processes for the purpose of controlling and perfecting them. To document their self-transformative work, diarists repeatedly invoked the concepts of "planning," "struggle," and "consciousness," core Communist values of the period of the first Five-Year Plans.

The young schoolteacher Vera Pavlova noted that she had divided her personal life into five-year plans, the dates of which corresponded to the official five-year plans established by the Soviet state. The construction targets she outlined for "my self," as well as her proud statements of production quotas met and exceeded ("on this front the Five-Year Plan has been met in two and a half years"), illustrate Pavlova's assumption that her personal life had to develop as part and parcel of the wider general plan of socialist construction. Repeatedly she voiced the need to control and rationalize her life, hoping to bring to light the realm of her "subconscious feelings." She also confided to the diary her dreams and fantasies, all her "crazy" thoughts, but above all a desire to "systematize" impressions and, ultimately, to live her life in "planlike," "systematic" fashion.[26]

Like Pavlova, the Moscow worker and Komsomol activist Anatoly Ulianov invoked the plan as a structure to bring order to his life and increase his work performance: "I want to transmit the planning of work to my daily life, both for my mental-physical [activities] and for leisure. I will try to make my work more manageable this way. Fewer of the usual tricks (walks with the 'perfidious' Katya, etc.)." Ulianov resolved to fight the entanglements of intimate relationships: "I must position myself on real rails, switch myself toward a rational mind, correct mental activity, a system." The writer Vera Inber advocated what she called "'technicizing the soul' . . . in other words, constructivism," to fight the "disorder in my soul" that she repeatedly diagnosed in her diary. In keeping with this mechanical imagery she remarked elsewhere: "Man is a factory. And the mind is the director of this factory." Consciously or not, Imber echoed Lenin, who had described the Communist party as a factory, with the Central Committee as its director.[27]

Diarists established a variety of related dichotomies to describe the composition of their self and the mechanisms of self-transformation in which they saw themselves engaged. These binaries included the opposition between the mind and the body, a diarist's "will" and his "heart," or individuals' "ideology" and their "psychology." Vladimir Molodtsov, a coal miner, described this last opposition: "It's interesting how much disparity there is between psychology and ideology. Ideologically, I mobilized myself to bridge the gap, and I do work actively, but the psychology still draws me back home, to my home environment. This is evidenced by the more frequent dreams of the past two days, in which I saw my mother. But ideology will improve psychology, this must happen."[28] "Psychology," in diaries of the early Soviet period, invariably had a negative ring. It was a lowly, chaotic, and dangerous force operating in the dark recesses of spirit and body, a force that diarists occasionally admitted to harboring in themselves. Ideology, by contrast, was attained through a person's conscious struggle against psychology. On the individual level it represented a subjective insight into a realm of higher knowledge of the laws of historical and social development, an insight that was institutionally claimed by the Communist party and bore the same name, ideology.

Stepan Podlubny, a kulak's son tormented by the "question of my psychology," assumed that he had inherited an ingrained kulak psyche from his father and would be unable to escape it. Vera Inber, hailing from the non-Communist intelligentsia, alluded to a "petit-bourgeois disorder" inside her that threatened to engulf her newly acquired rational worldview. Psychology could effectively be mastered only with the joint powers of the rational mind and the will. These two forces organized the individual's psycho-physical apparatus. As soon as they rendered psychology transparent and rational it ceased to be psychology, rising to the level of pure ideology.[29]

Because of its anti-Soviet connotation, diarists were more generous in recognizing the workings of "psychology" in others than in themselves. Following a conversation with a fellow worker of peasant origins who admitted having been attracted to a coal mining job by its high wage, Molodtsov indignantly commented on the man's "peasant psychology": "Sees only his personal gain and believes only in himself." Vera Pavlova, upon reading a newspaper report about the suicide of the Swedish "match king" Ivar Kreuger, reflected on the "psychology of the contemporary bourgeoisie"—a psychology indicative of the "material and spiritual crisis" currently reigning in the West. Her reasoning established a logical progression from "psychology" to spiritual breakdown to suicide.[30]

"Psychology" was also what diarists saw as the factor responsible for the many anti-Soviet crimes of which they learned in the course of the 1930s. Zinaida Denisevskaya, a teacher in Voronezh province, was bewildered when she read in the newspapers of a pernicious "Toiling Peasant party" in the province, which involved several of her acquaintances: "I don't understand all of this . . . Their psychology is completely alien to me. Who are they—fools, psychopaths, or bastards?" Lev Deich, an Old Menshevik, described the new conspiracy of Rightist-Trotskyist forces about which he read in the newspapers as a "nightmare" and felt unable to "understand the psychology of these people, what motivated them, and what they were banking on." In the midst of the political purges of 1937 the playwright Vsevolod Vishnevsky jotted down in his diary thoughts about "the enemies and their agents . . . the psychology of the traitors . . . Probably from their distrust in the strength of the people, the party . . . These are spiritual defeatists, spiteful and petty . . . Capitulators in the face of capital . . . I'm reading about Lenin, his stubbornness, his will."[31] If not actively engaged, psychology was weak and defeatist in spirit—as indicated in the diaries of Vishnevsky and Pavlova. Consciousness, by contrast, supplied individuals with a sense of purpose and thereby increased their willpower, on the strength of which they were to remake the world and themselves according to their conscious designs. Nobody possessed as much willpower as Lenin, the most conscious of all Bolshevik leaders. In studying Lenin's life, Vishnevsky sought to appropriate for himself a part of Lenin's iron will and thereby shield himself against the invisible but ubiquitous workings of counterrevolutionary conspiracy.

Diarists described the will as coterminous with a person's subjectivity. It was distilled in the work of channeling a person's unorganized psycho-physical forces. Once activated, it was an autonomous power that raised the self to the level of a historical agent. The diary had the crucial task of shaping and strengthening its author's will. While diagnosing in his diary the bad traits in his personality (which included his uncontrolled nature and inconstancy), Anatoly Ulianov attributed these to his weak will: "Willpower . . . its presence in a person should always guarantee him a good, conscious life. I don't have this will. This is why (by way of criticism) I am weak-willed, restless, frivolous, and hasty. My nervousness and my quick-tempered character unsettle me every time. Yes, the will is everything." The ideal to which Ulianov aspired was a "clean, mathematical life," to be attained through "willpower and political saturation." To realize this goal, he resolved: "Concretely, I am setting myself the task, for the period from January 1 to

March 1, 1933, to study at least the six-volume Lenin edition, to ponder over it, and to share with you [the diary] my opinions and all the unclear questions that may arise during the reading."[32]

Vladimir Molodtsov, the coal miner who had taken the appearance of his mother in his dreams as evidence of his backward psychology, corrected himself in a subsequent diary entry: "I was somewhat incorrect when I was writing about the contradiction between the will and the 'heart.' This contradiction is felt only when in one's head there is 'bread,' 'meals,' 'get up,' and 'go to sleep.' Down below in the mine there are no 'contradictions'; there is only unity and wholeness—production, coal, fill more wagons." As soon as the individual worker entered the work sphere, his body and psyche underwent a double transformation: they were collectivized, in joining the body and the feelings of the laboring collective as a whole; and they were organized, in entering the charts and graphs of the Five-Year Plan. Molodtsov experienced this process as the unfolding of his rational will. Thanks to its triumph he worked effortlessly, with highest devotion and clarity of purpose: "The highest feeling that I could experience in my short life is the feeling of being conscious of the fact that I am a part of the miners' collective."[33]

Stepan Podlubny described willpower in terms of a moral ideal: "For a long time, I have liked people with a strong will. No matter who this person is, if he has great willpower he is a good person." Podlubny assiduously recorded instances when he felt that his own willpower had increased, but unlike Molodtsov's, his diary was for the most part a record of his failures. Summarizing his performance at work and in life in general, he once concluded: "I lack the willpower to control myself. At the present moment I have a big, enormous, terrible impotence of the will. This is the source of all misfortunes and is my main shortcoming. A most dreadful, most dangerous shortcoming that can prove dangerous to life. Because everything depends on it." Yet the diary was more than a bulletin of a "sick" will. Writing was also a cure; Podlubny reasoned that by forcing himself to write regularly he would also increase his willpower.[34]

Willpower was attained through struggle. Diaries of the 1930s abound in references to life as continuous struggle. An entry from Molodtsov's diary reads: "Everybody is asleep now . . . Splendid lads! . . . Glory and honor to them. How good is it to live, while struggling. And to struggle, while living." Alexander Zhelezniakov, the rural party activist, described a hay harvest he directed. To take advantage of a spell of dry weather, he coerced the recalcitrant kolkhoz peasants into staying in the field until all work was finished: "We mowed until eleven at night, and the field was mown. The moon played a big role and helped me resolve this difficult task. Thanks to the party. It reared in me firmness and resolve in struggle, to win in the most difficult conditions. What great happiness! . . . I remember the words of Marx and Engels: 'Struggle is happiness!' The next morning it rained again."[35]

Work and struggle were indispensable attributes of Soviet selfhood, which was always defined as a work in progress. Nikolai Ostrovsky, a bedridden, blinded civil war veteran and author of the autobiographically inspired *How the Steel Was Tempered,* explained to his doctor: "Some strange people think that it is possible to be a Bolshevik without working every day, every hour on training one's will, one's character. One must constantly tend to this matter in order not to slide into the swamp of the petite bourgeoisie. A real Bolshevik constantly forges and polishes himself." As if echoing this exhortation, Vsevolod Vishnevsky noted with regret that he did not succeed in writing in his diary every day. This prevented him from attaining a "more systematic movement." Elsewhere he conceived of lapses in his quest for self-perfection as moments of stagnation or even regression.[36]

Several diaries from the 1930s contain end-of-year summaries, sometimes called "balance sheets," the express purpose of which was to diagnose the evolution of the self—its growth or, alternatively, its stagnation or decline. Podlubny's diary provides a particularly striking example of this habit, and shows that he modeled the practice on mechanisms operating in the public realm: "*12/30/1933* Throughout the entire Union and in countries everywhere they are reckoning up the annual work totals. Throughout the entire Union, in many cities, and in Moscow as well, conferences, congresses, etc., are being convened in order to review the year's work." In taking stock of his own development, Podlubny chose terms that were almost completely identical with the rhetorical language of official Soviet balance sheets. His end-of-year diary entry and a *Pravda* editorial summarizing the year's achievements both texts focused on the same notion of growth: Podlubny's personal growth and the "stormy cultural growth" of the Soviet population. The only discrepancy is that where *Pravda* affirmed that a "leap in consciousness" had taken place among Soviet citizens, Podlubny complained that his own consciousness was still underdeveloped.[37]

Constructing or Reconstructing the Self

While the concepts of plan, consciousness, struggle, psychology, ideology, and willpower were general attributes of diaries from this age, they proceeded from two qualitatively different notions of self. Diarists from the lower classes, chiefly workers and peasants, labored to construct a sense of self where previously, they believed, none had existed. Members of the educated classes, meanwhile, saw themselves as possessing a developed yet problematic self that required analysis and intervention in order to be transformed. Only a member of the educated classes could write what Vera Pavlova—whose father had been a factory manager–noted in her diary: "During the past days my 'self' [*moe 'ia'*] was subjected to a detailed analysis (my own), combined with criticism and reproach."[38]

Every Soviet citizen, to be sure, traveled from an old to a new life. Workers and peasants, too, voiced a conflict between old and new codes of thinking and behavior, but they rarely reified their lapses into "old" habits—such as heavy drinking, cursing, or abusing their spouses—into a full-fledged figure of an "Old Man" who had to die in order for the New Man to emerge. Their habits were the fruits of backwardness, results of the feudal-capitalist enslavement of the laboring people's souls, an enslavement that had kept them on the verge of a subhuman existence. A worker like Anatoly Ulianov regarded his ingrained coarseness as an indication of his "animal"-like existence, the beast within. The peasant-worker Leonid Potemkin described the need to work on his self in terms of material construction: he had to lay a foundation and build a frame surrounded by a scaffolding before he could proceed with setting up the factory, his finished self. His emphasis was on construction, rather than reconstruction, of the self: he did not foresee a need to tear down established old frames or accommodate preexisting building parts.[39]

The trajectory of Potemkin's and Ulianov's narratives was from a subhuman to a human state, from non-Man to Man. No diarist expressed this better than the kolkhoz activist Zhelezniakov. In anticipation of the sixteenth anniversary of the October Revolution, he exclaimed:

> There is not, was not, and will not be, in world history a generation more happy than ours. We are the participants in the creation of a new epoch! Do you recollect, enemies, you who surround us on all sides, that only twenty years ago we were insignificant insects, crawling on the masters' floors, and this insignificant person, who had been strangled by capitalism, realized himself as a class and shattered the whole world to its foundations on November 7, sixteen years ago . . . There is nothing higher

> than to be a member, a citizen of the Soviet land and to belong to Lenin's battle-hardened Communist party . . . Had the October Revolution not taken place, could I really have understood life in this way, and could I really have exchanged my personal life for the struggle for common goals? No! I would have remained almost an animal, but now I am happy.[40]

Evgenia Rudneva (born in 1920) expressed the same thought in a female register. Writing in November 1937, while preparations for the first elections to the USSR's Supreme Soviet were under way, which was to usher a new generation of purely Soviet citizens into political life, she noted: "I live a full-blooded life. How can I not love my Fatherland, which gives me such a happy life? In fact, what (yes, precisely: what, not who) would I have been, had I been born before the revolution? I would have been an ignorant girl, perhaps already a bride, who would harvest tomatoes in summer and bake bread in winter."[41] Rudneva suggested that lower-class women were even more oppressed than their male counterparts; in addition to their oppression as human beings they were enslaved in the domestic sphere. Hence female emancipation comprised the greatest possible span of human development, from not yet human to unfettered humanity.

By contrast, members of the educated classes—including representatives of the "bourgeois" intelligentsia as well as staunch Communists—had to cope with the fact that they inhabited problematic "personalities" shaped by prerevolutionary culture. They conceived of self-transformation in terms of killing the Old Man and rearing the New Man within. Unlike workers or peasants, who were weighed down by an uncultured past, members of the intelligentsia suffered from an excess of culture which needed to be stripped of its non-Soviet properties. In the words of the poet Johannes R. Becher, who converted to Communism in the 1920s, the intellectual, before joining the "proletarian fighting army," had to "burn most of what he owes to his bourgeois genealogy . . . Down with the vaunted and sacralized 'personality.' Down with its artificial inner and outward comportment, its exaggerated and paradoxical nature, all the capricious and moody posturing characterizing a 'personality.'" When Becher and others spoke derogatively of "personality," the term encapsulated a set of attributes marking the "old" intelligentsia: individualistic, narcissistic, passive, soft, and unfit for struggle—in a word, bourgeois.[42]

The struggle against his bourgeois essence was a prominent theme in the diary of the writer Yuri Slezkin; in fact, this struggle was what prompted him to keep a diary in the first place. On the opening pages of his journal, Slezkin, aged 46, took stock of the three decades of his literary career. The last decade had been especially "uneven and muddled"; he had neither written anything significant nor been able to publish, because of his "bourgeois" pedigree. The decade had been marked by the "painful need for restructuring" and by unsuccessful attempts to find himself. For the present and future, though, he was more confident: "Before me lies the last, and at the same time the first serious, obstacle: to rid myself of the past, to realize myself in the present, to overcome the inertia of my class. A Sisyphean labor, but doesn't what our country must now overcome demand the same sort of effort? Thus, a new decade, my fourth decade . . . May this diary be my witness, my critic and activator in the hours of creative exhaustion." Slezkin conflated the professional project of elaborating a new literary style with his personal quest to overcome his bourgeois past. Steeped in a realist aesthetic reaching back to the mid-nineteenth century, Slezkin believed that for his writing to be legitimate and truthful he had to personally partake in the very agenda of social transformation that pervaded the entire Soviet realm. One reason his past literary work had lacked substance and meaning was that he had failed to engage in the struggle against the former man inside, thus remaining bourgeois in essence.[43]

Yuri Olesha, another writer of "bourgeois" background, was prompted to keep a diary by a similar belief in the power of an autobiographical narrative to shape his actual life. Olesha turned to the diary in part in order to produce literature in the spirit of the "factographic" movement. With a degree of sarcasm, he commented on the new literary fashion of the day, which declared novels to be dead and regarded only documentary prose, such as the diary, as of value: "May everyone write a diary: employees, workers, writers, semi-educated people, men, women, children—what a treasure for the future!" Nevertheless, Olesha pursued his journal in earnest, not only as a literary experiment. He hoped that the pursuit of factography would also place his problematic bourgeois self firmly on a historical track and take him into the promised future. Applied to Olesha's personal life, however, the techniques of factography produced something else. To his consternation, writing a diary did not have a transformative effect. Instead of documenting his conversion to the new world, the factographic journal recorded the "useless" minutiae of his daily life and thus accumulated, rather than dissipated, the weight of his old, unreformed self. In writing and reading his diary, Olesha discovered with horror the incipient "truth" that he was a "petit-bourgeois individual who all his life has dreamed of becoming a big property-owner."[44]

Olesha obsessively recorded not only his thoughts but also his bodily symptoms, anxiously studying them for possible meaning: How did they situate him on the historical track? His inability to think like a progressive Soviet intellectual, and thus align his subjective self with the objective demands of history, eventually forced him to acknowledge that he carried in himself a wrong substance, spiritual and bodily. This "horrible" truth, he noted, had a physiological essence: it was "ingrained in my blood, in the cells of my brain." At its worst the crisis of Olesha's self generated fears of death: "I've had to interrupt writing—went to take a bath . . . In the tub. Hot—fear of death—have to listen closer: Is it the heart? Is there something happening to my brain?—isn't there? I think about death a lot. Some old man determined, by looking at my handwriting, that I think about death a lot. Morbidly, I think about death—too often (almost constantly)." In 1930, when Olesha generated this intense narrative of decline, his decline both as an individual and as a representative of a social class, he was only 30 years old. Yet, living in fear of death, he could not face the future with confidence. Instead he was drawn back into a past from which he found no escape. Recurrent rummaging in the past, another signature of Olesha's diary, was another mediated expression of the historical project that he believed was shaping his life as well as the life of the Soviet collectivity.[45]

While the teacher Vera Pavlova shared Olesha's social background as the child of a factory manager, the narrative of self-transformation she sketched out in her diary exuded a confidence and resoluteness unknown to the ever self-doubting Olesha. An unquestioning believer in historical materialism, Pavlova applied the laws of Marxist dialectics to her own life as much as to the study of social and historical phenomena. Marxist dialectics were especially important to her intelligentsia identity: as a conceptual tool they allowed her to divide her life into old and new component parts, to follow the struggle between them, and to salvage valuable parts of her old self in a dialectical spiral of unfolding consciousness:

> Recently some big questions, even problems, have become particularly acute. The problem of the old and the new is an enormous problem, capable of consuming a lot of thinking and a lot of time. That's because this problem can be resolved in various ways, while for me it looks like this: How does one unite (dialectically)

> that part of the old which is good, which is close to me, which is *mine,* which I have from the past (in my blood and from my upbringing), and for which I used to strive—the old, rich intelligentsia spirit—with the new that is around and *in me?* I feel in me powerful shoots of something new in terms of worldview, my attitude toward various aspects of life, in particular, everyday life and moral questions (the example of the "three letters" . . .). But what is referred to as the new spirit sometimes contains so much that is vulgar, boorish, and empty. This cannot be acceptable, it is disgusting and repugnant. How can one reconcile, unite, link strongly and firmly that which is to be mine from the old and the new? Is that possible? Yes. A product of the transition period—this is what I am.[46]

Even though Pavlova expressed revulsion at the vulgarity of parts of official Soviet culture, these reservations did not diminish her resolve to embrace the Communist idea and the promise of individual salvation that it—and only it—afforded.

When Pavlova wrote this entry she was being courted by an older colleague, Alexander Georgievich Polezhaev, who insistently invited her to visit his home to admire his butterfly collection. The old-fashioned comfort of his apartment, which looked to her as if it had not changed much since the revolution, reminded Pavlova of her own parental household and made her doubt that she could have a relationship with Polezhaev. In particular she wondered whether a union with this "old *intelligent*" would allow her to pursue her plan of entering the Communist party. At the same time Pavlova was attracted to another teacher, a certain Dulkeit. Her comparison of the two suitors shows Pavlova's externalization of what she conceptualized as her own divided intelligentsia self.

Polezhaev emerged as a "phlegmatic and slow person, who lacks fire, has no grip on life, and would rather retreat than enter a battle." Even worse, he was unable to lead his students and he complained about his teaching duties, which he regarded only as "a source of income, not more." Everything about him, his personal as well as his professional life, was deeply retrograde. "His relationship toward contemporary matters, toward the existing order is negative, decidedly negative." Reifying Polezhaev into an old *intelligent* was a technique that allowed Pavlova to isolate, before parting with, remnants of outlived intelligentsia values inside herself. Dulkeit, by contrast, essentialized the new self for which she strove. He appeared as "energetic, passionate, hot-tempered," and engrossed in his work. Pavlova concluded her assessment of Dulkeit in good Marxist fashion, moving from his individual virtues to their social meaning: "Dulkeit is also newer and more vital in a sociopolitical sense . . . He is a contemporary in essence, he involves himself in life, devotes his energy to it, is interested in it." In her comparison of the two men, which ranged from professional qualifications, work ethics, living environment, to their musical abilities, Pavlova refused to compare their physical features, holding this to be not just irrelevant but even "vulgar" *(poshlo)*. Her emphasis on their spiritual attributes was meant to suggest that she understood subjectivity in the Soviet order first and foremost as a quality of the soul, an inner disposition.[47]

In spite of her vacillation between the two suitors, her eventual choice had a preordained quality. She acknowledged as much when announcing a few months later that "the struggle between the old and the new has ended with the victory of the new, because the new is life itself." But as she also made clear in the diary, both men served as material for a dialectical project that transcended either of them. The ultimate focus of her diaristic reflections was not on the men themselves but on the dialectics of her personal agenda of self-transformation. One of her many comparisons of her suitors was accompanied by the remark: "Unwittingly, a flight of desire to analyze more deeply, and hence, to write." Once she had identified the dialectical underpinnings of her relationships with these men, Pavlova made no further mention of them in her diary. Three years later, in 1935, she married a professor of medicine.[48]

The episode surrounding Pavlova's two suitors illustrates the way she externalized the struggle against the Old Man within and assigned the Old Man a material reality. Her sociological rendering of people like Polezhaev into epitomes of the old intelligentsia enabled Pavlova to fashion herself as a member of the new intelligentsia. Her reasoning thus points to an interesting reciprocal effect between self-definition and the social definition of others. If we apply this mechanism to the denunciatory practices that were widespread during the 1920s and 1930s, we can understand denunciations as acts of identity construction on the part of the denouncing subjects. It was an identity that came at a price, as the shadow image that it cast—in the form of an old *intelligent* or a bourgeois enemy—ultimately had to be excised from Soviet society. In Pavlova's case, Polezhaev underwent merely symbolic death as a member of an "outlived" order, and her thoughts were confined to a diary, but nevertheless she formulated them at a time when the denunciations against the bourgeois intelligentsia were many and their consequences were material, often lethal.

The struggle against the Old Man within pervaded all spheres of life, as every thought or action on the part of an *intelligent* could be read as an expression of the state of the soul. Even such seemingly mundane matters as food and daily chores could figure as signposts of the diarist's spiritual journey. Members of the Soviet intelligentsia avoided complaining about the material difficulties of their daily lives, either passing over them in silence or hailing them as evidence of their success in renewing themselves. In her diary, Pavlova hardly alluded at all to the dire living conditions of the early 1930s. Most notably, she did not mention the famine of 1933, which she must have witnessed because she spent that summer in a village near Moscow. When editing her diary in the 1980s, Pavlova commented that this had been an extremely hard summer and that she had repeatedly been forced to travel to Moscow in search of bread. But for an *intelligent* during the 1930s, it was virtuous to repress one's craving for such base matters as food. Inversely, to articulate such desires, and thereby to question the policies of the Soviet state, was to reveal the old intelligentsia self. One of Pavlova's harshest criticisms of Polezhaev was occasioned by his attitude toward food: "[He engages in] the passive counter-revolution, faking assimilation to the new, but perhaps also gloating over and laughing in his sleeve. [He belongs to] the old intelligentsia, sighing for the past (even food), not joining the new life in earnest, giving it instead his energy only so far."[49]

This judgment could have been extended to another *intelligent,* the diarist Alexander Peregudov, who regretted that he had not kept a "great" diary in the 1930s. Peregudov's diary revolved almost exclusively around material concerns. His end-of-year summaries were conspicuously bereft of self-reflection. Instead they centered on the absence of goods: "*12/31/1939* The last day of the old year. The waning year has brought few pleasures: almost everybody is in need; almost everybody is hungry and without any clothes to wear. During the whole year there were long lines for clothes, shoes, and soap. And lately there is not enough black bread." Similarly, Ivan Sich, a retired French teacher who wholeheartedly identified with the old Russian intelligentsia and showed no inclination to transform himself, recorded in great detail the scarcity and high prices of diverse consumer goods, such as clothes, soap, cucumbers, and condoms. These attitudes were what a *Pravda* editorial identified as the essence of the "right opportunist" anti-party movement: it looked at the construction of socialism only from the point of view of supply, "betraying the complete narrow-mindedness of the philistine who lacks a historical perspective and a correct understanding of everything happening around him."[50]

It was legitimate for a Soviet *intelligent* to mention material difficulties only if doing so served a self-transformative purpose. Vera Inber, for example, proudly detailed her hardships in her diary as evidence of her new-found strength:

> Yes, there is a lot of work ahead. Such hard work, unbelievably hard! It's good that I have become physically stronger from all the running around, hauling these heavy bags, the trip to Peredelkino, and the lighter, less fatty food . . . I know the price of any physical and mental work. I know how to restrain my irritation, when you are in a vegetable store, standing in three lines at the same time: at the cashier's, at the reception, and then for the additional payment. Your feet ache, your parcels fall apart, your body is awfully hot in the oilskin coat, and there is a fly clinging to your face, but you can't shoo it away, because you don't have a third hand.[51]

Galina Shtange, the wife of a Moscow engineering professor, recorded in her diary the difficult circumstances of contemporary life as a way to underscore—and to communicate to future generations—the heroic sacrifices made by her generation in the building of socialism: "*1/1/1937* . . . It's just horrible when you think about how people live these days, and engineers in particular. I heard about one engineer who lives with his wife in a 9-[square-]meter room. When his mother came to visit, there was absolutely no place for him to do his work. So he put the lamp on the floor and lay down (on his stomach under the table) and worked that way, he couldn't put work off, he had a deadline. I wrote down this example so that those who come after us will read it and get a sense of what we went through." This passage would read differently if the last sentence, on the future reader to whom Shtange addressed herself, were omitted. Her comment on living conditions would signal despair and political criticism. The risk is to present a given statement isolated from the larger narrative context and strategy of which it formed an integral part. In the Soviet revolutionary period this context was defined by narratives of transformation and purification; these narratives girded Inber's and Pavlova's calls for perseverance, and they also informed the bleak statements by Sich and Peregudov, lending them explosive political meaning.

While working to eradicate their old, bourgeois essence, intelligentsia diarists also actively participated in the project of remaking the Soviet population into new men and women. This may appear paradoxical, for how could a class of such "impure" origins cast itself as a progenitor of purified humanity? Diaries reveal two major motivations that drew members of the intelligentsia to adopt this agenda. Thanks to its reservoir of education and culture, the intelligentsia was singularly suited to claim a teaching role in the Bolshevik state. The commitment to enlighten the "dark people" long predated the revolution and was integral to the professional and ethical vocation of the Russian intelligentsia. Moreover, their role as "social engineers" allowed members of the intelligentsia to externalize their personal quest for self-renewal by extending it throughout the Soviet realm, and on this basis to attain validation and absolution.

The ethos of reeducation suffused Pavlova's diary. Teaching for a time in a "dull, gray," and "backward" village near Moscow, she expounded on her daunting mission to remold the peasant youths. The young kolkhoz workers accepted her teachings only superficially, while "something instinctual, deeply ingrained in them," resisted her efforts at "reeducation." In a humorous episode Pavlova summed up the current state of village life, outwardly marked by the revolution, but in essence still permeated by backwardness. A fellow teacher, in her lack of culture almost indistinguishable from the rest of the villagers, had named her son after the October Revolution. Every so often Pavlova would hear shouts coming from the teacher's house, such as "October! Get off the [chamber] pot!" or "Where the hell is my little October?" Elsewhere in the diary Pavlova noted with evident pride: "I give knowledge, I teach how to work, I train new habits, I 'make' people! . . . It is a fascinating feeling to be the master of people (even if they are only youngsters) . . . And this consciousness of your meaningfulness and the meaningfulness of your work, this synthesis, it causes satisfaction, enthusiasm." After an arduous anti-religious campaign she had helped organize at Moscow's "Red Torch" factory, Pavlova wrote in a more exasperated mode: "How much time and work will still be needed to raise this mass to the height of real citizens of the socialist state? . . . How necessary the intelligentsia is for this task." In her capacity as a Soviet teacher she had no qualms about her problematic, partly bourgeois intelligentsia identity, which had given rise to so much anxious reflection in other settings. The task assigned to the Soviet intelligentsia—to act as teacher and rearer of the new man, to engineer the new man—validated the intelligentsia in its own difficult quest to renew itself.[52]

Private and Public, Personal and Social

Historians of the Soviet system often assume that only privately voiced statements are reliable indicators of individuals' "real" beliefs. They therefore endow the diary, understood as a private record par excellence, with a unique potential to express the individual self in undistorted fashion. Accordingly, diaries originating in the public realm—such as production or brigade diaries, or records written for the public eye—are dismissed as inauthentic records, especially in view of the pressures applied by the Soviet state, which forced diarists to practice self-censorship.

The problem of applying a public-private binary to Stalin-era diaries and subjectivities is that it projects a liberal understanding of selfhood into the Soviet context. The binary contains an assumption that Soviet citizens, like liberal subjects, strove for individual autonomy, and that hence their self-expression as individuals by definition evolved in tension with social or state institutions. Furthermore, the liberal model makes a universal claim that all individuals cultivate the private realm as a sphere of unfettered and authentic individual subjectivity. However, Soviet diarists raise questions about the universality of the pursuit of autonomy and of the private as a realm of integrated selfhood. The notions of private and public remain useful to the extent that they were employed as concepts in the Soviet setting, but it is important to grasp the historically specific meanings underlying these concepts and informing their use.[53]

In Marxist understanding, the concept of a private existence furthered antisocial instincts like individualism, particularism, and selfishness. Moreover, the private sphere served as an ideological device that upheld the capitalist system. Its function was to deceive the oppressed worker, to give him respite and make him oblivious to his fundamental state of alienation. With the abolition of private property, the socialist revolution would overcome humanity's self-division and allow humankind to regain its essence as a socialized species. Under socialism, any notion of the private was rendered anachronistic. Freed from his previous state of capitalist oppression and self-division, man would regain his nature as a social being. According to Marx, "what is to be avoided above all is the re-establishing of 'Society' as an abstraction vis-à-vis the individual. The individual is the social being." The society of the socialist future was not to function as an external bond, but to express the real internal unity of men. Freed from internal self-division and class conflict, each individual in the new world would identify with society.[54]

As committed Marxists, the Bolsheviks sought not only to eliminate private structures in socioeconomic life but also to purify the consciousness of the Soviet population from private concerns. The revolution was to take hold of all aspects of people's lives, and particularly of the realms that had been considered private and nonpolitical. As *Komsomolskaya Pravda* reminded Soviet citizens: "Everyday life is not a private affair, it is the most crucial zone of class struggle. Everyday life is inseparable from politics; and people who are not honest in everyday life, who are morally depraved, are depraved politically." Nadezhda Krupskaya warned: "A division between private life and public life sooner or later leads to the betrayal of communism. We must strive to bind our private life to the struggle for and the construction of communism."[55]

This Soviet imperative that individuals lead politicized lives, think about their existence in terms of its social utility, and not allow private concerns to undermine their universalist orientation is markedly present in diaries of the period. Stepan Podlubny made repeated mention of his "inner self" *(vnutrennost')* or his "soul" *(dusha)*. He sought to activate the self and imbue it with the revolutionary agenda of the Soviet state. As he understood it, the soul of a Soviet citizen was to be filled with a distinctly political spirit and should form a realm of enthusiasm. He was dissatisfied when he felt that "all the inside is asleep" or when he lingered in an "idiotic and nonpolitical mood." But when a sense of elevation toward the political sphere pervaded him, he observed with satisfaction the merging of his subjective, inner feelings with the objective, social world. Similarly, Anatoly Ulianov made a point in his diary of tying his personal life to his social existence, aware that a cultivation and reporting of personal concerns for their own sake would expose him as a philistine. He began his first diary notebook in a programmatic spirit, vowing to always link aspects of his "personal life," to the extent that they deserved to be recorded, to his "public life": "I only live in the latter, and all my personal interests are almost all the time tied in with my public ones." Only a few lines later, however, Ulianov changed the subject and began to describe his love life. Most of his diary from the 1930s was in fact devoted to his romances with women. Yet time and again Ulianov chided himself for his "petit-bourgeois" spirit, resolving to overcome the entanglements of his lowly, private existence and to embark on a higher, rationally determined life.[56]

It was not simply that Soviet citizens were to deny any personal side of their existence and were not expected to narrate them in their diaries. The binary that diarists established was not one of personal vs. extrapersonal, individual vs. social, or private vs. public. On the contrary, they sought to avoid any such binary pattern in their accounts. Resisting the tendency inherent in the diary medium toward a one-sided, self-engrossed, and latently individualist self-narrative, they were at pains to stress the politically conscious, activist, and socialized qualities of their selves. This emphasis, however, did not preclude an intimate relationship with the self. Ulianov addressed his diary as a personal friend and habitually ended his entries with a farewell, affectionately signed "Tolka." It never occurred to this Komsomol activist to reproach himself for the intimate, almost romantic tone in which he addressed his diary. To him the real problem was his abuse of the diary as an outlet for his weak, passive, and solipsistic instincts, and at one point he formally apologized to the diary for using it to discharge his "boredom and spleen."[57]

Intimacy as such—romantic dreams or episodes from family life—was not considered ideologically reprehensible. On the contrary, citizens were entitled and—increasingly as the 1930s progressed—admonished to cultivate their "personal life," which was regarded as a sign of how humane and developed socialist culture had become.[58] The more outstanding citizens were in their productive capacities, as

Stakhanovite heroes of labor or as polar pilots, the more developed their socialist personalities were assumed to be and the more they were to pursue their personal lives. Clearly in these cases the personal sphere did not clash with social commitments and desires but was one more expression of a citizen's socialist orientation.

This new validation of personal life is well expressed in the diary of Ariadna Chirkova, a Moscow biologist. Aged 32, Chirkova was a single mother who had been abandoned by her husband. Her infant son had died and she was left with a young daughter, yet had nobody—except the diary—who would understand her thoughts and feelings, all of her "inner life." Enviously Chirkova commented on a radio transmission from a group of aviators wintering at the North Pole. The telegraphist was, Chirkova noted, "so worried about his family that he even reminds his wife about all sorts of petty things she must not forget to do: read a certain book, subscribe to the journals, go to the theater, etc. I'm a skeptic, I don't believe all this . . . But I cried, as I listened to the transmission and then to his wife's detailed account of how the family had spent the day." Chirkova cried because what she heard on the radio, true or fictitious, reminded her that she herself had no such personal life, which she understood as a family life of love, intimacy, and the pursuit of education embedded in a larger heroic existence.

By contrast, the personal musings with which Chirkova's diary abounded had to be repressed because they did not amount to a full-fledged "personal life":

> My notes always and everywhere can produce a one-sided impression. This is only my inner world. My self. But I am preoccupied with this world only when I am writing these notes, and during a few other, completely unrelated and insignificant moments in the course of the day. For example, on my way to the laboratory. All my remaining time is taken up with work. Public life carries me

> away and enthralls me completely. For me struggle always comes first. These notes are just a small break for me, of no use to anybody but me, when I feed Irochka plums or oranges and think with horror about the thousands, tens and hundreds of thousands of children who don't have anything like that. And there are still many of those even in our country.[59]

Although Chirkova began by underscoring how insignificant the personal realm, the subject of her diary, was for her overall life, she identified this inner life with her "self" *(ia),* thereby implying that her professional life and social record were extraneous to her self. It seems as if in writing this entry she became aware of the risky implications of her choice of terminology, so she hastened to add that even in her most intimate moments, when alone with her daughter, she remained committed to the universal realm and remembered the "hundreds of thousands" of unfortunate children in the world who were hungry and lacked good maternal care. In fascinating detail this entry reveals the mechanisms of a distinctly Soviet conscience that prevented a Soviet citizen from indulging in her personal life, happy or unhappy as it may have been.

The double hierarchy addressed in Chirkova's diary, of personal vs. social and particular vs. universal, also figures in the definition of the term "citizen" in an official Stalin-era dictionary: "a conscious member of society, a person who subordinates his personal to his social interests." Broader social concerns also tower over the purely personal in the diary of Lev Deich, an erstwhile Menshevik activist who was in his seventies when he wrote the diary. Deich divided a given entry into two parts; he began with notes on the "political sphere" and then switched to his "personal sphere." While emphasizing the "big events" of the political sphere, he had nothing favorable to report on his personal life, which he described as "not particularly good," even "disgusting." It is indicative, too, that under the first rubric, Deich used the collective pronoun "we" ("we are expecting all sorts of good things from this"), while his personal life evolved in the first person singular.[60]

The unequal standings of the "personal" and the "state" spheres are illustrated glaringly in the diary of Nina Soboleva, a Leningrad high school student and daughter of a high-ranking local party official. In January 1940 Soboleva was nominated by her Komsomol cell to work as a "cultural enlightenment worker" *(kul'tprosvetrabotnik)* at a Leningrad toy factory. To prepare for the task she resolved to systematically study *Pravda* and also to keep a diary to record and reflect on her reading. An early diary entry said:

> *1/13/1940* Today in the newspaper:
> Stream of greetings for Comrade Stalin
> War in Europe. Berlin. The newspaper *Kölnische Zeitung* writes about the Anglo-French attempts to unleash a war in the North.
> Paris...
> London...
> Domestic news. "The case of the slanderous Napolskaya group" (on the anti-Soviet slanderous activities of the group. All five have received prison terms. Napolskaya, Ivanovskaya, and Gorokhov—20 years each, Mikhailovsky and Ionov—15).
> Well, after excerpting the papers in the morning, I wanted to write about myself, but there was this strange feeling—how awkward to follow the chronicle of state affairs with all sorts of personal nonsense. Maybe I should keep two diaries? One for the social sphere, and one personal?

If the personal could not be raised to the level of the political—a possibility that apparently did not occur to Soboleva—keeping two different diaries would prevent the political text from being tainted by petty individual concerns.[61]

Both Soboleva and Anatoly Ulianov began their diary projects with musings about how to reconcile their personal lives with their roles as social activists or citizens of the Soviet state. In the course of writing they became aware of the diary's potential to steer them into a fractured, solipsistic, "private" world unsuitable for a Soviet citizen, and both reacted by pointing out that the personal sphere was hierarchically embedded in their social existence. But neither was able to sustain the predominance of state language in their diaries. Just two weeks after the entry quoted above, Soboleva reduced her exegesis of *Pravda* to a single headline and went on to write: "To be honest, I don't feel like reading the newspaper today. I'd better write something about myself." From this point on her diary became increasingly personal, chronicling her friendships and her adolescent rebellion against parental authority. A year after the diary's inception the newspaper reporting was banished to the end of individual entries: "Before finishing, I want to at least summarize yesterday's news reports . . ."[62]

Not all Soviet diarists had conflicting feelings about recording intimate thoughts and dreams in their journals. Vladimir Zhelezniakov, as chairman of a village soviet, was aware of his duty to subordinate personal concerns to social interests: "*6/11/1933* At three in the morning my wife Maria saw me off. It was good to see her, but saying farewell was worse. Discarding all my personal interests, I stepped out briskly and hurried to catch the train. On my mind was the Pirogov village Soviet." Yet he was not embarrassed to adorn the pages of his diary with the graphic description of a personal dream. He had been dreaming about the Spanish Civil War, watching himself running his bayonet into fascist stomachs. Then his wife moved in the bed, waking him: "I regretted my interrupted dreams. Perhaps I would have seen heroic Madrid and the famed pilots, shooting down enemy planes . . . We are with you, heroic sons of the Spanish people! Fascism will be defeated! You, Wife, be more careful when turning over tomorrow night. I will be fighting fascism." Zhelezniakov could afford to narrate this dream in the diary because it was fully suffused with public spirit and therefore did not threaten the unity of his self. He might even have viewed it as evidence that his unconscious had become an extension of the battleground of his conscious life. Vladimir Biriukov, the ethnographer, did not dream about the Spanish Civil War; rather, the war itself, and his worries about the waning fortunes of the Republican army, caused him agonized, sleepless nights. Both Biriukov and Zhelezniakov lived in remote villages far from the Spanish battlefields, yet the war and the international class struggle assumed a strong presence in the chronicles of their lives.[63]

To be sure, not all Soviet diarists aspired to an exemplary life of exclusively public concerns, and even those who did almost inevitably fell short of this ideal. Nevertheless, the division between personal and social spheres or particularist and universalist interests, and the imperative to subordinate the former to the latter, were structuring facts that most diarists lived by. Even the critically minded history student Arkady Mankov once noted: "*3/23/1939* A person has two lives: one public and one private [*chastnaia*]. To date the two have been harmoniously joined only in the case of a few lucky people. For the overwhelming majority it has been like this: if the one did not succeed, they gave themselves wholeheartedly to the other." In spite of his diagnosis of the split between a public and a private existence, Mankov did accept the normative notion of a unified self embracing both the public and the private. He deplored the inability of the Soviet regime to kindle his subjective spirit and thereby integrate his self. Upon hearing of Hitler's occupation of the Memel region, Mankov concluded that he would have to go to war without an ideological purpose to fight for. Thus even a critic of the regime like Mankov adhered to an ideal of an integrated selfhood in which the personal would be raised to the level of the social.[64]

Several other diarists drew a distinction between "minor" and "major" keys when thinking about their intimate thoughts in relationship to the social world. When the voice in their journal was brooding, subdued, and depressed, they described it as in a minor key. Such lonely tunes were utterly unlike the resounding, unison cheer these diarists ascribed to the Soviet collective, and they also clashed with the ideals of confidence and strength that they themselves hoped to embody. After his return to Moscow, the former emigrant Nikolai Ustrialov was unable to find employment or to gain recognition as a full-fledged Soviet citizen. His despair, largely unaddressed in his diary, did come to the fore in an entry describing a parade of young athletes through Moscow. This was the collective to which he sought to belong, and it possessed everything that he himself lacked: "Cohorts and legions of youth, the wonderful early autumn sun, the orchestra scream of the loudspeakers, and the sounds—military, bravura, major. Songs of struggle, fervor, belief, and youth." Alexei Kirillov, a journalist who had been expelled from the Communist party because of his one-time support for Trotsky, voiced his despair and his frequent suicidal thoughts in his diary. Yet time and again he urged himself to write in an optimistic, "major" key: "I will try to be cheerful, and I am preparing myself to fight for the right to be in the party, for the right to be on this earth." Similarly, the literary official Alexander Arosev, when his credentials as a Communist were under attack, confided his melancholic thoughts to his diary while at the same time hoping to switch to a major key. Privacy in all these cases connoted a set of lonely, conflicted, and cheerless feelings, in contrast to the clamorous, vital, and militant chorus of public life.[65]

A related notion of privacy was the sphere of the secretive. Mankov noted in 1938 that yet another group of Moscow University students had been arrested, but that he was getting used to this situation and no longer thinking about his own possible arrest. "However," he added, "what do I have to worry about? So far only the diaries." Like Mankov, Stepan Podlubny was aware that the secrets in his diary would cost him dearly if it fell into the wrong hands, yet he did not stop writing. At the same time, he felt polluted and weighed down by his "black thoughts" and kept seeking a release from them. He had no positive notion of this secret space in which to anchor a sense of self and personal values diverging from public norms. Therefore he did not conceive of his diary as a record of a private sphere to be remembered. Rather, it served as a "rubbish heap" on which he could discard all the "garbage" that accumulated in his mind. He envisioned writing as a struggle from which he would ultimately emerge cleansed, suffused with public values, and rid of any alternative, selfish, and hence impure, private sphere.[66]

While searching for paper in her father's desk, the teenaged Nina Soboleva discovered a terrible document: a record of a party meeting at which her father had been accused of having denounced innocent Communists in 1937 and 1938. According to the document, he had defended himself by maintaining that these had been real enemies of the people. Soboleva did not know what to believe. She wrote: "After this inadvertent reading of father's papers a kind of heavy feeling has settled somewhere inside me ('in my heart'? 'in my soul'?)." Accusing herself of one of the most serious political offenses of the period, Soboleva declared that her knowledge of her father's secret had turned her into a "double-dealer": a person outwardly Soviet, but with an inner secret that violated the Soviet mandate of sincerity. The solution she adopted was to stop writing in the polluted diary notebook, hide it in a safe place, and continue with a fresh notebook. Her description of the diary as a repository of illicit and compromising thoughts suggests that she looked upon the realm of the secretive as a dark obverse of the ideals of revolutionary purity and transparency, a dark recess created by the Soviet striving for maximum light. It was an illegitimate gesture of concealment in the context of an all-embracing purificatory zeal—yet it was not (or not yet) a source of positive self-identity or the proud founding moment of a tradition of autonomous thinking.[67]

The concept of "privacy," as such, has no universal meaning. It acquires positive or negative valence depending on the ideological context in which the self articulates itself. In the Soviet case, given the public and collectivist ethos promoted by the revolutionary state, it may be not surprising that personal diaries were not kept to cultivate a private existence in contradistinction to the public sphere. Thus the application of the public-private binary in its liberal inflection, with the assumption that the private realm forms a locus of positive identity, is not useful for an understanding of Soviet subjectivities. This is not to say that diarists did not expound on their private lives: they narrated at length their intimate dreams, fantasies, and romantic encounters, reported on family problems, and recorded such mundane facts as the food they ate on a given day. Yet many of them chided themselves for sliding into such a "petit-bourgeois" or "individualistic" mode of narration, which they held to be illegitimate in Soviet culture. Most important, such private thoughts, disconnected from public values and public interest, threatened to undermine the ideal of an integrated personhood and were therefore repudiated when diarists began to reflect on the quality of their selves. Hardly a diary promoted personal ideals of autonomy, self-sufficiency, and individualism. Many were private in the sense of harboring secrets that their authors carefully guarded from intrusive glances, but these secretive thoughts were not systematized and extended into private identities.

Rather than using the dichotomy of private and public, diarists situated their personal and particular existence with respect to the social and general public interest. These descriptions evoke two trajectories—the small and limited subjective life of the individual, and the life of the collective, embodying the objective course of history—which ideally were to coalesce into a single whole. Time and again, diarists wrote of their efforts to merge their personal lives with the "general stream of life" of the Soviet collective.[68] A private existence in contradistinction or even opposition to the life of the collective was considered inferior and unfulfilled. The collective, imagined as a living, breathing body, was the ultimate destination of Soviet self-realization. In joining a collectivity the individual self became aligned and enlarged. An individual's relationship with the collective vastly surpassed any relationship with another person in meaning and the ability to furnish a sense of community. Anatoly Ulianov at one point broke off his "lonely" musings about Katya, whose heart he could not win, and Galya, whose advances left him cold, by declaring that he actually loved the party, who needed him as much as he needed her. His vow, fittingly expressed on a revolutionary holiday, was consummated some months later, when Ulianov joined the Communist party.[69]

While membership in the collective had the power to offset personal unhappiness in a Soviet citizen's "personal life" (witness also Chirkova's diary), losing this membership could engender total loneliness. This showed powerfully in the case of Julia Piatnitskaya, who had to watch as former acquaintances turned away from her and her sons also lost their friends. She concluded that "misfortune has some sort of smell," and that she and her sons were emitting an odor that would not wash off, in spite of daily baths. At times Piatnitskaya even felt estranged from her own children. When she confided to her older son, aged 16, her "evil, poisonous" suspicion that they were in the hands of a cruel and arbitrary state system, he would reproach her: "Mama, I find you disgusting at times like this, I could kill you." She also quoted her younger son, aged 11, as saying: "It's too bad they didn't shoot Papa; after all, he is an enemy of the people." In order to rejoin the revolutionary community and overcome her isolation in society, Piatnitskaya had to denounce her husband as just that: an "enemy of the people." This was what the state prosecutor, to whom she turned for help, suggested. Much of Piatnitskaya's diary describes how "tormented" she felt because she could not muster the strength to hate her husband and thus restore her ideological credentials as a Soviet citizen and member of the socialist collective.[70]

Rationality, Crisis, Salvation

Resolving to "prove, not for others, but for yourself . . . that you stand higher than a wife, and higher than a mother," Piatnitskaya indicated that two ways of apprehending reality existed: one from the standpoint of personal observation and the other from the perspective of ideologically mandated truth. From her viewpoint as an individual, and especially as a wife and mother, Piatnitskaya trusted her husband and wanted to defend his innocence. Yet her superior calling as a Soviet citizen obliged her to transcend personal feelings and accept, indeed embrace, his arrest as an act that served the interests of society and the state. Stalin-era diarists employed various mechanisms to channel these two differing realities into an integrated perspective.

Describing reality as a manifestation of ideological truth was the central mandate of the Stalin era's aesthetic doctrine, Socialist Realism. In the words of the party ideologist Karl Radek: "The greatest creations of Socialist Realism cannot . . . be the result of chance observations of certain sections of reality; they demand that the artist comprehend the tremendous whole. Even when the artist depicts the great in the small . . . when he wants to show the world . . . in the destinies of one small man, he cannot accomplish his task without having in his mind an image of the movement of the entire world." The painter Boris Ioganson defined Socialist Realism as a polar opposite of the "photographing of facts" advocated by "naturalism." Naturalism favored the "unreflected representation of isolated facts, without the use of thought in the process of cognition." By contrast, the chief distinction of socialist realist art was the "presence . . . of a will or purpose" on the part of the artist.[71] Diarists applied the aesthetic and cognitive imperatives of Socialist Realism to the composition of their self-narratives. They recurrently intervened in the production of their records to elevate confusing or disconcerting observations of daily life to a purposeful, rationally integrated, and future-oriented perspective. Conversely, many diarists who remained on the level of naturalist commentary linked this to a weakness of their own will or, even worse, to an inner disease. In so doing they recognized the power their secret thoughts had to shape or remake their very essence.

The diary of the Hungarian writer Ervin Sinkó, who lived in the Soviet Union between 1935 and 1937, illustrates such efforts to reconcile contrary perceptions of reality into a single truth. Unable to press his distressing observations of contemporary Soviet reality into the mandated ideological grid, he nevertheless managed a fusion of sorts by projecting himself into the future. In an entry entitled "Nightly Meditations; or, Letter to My Still Unborn Young Friend," Sinkó wrote of longing to catch a glimpse of the coming socialist order, so as to be able to "accept with less bitterness and more calm that intermediate station, that road, leading from the past to the future, which is called 'Soviet Union' . . . And because I believe in a Tomorrow, in a socialist Tomorrow, which is bound to recognize the current state of the Soviet Union as a phase of backwardness, of inhuman arbitrariness and inhuman bureaucrats, I rise up and try to reach beyond the wall of time, to give my hand to a young person who will live at a time when the view back on our time remains only a bad memory, recorded only in schoolbooks, to a happier humanity."[72]

The writer Kornei Chukovsky displayed more ease in raising his personal observations to the level of Socialist Realist truth. Vacationing in the Northern Caucasus, he visited a small town:

> It's hot and dusty, there is a lot that is vile and a lot that is wonderful—and one senses that the wonderful is here for a long time, that the wonderful has a firm future, while the vile is temporary, for a short period. (The same feeling that one senses throughout the entire USSR.) The Grozny oil plants, which did not even exist in 1929, the workers' settlement, the river, whose course has been diverted to the left, are all wonderful . . . And the vile things: dust, the high cost of living, Asiatic backwardness, contempt for the human personality.

In the span of a few lines, Chukovsky managed to remake a dusty construction site into an emblem of the perfect socialist society, by situating it in the eschatological temporal frame of Communist ideology. The certainty afforded by this temporal grid allowed him to distinguish between lasting achievements of the Soviet order—technological progress, expressed in the plants; the socialist welfare state, represented by the workers' settlement; man's rule over nature, conveyed by the diverted course of the river—and bad, but ephemeral aspects: dust, disorder, and "contempt for the human personality," which may have referred to his observations of how the workers were abused at the oil plants.[73]

In contrast to Chukovsky, Arkady Mankov denounced the socialist realist conception of revolutionary time as a propagandistic ploy by the Communist regime. Upon reading a story by Alexei Tolstoy, which projected an industrialized future Soviet order, Mankov noted: "the device of a tendentious and speculative merging of times—another subterfuge of our 'socialists,' directed toward influencing people's consciousness for the purpose of controlling them. Such is the genesis of a mass of illusions which nowadays are rooted in the minds of the people." Yet Mankov's diary also illustrates his persisting doubts about the validity of his own interrogation of ideological truth. Following a critical commentary on the decline of living standards, Mankov paused:

> But what if everything I've written is incorrect. Short-sighted. What if it's only the external aspect of phenomena, the outward appearance, which is absolutely necessary and historically inevitable, so to speak, but behind this appearance is hidden the bright and radiant essence?!? And I missed this essence, because I am insignificant, short-sighted, capable only of obscuring the truth, but certainly not of disclosing it? . . . Perhaps there is indeed a decrepit little yellow devil sitting inside me, the class enemy, as they write in the papers?? Is it possible? Is it possible?[74]

Mankov's explanation of his criticism of official policies as the voice of a class enemy within him was shared by a number of other diarists of nonproletarian and thus "class alien" background. Vera Inber concluded that her "inability to link the personal with the public" (specifically, her difficulty in reconciling maternal duties with her obligations as a Soviet writer) was an indication of her "intelligentsia roots," which had yet to be pulled out. Vera Pavlova attributed her doubts about whether freedom was really the recognition of necessity, as the official Soviet definition held, to the "rotten intelligentsia spirit" still besetting her mind. Stepan Podlubny traced his ideologically "reactionary" thoughts to his failure to eradicate his kulak essence, and he even diagnosed a similar disposition among several of his acquaintances who were also of class alien origins. Finally, Nikolai Zhuravlev, who was an offspring of the landowning gentry, linked persisting impurities in his mind to his "misfortune" of having "lived sixteen years under tsarism, and moreover under the roof of a landowning daddy. 'A grave heredity,' one is inclined to say, using the language of psychiatrists." In challenging the rationality and systemic quality of Soviet ideology, these diarists also questioned the Soviet essence of their own selves. Thoughts that could not be integrated into the rationalist Soviet outlook had the power to recast their authors as kulaks or feudal landowners. In the course of writing, diarists transformed themselves into sociological expressions of their secret moods.[75]

To avert the final consequence of this logic, some diarists split themselves into two distinct voices, one Soviet and one anti-Soviet, and asserted that the critical voice did not express the totality of their selves but was the voice of an enemy within. In a parallel to the show trials staged by the regime at around the same time, Soviet citizens thus used their diaries to put themselves on trial and to expose the inner enemy, in the service of restoring the purity and integrity of their Soviet selves. The ethnographer Vladimir Biriukov was a master at applying this technique. His journal never reached the level of introspection and desperate soul searching of many other diaries, because Biriukov invented another person he called the "philistine" into whose mouth he placed thoughts critical of Soviet policies. To this person he then replied, adopting the stance of a conscious Soviet citizen: "Feuchtwanger writes in his book *Moscow, 1937* that the Zinoviev-Kamenev trial allegedly made a bad impression in Europe . . . If a philistine were to say that the defendants were Protestants opposing the ruling regime, then it turns out that these so-called Protestants have in fact been spies and provocateurs since the times of the Nikolaevan regime . . . Strange Protestants, indeed!" Biriukov used this narrative device repeatedly, and one can but assume that the "philistine" position stood for thoughts he entertained himself—why else would he write them down? Yet by disclaiming authorship of them Biriukov sought to avoid the problem of contamination that other critically minded diarists had to contend with.[76]

The strategies of splitting up the self and cutting off bad, corrupted parts shed new light on self-censorship in the Stalin period. Scholars often consider self-censorship in contradistinction to sincerity. They interpret it as a fear of disclosing a subjective truth to others, to the extent that it is completely repressed. Yet it appears that Soviet diarists censored themselves not so much to conceal a dangerous truth from people around them but to preserve a truth they entertained of themselves. Self-censorship thus also functioned as a means of self-preservation. Silence, Ervin Sinkó reported in his diary, was a preferred mode of public communication among Communist officials in Moscow in the mid- and late 1930s. In a different context, he extended this to himself: "I would rather bite off my tongue than say a single word that someone could interpret as meaning that I stand in 'opposition' to the goal whose sole guarantor and protector currently is this Soviet Union."[77] Nina Soboleva's diary illustrates the use of self-censorship to cut short a disturbing thought pattern that threatened to violate the boundaries of ideologically correct Soviet reasoning. Soboleva worked as a Komsomol agitator in a Leningrad toy factory, where her task was to explain the headlines of *Pravda* to elderly and barely literate women workers. In February 1940 she reflected in her diary on a speech by Hitler, printed without commentary by *Pravda,* in which Hitler justified his war against Britain and France by comparing their ratios of state territory and population size with the German ratio. Whereas the British Empire, according to Hitler, held close to 40 million square kilometers for 46 million inhabitants, the German Reich consisted of only 600,000 square kilometers for a population of 80 million. Soboleva found Hitler's reasoning sound, and she suggested that all across Europe state territories should be repartitioned to fit demographic exigencies. She even recommended that the Soviet Union might first offer some of its territory to the Germans, given its colossal size and the exemplary worldwide moral standing of the Soviet regime. In view of the recent current of militant Soviet patriotism, Soboleva doubted that her government would undertake such a step, although she added that she found the Russian tradition of imperial aggrandizement, to which the Soviet state owed its territory, reprehensible. At that point she hesitated: "No, I'd better stop here, since God knows where these thoughts would lead me. But isn't it funny—before I began reading the papers everything was more or less clear to me and I never had any thoughts like these, but now every day I discover more and more things that don't make sense."[78]

The source of Soboleva's heretical thoughts was not some underground or émigré publication, but *Pravda,* the official voice of the Soviet Communist party. Critical opinion in Stalinist Russia did not have to depend on exposure to alternative sources of information beyond the reach of the totalitarian state. What triggered Soboleva's heresy was a literal comparison of Soviet policies in 1940 with the revolutionary agenda of 1917. Even more strikingly, Soboleva was not driven by any political agenda or desire to expose the regime. To the contrary, she was desperate to understand and believe Communist ideology and pass it on to her semi-literate audience, and as part of her preparation for this task she attended a class for political agitators in which she was trained in the exegetical reading of *Pravda.*[79] The actual source of her heresy lay in the mandate to understand and master Soviet ideology in its totality so as to be able to propagate it to others.

This incident was not an isolated occurrence; reading the paper, Nina kept finding inconsistencies and contradictions she was unable to resolve on her own. For help, she turned to her father, a leading Communist official. He chided her for infantile reasoning and lectured her about Soviet "state interests" that necessitated all the policies she failed to understand. Not fully convinced, Soboleva read the paper with ever greater apprehension: "Every day when I open the new edition of *Pravda* I begin by fearfully examining the headlines." She gave up her attempts to comprehend and rationalize Soviet policies in her diary. And she noted with relief that the factory workers did not press her for explanations of her political readings: "At least it's good that they no longer ask questions. They listen to everything in silence, thank me, and leave." However, when she offered to read other literature—fairy tales and short stories, the women were "ready to listen for hours, although they all have children and families."[80]

Other diaries also reveal that heretical thoughts jolted their authors from the heights of ideological reading into a confusion that could develop into a veritable sickness of mind. Olga Berggolts, writing in 1939, described her difficulties in retaining her earlier ideological commitments after a six-month prison term as a suspected enemy of the people. Before her imprisonment, her thoughts had been "clear" and organized in a "harmonious system." But her Communist self had been besmirched and shattered in prison: "They took out my soul, poked around in it with stinking fingers, spat on it, defiled it, and then they shoved it back in and said: 'live.'" Berggolts described feeling "crippled" by the "poison" of doubts that had arisen in her after her experience of injustice and inhumanity in prison. She particularly worried about living on as a Soviet writer with shattered Communist convictions: "How will I write a novel about our generation, a novel on the subject of the epoch, on the subject of its consciousness, when this consciousness after prison endured such pogroms, and lost the equilibrium that it had before prison?" Several months later Berggolts returned to the same topic; this time she diagnosed herself as psychotic: "Should I seek medical treatment? After all, I've been free almost six months, but not a day or a night passes that I don't think about prison . . . Well, no, it's a psychosis, it's probably a very real disease." Yet she also mentioned that while in prison she had given recitals of poems devoted to Stalin and that her audience had thanked her and been moved to tears. Her odes to Stalin had the same rationalizing function as the diary—both were deployed to fight an incipient disease of the self and restore the harmony and clarity of her rationalist worldview.[81]

Metaphors of pollution and poisoning were pervasive in diaries of the 1930s. Podlubny likened his diary to a "rubbish heap," which was to collect all the garbage flowing from his mind. Mankov called his diary a repository of his "dirtiest and most loathsome thoughts." Piatnitskaya condemned her own belief in her husband's innocence as "terrible," "poisonous," and "evil." Communists and non-Communists alike wrote of their inability to rise to the required level of ideological understanding as indications of a grave illness—a "sickness of will," a "paralysis," a "poisoning." Mankov likened his obsessive urge to criticize Stalinist policies to masturbation, and chided himself for this sickness, which only bred individualistic and narcissistic instincts but was entirely devoid of social use. Sinkó regretted that he did not belong to the "great warring community" and hence would not ascend to "salvation": "I simply can't achieve this . . . This consciousness even paralyzes me." Writing in her diary, Nina Lugovskaya oscillated between fierce denunciations of the Soviet system, including her idea of killing Stalin, and descriptions of bouts of "pessimism" and "hopeless thoughts," which were particularly acute on revolutionary holidays, when she listened to the parades on the radio and felt her "painful" separation from the "life around me." She was 14 when she noted that she felt "so old now, so hopeless and despairing . . . My entire life will go by in this hopeless pessimism." Her negative feelings reminded her of Chekhov's characters: "misfits, dissatisfied with life," but unable to bring about change. Nina also wrote that, to be able to act and live in a fundamental sense, she required a collective of like-minded, spirited individuals. Yet she was unable to find them, neither with her peers at school, among whom she suspected the presence of secret informants, nor among her sisters, who did not share her passion for politics. Repeatedly Lugovskaya wrote about wanting to kill herself—following the example of a Chekhovian character who committed suicide. She was arrested in 1937 and sentenced to five years of hard labor.[82]

While portraying revolutionary subjects in spiritual crisis, diaries also functioned as catalysts of their authors' renewed spiritual health, purity, and clarity of mind. The very definition of microbes, poisonous substances, and dirt that diarists located in their souls suggested the possibility—indeed, the necessity—of a curing or cleansing intervention. During her time as a social pariah, Julia Piatnitskaya wrote: "How vigilantly one has to watch one's thoughts, how much one has to care for their purity, and how short human life is! Every life ought to give something to those who are close to it in spirit. Every life ought to give as much in return as it has taken from society." Piatnitskaya's diary of this period was full of references to purity and cleansing. In passages seemingly unrelated to the confession of her confused state of mind, she described cleaning the apartment, doing laundry, ironing her son's white pants, or taking baths. Piatnitskaya appeared obsessed with cleanliness, yet none of these activities satisfied her goal of emerging clean in her mind. Piatnitskaya also related that her son no longer went to school after his father's arrest. He would leave the apartment only after dark and spent the days at home, also engaged in obsessive washing and ironing.[83]

Diarists hoped that emptying their dirty and unhealthy thoughts into a diary would let them become purer and healthier persons, free of doubts, with renewed willpower and mental clarity. Indeed, the work of purification to which these diarists committed themselves made sense only in an environment of impurity. The process of self-constitution into a perfect, fully transparent Soviet citizen by its very definition depended on the presence of impurities to be overcome, as these impurities—understood as weaknesses of the mind—functioned as stepping stones of the will. Thus diarists kept producing new impurities to be exposed and new instances of contamination to be neutralized. To this extent, we might understand their diaries as a means of making themselves transparent.[84] Piatnitskaya articulated this mechanism when referring in her diary to "all my grave thoughts, as they appear from time to time and then go away, after some work on myself." She also lamented that her husband's absence robbed her of the confessor to whom she had turned to absolve herself of the weaknesses of her mind. "I told him everything, everything, although I caused him pain at times, and we'd had our quarrels, but my soul was untroubled, I felt like an honest person. I didn't hide anything from Piatnitsky." Now the only catalyst of salvation left to her was the diary itself: "I want to blurt it out on paper—I've already gotten used to this, plus Piatnitsky's not here."[85]

In their quest for total transparency, diarists emphasized how sincere they were in baring their souls and revealing their innermost thoughts. Reflecting in her diary on an autobiographical novel she had written, Vera Inber remarked: "Let them see how the writer is constituted. Without any secrets." Vishnevsky wrote in 1939: "The past decade passed in enormous tension, an immense amount of energy was spent, ups and downs, dramas, passions . . . All this inexorably affects the soul, the nerves, and the heart . . . I didn't want to write about this, but 'objective' reality demands it." In fact Soviet narratives of disclosing the soul *depended* on a mode of sincerity, as becomes clear in a passage in which Olga Berggolts complained that her diary had been besmirched by a state prosecutor who had used it as incriminating evidence against her: "Commissar Goglidze himself searched in my words about Kirov, words filled with mourning and love for my native land and Kirov, for grounds to accuse me of terror. Oh, how base, how base. And the fault-finding, questions, and underlinings in the diaries that the prosecutor made? On the most exalted, the most bitter pages!" Berggolts was incensed that her diary, in which she had been at her most sincere, could be used for such an incorrect analysis of her soul. This experience forced her to overstate her convictions in the diary and to avoid any possible ambiguity so as not to be misunderstood a second time: "And those abused, befouled diaries are there in my desk. And regardless of what I should write about now, it seems to me that this and this will be underlined with the same red pencil, with the special purpose of accusing, slandering, and backing me into a corner. I hurry to add some sort of explanation 'for the prosecutor'; or else I lose heart, remain silent, and don't reveal on paper what is most painful and most unclear to me . . . Oh, shame, shame, shame! . . . No! Don't think about it! But there has not been any greater lack of freedom than now."[86]

Worst of all for Berggolts was that she could no longer voice her doubts and fears for the purpose of ordering and fitting them into a rational grid, and thus deploy the diary as a tool of purification. She feared that if she did so the NKVD would isolate these statements and interpret them as expressions of her total self. Her fears were justified—in the context of the Great Purges expressions of doubt amounted to severe counterrevolutionary acts. Moreover, even expressions of loyalty by a suspected counterrevolutionary were distrusted: the more loyal they were, the more the enemy was able to dissimulate behind the mask of a good Soviet citizen. In studying Berggolts's diary, Commissar Goglidze was undoubtedly aware of a famous precedent for her mourning over Kirov. At the January 1937 Moscow show trial, state prosecutor Andrei Vyshinsky exposed the hypocrisy of the defendant Georgy Piatakov. Back in 1934 Piatakov had publicly sobbed over the corpse of Sergei Kirov, whose murder, Vyshinsky asserted, Piatakov himself had instigated. Portraying Piatakov as concealing a counterrevolutionary essence behind his Soviet appearance, Vyshinsky described him as looking at himself in the mirror, admiring his ability to dissemble.[87] Reading Berggolts's diary in the light of Vyshinsky's diagnosis, her prosecutor was bound to interpret her professed love of Kirov as a deceptive ploy, a counterrevolutionary gesture of the vilest sort.

Unable to restore the purity of their minds, several diarists yearned for support from none other than the NKVD. They represented the Stalinist secret police as a moral authority, able to both understand and cure their diseases. Podlubny expected the NKVD to rectify his thoughts and to rear him as a good socialist citizen. Instead, the secret police continued to remind him of his kulak origins and block his transformation into a new man: "Instead of curing me, they are making a cripple of me." Piatnitskaya expressed her hope that the NKVD would ensure her growth into a full-fledged socialist citizen: "I sincerely ask the NKVD for humane assistance. I ask for a harsh life for myself, but this would still be life (struggle, work, and an unmistakable growth as a person and consequently of human and, consequently, civic spirit)." She yearned to confide all her "good thoughts" to NKVD chief Nikolai Ezhov. Ultimately she hoped that the NKVD, or Ezhov himself, would assume her husband's former role of confessor: "The only thing that I would like to have . . . is trust of the NKVD. Such trust that I could speak about everything that worries me, all my grave thoughts, when they appear from time to time and then go away, after some work on myself—that I could speak about all this with somebody from the NKVD. I would have what I had with Piatnitsky." Piatnitskaya also emphasized that she never even considered hiding anything from the NKVD: "this is a principle of mine." Elsewhere she remarked: "Regardless of everything, they [the NKVD] are closest to me." Similarly, Podlubny hailed his encounters with the NKVD as rare moments of total truth and absolution, since they alone knew about his real social essence as a class alien: "Somehow you cleanse your soul of some sort of trash. After all, you speak sincerely and truthfully, while at the same time everywhere else your entire life is a lie." For Podlubny and others, both their diaries and the NKVD functioned as agents of transparency.[88]

While some diarists experienced the Stalinist purges as a successful test of their willpower and emerged from them feeling stronger, younger, and purer, others did not. Following a series of attempts to cleanse herself from her impure thoughts and to gain readmission into Soviet society, Piatnitskaya seemed to realize gradually that her struggle was in vain: "After all, there were months when my head was clear. I could hold myself together, I tried to struggle for my life, and I had no conflicts with Soviet Power. But now something new has happened: either I am sick, or I need to be isolated from my fellow citizens. I see a lot of disgusting things in the newspapers. And when I look in the courtyard, I also feel nauseated." If she was "sick," she could still entertain hope of being cured, although this was very difficult, now that she had no healer of souls to turn to—neither Piatnitsky, who had acted as her confessor prior to his arrest, nor the NKVD, which failed to take up this role for her. At the same time, Piatnitskaya saw herself confronted with increasing evidence (some of it on the pages of the diary itself) that she was an irredeemable counterrevolutionary. This would mean that not just a part of her soul but all of her self had become infected with an incurable, evil essence. The only remaining solution was to isolate herself from the rest of Soviet society, so as not to infect the healthy social body. Piatnitskaya even went to the state prosecutor and informed him "about my mood and my thoughts that would require me to be isolated from society. I told him that for this whole period I had isolated myself—it's been nine months already—but that it would be advisable to remove me to the fullest extent officially." Piatnitskaya was arrested later in 1938 and sent to a prison camp in Kazakhstan, where she worked as an economist. Her son Igor was in the same camp system, and they saw each other one final time in 1939. Julia's fate was sealed when she resisted the sexual advances of a camp commander. He had her sent to do heavy labor at a dam-construction site. In the fall of 1940, too weak and sick to work any longer, she was shunned by the camp population and left to die in a sheep pen. Her lifelong struggle to join the laboring collective and help build the radiant future ended in total isolation from society and from the human world.[89]

Self-definition in the Stalin era—the question of personal identity, whether a person was strong or weak, clear-minded or crazy—was intrinsically linked to the ability to master ideology. As diarists struggled to regain their ideological convictions, they struggled by the same token to regain themselves. Many of these diaristic self-projects proceeded under a tyranny of rationality which forced diarists to cut out, suppress, or rework thought patterns that stood in the way of a fully rationalized worldview. Unlike its present-day psychological usage, "rationalization" in this period was not an attempt by unstable and weak individuals to "rationalize away" uncomfortable truths. To the contrary, rationalization was essential for Soviet citizens, who were supposed to believe in scientific laws of development and the rationality of their existence. Soviet citizens were thus constantly asked to rationalize, to make their daily observations fit ideological mandates. The more their observations departed from the required viewpoint, the more they were expected to struggle to reinhabit the grid. The ability to rationalize a phenomenon was thus a characteristic of mental strength. Rationalization bred willpower, determination, and youth. Conversely, individuals who failed to rationalize their observations, who surrendered to the torrent of chaotic or critical thought, were cast as weak-willed, mentally disordered, and ultimately doomed.

Beyond denoting an intellectual quality, rationality had strong moral connotations, as diarists' interchangeable use of rationality, clarity of mind, and spiritual purity makes clear. In addition the ideal of rationality had an important sensory dimension, as it was by virtue of their rational, pure minds that individuals achieved integration into the collective and thereby gained a true sense of belonging. Conversely, those who were pushed outside the ranks of the collective were bound to feel crippled, isolated, and unable to live on their own. Speaking in 1925, Martyn Liadov, rector of Sverdlov Communist University, invoked the sensory dimension of Soviet subjectivity when he described the future Communist society: Communism would restore the unity of personal and social pursuits; it would yield a society in which "every person will feel pain, will feel burdened, if his personal interests in any way contradict the interests of the collective. But that will be an anomaly . . . [In Communist society] there will no longer be any coercive power. In each of us, inhibitive centers will be developed by life itself, by the force of collective creativity . . . I will be capable of experiencing only the general pleasure, the general satisfaction, the unlimited pleasure that will reign all around me."[90] More than a decade later Julia Piatnitskaya described in her diary exactly the kind of pain referred to by Liadov—a pain caused by the individual's severance from the collective. But her pain was not entirely occasioned by an inhibitive center within her, as Liadov had predicted. In Piatnitskaya's case, as in countless others, the force of her conscience combined with the coercive mechanisms of the state apparatus (state prosecutor, NKVD investigators) and powerful doses of social stigmatization (on the part of former colleagues and neighbors) to create feelings of painful exclusion from the overall current of Soviet life.[91]

Communist subjectivity in its Stalinist guise operated not only through the intellectual appeal of Marxism and its promise of individual emancipation and transformation but also through the seduction and absorption of the lonely individual into the "mass ornament," to use Siegfried Kracauer's contemporary metaphor.[92] Studies of subjectivity in the Stalin era remain incomplete if they fail to consider the crippling and anesthetizing effects on individuals who were expelled from the nurturing collective, a punishment that could be incurred by as little as a series of idiosyncratic private thoughts. Rather than heroic liberal agents, doubting Stalinist subjects more often appear as atomized selves in crisis, longing to overcome their painful separation from the collective body of the Soviet people. The search for inclusion in the revolutionary universe and the fear of expulsion from it are at work in each of the four life stories to follow.

4

Intelligentsia on Trial

ZINAIDA DENISEVSKAYA

Zinaida Denisevskaya was a 30-year-old schoolteacher in Voronezh, a provincial capital in Russia's agricultural heartland, when the Bolsheviks came to power in the fall of 1917. In her diary she had few favorable words for the new regime: "The Bolshevik victory worries and frightens me. I don't trust them. They have neither honesty nor intellect; I'm not talking about the exceptions, but on the whole they are dark and evil." Less than twelve years later Denisevskaya recorded a transformation she had begun to undergo: "Over the whole last year I have unconsciously become a 'socialist,' I am beginning to understand communism." Another year later she confided: "Life has reeducated me over the past twelve years," and "only recently have I come to trust the party and the state." Her previous outlook on life now appeared to her "bizarre and ridiculous." Castigating her past "ignorance," Denisevskaya effectively reverted from a teacher, chiding the Communists' lack of culture, to a student avidly learning the new forms of life.[1]

Denisevskaya kept her diary from 1900, when she was a 13-year-old schoolgirl, until her untimely death in 1933. It is an extraordinary record, given its volume and its self-reflective quality. On one level, the journal charts the succession of thoughts and often startling revelations that brought Denisevskaya from condemning the Bolsheviks in 1917 to embracing them—quite literally—by the end of the 1920s. But the framing dates of the diary allow for a broader perspective on her evolving self-exploration across several decades of cataclysmic political and social changes—the breakdown of imperial Russia, the turmoil of revolution, and the early years of a new regime intent on remaking human relationships and creating a new world. Denisevskaya's self-reflection predated the Soviet order; she entered the revolution of 1917 with developed and articulated notions of her own "personality." It was

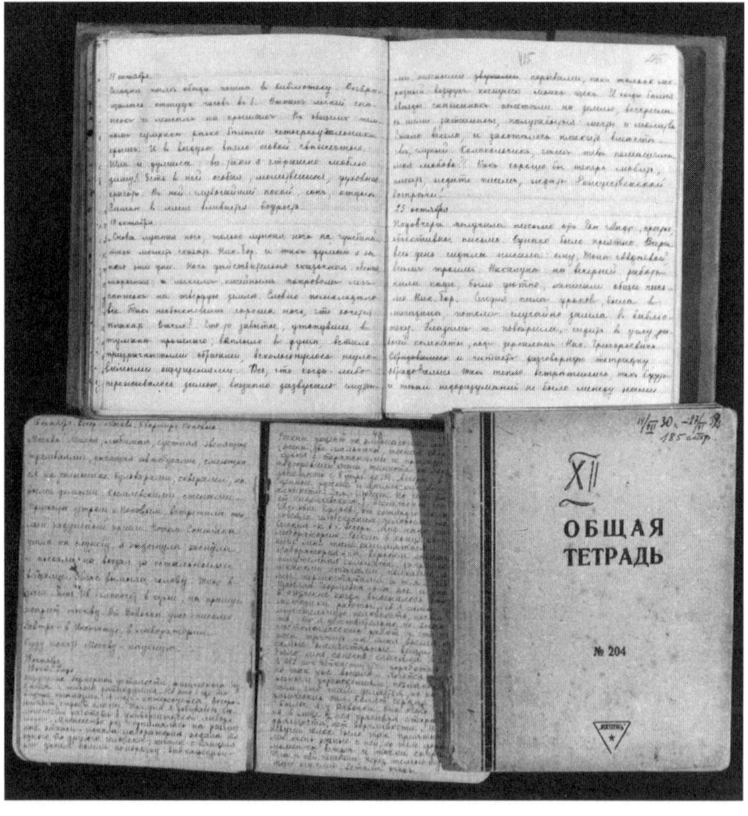

The diaries of Zinaida Denisevskaya
© Manuscript Division, Russian State Library, Moscow.

precisely from this vantage point that she criticized the Bolsheviks as uncultivated and faceless. And yet over the years she came to trade her personal autonomy for a value that appeared infinitely higher, larger, more meaningful. In detailing this woman's critical engagement of her self between the extreme poles of "individualism" and "collectivism" through a continuum of political revolution and social transformation, her diary differs markedly from customary accounts of the collectivist Soviet system encroaching on the autonomy of its citizens.

Throughout her life Denisevskaya retained a commitment to cultivating her personality, thereby revealing her engagement in the ethos of the Russian intelligentsia, that group of educated and critically thinking individuals which defined itself above all by a commitment to the creation of a perfect social order inhabited by harmoniously shaped, fulfilled, and integrated human beings. The continued pursuit of her diary was in some measure an expression of Denisevskaya's sustained aspiration toward such an ideal type of personality. In light of this longer-term commitment, Bolshevik ways of thinking and acting on the self appear less original, and more situated, as variants of a preoccupation with working on and perfecting the self that characterized larger segments of Russian culture—late imperial and revolutionary as well as Soviet.

Another continuous theme in the diary, and in fact its overriding theme, was loneliness. Over the years Denisevskaya kept dreaming of, but never experienced, a lasting love relationship (though she was married for a few months late in her life). Feeling not understood, lacking the resolve to speak up and being instead subjected to the vocal opinions of her friends and colleagues, she turned to her journal as her strongest "friend and support." Even as a 13-year-old she cast herself as a loner, "overly serious and calm" and prone to introspective dreaming. When a friend at school jokingly nicknamed her "nun," she noted: "Yes, I am a nun, a hermit. But it is not out of my own will that I have locked myself in this stifling monastery." Thirty years later, amid the turmoil of the Stalinist revolution and in starkly different conditions, she still sounded the same tone: "I'm experiencing a most profound sense of personal loneliness." Of the incredible 5,623 pages of Denisevskaya's diary writings, many, if not most, resonated with the melancholic sound of her voice, a backdrop of loneliness against which her desires for completion and communality unfolded.[2]

In the course of her life, loneliness meant a variety of things to Denisevskaya. It referred in part to her predicament as an unmarried woman, but it also connoted an existential solitude, a sense of being unsheltered in the world. After 1917 she increasingly came to understand her lonely condition in the context of class. The notion of the "laboring collective," ardently proclaimed by the Soviet regime, resonated to her with a promise of deliverance from loneliness and eventually proved stronger than her abhorrence of the coarse Communists around her. The question remains to what extent her loneliness was a personal characteristic, responsible for her eventual embrace of the Soviet idea, and to what extent loneliness was ingrained in the intelligentsia's self-image in an age of rising masses and collectivities.

Intelligent, *Woman, Human Being*

Zinaida Denisevskaya was born in 1887 into a family belonging to Voronezh's educated elite. She appears to have been the oldest of at least four children. Her father was a science teacher in the private girls' school which she later attended, and at least at one point he was the director of that school. In 1907 Zinaida enrolled in the Women's Higher Courses in Moscow, a university-level institution founded in the early 1870s, which provided high-level training in scientific subjects as well as the humanities. She majored in natural sciences. After completing her studies in 1912, she moved back to Voronezh, where she worked first as a teacher in local gymnasia and elementary schools and later as a librarian in the city library. In 1920 she left the library to take up work at the experimental station of the Voronezh Agricultural Institute. She remained there for the rest of her life, working with a team of agronomists who experimented with innovative methods of agricultural production and labor and sought to spread them among the local peasantry.[3]

Denisevskaya began keeping a journal in 1900, at the age of 13. Her diary notes of the years up to 1919 are preserved in five thick, bound volumes, each containing about seven hundred pages. Their appearance stands in stark contrast to the thin, brittle notebooks in which Denisevskaya recorded her life in the Soviet period, from 1919 to 1933. For much of her life Denisevskaya wrote diary entries often at daily and rarely at less than weekly intervals. Many of the diary entries keep revolving around the same themes, and do so with the same yearning and fatalism. She described her family life as conflicted and unhappy. While Zinaida portrayed her father as tender and loving, her mother appeared as cold, harsh, and unjust. Yet the diary also notes Zinaida's mother alternating between hysterical outbursts and numbed suffering over her husband's infidelity.

Nowhere in her early diary did Denisevskaya define herself clearly in social terms, but her family background as well as her educational and professional aspirations marked her as a member of the intelligentsia, if adherence to this group is defined by an overriding moral commitment to serving the needs of society. This was exactly how she described her father: "He is completely preoccupied with his idea to serve society and has given himself completely to it." The daughter aspired to become a teacher herself, a goal shared by most Russian girls who attended private gymnasia in the early 1900s. To become a village schoolteacher and educate the "dark" peasantry was their profession of choice, whereas boys from the educated classes wanted to become doctors and scientists. Together with an increasing number of young women her age, Zinaida also sought to obtain a higher education. Like others of her generation she saw a university education as essential "to become a fully developed personality, live a conscious life, take part in the life of society." To become a member of the intelligentsia was to turn into a "critically thinking person, to cultivate a rational worldview," as the liberal politician Ariadna Tyrkova-Williams wrote, looking back on her youth and moral education in the 1880s.[4] Personhood, thus defined, referred not to any individual's empirical life but to a more abstract and general idea of the human personality *(lichnost')*. In working on themselves, members of the intelligentsia attempted to fashion themselves according to an idealized image of humanity.[5]

The commitment to the development of a moral personality with an integrated worldview showed well in Denisevskaya's case. She was 17 in 1904 when ever-larger sections of Russian educated society began to clamor for constitutional concessions from the autocratic government. For this young woman who sympathetically recorded the evolving protest and strike movement of 1905, the political sphere promised an escape from her lonely and sad personal life into a world of joyous communion with fellow citizens. Beyond tracing the "rising enthusiasm of society," she hoped to inscribe herself into what she perceived as a generation on the rise: "[to] participate in the important work of a whole generation . . . To prepare myself for this I must read, develop." The revolution served as an impetus for her to develop a worldview of her own: "I must clarify to myself my political and social views, and formulate them if they are not there." "The main thing is to work out my worldview. But it just won't be worked out—an absolute standstill—anguish and despair." Five years later she still complained: "I lack an integral worldview; because I can't clearly and logically explain all of life to myself."[6]

And yet, while the revolution provided her with a new sense of community ("standing together with ten thousand people at the People's Palace, I for the first time conceived of myself as a human being, a member of society"), she felt more comfortable on the sidelines of the revolutionary movement, from where she followed with a mix of envy and resentment the celebrations of her politically active peers. In the first place she blamed her poor health for keeping her locked at home with an aching heart, while down in the streets of Voronezh "life is in full swing." But most of the politically active youth were socialists and fought for radical positions that she could not bring herself to support. By virtue of "character, nature, and education" she belonged to the party of "cultural reformers" and "gradualists." "And I hate myself for this. I envy them, the young people who take on risk and sacrifice, who live with all the strength of their young bodies. And I'm annoyed at myself." At the same time, she rejected the "fanaticism and intolerance" of political parties and condemned their "expropriations and killings." She particularly rejected Communist ideology, which "completely suppresses and smothers individuality." As for her own political commitments, she valued "education and humaneness above everything else. It's not enough to be a conscious proletarian, one must first and foremost be a human being."[7]

Denisevskaya's observations on political life intersected with another sphere in which she began to reflect on herself as a "human being." This was her sexuality. The theme first surfaced in an entry for February 1907. In concluding a glowing account of the first opera she had ever attended—*Carmen*—she noted that "something new" was happening to her. She was becoming "flirtatious" toward a 29-year-old male friend, to whom she was beginning to relate not as "an abstract being," but as a "physical person": "Again I see in myself that which I am trying to kill off, that which I find disgusting—sensuality. In my soul I am sinking to the most hidden and disturbed thoughts and desires, I see that I want casual caresses from him."[8]

Throughout the Russian reading world there appeared a new obsession with instinct and sexuality in the wake of the 1905 protests that could be only partly explained by the press reforms and the ensuing rise of the boulevard press. The preoccupation was not with sexuality as such but with the claims to self-realization that were attached to it. At the center of a debate that polarized the opinion of educated society for several years was Mikhail Artsybashev's erotic novel *Sanin* (published in installments in 1907), whose philandering eponymous hero convinces the women he seduces that sexual impulses improve rather than degrade their personalities. Secondary only to *Sanin* in influence was another novel, Anastasia Verbitskaya's *Keys to Happiness,* which more specifically addressed a female audience. Its heroine, Manya, pursues a way of life that combines personal autonomy, professional success, love, and sexuality. She learns from a man that women can and should allow themselves physical pleasure without becoming slaves of love, that personal autonomy and sexual satisfaction without emotional involvement constitute "the keys to happiness."[9]

Contemporary critics apprehended the appearance of these novels as an indication of a cultural sea change. The ethos of revolutionary struggle and self-sacrifice for society, propagated by the radical intelligentsia since at least the 1860s, seemed discredited in light of the failed revolution. Social and political commitments were eroding among contemporary youth, the designated heirs of the intelligentsia. The collective strength and the moral standards of the revolutionary movement were dissipating into base individualistic urges. Sanin was the antihero par excellence, an opposite of the self-sacrificing underground fighter who had inspired the intelligentsia in the past. He was an extreme individualist, who lived in order to satisfy his "natural" needs and despised social morality and politics. Most shocking was not Sanin's notion of free love—after all, Chernyshevsky had advocated a ménage à trois back in the 1860s—but the disconnection of sexuality from an agenda of social emancipation and its proclamation as a highest goal in itself. Both *The Keys to Happiness* and *Sanin,* to be sure, were only symbolic expressions of a trend toward individualism and subjectivity in Russian and European culture of the 1900s and 1910s. It was a trend marked by Nietzschean ideas (which Artsybashev acknowledged as an influence) and neo-Kantian philosophy, but also by the reform policies of the autocratic government, notably Prime Minister Stolypin's wager on the "strong peasant" and the decision to break up the peasant commune.

Denisevskaya took up the language of the new literary individualism for the purposes of her own self-analysis. Reflecting in her diary on her relationships with several male friends, she wondered whether she had sufficiently "expressed herself in life. Was I independent and individualist in my personal life?" Was she an equal and independent partner to these friends, or had she become their "slave"? Even if outwardly she appeared submissive, Denisevskaya concluded, she had to remain true to herself: "I cannot allow my soul to be violated." After leaving Voronezh to study in Moscow, she became involved with a man who in the diary is called merely "the student." Her description of him was embedded in the most burning question about the student movement: Was it still a progressive force, or had it been fatally corrupted by the new individualism? Denisevskaya's diagnosis was sobering. Clearly there were sides to the affair that she enjoyed: "I like it when he slides his hand over my shoulders and breasts . . . Nobody has ever caressed me like this. People would like or admire me, put me on a pedestal, they would caress my soul, but not my body. Even my mother did not caress her little girl. And now it feels good when he caresses me." But she was beset by moral qualms: Had "the student's" mission to educate her senses degraded her as a person? Part of her wanted to brush aside these doubts. Her ideal woman, after all, was not Faust's Gretchen, or Turgenev's Liza (from *A House of Gentlefolk*)—submissive, virtuous women, passive victims of men—but a modern, self-affirming, socially active and committed individual, like Chernyshevsky's Vera Pavlovna, or like Elena, from another of Turgenev's novels (*On the Eve*). "They all lived, loved, and knew men, which did not taint them in the least, on the contrary, new complex experiences raised the personality of each of them, made it develop." With these literary heroines, who served as models of personal and social behavior for generations of young Russian women, Denisevskaya insisted on her personal right to express her sexual instincts, and she linked this self-affirmation to progressive values of the day—"individualism" and "individual freedom for everybody."[10]

It remained to be seen, however, whether this individualist and materialist definition of the self could be reconciled with Zinaida's intelligentsia background and her commitment to a morally defined notion of "personality." The heroines from Chernyshevsky's and Turgenev's novels, she had to recognize, were not viable role models in the morally depressed climate of the post-1905 student movement. The free love advocated by Vera Pavlovna as a socially progressive ideal logically degenerated into blind physiological impulses as soon as it was divested of a social purpose. Such naked individualism was not emancipating, but debasing. Denisevskaya described how in the course of her Sanin-like experiments her moral self became a prisoner of her body. The moral humanism underpinning her self-definition as a human being *(chelovek)* and as a person *(lichnost')* made it impossible for her to fully accept the idea that her instincts were expressions of her human "nature," for that would reduce her to an "animal." In the end she felt nothing but bitterness toward the student who had posed as her "'teacher of life,'" but had aroused in her merely "the instinct of a woman," then had left her and "indifferently" returned to his wife and children. "Woman" in Denisevskaya's vocabulary had a decidedly negative ring, connoting bodily instincts, irrationality, and the art of lowly intrigue: "I have become more experienced, I have learned to lie and be deceptive about my feelings. I'm no longer a sincere little girl, I have come to understand my power and role as a woman." To be a "woman" was to feel and act sexually—in marked contrast to the conscious and moral "human" will. In some ways, Denisevskaya's understanding of "woman" was analogous to her representation of the political sphere: both were realms governed by passions and selfish interests, in opposition to the higher, universal spheres of "humanity" and "society."[11]

Denisevskaya discovered the possibility of synthesizing her understanding of "woman" and "human being" in an article by the Russian feminist Alexandra Kollontai entitled "The New Woman." Writing in 1913, Kollontai proclaimed the emergence of a new type of woman as a social fact: young female workers and office employees, products of modern economic life who were appearing in large numbers in Russia and abroad. They were materially self-reliant and assertive, legally single, and psychologically independent and free. They stood in opposition to the "woman of the past" who was a mere appendix to her husband, an object rather than a subject. The modern woman fought against her traditional position of "impersonal submissiveness." Her defiant outlook forced the "new woman" into loneliness, as she could not expect to be truly loved by men who only wanted to possess and thus objectify her. All that men could offer her for now was physiological satisfaction, while her self-realization was to occur through work and public service. Yet she knew that at some distant point in the future people (meaning men) with a "different configuration of the soul" would appear. They would be able to experience and dispense true, comradely love, which did not entail the objectification of women.[12]

In reading this article, Denisevskaya wrote, she came to "understand" herself as a "new woman." She could lead a socially and morally meaningful life without having to repress her instinctual desires. The model was attractive not only because it married physiology to morality and appeared new and progressive but also because it provided an explanation for her plight as a single and lonely young woman. One of the literary heroines cited by Kollontai kept a diary which sounded the theme of loneliness familiar from Denisevskaya's own record: "I'm used to being alone, but today I feel so lonely . . . Does this mean that I'm not independent, not free? I'm terribly lonely." Commenting on this diary, Kollontai confidently offered a solution to the heroine's torment: "Don't we hear in this complaint a woman from the past who is used to being surrounded by familiar and beloved voices, and to feeling someone's habitual caresses?" Kollontai's new woman resolutely withstood such traditional longings: "She goes away, quietly smiling at him at parting, she goes to seek her dream of happiness, she goes, carrying her own soul with her, as if . . . it was necessary for her to build a new life for herself." Solitude in this reading was less a curse than an achievement, a first step toward self-realization as a modern woman.[13]

Yet Kollontai's advice did not appear to change Zinaida Denisevskaya's life in appreciable ways. After graduating from the Women's Higher Courses in Moscow, she returned to Voronezh and lived in her parents' household, as traditionally befitted an unmarried young woman. And she continued to deplore the lack of love in her life. Most significantly perhaps, the lexicon of the new woman disappeared from Denisevskaya's diary in subsequent years—a remarkable development given that these were the years of the revolution, when the ideal of the new woman was in full swing.

The Old Intelligentsia

After the outbreak of the First World War Denisevskaya "attentively" followed both "the war and Russia's public life" and regretted being unable to take part in the "rebirth of Russian society" that she was reading about in the newspapers. She greeted the outbreak of revolution as a climactic event, enabling "Russian society" for the first time to exercise political power for the good of the people. As a teacher, she could claim a modest but significant role in a nationwide campaign to impart civic education to the people, as she explained to her students the "significance of the most widespread current terms: constitution, monarchy, republic, supreme power, etc." Denisevskaya repeatedly stressed her interest in public events, and she noted apologetically that her diary, which continued to deal for the most part with personal reveries and her loneliness, reflected but a fraction of her interests and pursuits.[14]

Yet amid the increasing social and political polarization of civil war, Denisevskaya's idealized notion of a unified, organic Russian society evaporated. It had vanished from her vocabulary by the fall of 1917. From the vantage point of an imaginary middle, she observed the fracturing of the political landscape. She was harshly critical toward the Soviet government, a regime staffed by corrupt, power-hungry, and uneducated elements who had nothing in common with the lofty socialist ideals of brotherhood and justice. But she was at least equally critical of the "so-called intelligentsia"—educated members of society who commented with "resentment, hatred, and malicious joy" on the blunders of the Bolshevik regime and in the process lost sight of their duty to work for the people. Even the danger of being accidentally crushed by the "wheel of the general machine" was no reason to relinquish this duty, for the laws of history continued to work. The current era was a "transition period," marked by "the people's passing from infancy to adolescence." It was in denouncing the socially irresponsible "narrow-minded egoism" of this social group that Denisevskaya claimed for herself the role of a true member of the intelligentsia, in its more traditional and inclusive understanding as an engine of education and progress and a midwife of the future Russian nation. Even in this time of chaos and extreme violence, she looked for a life-ordering principle,

an ideology from which to derive a personal worldview. An ideology was legitimate if it corresponded to the lawful progression of history and served a general interest, which in the context of revolution could only mean the interest of the "people." This explains why she never sided with the White Army and was closer to the Reds in spirit, but at the same time she wondered how the latter's brutality could possibly express the socialist "principle of brotherhood and equality."[15]

The civil war affected Voronezh in especially harsh ways. Held by the Whites in the early stages of the conflict, the city was seized by Soviet armies in the fall of 1919. Denisevskaya's diary is filled with accounts—for the most part not first-hand, but based on conversations and rumors—of searches, confiscations, arrests, and drunken acts of violence, including random murder. Classified by the Red government as members of the propertied classes, Denisevskaya and her parents were at least once subjected to a forcible tax ("contribution"). Such practices left her wondering how teachers, as members of the "proletarian intelligentsia," could be possibly grouped among the "bourgeoisie." Ultimately, she confessed feeling too exhausted and weak to fully "'accept' reality": "I lost my head under the pressure of the revolution, faced with this permanent risk of death, robbery, fright, and the loss of people dear to me." She retreated into a life centered on her work at the city library and "far removed from politics and party questions, from the common life of Russia . . . I don't want to find my way amid the details of contemporary life, to find out who's right and who's guilty, who's achieving victories and who has made mistakes."[16]

Paralleling this retreat from secular politics, Denisevskaya increasingly sought escape in religion and the hope of an afterlife. She had been religious all her life, though she often stressed the modern and

---

Staff members of the Voronezh city library, 1919. Denisevskaya is standing at center right, wearing a dark hat. © Manuscript Division, Russian State Library, Moscow.

scientific form of her belief. God to her existed as a "substance," "a special kind of energy," a force like electricity that showed when people were animated by love and committed good deeds, and this godly energy was imparted to individuals by Darwinist laws of evolution. In the initial stages of the revolution Denisevskaya had seen socialism as superior to religion because in addition to incarnating the best principles of Christianity it was a progressive force based on scientific laws. But in the face of mass death and violence, her Christian belief rebounded. Suffering from chronic heart disease and an acute case of yellow fever, Denisevskaya did not expect to survive these apocalyptic times.[17]

Yet she came out of the civil war stronger, and with a new sense of direction. In 1920 she relinquished her position at the city library and left her parents' home, to take up work as a researcher at an experimental station outside of the city. In her own words, she transferred from a "mental" world of "abstract ideas" to hands-on, scientific, "factual" work. In an immediate sense, collaboration with the agronomists from the region and from Moscow who visited the farm promised escape from her loneliness. But her move was also an attempt to shed the mental and bookish domain of the traditional intelligentsia, as it was caricaturized by the radical socialists, and to embrace a principle of applied labor with and for the toiling people. Her writings of this period expressed an increasingly critical view of the social and moral ideals of her past, to the point that she equated the spirit of the intelligentsia—which she had once seen as service to the people—with bourgeois individualism. Yet her repudiations of past allegiances coexisted in the diary with descriptions of her work for the people which evoked a traditional intelligentsia ethos. In describing the difficulties of conducting agronomical research in conditions of appalling "backwardness," Denisevskaya cast herself as a beacon of education and morality, a guiding force for both erring Communists and the benighted people. Her claim to cultural and pedagogical preeminence stood in marked contrast to her programmatic spirit of abdication and subservience to the laboring people.[18]

Several years into her new profession, Denisevskaya's initial enthusiasm was gone. The experimental farm, which had earlier appeared to her as a "happy island," turned out to be an isolated spot of culture in the midst of an interminable "swamp." This was brought home to her when the new director of the region's agronomical stations, Pavel Pistsov, visited the farm:

> I experienced a strange and unpleasant feeling of envy for this stocky, short, blue-eyed man. He lived in China and Japan for a long time, he has seen, knows, and understands much. His vocabulary is peppered with foreign words. He is a cultured European, or more exactly, not a European but an internationalist. I sensed him to be a person at the highest level of culture and envied him strongly . . . He is Russian, but I am as strange to him as Dunya or Marisha [peasant assistants] is to me. He wears cultured clothes, while I walk around in felt boots and an old-fashioned blouse. He has seen and knows the world, he talks about scientific work conducted all over the world, as if these were things that were close to him; and I don't know anything, I sit from morning till night, doing mechanical work, I've grown old, let myself go, become unsociable.

Pistsov seemed to fit Denisevskaya's idealized notion of the intelligentsia: highly educated, refined in dress and speech, engaged in cutting-edge scientific work with a universal scope. These features underscored her own material and cultural destitution. Most striking perhaps was that she saw herself appearing old and wasted compared with the director, though she was only 39 years old—exactly Pistsov's age.[19]

The latter half of the 1920s was a time of personal crisis for Denisevskaya, dramatically punctuating the quietist tone of her earlier diary. She described a veritable loss of self, brought about by her crushed convictions and lack of a personal mission. She felt she was drifting, incapable of directing her sick body and nerves: "Everything is so unstable, confused, unexpected. From all directions misfortunes, illnesses, suffering, and death come down on you . . . I have lost my philosophy, I have lost control of my nerves, I've become like seaweed, swaying in the surf." Materially she enjoyed basic comforts ("I have a warm room, a soft bed, I can live, eat, drink, and work"), but spiritually she felt utterly void. The "main thing" she lacked was love. "That is why I have nothing to write about . . . Always one and the same story: loneliness, shifting moods. Up—and down, up again, and down again . . . And invariably the downfalls are deeper and last longer than my peaks."[20]

The questions about her life and social mission that Denisevskaya posed in personal terms in her diary were also subjects of debate at the very center of Soviet power. At issue were the "bourgeois specialists," professionals like Denisevskaya, who had been educated and formed before the revolution and now lent the regime their expertise without embracing the Communist cause. Communist activists disdainfully contrasted this "old," "bourgeois" specialist to a "new," yet to be formed, Soviet intelligentsia, which was to be devoted to the political regime body and soul. In turn, members of the embattled group sought to retain a degree of political independence while stressing their basic loyalty to the Soviet order. At a public debate in Moscow in 1925, a scholar defended the intelligentsia's cultural credentials, which were epitomized in the "heroic type of the female village teacher." Coping with political adversity, a meager income, and miserable living conditions in a backward village, far from the outposts of civilization, this beacon of the intelligentsia "created" with the utmost energy her "modest, yet great deed."[21]

This plea for political autonomy met with a fierce rebuttal from the Bolshevik party's chief ideologist, Nikolai Bukharin. Politics and culture could not be viewed as separate fields of action, Bukharin insisted: "You build the edifice in such a way that the cultural row appears to be independent from the political one. But such a thing doesn't exist." The intelligentsia was further crippled in its stance toward revolutionary action, according to Bukharin, by its traditional faintheartedness. This trait was rooted in an ingrained individualism which prevented the class of bourgeois specialists from appreciating the collective power and historic might of the working class. Bukharin attacked the intelligentsia's ethical reservations about the policies of Soviet power, which he characterized as its fear of dirtying its hands. In the present situation of intense class struggle, revolutionary politics could not be carried out without recourse to violence. Under these conditions those who professed a fear of "stepping over corpses" were in fact covert reactionaries. The central charge brought by Bukharin, however, was that, in spite of its professed populism, the intelligentsia was not really committed to emancipating the people, being reluctant to give up its monopoly on enlightenment. It preferred to preach and speak on the people's behalf rather than letting them speak for themselves. In concluding, Bukharin invited the intelligentsia to join the Communist regime in realizing its "gigantic universal standards" and in rearing a new, Soviet intelligentsia: "We will produce educated individuals in great numbers, we will manufacture them just like in a factory . . . If we set ourselves the task of going toward Communism we have to infuse everything with this task."[22]

In strikingly literal fashion, in the following years, Denisevskaya appropriated for herself the scenario outlined by Bukharin. She turned against the "old intelligentsia"—both inside her and in her social environment—confronted the faintheartedness ascribed to her, and assumed a more "party-minded" stance toward politics and the building of a socialist society. This was a stunning turnaround. How did it come about?

The relentless propaganda generated by the Soviet regime against the "old," "bourgeois" intelligentsia undoubtedly played an important role in structuring Denisevskaya's choices and preferences. This largely verbal violence was broadened and systematized toward the end of the 1920s, culminating in brutal harassment, arrests, show trials, and executions—some of them in Denisevskaya's immediate vicinity. This massive violence appears in Denisevskaya's diary only in 1930, well after the onset of her conversion to the Soviet cause. The decisive point is that the Soviet vision as outlined by Bukharin was immensely appealing to Denisevskaya. Several of her lifelong commitments—the quest for a coherent worldview, a meaningful mission in life consonant with the laws of history, and the creation of a perfect human personality and society—were now brought to her by the state. Beyond their intellectual substance, these ideas were tantalizing for their integrative potential. It was for the sake of integration into the collective that she distanced herself from the "old intelligentsia," which she defined as individualist, selfish, marginal, and negative, and embraced the universalism propagated by the Soviet regime. Denisevskaya built a new home for herself in an edifice of socialist subjectivity. Socialist subjectivity had differing meanings for different individuals; for her it afforded a large, communal life, filled with warmth, love, and a sense of belonging that mitigated her personal loneliness.

Alyosha

The strength of these new ideas can be gauged by Denisevskaya's evolving characterization of several people close to her between the mid-1920s and the early 1930s. There were the Ferdinandovs, Vasily Vladimirovich ("V.V." in the diary), her supervisor on the experimental farm, and his wife, Juliana Vasilevna ("J.V."). Denisevskaya lived in the same building as the couple—quite possibly in the same communal apartment—and she described their household as an outpost of culture in the forbidding steppe. When, in late 1926, the Ferdinandovs moved to the city of Voronezh, where V.V. had been appointed to a newly established veterinary institute, Denisevskaya thought with horror about the "thousands of conveniences and pleasures" she would soon lose, including J.V.'s piano recitals and cherished evening discussions on cultural and political themes. V.V.'s new appointment, she remarked, was another indication of how "completely muddled" Soviet power was. Courses were to begin within a week, even though the institute existed only on paper and lacked a building, teaching staff, and money. "It is so dull and repelling to live in Russia right now!" she concluded. It is likely that her words echoed V.V.'s own indignation, and thus convey a sense of her conversations with the Ferdinandovs.[23]

However, only a few months later, when Denisevskaya visited the couple in the city (for the "Old Christmas" holiday, as she pointed out), there was a note of estrangement in her description, a gap that was to widen in the months and years to come: "J.V. is like a picture from a fashion journal. V.V. appears urban and distant." From now on, her visits to the Ferdinandovs would be followed by critical remarks on their "intelligentsia" milieu. She took exception to the permanent sarcasm and bickering with which members of the intelligentsia commented on one another as well as on social and political developments. At the same time she seemed to be afraid to articulate her own views:

> I'm getting tired of keeping silent, of not speaking out, and of the discrepancy between my thoughts and the thoughts of the people around me. I am amazed by the narrow personal outlook on life that most of these people have. If there is no white bread or no

> white cloth, it means life is bad. But the fact that other people's lives have become better in many respects is not taken into account. And they gloat over everything, speak ironically about everything. One becomes bored with this constant hostility toward everything.[24]

As Denisevskaya recast the Ferdinandovs as representatives of an old and outlived world, she showed greater sympathy to a young generation of Communists and specialists whom she saw as the mainstays of the Soviet order. This change in perspective was spurred by her new professional duties: in 1928 she took up a teaching position in the poultry farming division of the same veterinary institute at which V.V. worked. She did not give up her work on the experimental farm, but commuted more frequently to the city and the institute. It was there that her enthusiasm for the young people, initially not without reservations, overtook her.[25] As she encountered her new colleagues, she spontaneously divided them into "old" and "new" generations, proclaiming her attraction to the new: "My heart flew to the new." She immediately took a liking to an intern assigned to her, Antonina Tatarskikh, who possessed strength of mind, a practical orientation, and an unshakable optimism and cheer. Virtually the same features appeared in the diary to characterize another young colleague, Ivan Sergeevich Smychnikov, a 29-year-old specialist from Leningrad on a visit to Voronezh. Denisevskaya studied these people "attentively and carefully," recognizing in them prototypes of the emerging Communist new man. "A new type, vital," she remarked on Smychnikov, and Tatarskikh she described as "some sort of a new woman," with a "new, human-female essence." Both hailing from distant provinces, the Tambov region and "the depths of the Perm forests" respectively, these new people could not display the same cultured manners as J.V. and her circle, but were infinitely superior to them because of their active participation in social and political life and their commitment to building the future: "They are the heirs to what I valued and loved about the Russian intelligentsia."[26]

In the midst of these reflections on the young and new people, Zinaida Denisevskaya fell in love with one of them. His name was Alexei Stepanovich Dankov; she called him Alyosha. The two had known each other for several years, but only after developing her romance with the young generation did Denisevskaya become seriously involved with him. Their relationship is well documented, thanks especially to a series of letters she sent to him and copied into a notebook. The history of their relationship, which ended in 1932, allows us to trace Denisevskaya's gradual redefinition of her view of herself and of her partner, whom she remade into an icon of the new generation. Denisevskaya's description of this relationship was highly personal, brimming with feelings and desires, but it can also be read as an inquiry into the social and political relationship between the old, bourgeois intelligentsia and the new, Soviet one. The semantics of personal love and ideological orientation were so intertwined for Denisevskaya that the question of whether she and Alyosha could truly understand each other and become a loving couple was at the same time a question of whether she as a representative of the old order could find a permanent home in the new Soviet system.

Alyosha was sixteen years younger than Denisevskaya; they seem to have known each other from the early 1920s when he joined the experimental farm as an apprentice. He was then about 20 and she in her mid-30s.[27] He left the farm in 1925 to study in Moscow. Details of their early relationship are unknown, but he wrote to her from Moscow that he still loved her and that she meant everything to him. To prove this, he added—in the contemporary Communist language of love—that he could not stop masturbating. Denisevskaya felt sorry for him. As she noted in the diary, he had misinterpreted her tender, motherly affection and become aroused: "He was unable to master his instinct and let himself be enslaved by it." Her attitude toward him was patronizing. She reported trying to enlighten him about the difference between simple physiological urges and the complex psychology of love, but ultimately gave up: "He doesn't understand anything, when I try to make him understand himself." To a friend she confided that Alyosha bored her: he had come from Moscow for a visit, but had nothing interesting to say about the capital, because he had been studying all the time.[28]

Alyosha then disappeared from the diary for three years, until September 1929, when he visited Voronezh for two weeks—and proposed to Denisevskaya. She turned him down. In a revealing diary entry she explained: "Ah, if I could only alter just a bit, some minor traits in his manner and character . . . perhaps the feeling of alienation inside me would die away, [a feeling] which prevents a reciprocal tenderness from swelling up inside me. The way he nods when saying farewell, his clumsy figure, his manner of speaking . . . I want to cry from pain for him and for me." She evaluated Alyosha entirely through the lens of the cultured intelligentsia, feeling embarrassed by his unrefined behavior: "It feels good to be in his tender, strong arms when we are alone, but it is unpleasant to see him clumsy and awkward, lacking any cultural skills, which unintentionally makes Juliana Vasilevna want to protect him." On a conscious level she no longer wanted to respect the opinions of the old intelligentsia, but she could not help relating to Alyosha as J.V. did, and she hated her old friend for that, and herself as well.[29]

Being with Alyosha brought out the village schoolteacher in her. When she wrote to him after his return to Moscow, she addressed him condescendingly, as a willing but intellectually limited student, with a mix of encouragement and reproach. It was "absolutely impossible" for them, she explained, to reach a mutual understanding, for they were "people of different worlds, of different generations. Our last encounter turned something upside-down inside me. Sometimes I want to cry because you are not as I would like to see you." She acknowledged that his personality had grown over the years, and she commended him for the "sincerity" and "purity" of his feelings, but she wondered whether his "psyche" had developed commensurably, and become "more refined" and "profound." The letter, didactic throughout, ended with exhortations: "At least once in your life, write, please, a sensible, detailed, sincere letter. Only this will decide which form our relations will assume in the future. Don't rush, it would be better to write the letter over several days. All the best!" She also remarked that while she intuitively addressed him with the informal "thou" *(ty)* he should always address her formally and respectfully, because "'You' *(Vy)* means more to you than 'thou.' You address everybody with 'thou'." In the only surviving letter from him he indeed addressed her as "Zinaida Antonovna." By contrast, she invariably called him "Alyosha."[30]

Unexpectedly, perhaps, the relationship did progress. In late October, a few days before Alyosha was to visit again, she noted in the diary that she had agreed to marry him, though only "unofficially" and physically, meaning not with her heart. During this visit she came to see him in a new light, as she recognized his investment in the Communist party, his political and social development. Denisevskaya couldn't help scrutinizing her young husband; he was one of the new people whom she read "like new books . . . attentively and intently." Personal characteristics of Alyosha that Zinaida had previously dismissed or ignored, like V.V.'s praise that he was "vital" and "active" or her own acknowledgment of his sincerity, purity, and strength, began to resonate in new ways, recasting him into a model new man. This was a sweeping reconsideration of a person whom until shortly before she had ridiculed as an awkward boy with no manners.[31]

A new stance toward politics defined Denisevskaya's reappraisal of Alyosha. Political consciousness replaced culture as the yardstick of "personal development," and in this domain Alyosha was "a hundred times" more mature than she was. Denisevskaya now proclaimed a new closeness with the political sphere, and specifically with party politics, which she had formerly abhorred as egotistical, violent, and unjust: "Even class politics—the thing that I as a member of the solitary intelligentsia could understand least—is beginning to make sense to me." Along with her deepening intimacy with Alyosha, she wrote, she was undergoing a change in her political views: "The common life of Russia has become more dear to me, everything in [Russia] has become more understandable." The term "understand," which Denisevskaya used repeatedly in this context, was revealing: this former teacher, who had long sought to teach Alyosha lessons of culture and polished manners, now considered him a political teacher of sorts. Her view was very close to the way party leaders at the time represented the proletariat vis-à-vis the intelligentsia. The proletariat was to act as an "educating class," imbuing those bourgeois specialists who did not oppose the Soviet project with ideological steadfastness and willpower.[32]

Overall, the change in orientation that Denisevskaya documented followed the steps Bukharin had stipulated for the intelligentsia: it had to abdicate its cultural prerogative, break out of its caste-like isolation, and proceed under the firm, guiding hand of the Bolshevik party. She enacted this program in literal fashion by marrying a young Communist. But it is noteworthy, too, that Denisevskaya's new description of Alyosha and herself elaborated rather than repudiated her previous assessment, and had thus a remarkably organic character. She was not an "old *intelligent*" who capitulated under pressure and renounced her previous views. Instead her ongoing redefinition retained a number of traditional features while incorporating new traits. As before, Alyosha was an object of her education (a "boy," a "son"), but in addition he emerged increasingly as a developed personality ("human being"), an ideological partner ("brother") and a potential psychological soul mate ("husband").[33]

In marrying Alyosha, Denisevskaya ran into a series of conflicts, struggles, and misunderstandings. It was one thing to study the new Communist generation with ethnographic passion, and another to engage in a relationship with a dedicated Communist. In one of her first letters to him after their wedding, she wondered how they could possibly "combine, agree on, and reconcile" their contrary expectations. Because she was older, she was more "demanding in love than you are. I want more complex feelings, more profound joys, more mutual nurturing than the two of us are experiencing . . . While you want from me better health, better understanding of your interests, the ability to argue and demonstrate greater political and public development . . . Isn't this true?" Denisevskaya persistently sought to cultivate a psychological dimension of love. Alyosha was away from her nearly all the time, so she formulated her views on their common future in letters to him. Alyosha rarely answered, and when he did, he limited himself to brief notes:

> *12/17/1929* Yesterday I received a postcard from Alyosha. Once again the usual thing: he is terribly busy, he has no time to write and doesn't know how; he agrees with me about some things, while disagreeing about others. He finds many of my questions strange. To him it seems that everything is clear, that everything goes without saying. And . . . not a single warm word, not even a hint of affection . . . He doesn't know how to love.[34]

With great anticipation she awaited his next visit to Voronezh, in February 1930. Alyosha stayed only two days, but that was long enough to shatter her expectations. As she confided to the diary, she had wanted to see him, for the first time, totally naked, so as to experience his feelings for her directly and totally, but instead the sight tore apart the mystery of love, revealing a male body governed by physiological urges. To her the experiment proved that there existed between them no "real love," "which would fill our entire being": "This is not love, but just a 'liaison.' We are so different in our nature that we don't have a real spiritual closeness, and we don't have real, spiritual intimacy, and there's no passion that would go to one's head and set our bodies on fire. What is it then? For him—the satisfaction of a 'need,' and for me a 'game of the imagination.'" Alyosha, in turn, disdained her "old-fashioned notions of love, and of how to express it." He reproached her for her lack of political consciousness, and he also blamed her for work problems on the experimental farm. Meanwhile he refused to discuss his party activities, thereby showing his distrust toward her as a non-Communist and a class alien. At least once she felt subjected to a veritable interrogation, as he questioned her about the whereabouts of a colleague and made her lie to him. All in all, she had major doubts about a union with a Communist whose commitment to the party defined all aspects of his life.[35]

The most remarkable thing about the multiple dysfunctions that characterized this relationship is Denisevskaya's interpretation of them. Alyosha's inability to cultivate a "personal life" or to "love," she mused, pointed to a defect not only of him individually but of his entire historical generation—the generation of the emerging "new man." This generation was "doomed" because the laws of history required that they sacrifice their personal lives for the building of the Communist world. Strained to exhaustion by affairs of state, their psychological development could not but be crippled. By historical necessity, the "young generation" of the transition period, the young men and women who built—but could not yet inhabit—the new society, were self-sacrificing beings whose lives were "somehow not authentic," because they lacked developed individual souls. As she said in a letter to Alyosha, "History has 'doomed' you to rushed and ceaseless work . . . You should not be blamed for this. But knowing that you are 'doomed' makes me sad."[36]

This interpretation showed her that she had been mistaken in wanting to form a psychological relationship with him. To expect a spiritual communion of their souls was to make a historically impossible demand. He was a "man of modern style" who had no developed soul and for whom love, as she understood it, was meaningless. The voice of historical reason had the power to situate, even dissolve, her psychological needs: "No letters from Alyosha. There are times when I miss him extremely, but when I read the newspaper in the evening I understand his silence." Reading the paper, the record of history's progress, reminded her of Alyosha's mission and subdued her anachronistic desires. In light of this historical explanation, it became clear to her that she had misunderstood Alyosha much of the time. She now understood that his party idiom, which she had considered clichéd and an obstacle to personal expression, was in fact his personal language, the sober and factual language of modern times.[37]

History explained not just Alyosha and the young generation, but herself as well. She too was a historical type, suspended between old and new: "My views, my behavior, and my life have always kept me apart from the older generation. At the same time, I don't have the strength and health to endure the pace of life of the new generation." This historical predicament also explained her lonely existence: ideologically removed from the old generation and close to the young, yet biologically (in terms of age, health, strength) incapable of marching with the young. But she drew comfort from being a harbinger of the new generation. All her life she had been working for this young generation—and this, she added, also explained why her feelings for Alyosha carried so many motherly overtones.[38]

Denisevskaya was not alone in reflecting on the young generation in such terms. Novels, medical publications, and public debates of the period discussed the extraordinary stress and the manifold disruptions inherent in the revolutionary project of tearing down old forms of life while constructing the new order. The interim between the outdated old world and the not-yet-present new one was inhabited by a generation of young, self-sacrificing Communist men and women. Literary representations of this generation differed starkly from the harmonious, emotionally and physically integrated hero who would come to characterize later socialist realist prose. Consistent with their dialectical role in history's progression, the heroes from the 1920s were one-sided ascetic and self-renouncing warrior types. They were covered with dust and wounds, often sick, and unable to form personal relationships. They did not embody the "new man" of socialist society but acted as its precursor, progenitor, or educator.[39] Denisevskaya too saw the laws of historical progression as responsible for the creation of this unbalanced generation. In part her characterization of Alyosha also echoed the writings of Alexandra Kollontai, who had spoken of the "new woman" as a "transitional type," living an incomplete life but receiving validation from her dedication to constructing the perfect and complete future.[40] Even if Denisevskaya admitted to an anachronistic yearning for real love from a "historically doomed" person like Alyosha, her very emphasis on intimate love as the measure of a personal relationship suggested that there were certain "individualist" and "bourgeois" notions of self that she was not (yet) ready to forgo.

In the end the union with Alyosha, which generated so much hope, reflection, and struggle, turned out to be but a brief "autumn fairy tale," as Denisevskaya noted wistfully, referring to the autumn of 1929 and possibly also to the autumn of her own life. There was a distinct irony to the ending of their relationship, but it was lost on her. While for a long time she had rejected Alyosha's advances, fearing that his *cultural* backwardness would embarrass her, she now concluded that they were *politically* incompatible: people would suspect that there was "some sort of a selfish, egoistic lining" in her relations with a "young party worker with a potentially brilliant future . . . I also remembered various remarks you made at different times about ordinary people ingratiating themselves with party members. And I felt your party membership and your youth to be an insurmountable wall between us, created by the conditions of life, and I step back from this wall." Following the break-up Denisevskaya fell back into loneliness and despair, but a month-long stay in a sanatorium helped her recognize the benefits of the relationship. For one, Alyosha had taught her a lesson or two

Portrait of Zinaida Denisevskaya, 1931.
© Manuscript Division, Russian State Library, Moscow.

in sexual expression, allowing her to accept her previously repressed "physiological urges." More important yet, she had begun to understand the low significance of personal love, whether psychologically or physiologically defined, and the enormous plain opening up beyond it—sublimated love for the collective: "It turns out that sexual attraction is just a tiny, minuscule part of life; love is a secondary feeling; and loneliness is destroyed by the collective . . . I have discovered a new world for me in Marxism. I read with deep interest."[41]

Denisevskaya had longed for a man in her life, and yet through him, she had discovered the collective. Unable to forge a profound personal bond, she became aware of the prospect of comradely, collectivist love. And the teacher who had helped redirect her love was her former student Alyosha himself. He was now gone, but before leaving he had impregnated her with the Soviet idea, a view of the self that held personal life to be subordinate to the life of the collective and regarded the collective as the ultimate measure of individual happiness and fulfillment.

The Old Self on Trial

The romance of this unlikely couple took place against the backdrop of collectivization, a campaign decreed by Stalin in late 1929 that unfolded in orgies of violence in the following years. Collectivization was a euphemism for the systematic annihilation of the traditional peasantry and its forcible transformation into a class of industrialized rural workers. The campaign was sweeping and spared no agricultural area of the country, but it was especially brutal in the Black Soil Region, Russia's traditional agricultural heartland, which included the Voronezh region. Along with the peasantry's traditional way of life, collectivization also targeted a great part of the agronomic profession to which Denisevskaya belonged. The 1920s had been a heyday for Soviet agronomists. Working from experimental farms, scholars and technical specialists cooperated closely with selected peasants to promote innovative agricultural methods and tools, and they encouraged the peasantry as a whole to join the cooperative movement. Leading agronomists, notably Alexander Chayanov and Nikolai Kondratiev, publicly advocated visions of a socialist system of agriculture to be achieved through the peasantry's gradual and voluntary self-collectivization, in harmonious interaction with the country's industrial development. But these visions and their authors came under heavy attack in the late 1920s. In an open letter, published shortly after Stalin had decreed wholesale collectivization, Chayanov confessed that he had erred and had now come to understand the party's "general line." Nevertheless, at a national conference of Marxist agrarians that opened a few days later, he was denounced as a covert agent of capitalist agriculture. Stalin, in a speech at the conference, singled out Chayanov's "antiscientific" and harmful theory that capitalist peasants could peacefully convert to socialism. Stalin's criticism was ultimately aimed at his political rival Nikolai Bukharin, a former ally who endorsed an evolutionary road toward socialism and favored persuasion over physical force. At the conference, Stalin also issued the signal for "dekulakization," the destruction of the strong peasant households that were essential to Bukharin's economic vision as well as to the experimental work conducted by Soviet agronomists.[42]

Until this point the debate over the course of Russian agriculture had received little attention in Denisevskaya's diary, but it is indicative that well before the launching of collectivization she sided with the emerging kolkhoz movement, in part because this was where many of the young people worked whom she admired so much. As the brutal campaign unfolded in the winter of 1930, Denisevskaya did not once question her support of it, even though her proximity to the battleground might have given her pause. While she claimed to be aware of excesses and wrongdoing ("I know that in different places different things are being done, including bad things"), to her such practices were peripheral and should not deflect from the "main background to life—the serious and active creation of new forms of life." She concluded on an optimistic note: "I am made terribly happy by knowing that mankind has set out on the right path. We will have a different life, and different people."

Denisevskaya wrote so affirmatively, in part, to respond to the skepticism and despair of the "old" generation surrounding her at work and in her personal life. But she also sought to ward off a protesting inner voice that, if it had room to speak, would expose the old self in her. She had to play down the brutality of the regime's policies so as not to undermine her conversion. Otherwise her incipient doubts threatened to realign her with the "old," "critical," and "selfish" people from whom she had sought to escape. As things were, the collectivization campaign clarified her position as a resolute defender of the new order ("of our power—the power of workers and peasants") who was "deeply disappointed with the contemporary intelligentsia." Denisevskaya rarely reported on the campaign without bringing up the question of the old intelligentsia and the new people, without positioning herself between the dying old and the emerging new order. Almost invariably her favorable accounts of the kolkhoz movement were followed by biting comments on the regime's critics. Her reporting on collectivization thus bore a highly conceptual character, as it kept raising issues of universalism vs. particularism, individual self vs. community. These questions, and especially the question of her self, drove her perception of the events around her.[43]

Denisevskaya first saw a collective farm in August 1930. On a mission to give lectures on poultry farming, she traveled to a kolkhoz in Kozlov district, where collectivization had been achieved with particular ferocity. A kolkhoz organizer in one of the district's villages had declared: "We will first have to destroy two-thirds of the village; only then will we be able to build the new life." Visiting a few months later, Denisevskaya was dazzled: "I was there for only five days, but it seems that I glimpsed a new world—beyond time and the passing of days." She was struck by her close relations with her student brigade, and by the kolkhoz workers' "love" for their communes. Both points reinforced her recently discovered notion of sublimated love for the collective.[44]

These newfound convictions were severely tested by a series of events that descended on Denisevskaya and her division of poultry farming with catastrophic force in the second half of 1930. First came news of apartment searches and arrests of a number of Voronezh agronomists. Then, on September 22, *Pravda* featured extensive reports on a trial of an organization of "wreckers," high-ranking officials in the country's food-supply administration who in collaboration with foreign powers had worked to induce famine and weaken the Soviet regime. One of the accused men named the agronomist Alexei Chayanov as a spiritual ringleader of the organization. Three days later the newspaper reported that forty-eight members of the wrecking organization had been sentenced to death and shot. Denisevskaya was "shocked" by these reports, not so much by the executions as by the supposed deeds of the defendants: "How could they, how could these professors sell their soul, their conscience, and their honor for money! . . . I understand *open* hostility, but these *mean* and *deceptive* forms . . . Oh, how disgusting and base."[45] The arrests of agronomists in Voronezh, both at the Agricultural Institute and at the regional experimental station, continued through September and October and included some of her close colleagues. The combined force of "this whole nightmare of wreckings, arrests, executions" nauseated her, yet she insisted that her colleagues, with whom she had collaborated for many years, could not possibly be conscious wreckers.[46]

The story of the arrested agronomists took a sensational turn in early November, when the Voronezh party leadership announced the discovery of the "Toiling Peasant party" (*Trudovaia krest'ianskaia partiia*, TKP), an underground organization operating throughout the Soviet Union. One of the party's centers, the paper claimed, was the Voronezh Agricultural Institute. The party, functioning as a scientific branch of the Communist "Right Opposition," was bourgeois to the bone; it opposed collectivization and pursued a course of "kulak-capitalist restoration." Eventually it hoped to turn Soviet Russia into a colony of foreign imperialist powers. Among the leaders of the Voronezh branch of the party, all employed at the Agricultural Institute, *Pravda* named Pavel Pistsov.

Denisevskaya's diary entries for the fall and winter of 1930 suggest how thoroughly the arrests had shattered her morale. Working side by side with V.V., she found it "painful" to watch him await his own arrest and in the process almost lose his mind. Furthermore, the institute's administration, depleted by the arrests, seemed unable to resist incursions by rival institutions to take over some of its buildings. The odium of rightist deviation hanging over the institute was very much like the odor of death inviting the vultures to devour its remains. Finally, Denisevskaya mentioned how sick she was, how dire her existential situation had become as a result of bad health and undernourishment, and how tired she had become of this life.[47]

Paradoxically, perhaps, Denisevskaya managed to restore her Soviet commitment upon learning of yet another supposed counterrevolutionary plot. In November 1930 Soviet media disclosed the existence of an "Industrial party," an anti-Soviet association concentrated in the engineering profession. The charges against its supposed members were as fabricated and outrageous as the story of the TKP, but in this instance Denisevskaya had no direct personal knowledge of the accused that contradicted the official charges. Besides, the members of the "Industrial party" were openly put on trial. In reading the defendants' detailed confessions, she was "seized with terrible indignation, and you begin to feel that you are ready to make any sacrifice for the defense of our homeland, the 'land of the Soviets.'" By contrast, the lack of transparency of the TKP affair had caused her to remain suspicious about the case.[48]

The show trial, propagated in the newspaper as well as through lectures organized by the institute's party cell, had a notable educational effect on Denisevskaya. Thanks to Alyosha she had already come to view her personal emotions, specifically her longing for a loving personal relationship, as a set of individualist impulses which she had to renounce to open herself to the more fulfilling prospects of comradely love. Now the trials gave her a second major insight: that her professional life was fulfilling only insofar as it expressed the social and political currents of the day. Science was "boring and senseless" if it was conducted "for the mere sake of one's personal curiosity"; it could "in essence not be apolitical." Armed with this new vision, Denisevskaya looked back at her ten years of work at the experimental station and was struck by her past ignorance and detachment from life. She concluded the entry with reflections on the wrecking activities that probably explained her and her colleagues' poor work record: "All the same, the sabotage became apparent. I remember Pistsov's visit to our farm. He was little interested in us workers. And we never had any money." This was the same Pistsov whom four years before Denisevskaya had described as a progressive and cultured European, and yet she now saw him as an entirely different person—deliberately evil, subhuman, and antiprogressive.[49]

The trial of the old self unfolded in a series of subplots on the pages of Denisevskaya's diary: her critical reporting on the wrecking professors; her attempts to distance herself from old friends and acquaintances; and her struggles against the old self within her. This extended trial required a steady input of labor and vigilance on Denisevskaya's part. Answers and solutions to the monstrous stories of wrecking, greed, and betrayal that engulfed some of her colleagues did not come easily to her. Only a "conscious," wide-open mind that situated every occurrence in the larger picture of class struggle and historical inevitability could rework unbelievable misdeeds into an unbroken pattern of Communist belief. This "belief," Denisevskaya's case suggests, was not merely a naive or desperate escape measure for those who refused to accept the disillusioning truth about Stalinism. It was really a complex and laborsome process, an ongoing effort to sustain a coherent worldview in spite of scattered observations that often contradicted the ideological mandate. Denisevskaya acknowledged as much when, in the midst of the TKP case, she wrote: "In its fundamental ideas, the party is now correct and I'm forcing myself to overlook petty details. One must not confuse the particulars with the general. It is very difficult to maintain a broad view all the time, especially for a non-party member." Denisevskaya's manifold statements of belief in the Soviet cause should not be read at face value; they were deployed to generate the type of belief that they ostensibly documented. The tension and labor involved in these efforts are evident in Denisevskaya's frequent use of qualifiers: "no matter" what others thought, or "in spite of" the regime's cultural backwardness, she would not give in. Working through contradictory "petty details" was essential, because not to do so was to risk being exposed as a member of the accursed old world—as a bourgeois philistine who lacked understanding of the inevitable course of history and the sacrifices necessary for the creation of the future.[50]

Joining the Soviet Home

Denisevskaya's reflections resonated with a commitment to move on: not to let herself be stopped by appearances that clashed with her newfound certainties, for this would make her fall out of step with the "movement," the imaginary Soviet collective that under the leadership of the Communist party was building the new life. It was almost irrelevant which shocking conspiracy she read about in the newspapers, or which of her colleagues was arrested as a counterrevolutionary agent. Any such incident presented itself as an obstacle to her worldview and demanded to be explained, and if it did not entirely disappear in the light of ideological reason, its inexplicable residue had to be discarded and repressed from memory. This dynamic was determined less by the shape of any given obstacle than by the nature of her commitment, which demanded that she move on. For this reason it is useful to shift the perspective away from the chronology of contingent events—cultural revolution, the collectivization campaign, the TKP affair—to Denisevskaya's elaboration of her self-understanding and how this work on her self impinged on the events and the people she encountered. Seen in this light, the same events that have appeared as primary assume an anticipatory character. Denisevskaya reacted to them with a specific disposition, a way of looking at and understanding herself, which determined her selective focus on themes, categories, and problems in the diary. She looked at herself chiefly through the prism of loneliness.

Loneliness was the main underlying motif of her diary. She wrote of feeling lonely in every sphere of life: in her family, where she had to contend with bickering parents and an unaffectionate mother; in public life, where her chronically ailing body blocked her desire to become more of an activist; in her failed relationships with men; and in her interactions with peers and colleagues. Denisevskaya always believed her loneliness signified more than a purely personal predicament. She interpreted it in historical-sociological terms, as a component of her intelligentsia self. Before the revolution she looked upon her lonely state with some pride, as an expression of her developed personality. She was a new woman, ahead of her time, and she derived comfort from the belief that in some future time all people—especially men—would be psychologically more mature, so as to create a world of true, comradely friendship and love. After 1917, with the culture of individualism and the traditional intelligentsia in disrepute, what she had once been proud of turned into a burden, doubling her loneliness. Her developed "individuality" appeared now as a token of her adherence to the outlived, bourgeois order, whereas the present and future belonged to collectivities. As late as February 1928 Denisevskaya complained to a devout Christian friend about the isolating effects of her "individuality," and her hope that this condition would cease to afflict her after her death.[51]

Her individuality was a historically conditioned affliction: she hailed from the bourgeois order, which put inescapable limits on her attempts to join in the new collectivist age. It was from the point of view of a "member of the solitary intelligentsia,"[52] a sympathetic bystander, that she followed the Soviet project and its creation of collectivist life forms, including the kolkhoz system. She also commented favorably on Soviet attempts to abolish traditional family life and create socialized forms of childcare and upbringing, projects that promised at least symbolic deliverance from the oppression she herself had experienced in her family. But the collectivist forms that fascinated her most were Soviet marches and holiday parades. Her autobiographical narrative contains tangible descriptions of the marching collective and provides a strong account of the ritualistic power of Soviet holidays to reforge an individual's sense of self. The parades directly spoke to the central issue in Denisevskaya's life. They appeared in her diary as concentrated symbolic expressions of collectivism, and as such they contained a response to her personal loneliness, which she interpreted as a historical predicament of the Russian intelligentsia. The big question lurking behind her descriptions of the parading masses was: Could she join in the march?[53]

In the fall of 1928 she reported attending a parade in Voronezh in celebration of the eleventh anniversary of the October Revolution, the first such parade she attended in Soviet times:

> I saw the face of the people who hold in their hands the red banner. It is a diverse sight, gray as a whole, but true to reality. There are just a few strokes of the intelligentsia present. This doesn't diminish [the intelligentsia's] role, but puts it where it belongs in reality. For a long time I had wanted to see this reality, but could not for one reason or another . . . I am not idealizing, I am not judging anything, I simply am watching and understanding what Russia, the Revolution, "Soviet power," etc., mean, what is poverty, hunger, philistinism, what it means when people of different development and different degrees of prosperity don't understand one other. And all this complex human life made itself heard in thousands of shouts. I listened to it, I followed with my eyes the columns of demonstrators. I am unable to express in words all that I heard.[54]

The ambiguity of this description is striking. Denisevskaya sought to understand the new historical order, but she could not muster a sense of emotional belonging to it. She acknowledged the marginal position of the intelligentsia, who had abdicated as a historical force, yet she continued to look at the "gray" masses through the prism of individualism, which made the few representatives of the intelligentsia stand out in the picture. While admitting her curiosity, she stressed that curiosity alone had not brought her to the scene; she had been in town anyway because she had to schedule an operation in the hospital. She had recently been diagnosed with breast cancer.

Fifteen months later, in the midst of her romance with Alyosha, Denisevskaya talked about the collective from an entirely different perspective. She now felt with the masses. Too weak to take to the street, she depended on the radio and the newspaper to bring her into communion with the parading masses: "The radio has been fixed and I'm again relishing the sensation of a common life. Today is the twelfth anniversary of the establishment of the Red Army. Both yesterday and today, spontaneously, with everybody else, I have been celebrating, taking pride, hoping, and believing." It was vital that the radio had been fixed, for its reporting had the power in turn to fix her troubled soul. Only three days before, Denisevskaya had complained of feeling "most profoundly" lonely on the experimental farm, where all her co-workers were at one another's throats. The Red Army holiday allowed her to escape this stifling, bickering world. Rapturously she "listened to the roaring of thousands of voices and felt my union with them. This made me happy."[55]

Still, hers was only an intermediate position between the old and the new worlds. The very fact that she continued to have bouts of personal loneliness indicated the distance that still separated her from the Communist universe, which supposedly was free of any possessive, self-centered feelings. She envied dedicated Communist activists, who were receptive to the "party spirit," which filled them with a "sense of brotherhood, comradeship," and which effectively solved the age-old problem of "human loneliness." The chief agent preventing her absorption into the collective organism of Soviet activists was her failing body: "I don't have enough physical strength to join their ranks. I am doomed to loneliness until I die."[56]

In the final phase of her life, Denisevskaya proceeded to dismantle this residue of individual separation and become a Communist in body and soul, if not on paper. This final step was facilitated by her transfer to the Voronezh Agricultural Institute, where starting in January 1931 she taught and supervised doctoral research on topics such as the "dialectics of the poultry egg."[57] Her daily contact with members of the young generation as well as her heavy workload reinforced her sense of involvement and historical mission. On May 1, 1931, she celebrated Labor Day with students and teachers from all over the city. For the first time in her life she marched in a demonstration, reveling in the much anticipated oneness with the collective:

> Yesterday—an evening meeting in the barracks. Today—the demonstration. Exhaustion hampers my feelings of joy. But more important is the sense of a merging with everybody who celebrated this day. All of us, our institute, all the Agr[icultural] Inst[itutes], all the other institutes, the workers' faculties and schools, all the workers, all the Red Army soldiers, all of us—were one. We all marched together—with the same songs and thoughts. This time I did not see the "face of the people," because I myself was a part of it, I was a drop in the sea, I was forming the "1st of May," and wasn't just an onlooker . . . I'm extremely tired. First we waited for three hours, then we marched quickly. I almost got sick . . . I barely managed to get back home, but I am happy to have done this. Perhaps this was my first and last time to participate in a demonstration.

When Denisevskaya referred to herself as a "drop in the sea," the proud emphasis was on the enormous sea, not on the vanishing drop. There was not a trace of sad commentary on the individual drop dissolving in the larger whole. Here as elsewhere she identified all that kept her apart from the marching collective with her failing individual body. In fact her poor health forced her to push her physical resources to the limit in order to survive in the labor-intensive Soviet environment. But the primary attribute of the individual body in Denisevskaya's representation was not that it was sick but that it was a selfish, particularizing force. She invariably pitted the instinctual cravings of her body against the voice of her socialized consciousness—as one became weaker the other surfaced and triumphed. Her unfolding consciousness had the power to soothe the pain of her body and drag it along. But the relationship could also be reversed. When in connection with the arrests of agronomists Denisevskaya confided her doubts about the correctness of the party line, her ailing body called attention to itself, acting in somatic concert with her wounded worldview. In this situation her body regained the first and the last word:

> My heart pains me very much and this interferes with my ability to think and feel correctly. The situation of our division is now catastrophic: no director, no money, no people. They are kicking us off the farm. We have nowhere to live and no place to work . . . I am trying to convince myself of the need to endure this transitional period, to bury the old and assist with the birth of the new. But the pain in my heart drains all my good spirits.

Noting that V.V. lived in anticipation of his own arrest and was now "verging on a psychosis," Denisevskaya added that she herself suffered from intense headaches, but vowed not to give in to her "depression."[58]

Denisevskaya could not imagine acquiescing to the lowly forces of her body. Her body contained a coded reference to autonomy, but this autonomy was undesirable and bourgeois—it was maintained by people who spoke through the base needs of their bodies, not their conscious minds. Even the most despairing confession was regularly enjoined by an appeal to renew the fight for a restored worldview. If such an appeal did not come immediately, it was sure to follow in a subsequent diary entry. On November 6, 1930, when Denisevskaya first learned about the TKP, she confessed to finding the news absurd and incomprehensible. The following day was the revolutionary holiday, and its rituals—the marching and music transmitted by the radio—offered her an opportunity to realign herself with the revolution's "general line": "For the whole day I have been in touch with the holiday through the radio and the farm. For the whole day I have felt not alone . . . How much has changed over these thirteen years, both within me and around me! Life has been reborn! And I have been reborn."[59]

Denisevskaya described herself as driven by a material and sensory quest to join "human society, feel it like an individual, a multicellular, complex, but fully definite being." Socialist society afforded her communality, shelter, a new home. Through the radio transmissions of the May Day parades, she was able to "visit the whole of Russia. Yesterday I was sad that I knew nobody whom I could visit [for the holiday], but today I was among my own family—on Red Square in Moscow, at the People's Palace in Voronezh, in Baku, Kiev, and other places." The Soviet collective was her new family, the territory of the Soviet Union her new home, the parade grounds "corridors" of this home, and the aims of the Soviet project the essence of her "true," newly discovered self.[60]

In March 1933, shortly after discovering her new home, Denisevskaya died. The exact circumstances of her death are unclear, but the diary suggests how distressing they must have been. She complained of chronic "suctorial stomach pain," fearing that it was cancerous. In late 1932 her pay had been cut severely, and there were rumors that the institute would be closed altogether. Denisevskaya noted laconically: "It's very difficult to live now, there is little food at the market, and everything is very expensive. Because of the poor diet my health is bad, I have no strength, and my spirits are fading."[61] The fall and winter of 1932–33 brought the great famine, a manmade calamity caused by the relentless Bolshevik drive to extract grain from a rural economy in turmoil. The famine hit hardest in the grain-producing areas of the Soviet Union, including Voronezh province. While the cities continued to receive privileged bread supplies, rations were reduced to an all-time low. In Denisevskaya's mental repertoire these distressing facts represented the "minuses" of life that gnawed at her, sapping her physical strength and threatening to sever her from the socialist collective. Yet no matter how formidable the pull, she refused to let go: "Hunger, cold, and disease all around . . . And the party's policy is absolutely incomprehensible . . . How is one to live? Just live for the present? Through small, piecemeal work, the way I lived earlier, before I came to believe in the purpose and greatness of the gigantic construction in our country? That is no longer enough for me."[62]

The final entry in Denisevskaya's diary is dated February 19, 1933. She announced that the institute would be dissolved and the staff disbanded shortly, without ration cards or work—a likely death sentence in the context of the famine. It was a short entry, concluding with the words: "There is nobody to blame for that . . . Am feeling unwell. My head and throat ache . . . It's good that Father is still alive. After all, it's at least moral support. We will live through this somehow . . . until we die." Denisevskaya reportedly died on March 16, 1933, at the age of 45. Amid near-universal death and suffering, her fate stands out as tragic, because she was killed by the ruthless measures of a regime in which she believed herself to have found a permanent home. Compounding the tragedy was her consent to being crushed by political events, if these expressed the inexorable course of history, for it was her understanding of these laws that ultimately grounded her claim to be at home in the Soviet project.[63]

Forty-four years after her death, a parcel containing Zinaida Denisevskaya's diaries arrived in the manuscript division of Moscow's Lenin library. It was sent by Veronika Khrizonovich, Zinaida's cousin, who at one point had worked with her on the experimental farm. Introducing herself in an accompanying letter as a "Communist since 1947," Khrizonovich recommended the diaries to the archive's attention as the record of a Soviet citizen's difficult but eventually victorious road toward consciousness, self-mastery, and self-perfection. There was no trace of tragedy in Khrizonovich's account, which presented her cousin's late epiphany as the defining moment of her life: "As you read the final notebooks of Zinaida Denisevskaya's diary, your heart becomes filled with joy. You see how brightly the civic face of this person lights up, the face of a Soviet person who was deeply passionate about educating and rearing the liberated people, builders of the new life. She herself grew together with them and built this new life." The letter is dated June 13–October 24, 1977. Veronika Khrizonovich, an archivist's note reveals, died on November 24, 1977. It seems that in the final days of her own life Khrizonovich sought to partake in the brightness of pure and total vision that her cousin Zinaida Denisevskaya had labored to achieve.[64]

The Intelligentsia Transformed

In one of the most vivid scenes of her diary, the parade of Voronezh teachers and students on May 1, 1931, Denisevskaya described her merging with the collective as a triumphant moment of self-realization. The parade, as well as the barracks meeting the evening before, were sites from which she could extract the principle of collectivism toward which she had been striving in the final years of her life—working with and for the people, chanting in a unison of "thoughts and songs," marching with history. It did not occur to her in this age of barracks life and collectivization to fight for a position of personal autonomy, to protect her frail body or privilege a personalized point of view. To have done so would have not only undermined her purpose in life but discredited her socially and morally, making her appear outdated and selfish, in a word—bourgeois. And yet Denisevskaya was familiar with positions of autonomy, having proclaimed herself an "individualist" earlier in life. It was not for lack of other intellectual resources that she embraced the Soviet collectivist ideal.

To Denisevskaya, joining the Soviet system above all promised respite from lifelong loneliness. In the diary, her desires for completion and communality unfolded against the steady backdrop of her melancholic voice. Yet in sounding these themes, she addressed more than her own personal predicament, suggesting that loneliness was ingrained in the intelligentsia's self-image in an age of rising masses and collectivities. She was at pains to stress the historical dimension of her lonely existence. Before the revolution, she styled herself as a new woman, a woman ahead of her time and therefore alone. Her loneliness was reinforced by the Bolshevik politics of class, which branded her, along with other members of the "bourgeois" intelligentsia, as class aliens–marginalized and "selfish" individuals, doomed to extinction. At the same time, the Bolshevik system offered the tantalizing prospect of breaking the caste barriers and joining the party-led movement, if only she could acknowledge its historical righteousness.

The trajectory of Denisevskaya's diary across the political and social dislocations that marked the first three decades of Russia's twentieth century provides a rare insight into the continued ethical commitments of a member of the intelligentsia, one who initially condemned and later embraced the Soviet regime. Throughout her life Denisevskaya cultivated her "personality," which she defined by the possession of an integrated, universalist "worldview" and the dedication to working on behalf of history's progression. In the end she came to consider the Soviet regime the sole legitimate carrier of these core intelligentsia values. In her diary the Bolshevik project of creating a new man appears as but a variant of a preoccupation with perfecting the "personality" that defined the Russian intelligentsia as a whole. Denisevskaya's diary shows that this shared agenda provided room for considerable creative engagement between the Bolshevik state and a member of the "old" intelligentsia.

This commonality should not, however, obscure the major break that the imposition of the Soviet system signified for Denisevskaya's understanding of herself as a person and a citizen. The Bolshevik project's activist thrust jolted her out of her habitual passive longing, forcing her to work on herself, and not only on the pages of her diary. Prior to the revolution Denisevskaya's self-representation as a "new woman" amounted to little more than a pose, a play of her "imagination." In later years she began to rework fundamental aspects of her personal, professional, and social life, in an attempt to live—not only imagine—a collectivist existence. Moreover, the self in Bolshevik understanding was politicized to the core. Denisevskaya, by contrast, habitually differentiated between a sphere of political action and nonpolitical realms of her "personal life," a distinction she would later no longer uphold. By the early 1930s no sphere of her life, not even questions of love or sexuality, remained autonomous of the political.

This sweeping transformation is illustrated in her changing attitudes toward the diary. In the politically heated aftermath of the revolution of 1905 she apologetically noted that her poor coverage of politics resulted not from indifference but from fear that her diary might be confiscated by the police. Her personal life seemed a safer topic: "My soul, my heart and my feelings, the police don't need them, they are interested in public life." As late as 1925 Denisevskaya considered her diary politically uninteresting. Who was interested in "the reflections of a living woman's soul," especially in the 1920s, when psychology was being widely discarded for physiology? Five years later it no longer occurred to Denisevskaya to use such terms. As before, the diary was the record of her innermost feelings, her hopes, worries, and doubts, but she was now aware of the political valence of these feelings. In a political system that measured individuals according to the totality and sincerity of their "belief in the cause," the life of the individual "soul" was no longer a mere personal appendix to public political dispositions, but the very heart of a politicized self. In Denisevskaya's final reflections on loneliness and love, past and future, the division between the political and the nonpolitical was erased, along with the boundary that distinguished the individual from the community. The world of her personal life had been extended to "at least the borders of the USSR"; in her thoughts and feelings she "shared the interests, hopes, and dreams of the USSR."[65]

5

Secrets of a Class Enemy

STEPAN PODLUBNY

Stalin's industrialization campaign swept millions of people from the villages of the vast Soviet land into the cities and onto the sprawling construction sites of the First Five-Year Plan. They formed an indispensable workforce for the project of remaking Russia into a socialist state. While helping bring the new world into being, these peasant-workers also were to remake themselves. Stalinist planners conceived of the emerging industrial landscape as an extended factory of the soul. The peasants arrived there as "old human material," weighed down by the forces of tradition, superstition, and narrow egoism. Under the combined influence of collective labor and attendant political education they were to remold themselves into socialist citizens. Factory managers avidly recruited peasant laborers who arrived in search of a better future, or merely to escape villages where class war had made their lives unbearable.[1] Party officials, however, were alarmed. They suspected that scores of kulaks—members of the exploiting rural bourgeoisie—had gone into hiding amid the uncontrollable rural-to-urban flow. It was feared that these kulaks assumed the guise of good workers to deceive the regime, but at their core resisted the spirit of socialist re-education and plotted to bring down Soviet power. They were, in the language of the times, "wolves in sheep's clothing." The only effective way to deal with them was to tear off the false cover and bare their hostile essence. To check workers' documents was one way of identifying enemies in disguise. Yet documents could be forged. Ultimately only Bolshevik vigilance, the constant probing into individuals' deeds and thoughts, could tell who did and who did not pass the litmus test for acceptance into the classless socialist society.[2]

Stepan Podlubny was one such wolf in disguise. The son of a kulak, he fled his Ukrainian village during collectivization and settled in Moscow, pretending to be of working-class background. Podlubny kept a diary from 1931 until 1939, then from 1941 to the end of his life. In it he documented his strenuous efforts to blend in with his new environment in a climate of witch hunt and unremitting exposure of class enemies. But Podlubny's diary also makes clear that he looked upon his new life not merely as a matter of dissimulation but as a chance to achieve a total reconstruction of his self, with the goal of becoming a genuine member of socialist society. Though a victim of Bolshevik repression, he remade himself into an agent of revolutionary self-change. The central problem he grappled with was the tension between the forces of the old and the new within him. He expressed much hope that the integrative side of Bolshevik ideology, which stipulated that anyone could join socialist society if he partook in its construction sincerely and wholeheartedly, would apply to his case. At the same time he remained aware of the regime's persecutory zeal and the danger that he might be indelibly stamped as an enemy. Two contradictory questions marked his life throughout the 1930s: Could he successfully mask his alien identity and escape the punitive gaze of the Soviet regime? And, in the longer term, could the wolf turn into a sheep?[3]

Podlubny was born in 1914 into a peasant household in the Vinnitsa district of Ukraine. An only child, he grew up in a family that for generations had lived from agriculture and trade and had acquired considerable wealth. When Stepan's grandfather Evdokim died, each of his six sons inherited fifteen desiatinas of land, most of which was lost in the course of the revolution. Stepan's father, Filip Evdokimovich, who was drafted as a soldier in 1914 and soon captured by the Austrians, was stripped of all but four desiatinas of his landholdings after his return home in 1918. Nevertheless, the Podlubnys were regarded in the Soviet village of the 1920s as members of the kulak class of peasant exploiters. Stepan spoke Ukrainian at home and attended a Ukrainian seven-year school in which Russian was taught as a foreign language. He had difficulty learning because his father took him out of school every spring to work in the fields. During the annual summer vacation the family hired a tutor who taught Stepan the parts of the syllabus he had missed.[4]

With the launching of the radical industrialization campaign in the late 1920s, official policies toward kulaks turned increasingly hostile. In the spring of 1929 the government introduced the principle of "self-taxation," transferring to local soviets the power to determine the amount of grain each local household owed in taxes. The village soviets imposed the overwhelming part of the grain tax on kulak households, thereby forcing them into destitution. Households that did not fulfil their quotas were heavily fined. In most cases, this vicious circle ended in the confiscation of the entire farm. This was the fate of the Podlubny family. A certificate issued by the Beryozovka village soviet, dated October 1929, stated that Filip Podlubny's property included a house, a barn, and four desiatinas of farm land. The certificate further declared that Podlubny did not own any farm tools and had transferred his entire inventory to the village soviet in the preceding spring as part of his grain delivery obligations.[5]

In the winter of 1929–30 the Podlubnys' property was completely expropriated. Because of his failure to fulfill his obligations to the state, Filip Podlubny was arrested and deported to Arkhangelsk for a three-year sentence of administrative exile. Filip's wife, Yefrosinia Danilovna, and Stepan were spared for the time being, but they had to leave their home, which was handed over to a family of "proletarian peasants," and settle in an abandoned hut on the edge of the village. In a widely published article, Stalin reiterated the goal of the Communist state: to "liquidate the kulaks as a class" and free Soviet society of its "most beastly, rawest, and most brutal exploiters," the "spiders," "vampires," and "bloodsuckers" who had enriched themselves at the cost of the laboring people.[6]

In the spring of 1930 Stepan's mother left the village of Beryozovka and joined her husband in Arkhangelsk, using the personal documents of a cousin who shared her first name but was not classified as a kulak. Stepan remained behind to complete his final year at school. As the son of a kulak, he could be legally barred from attending school, but the school director allowed him to finish the year. The director secretly issued him a graduation transcript, but urged him to leave the village as quickly as possible. Indeed, as Stepan learned years later, Komsomol activists in the village had been preparing to have him arrested. With the support of friends, Stepan obtained a train ticket to Archangelsk. On the train the police confiscated all his documents, and his journey seemed over. But thanks to a string of lucky circumstances, he ultimately reached Archangelsk and found his parents.[7]

In the following winter, 1930–31, Stepan and his mother left Archangelsk, intending to return to their home village. By now Stepan, too, had forged documents showing him to be of worker origins. At the Kievskaya train station in Moscow they encountered fellow Ukrainian peasants, who reported arrests of kulaks' family members and dependents and urged them not to travel any further. Mother and son remained in Moscow and looked for work. Within a few months both found steady employment, Stepan's mother as a janitor, and Stepan as an apprentice in the factory school of the *Pravda* printing plant. They lived in central Moscow, in a humid basement room of the building in which the mother worked. It was an ironic twist of fate that the new home of these two class aliens in disguise was located on Red Proletarian Street.

Podlubny began to write in his diary notebook just before he joined *Pravda*. The first pages were filled with writing exercises—texts of Russian folksongs—which, as Podlubny noted, were dictated to him by an acquaintance in April 1931. These dictations were followed by several more lyrics composed by Podlubny himself. The songs belonged to the repertoire of traditional Russian folk culture, revolving around young people's adventures and romances. Podlubny probably wrote the lyrics to gain proficiency in Russian, which was still a foreign language for him at the time. As the many grammatical errors and Ukrainianisms dotting his early diary writing illustrate, expressing himself in Russian did not come easily.

The actual diary began on the back of the notebook and was entitled "Work Diary of the '9th-Komsomol-Congress' Brigade and Daily Notes of the Brigadier and Student Stepan Filipovich Podlubny." The first entry was dated May 31, 1931. On that day Podlubny had been nominated as leader of a brigade comprising ten workers. The entries of the following days and weeks recorded personal achievements—his acceptance into the Komsomol, his appointment as editor of a wall newspaper—as well as the performance of his brigade. Stepan noted in particular those whose work performance was unsatisfactory. One female coworker, identified only by her last name, Borodako, came up almost daily: she would arrive late at work, sing and dance in the factory shop, or spend an inordinate amount of time washing herself in the bathroom. An article denouncing her attitude, entitled "Sing, Borodako, sing . . ." appeared in the wall newspaper. Signed "V.," it was probably written by Podlubny himself. His diary records Borodako's reaction: "If I knew who this 'V.' is, I would punch him in the mug." As part of his efforts to rectify Borodako's behavior, Podlubny sent two female brigade members to her home. They found her mother to be "a good person" but unable to do anything about her daughter, who was "carousing at night" and "behaving badly." At a mock trial staged by the Komsomol, Borodako was publicly reprimanded; her behavior improved for a few days, but she soon reverted to her customary ways.[8]

From the very beginning of his new life in Moscow Podlubny actively engaged himself in the policies of normalization practiced by the Soviet regime. He extolled the norms of discipline, socialist competition, and achievement, prodding his co-workers not only to conform to them at work but to adopt them in all spheres of life. The Borodako incident could not but make him aware of the importance of his own work performance for his standing in society. Should he fail to do outstanding work, a similar background check might be applied to him. His new life took place on an intensely monitored social stage.[9]

Starting in 1932, Stepan's diary changed character, shifting toward a record of his personal hopes, longings, and fears. The earlier passages, he explained in a retrospective entry, had been "objective" in tone and had "related only to the workplace." His task now was to keep a diary in the real sense, "for the purposes of my overall development." This shift was in part induced by the literary circle in which Stepan had enrolled soon after joining *Pravda*. Referring to the circle, he admonished himself to write better, more fluently and in a literary vein, an indication that the diary was to be a training ground for the aspiring writer. Literary circles exploded in size and membership during the First Five-Year Plan. Communist activists and non-Communist writers alike called for literature to enter the industrialization campaign and serve its mobilizing and transformative goals. Factories established their own literary circles in which experienced writers imparted the skills of the craft to proletarian workers, who were to become chroniclers of both the building of socialism and their own transformation in the course of industrialization.[10]

Dreaming of becoming a writer, Podlubny regarded it as his task to write a personal memoir that would also be a "chronicle" of the "1930s." He wanted this memoir, which he planned to write in the form of a novel, to capture his specific experience as a kulak offspring in the Soviet system. He even had a title for the project: "the life of an outdated class, its spiritual rebirth and adaptation to new conditions." Podlubny mentioned models that were to help him compose the memoir: works by Alexander Herzen, Leo Tolstoy, and Maxim Gorky, progenitors of the Russian autobiographical tradition who were held in high esteem in the Soviet system as "socially progressive" writers. In the memoir he wanted to "remember life, not just family life in the narrow sense, but also the course of political events. And compare these, by then already past events, with what happens in reality, which up to now is only a dream for the future."[11]

The longer he wrote, the more Podlubny cherished yet another motivation for keeping the diary: it had become his "sole friend." Only to the diary could he confide the secret of his past and the fears and doubts that accompanied his attempt to fit into the new society. His hope was to free himself from his torments by releasing them on paper. The diary served as a "rubbish heap" onto which he could discard all the "garbage" that had accumulated in his mind. Elsewhere he referred to the diary as the "mirror of my soul," or as a medium revealing "the seamy side of a person." Podlubny's secret and his recording of it in his diary interfered with the projected use of the diary as a literary training ground. Other members of the circle read aloud from their diaries and showed them around. Podlubny kept his own locked away and even concealed its existence, being acutely aware of what might happen to him if it fell into the wrong hands.[12]

While deployed for various ends—as "rubbish heap" for useless thoughts, training ground for developing consciousness, emotional source of relief, best friend—Podlubny's diary also served an overarching purpose. It was a laboratory of his self. The desire to become purer in the course of discharging his "black" thoughts ran parallel to the purpose of his decidedly less black memoirs. Both projects were to provide evidence for his claim to membership in Soviet society, and both were tied to his personal struggle for moral self-improvement. Public and private ends were effectively fused in this project of a class alien in search of political integration, social acceptance, and self-respect.

The Problem of the Kulak Past

Podlubny's ambiguous social standing resulted from an unresolved tension in Bolshevik attitudes toward kulak descendants and other class aliens. Throughout the New Economic Policy period, the Soviet state grudgingly accepted the existence of a class society, including remnants of the "old," "feudal-capitalist" order. Politically, however, kulaks as well as former priests, policemen, and landowners were disenfranchised.[13] When the regime embarked on its radical industrialization campaign, an official decision was reached to "eliminate the kulaks as a class." The rationale was that in a classless socialist society there would be no place for capitalist exploiters. Beginning in the winter of 1929–30, the property of peasant households deemed "kulak" was systematically expropriated and several million kulaks were deported into administrative exile. The kulak peasantry was divided into three categories, according to the degree of danger they allegedly posed to Soviet power. Members of the first group, the "counterrevolutionary kulak aktiv," were deemed incorrigible, inveterate enemies of the Soviet system, and thousands of them were executed. Kulaks of the second and third categories, considered less politically active and hence less dangerous, were exiled to nearer or more distant localities depending on the degree of their anti-Soviet attitudes.[14]

Soviet laws of the early 1930s stipulated that kulaks in the last two categories could be rehabilitated if they demonstrated that they had performed at least five years of honest labor for the Soviet state. The regime was thus not in principle opposed to the integration of former kulaks and especially their dependents into the social body, provided that they proved they had shed their class-alien essence. Resting on the belief that individuals could remake themselves through their own efforts, these laws expressed the universalist pretense of Bolshevik ideology. This explains why Soviet officials showed themselves reluctant to determine class identity genealogically, so that the son of a kulak would also be branded forever a kulak. Membership in a social class was first and foremost a quality of individuals' will, regardless of their social origins. Podlubny—like many other class aliens—clung to this voluntarist interpretation of class in seeking work in a factory. He hoped that by working in a proletarian environment, by "stewing in the workers' cauldron," he could shed his kulak essence, purify himself, and acquire the ideology of a true proletarian.[15]

Yet this integrative orientation of Bolshevik ideology was counteracted by a host of discriminatory practices against class aliens in Soviet daily life. Up to the mid-1930s they were barred from higher education and perennially at risk of being dismissed from their jobs. These attitudes were rooted in a suspicion that class aliens were inherently opposed to the Soviet order and could not completely remake themselves into loyal citizens. The regime engaged in frantic vigilance campaigns and attempts to unmask class aliens who were believed to be hiding in factories, institutes of higher education, and the state administration.[16]

Podlubny's diary shows that he responded to the mixed signals of the state in equally complex ways. He knew he had to conceal his past and thus engage in some form of outward dissimulation, a need that was especially acute whenever the regime stepped up its repressive measures. At the same time, he exuberantly noted every indication that class aliens might redeem themselves if they worked sincerely for the socialist state. Yet in seeking integration he faced a considerable problem: his concealment of his background was bound to be interpreted by the authorities as subversive and counterrevolutionary.[17] Making things even worse, the combined strategy of concealment and transformation undermined Podlubny's own sense of his sincerity. His ambivalence about his new identity showed in the title of his projected novel on the class alien's "spiritual rebirth and adaptation." If the first term signaled genuine inner transformation, the second suggested accommodation to a qualitatively different reality, and thus raised questions about the validity of the quest for transformation.

Throughout his years in Moscow, except for a brief lull in the mid-1930s, Podlubny lived in an atmosphere of witch hunt against hidden class aliens and political counterrevolutionaries. How such "Bolshevik vigilance" was practiced in daily life can be gleaned from the diary of the coal miner Vladimir Molodtsov. For the ardent komsomolist Molodtsov, the attitude of a fellow worker of peasant background sparked an urge to unmask him as a kulak: "I got into a conversation about production with Suvorov, and he declared: 'I've come here to earn more money and equip myself.' There it is, the peasant psychology! Sees only his personal gain and believes only in himself. True, not all of the peasantry is like this . . . The new kolkhozes are educating new people. I just had a thought: Isn't Suvorov perhaps a kulak henchman, wasn't he sent here to demoralize the workers? Anything is possible." A few days later Molodtsov noted that he had not been able to confirm his suspicions about Suvorov. He next directed his ire toward another peasant worker who had received a package of pork from his village—a sure indication of his kulak origins. This colleague gave Molodtsov some of the meat, then asked him for tobacco in return. Molodtsov was furious: "This whole story has given me a clear picture of how the kulak buys off the peasantry . . . Only you won't buy us off, we can now see through a kulak's soul."[18]

Podlubny's diary addressed the same issue, but from the other side. It documented the fear of a person who saw himself surrounded by enemies waiting to expose his newly claimed identity as a sham. Given their watchfulness, any nervous gesture or slip of the tongue could have catastrophic consequences. When Podlubny's Komsomol group organized a summer camp on a kolkhoz near Moscow, he as a group leader suggested that everyone get up before dawn, work until eleven A.M., and then break until late afternoon to avoid the scorching sun. Others, who wanted to sleep later in the morning, disagreed, but his position prevailed. In his diary Podlubny reproached himself for his stance. Others might suspect that he was of rural background, and then investigate his background. He resolved to work more sloppily the next few days so as to not appear to be a skilled peasant worker.[19]

His diary was filled with reminders not to give in to urges to confide personal problems and worries to friends and colleagues. These impulses were "superfluous" and dangerous, as they allowed others glimpses into his problematic inner life. Even more worrying were encounters with people who had known him in his prior life. On the street Stepan and his mother once ran into "Vova and Itta," former neighbors who had come to Moscow to flee the famine raging in Ukraine. The Podlubnys helped them find shelter in the city. Stepan reported that while he was happy to see people from back home, he also sensed the danger of such contacts: "If you can't prevent yourself from spilling words that are harmful to you, forget about controlling others' flapping tongues. All you can do is wait and see. My arms and my legs are tied. This is not good, not good at all." At the same time, Podlubny was eager to know what the people around him talked about and thought, so as to sense potential danger and react as quickly as possible. Reminding himself always to be "professionally cautious and observant," he was engaged in the same hermeneutics of suspicion as Molodtsov, except that in his case they served as protection from Bolshevik vigilance.[20]

Another way to navigate the treacherous terrain of his new social environment was to emulate the behavior of people who appeared strong and popular. Once he had gained their "authority," Podlubny believed, he would be less vulnerable. In the early parts of the diary a Komsomol secretary figured as such a role model: "I exactly copy his actions and manners." In later years he was replaced by the director of the factory school, whom Stepan called the "mirror into which I avidly look every day."[21]

Podlubny's adaptive techniques proved highly successful. Both in school and at work he soon stood out as a model apprentice. His successes showed in good grades at the factory school, a budding career in the Komsomol administration, and his own satisfaction at having acquired "authority" among his peers. In the fall of 1931, a few months after he joined *Pravda,* his picture appeared in the factory newspaper, acknowledging his achievements as brigade leader and shock worker. Other photographs demonstrate the remarkable outward change that Podlubny underwent after his arrival in Moscow. The peasant boy, who in a 1929 shot of his primary school graduating class appears younger and smaller than his classmates, by the winter of 1932 had turned into a fashionably dressed, urban young man. The 1932 photo shows Podlubny with two fellow workers from the *Pravda* printing plant. The colleague on his left (at right in the photo) wears the felt boots of a villager; the other apprentice's collar is disheveled. Standing in the middle, Podlubny appears as the best dressed and groomed of the group, and he also conveys the most self-assurance. All three, to be sure, wear similar soft caps to pass as sophisticated young urbanites. In a 1934 photograph of Podlubny with classmates from "Red Banner class no. 5

of the *Pravda* school," he is the only man wearing a suit and tie. He and one other student wear badges on their jackets, possibly medals awarded for sports or "shock work."

The photographs tell only part of Podlubny's life story. As his diary

Stepan Podlubny (center) and other apprentice printers, 1932.
© Marina Gavrilova, Moscow

makes clear, his successes at work did little to alleviate his anxieties. Outward conformity to his new environment was indispensable for his survival, but it was insufficient to resolve his problematic standing as a class alien. The more fundamental challenge for him was to change inwardly, to remake his inner disposition to match his outward appearance as a citizen of the socialist state. This type of self-change involved far more than donning new clothes.

Podlubny articulated the problem of his inner disposition in a diary entry devoted to his work performance at the printing plant. Assuming that for a real proletarian in a socialist state, labor was an arena of natural self-realization and thus effortless, he wondered why work cost him so much effort:

Podlubny (left rear), with fellow students of the Pravda school, 1934.
© Marina Gavrilova, Moscow

> My successes in production work don't make me happy. A thought that I can never seem to shake off, that sucks my blood from me like sap from a birch tree, is the question of my psychology. Can it really be that I am different from the others? This question makes my hair stand on end, and I break out in shivers. Right now, I am a person in the middle, not belonging to one side or the other, but who could easily slip in either direction. But the chances are already greater for the positive side to take over—but still with a touch of the negative left. How devilishly this touch [of the negative] torments me.[22]

At the root of his problem was his "psychology," the same force that Molodtsov had identified in his fellow miner whom he suspected of being a kulak in disguise. The word referred to the unorganized psychic-physical forces working inside the individual; psychology was what constituted an individual before his conscious self-organization. In Podlubny's case, "psychology" referred to the shaping influence of his background as a kulak's son steeped in village culture. From this "old wound of my origins and memories" flowed everything that was bad, reactionary, backward inside him.[23] Podlubny implied that this negative side of his self was the inner class enemy who threatened to take possession of him. But there was also a positive side in him, represented by the forces of consciousness, which could mold and transform psychology. Strengthening consciousness was the way to acquire a proletarian identity and thus to become a new man. Podlubny stood "in the middle," between his discredited past and his anticipated future identity.

One way to develop consciousness was to read and internalize the fundamental Soviet texts: "[I] asked the leader of the political circle: What should I read first, Marx or Lenin? He said I should read both at the same time. That is very significant. He advised me to work with a pencil. In Marx, in his philosophy, he says so many obscure things, so much in it is difficult to understand, there are such depths, that you read it for the third time and still discover some new meaning."[24] A few weeks later, however, expressing a sense of futility, Podlubny dropped Marx from his agenda. He showed greater perseverance in reading novels and going to museums and theaters—expecting to find guidelines for his own thought and behavior. A particularly disappointing experience was reading the three volumes of Gorky's *The Life of Klim Samgin.* Podlubny admired Gorky as the leading Soviet writer and as a proponent of the idea that class aliens could be reeducated through labor. Yet he found the novel "boring, monotonous, and foggy," and deplored the fact that Samgin remained an "undefined" person throughout the book. Podlubny expected to find in Soviet culture models of determination and a clear way to think, not merely replicas of the "indeterminable" and "unsystematic" life he was still leading.[25]

Inner desire and the need to adapt outwardly were densely interwoven in Podlubny's understanding of self-change. The combined coercive and self-willed dimension of transformation is well stated in a retrospective entry devoted to his former life in the village, "when no external or internal forces whatsoever intervened in my fate." The external, coercive impact of collectivization, his wording suggests, unleashed in him an inner desire for self-renewal. Back in the old days, he added, his "horizon [had been] very, very narrow." The years since had witnessed the "reconstruction of my life and situation."[26]

As he turned from the past to the present and future, however, Podlubny was less confident of the prospects of personal transformation. In particular, he remained uncertain about how ingrained or amenable to change his psychology was. Even his program of mastering culture, conducted for the purpose of self-renewal, could be read as an inordinate obsession with culture characteristic of class aliens. Such doubts and self-distrust came to the fore in late 1933, when Podlubny transferred from the shop floor to the library of the printing plant. He wrote that a dream dating back to his childhood had come true: to be surrounded by books and work in a "cultured" environment, in the company of educated colleagues. Furthermore, the transfer had brought him closer to the realization of his goal to become a writer. But Podlubny worried about the implications of turning his back on the factory shop floor. There he had been in the ranks of the working class, where the attainment of proletarian consciousness was virtually guaranteed. The library, by contrast, was a haven that attracted class aliens seeking a niche in Soviet society. Podlubny was concerned both that the state would look for enemies especially in places like the library, and that his new workplace afforded less opportunity for socially useful work and hence for reeducation:

> No matter how much you feed the wolf, he still looks to the forest. It's the same with me. No matter how much I try to reeducate myself, I simply can't get rid of the habits of a useless person. It's true that they are small, not even noticeable to an outsider, but to me when I observe myself everything is noticeable. How careful I am, I watch what I say, but just one ingrained habit could be the end of me, perhaps forever.[27]

Several years into his new life of learning and remaking himself, Podlubny still believed himself in some sense to be a wolf in disguise. In part this had to do with the very magnitude and elusiveness of the task of reforging an ingrained psychology. Even more important, his project of self-change unfolded amid repressive measures of the Soviet state that forced him to hide, and thus retain, the very wolflike nature that he wished to shed.

Subjectivity and the State

Early on in his diary, Podlubny described learning an important lesson, a lesson of the kind that, he noted, you did not read about in textbooks but experienced only in real life. The setting was the *Pravda* print shop, a place where work stoppages caused by mishandling of technical equipment by untrained or exhausted workers were frequent. These breakdowns in production were habitually followed by calls to unmask the "saboteurs" intent on bringing down Soviet power. As a brigade leader responsible for a mixed team of workers, Podlubny was in an exposed position. Furthermore, he kept being harassed by an old technical instructor who apparently could not stand his ardent and outspoken Komsomol activism. Podlubny characterized the print shop as a "snake pit" filled with "enemies" waiting to denounce him as a wrecker and a class enemy. After an incident in which he had been accused of damaging a machine and reprimanded by the Komsomol secretary, Podlubny decided he had discovered a fundamental rule: "I've worked out a new approach to life . . . You always have to reach out to the interests of the state, and of production in particular, and not follow the moods of the other guys and let yourself be contaminated by them."[28]

Podlubny experienced the state as the ultimate force that decided his fate. It was for the state that he worked, whether in the production process, as a Komsomol activist, or in school, and on this basis the state determined his very identity. Persistent work for the "interests of the state," he believed, would save him from falling victim to the intrigues at the workplace and ultimately assure him integration into the Soviet system. In diary entries Podlubny described the state as an external and, indeed, hostile force, to which he had to adapt as a small and always vulnerable creature. But he also expressed hope that one day his problematic class identity would resolve itself, enabling him to identify with the interests of the Soviet state out of genuine personal conviction.

The young apprentice in the *Pravda* print shop outlined his hopes for integration at a time when the regime was far more active in weeding Soviet society of unwanted elements than in inviting class aliens into its fold. This was made dramatically clear to Podlubny in two sets of events in the fall and winter of 1932–33. In October 1932 he was approached by officers of the secret police (GPU), who asked him to work for them as an informer. In all likelihood the GPU had taken notice of Podlubny because of his outstanding record as brigade leader and Komsomol activist. The irony was remarkable: in an effort to conceal his problematic past, Podlubny excelled as a Soviet activist, and on the basis of his success the GPU entrusted the "komsomolist"—this was the code name assigned to him—with the task of unmasking disguised class enemies just like himself.

As an informant Podlubny would meet with his GPU contact officer periodically and at different places—either in janitors' apartments or at the secret police headquarters. He had to sign a document agreeing to the terms and promising to keep his assignment secret. In a short diary entry written a few days after his recruitment, Podlubny voiced regret over having "involved himself" with the GPU, a word choice that suggests a degree of active compliance on his part and the possibility, forgone by now, that he could have turned down their offer.[29] But his agreement to work as an informant was consistent with his philosophy of always defending the interests of the state. Turning his back on the GPU would have risked undermining the organization's impression of him as a devoted Soviet citizen and might have aroused even more far-reaching suspicions.

But his encounters with the secret police strained his life to an extreme. The need to control every word and every gesture was intensified now that he dealt face to face with the very authority that specialized in unmasking people like him. A diary entry of November 1932 describes him and his mother sitting in their basement apartment with a summons lying on the table in front of them: "Perhaps it's the last evening that we are sitting together, and there [at the GPU meeting], we'll be torn apart. One will not know of the other (Mama). Terrifying. Awful, but said as a joke, laughing. Ah, here goes! We are toys in fate's hands, as the old proverb says. Almost two A.M., but we don't even think of sleeping." By the time Stepan left to answer the summons the next day, his mother, wearing five skirts, had packed up her belongings. If he did not come back she was going to escape and rejoin her exiled husband in Arkhangelsk. The meeting to which Stepan was summoned turned out to be routine.[30]

Podlubny's dealings with the secret police, which more than any other state organization incarnated the revolutionary principle of purification, constantly reminded him of his own impure origins. The GPU prompted him to think of himself in precisely the terms he wanted to avoid, namely, in an opposition between private thoughts and outward behavior. This resulting split mind was a far cry from the integrated socialist personality who thought and acted uniformly and as a matter of inner conviction: "My daily secretiveness and the secret of my internal life don't allow me to become a person with an independent character. I can't come out openly or sharply, with any free thoughts. Instead I have to say only what everybody says . . . Unwittingly I'm acquiring the character of a toady, of a cunning dog: soft, cowardly, and always giving in. How trite and how disgusting!"[31]

Podlubny's work for the GPU was not entirely a matter of concealment and adaptation. The reports he wrote on the "moods" of the young workers in the *Pravda* plant evolved from observations that predated his recruitment as an informant. His diary of 1932 repeatedly mentions a certain member of his brigade, a worker named Anisin. In

May Anisin caused a scandal by typesetting a counterrevolutionary slogan. While the Komsomol investigated Anisin's background, Podlubny received a reprimand as brigade leader. Later that year Anisin, who also attended the literary circle, read sections from his diary to Podlubny. Interpreting the passages as direct expressions of Anisin's character, Podlubny was appalled: "How opposite our writings are. He's such an egoist. Amazing. He wants to be a person who looks upon his environment with indifference. That's deadly boring. True, he's an indeterminate sort of person, and, true, it's hard to say what sort of fellow he is, you can't figure out what his ideas are." In November the GPU assigned Podlubny to observe Anisin, who had meanwhile been expelled from the Komsomol. Podlubny's report is not available, but in his diary he characterized Anisin's behavior as "suspicious and deceitful," seamlessly elaborating on his earlier views of his "indeterminate" coworker.[32]

"Counterrevolutionary" moods were widespread among young workers in the plant, Podlubny noted in his diary. He called upon the GPU to step in and intensify its "educational work." He cast the secret police as a moral authority, whose vocation was to correct the consciousness of erring individuals and thus restore their shattered psychological health. Podlubny also supported the GPU's concern for social hygiene. He once reported to his contact officer that he had been approached in a park by a man who wanted to have sex with him. Podlubny provided the man's name, which he had made a point of obtaining. The GPU showed interest in the case and told him that the suspect would be "unmasked" shortly. Podlubny's reports were not confined to the moral health of Soviet youth. Preserved among his papers is a denunciation of his foreman at work, Zakharov, the instructor who had harassed him during his apprenticeship. Podlubny denounced Zakharov as an inveterate "reactionary" who talked only about the shortcomings of Soviet life while failing to mention its achievements. Moreover, he charged Zakharov with seeking to impose his "old views" on the apprentices, some of whom had fallen under his sway and begun to exhibit "passive" and "backward" attitudes. Taken as a whole, these reports demonstrate a considerable degree of overlap and interaction between the GPU's political taxonomy of Soviet society and Podlubny's private views of himself and his social environment. With their stark emphases on unhealthy, bad, passive, reactionary views of youth, Podlubny's reports for the GPU read like an extension of the work of self-transformation in the diary, in which he sought to rid himself of his own black thoughts.[33]

Shortly after Podlubny was recruited by the GPU, he and his mother faced another formidable challenge. A government decree of late December 1932 announced the introduction of passports for all urban citizens. By making it mandatory for individuals to register with the city administration, the Soviet government sought to assume a degree of control over peasant in-migration to the cities. With the agricultural crisis induced by collectivization, and with the first indications of a famine spreading over the countryside, peasants left the villages in unprecedented numbers, threatening to exceed the resources of the rationing system in the cities. But the passport law was also introduced to purge the cities of class aliens and chain the peasants, who did not receive passports, to the newly established kolkhozes.[34]

Verification commissions, staffed by the GPU and the Moscow criminal police, went from building to building, checking papers and confiscating documents from disenfranchised persons as well as from peasants who had fled from collective farms. Police agents confiscated forty ration cards in Podlubny's building alone and ordered their owners to leave the city immediately. The Podlubnys had already packed up just in case, but they were allowed to keep their ration cards, presumably because of the plausibility of their forged documents and because they both had employment in Moscow. Like everyone else, however, they had to wait and see whether they would receive passports.[35]

In his diary Podlubny struggled to identify the purpose of the passport campaign. The challenge for him was to discover the state interest in order to conform to it and thus be saved. An initial entry, recorded when he first heard about the new passports, expressed disorientation: "How am I supposed to live?! What is to be done?!! Where will I see the mirror of myself? How should I beha-a-a-ve . . . ? How do I look!!! Why is there nothing to read on this!?" Later, after the verification commission had come through his building and he had heard what other people were saying about the passport campaign, Podlubny believed he understood its rationale. The purge was a social hygiene measure, "a machine for human cleansing of the newest type. Those who are needed pass through the sieve, and as waste remain the people with a wealthy past." The state proceeded to "sift out" and discard those elements of society which it did not need for the ongoing construction of socialism. The groups targeted by the purge included "speculators," "alcoholics," and "thieves" as well as disenfranchised people and, generally, those "with a wealthy past." What distinguished these people was their tainted psychology, which made them incapable of performing socially useful work. To this group he opposed the exemplary "honest citizen": earnest and hardworking, dedicated to the interests of the state. Podlubny hoped that the new passports would create a contract between state and citizen, a firm social contract requiring each individual to work harder but in turn granting distinct benefits: not only a ration card and a salary but, more important, membership in the "family" of the Soviet state and thus an inviolable sense of self, sanctioned by the Bolshevik regime.[36]

But the diary also shows how unstable this subjectivity defined by useful work remained in the face of an unending search for hidden enemies. A young woman who worked with Podlubny tried to kill herself with rat poison after she had been unmasked as the daughter of a tradesman and threatened with expulsion from Moscow. A party official speaking in the plant formulated the goal of the passport campaign: 50 percent of all apprentices were to be purged. Podlubny guessed that the same percentage of Moscow's citizens would be deported.[37] These events prompted Podlubny to modify his self-definition. Convinced that he would not make it through the human cleansing machine, he referred to himself as "weed" that the sifting process would discard from the "chosen seeds." In the same entry he mentioned that he and his mother had changed their "tactics of adaptation." This made sense, for if he knew himself to be alien to the new order, the only way to prevail was to deceive the regime. His tactic was to become a "toady" who pleased the authorities; his mother's was to be an excellent student. Still, he feared they were doomed: "We're headed for disaster. With a calculation of 95 lost and only 5 will win."[38] When he sensed that the state was willing to rehabilitate former class aliens, Podlubny considered himself a good and committed Soviet worker. Yet as soon as integration appeared to be withheld, he defined himself as a non-Soviet element, a bad seed that could make it onto good socialist soil only by way of cunning or chance.

In April 1933 Podlubny and his mother received their new passports. This seemed to cement their identities as good workers chosen by the state. In a euphoric entry written several weeks later, Podlubny no longer portrayed the Soviet system as something he had to fight or adapt to, since he had become an organic part of it. His own interests and the interests of the state had fused:

> Lately I've come to view my social work not as careerism but as a system, as a component part of my body and my existence, as the bread that is indispensable in order to exist, not a struggle for existence but a system that I willingly embrace. And with every day

> this constancy, this system, which is necessary for my organism, becomes stronger, becomes more firmly established. I have noticeably reeducated myself from careerism to a system that is necessary like food, to which I devote my time without any effort. That's good. I'm happy about it.[39]

Over time, however, the familiar uncertainties resurfaced. The atmosphere of vigilance, whether at the workplace, in the Komsomol, or in the GPU offices, did not diminish, and it threatened to undo at any moment the structure that Podlubny had built for himself. The unresolved question of his identity was glaringly expressed on the cover page of his new diary for 1934. Executed in constructivist style, it featured a huge red question mark and the caption "Again you hang above me like a boa [constrictor]."[40]

A poem Podlubny composed around the same time imagined the nightmarish vision of his public unmasking. What he feared most was ostracism, the prospect of a lonely existence outside and beyond a world he measured in terms of collectivities and usefulness to society:

> Today—the office
> And questions will be raised about me there
> I'm gripped by fear
> Perhaps I will return
> No longer Podlubny,
> A pleasant fellow
> And authority for everyone
> But will walk out
> Known everywhere
> Terrifying to everyone
> Needed by no one,
> Completely alone.[41]

Sooner or later, Podlubny knew, his "game" would end with the discovery of his origins. At the very latest, this had to happen when he came up for the military draft at the end of his apprenticeship. The required background check would bring to light the deceit on which his

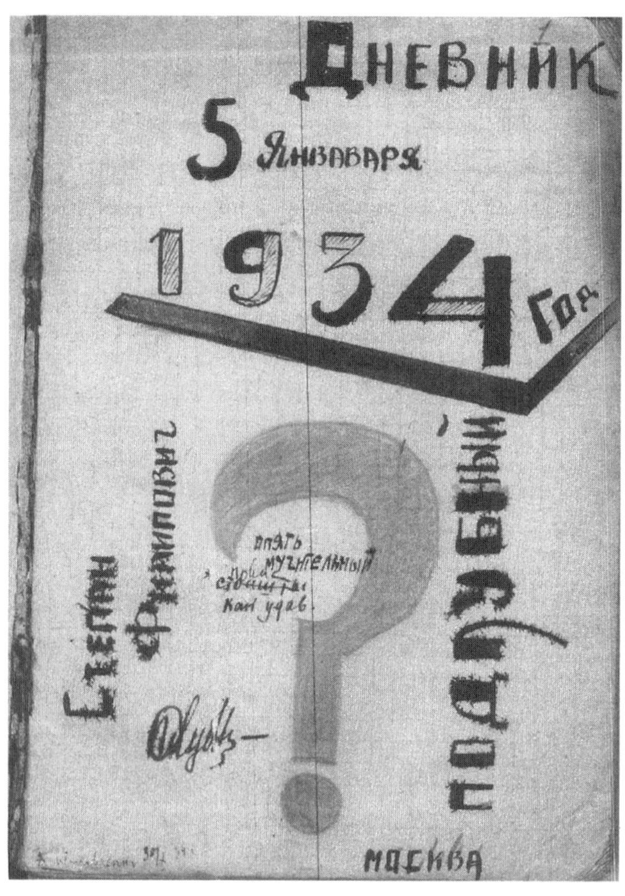

The title page of Stepan Podlubny's 1934 diary. Podlubny's drawing.
© Marina Gavrilova, Moscow

life was built. In October 1934 the event he had been dreading took place. He was at a regular meeting with his secret police contact officer, in the presence of the officer's supervisor. "Totally unexpectedly they asked me these terrible questions. I don't know why, but I didn't really lose my composure. Blushed, didn't answer, just listened carefully. They didn't ask many questions. If I understood it correctly, they were mainly upset about why I had concealed it from them. The whole conversation didn't last more than ten minutes . . . We talked very openly and coolly."[42]

One reason Podlubny did not lose his cool was that just days earlier Soviet newspapers had published decrees granting civic rehabilitation to kulaks and other class aliens who could demonstrate that they had worked sincerely for the Soviet state for five years. In light of this new legislation Podlubny thought the repercussions of his unmasking would not be too serious. At the very least he expected the state to give him clear guidelines on how to behave. Thus he hailed his unmasking as a "historical moment," the end of his "illegal" life. But all that his NKVD contact officers told him (the GPU had been renamed the NKVD in the summer of 1934) was that he would not be punished as long as he continued to do good work for them.[43]

In the spring of 1935 a colleague of Podlubny's was exposed as the son of a kulak. Surprisingly, nothing happened to him. To Podlubny this indicated that the state was changing its policy toward class aliens. What mattered was no longer one's past but one's current work performance. Once more he believed he was witnessing a "historical moment":

> Perhaps from here on my new worldview will begin to emerge. The thought that I've been made a citizen of the common family of the USSR like everybody else obliges me to respond with love to those who have done this. I am no longer with the enemy, whom I fear all the time, every moment, wherever I am. I no longer fear my

> environment. I am just like everybody else, and therefore I should be interested in various things, just the way a master is interested in his farm, and not like a farm laborer toward his master.[44]

Time and again Podlubny voiced the expectation that he would be fundamentally transformed as soon as he received legal standing in Soviet society. He saw his illegal standing as the source of his problems. It forced him to view his environment as hostile. He could adapt to its forms of life, but he could not organically merge with them. In crossing the threshold of legalization, Podlubny expected to discover a new sense of uncoerced and total devotion to the state—love. At the same time he would outgrow his ingrained psychology, become a member of the Soviet family, and acquire an integrated worldview befitting the socialist "personality."

In the fall of 1935 Podlubny was accepted into Moscow's Second Medical Institute. For years he had dreamed of becoming a student, but his social origins had seemed to prevent the fulfillment of this dream. The biography of each candidate for admission to a university was thoroughly scrutinized, and Podlubny had to fear that the authorities would discover his kulak past. Yet, with recommendations from the Komsomol and the *Pravda* plant, he was admitted to the institute. On the face of it, he now conformed to the ideal of a socialist new man. A professional career in medicine seemed to be within his reach.[45]

Fashioning the Social Environment

Podlubny's quest for transformation determined in great measure the relationships he forged, as well as those he severed. His desire for a new form of life, in tune with the reformed "psychology" he hoped to acquire, affected his interactions with friends and colleagues in Moscow, as well as with acquaintances from his former home in Ukraine, and it dramatically cut into his personal and family life. In the first instance it redefined his relationship with his father, Filip Evdokimovich. Stepan's memories of his childhood, sketched out in various places in the diary, evoke an abusive father who punished his only son at every step. Stepan experienced a moment of liberation when he was separated from the "tyrant" after his father was sentenced to administrative exile during the dekulakization campaign. That was a turning point in his life: only then did he start to gain consciousness and "grow." This, to be sure, was a retrospective account, written nearly three years after his father's arrest.[46] Whether Stepan had thought about his father this way at the time is unknown. The fact that Stepan and his mother chose to join Filip in his exile suggests otherwise. But Stepan's self-definition as an urban citizen in Stalin's Russia called for a repudiation of his old life, epitomized by his father, in such stark terms.

Filip Evdokimovich was reunited with the family in Moscow in April 1933, upon completion of his three-year term of exile. He found work as a loader and obtained a temporary residence permit. While precarious, his standing in Moscow was legal, but the fact that he lived with his wife and son threatened to betray their concealed social background. Stepan blamed his father's imprudence for putting the family in danger. He was even more upset, however, by his father's unreformed ways. Despite the opportunity to remake himself in exile, he had remained "old," "backward," and "useless." Stepan portrayed his father as a "useless old man," not because of his biological age (he was 45), but because he made no effort to become a socially useful Soviet citizen. Throughout the diary Stepan emphasized his emotional and intellectual detachment from his father. Calling him a "father by conception but a stranger by education" or simply his "former father," he made a point of contrasting relationships based on blood to those forged by consciousness. Bonds of consciousness superseded those of kinship and thus justified Stepan's claim to be recognized as a member of the new order in spite of his blood ties to the old.[47]

Podlubny's account of his relationship with his father can be interpreted as more than just an adolescent's struggle for identity: the concepts and emphases he selected can be situated historically as part of a larger cultural text. Podlubny couched the opposition between himself and his father in terms that were central to the battle for Soviet industrialization: a struggle between "old" and "new" elements in society, "backward" and "progressive," darkness and light. His reproaches of his father all revolved around the central revolutionary mandates of growth, self-change, and service to society. Not only did his father fail to "work on himself," develop into a strong character, but he failed to demonstrate his usefulness to society. Moreover, in the past he had tried to stem his son's "growth" by keeping him out of school to tend the goats.

And yet, while Stepan condemned his father in the revolutionary language of Bolshevism, he did not confront him in ways that befitted a committed Bolshevik. The party appealed to youth, especially to those with tainted backgrounds, to dissociate themselves from their fathers and denounce them as class enemies. Ritualistic declarations by sons and daughters of class-alien heritage filled the local and national press, repudiating their parents and stating that they had severed all ties to them. Among these sons was the famous Pavlik Morozov, who allegedly reported his kulak father to the authorities and was then killed by his uncle. Pavlik was declared a martyr and a model to be emulated by Soviet youth.[48] Stepan Podlubny stopped well short of such behavior. Not even in his diary did he vilify his father as a "kulak" or an enemy; much less did he entertain the thought of denouncing him publicly. Even so, his hostility toward the "old man" was real enough. The diary records altercations between father and son, provoked by

Filip's drunken fights with his wife, that suggest how the patriarchal world of the peasantry had come tumbling down, and how much the Communist values of sobriety, discipline, and individual self-respect appealed to peasants' dependents as sources of empowerment and moral authority. Filip stayed with his family for only a few months in 1933. That summer he and Yefrosinia visited their Ukrainian home village, where he hoped to resettle. They were chased away by the local authorities. After they returned to Moscow, Filip moved to a place of his own.

Stepan greatly admired his mother. He praised her for the "proletarian views" she had gradually come to exhibit, implying that, like him, she had accepted the need to rework herself. His mother attended evening school and performed outstanding social work for which she received awards. Stepan's diary cites a letter she wrote to him from a summer work camp where she had been sent to cut peat: "Received a letter from Mama. Am very happy that she has reeducated herself a little in the course of her 'emigration.' She writes that, in spite of the great difficulty of the work, 'I'll stay for the entire month until the victorious end.' This is very good. This is the proletarian way."[49]

In his interactions with people Podlubny was at pains to represent himself as a bearer of progressive and "cultured" values. He emphatically rejected language or attitudes that smacked of primitivism and village "backwardness." A wing of his building on Red Proletarian Street was occupied by the Rodin family, peasant in-migrants from Kaluga province. Stepan called their apartment the "Rodin village," because the family gave temporary shelter to all their relatives and acquaintances who came to Moscow in search of work.[50] Stepan and his mother, too, had stayed with the Rodins when they first arrived in the city. The apartment was also a meeting point for youth, and Stepan went there on occasion to chat and have a good time. Nevertheless, he consistently portrayed the "Rodin village" as a bulwark of peasant backwardness and barbarism: "The young people come together to dance and sing in the Rodins' kitchen. These young people are all from the village—girls and boys from a backward, extremely low milieu. You stand there and look at them, a pleasant picture at first sight. But when you think about it more carefully, you draw back, because you remember that these are living people. People! Not animals. But their relations with one another, their thoughts and manners are just animal-like."[51]

This drunken scene supplied Podlubny with a contrast against which he could establish his sense of himself as a new man. In as much detail he described his activities with other apprentices who shared his striving toward education, moral self-improvement, and proper attire. These were the pursuits that distinguished "cultured" youth: "Today the three of us, Kolya Galankin, Fyedka Kondratyev, and I, spent a cultured and very good evening at the theater. Remarkably pleasant feelings of the heart. It reminded me of something grandiose, adult, and new at the same time. It's not the same as going to the movies around the corner for a ruble. No, to the theater, a serious, cultured matter, and for five rubles. It has a huge moral significance, how much you pay."[52]

A portrait of Stepan Podlubny, taken in 1936, emblematizes the ideal of the cultured person. It shows him posing in a photographer's studio, wearing a fashionable suit, his hand resting on an Empire-style banquette. The setting, with heavy curtains in the background, illustrates the neoclassical aspirations of Stalinist culture. Having his portrait taken required an investment, symbolic and material, on Podlubny's part; it bespeaks the importance he attached to representing himself as a developed individual of the socialist age.

Another moment of upward mobility, in a quite literal sense, took place in 1935, when the Podlubnys managed to escape from their humid basement room. A government office had been vacated on the second floor of their building, and in the ensuing battle among would-be tenants, mother and son managed to claim half a room and two windows for themselves. Another tenant lived in the same room, behind a makeshift screen. The apartment was shared by thirteen families.

While seeking the company of educated and refined youth, Stepan noted with some concern that when it came to girlfriends he seemed to do best with "uncultured" types, "from the lowest class." For a while he

Podlubny in 1936.
© Marina Gavrilova, Moscow

dated a girl named Tanya, whom he liked for her looks and her sincere love for him. But he feared that if he remained with her, this would signify that he, too, was from the lowest class, a psychologically and intellectually inferior type of person. As if to counter this suspicion, he wrote her rambling letters, one of them fourteen pages long, about his contradictory feelings toward her, even though he knew she was not literate enough to read and understand them. His long letter in fact was addressed to her more "developed" girlfriends, who, Stepan was certain, would read and explain it to Tanya. When he received Tanya's reply, he burst out laughing. The few lines were written phonetically, with spelling mistakes in almost every word. The letter confirmed his feeling that Tanya, like other girls he had dated, was mere "cannon fodder" and could not possibly become his steady girlfriend or his wife. He quickly broke off the relationship, explaining in another letter that he felt touched by her "sincerity" and "loyalty," but that her "complete illiteracy" and the "crudeness" of her expression had turned him off.[53]

A diary entry captures the two contrasting "milieus" between which Podlubny saw himself suspended. One was defined by Tanya, the other by Polina, a university student:

> On the evening of the 23rd I was at Tanya's name-day party . . . A black, dreadful cellar apartment consisting of a small room and a kitchen. After I read pages from the calendar and the old newspapers, which are glued to the wall, or more precisely: after an hour of boredom, the table was laid. There wasn't much to drink, not much food, and no music. Awful boring. All in all, Galankin made the right conclusion: What can you expect from these people?
>
> On the 22nd Polina Lakernik called. She invited me and Nikolai [Galankin] to a dance at her apartment. The dancing was splendid, I got to know a different society, more cultured and totally different from the one with which I have mingled so far . . .

> On the 27th I went ice-skating with Polina on the skating-rink of the Central House of the Red Army.[54]

Stepan sought the company of Polina, Nikolai, and others not for the sake of their "cultured" appeal alone. He voiced a need for friendship, for people with whom he could share his worries, conflicts, and doubts, his innermost essence. Yet these desires ran up against the necessity to remain guarded, to be sure the secret of his class origins would not leak out.

Letters written to Podlubny by friends and colleagues indicate that his watchful behavior did not escape their attention. In 1933 he became involved with Veronika Ivanova, for once a "cultured" and educated girl hailing from the "Soviet aristocracy." They started a correspondence in which they discussed their feelings for each other in light of the personality ideal of the time. His goal, he told her, was to "suppress the outpouring of inner feelings with the power of the brain." By living a strictly rationalist life in the image of a machine, he hoped to incarnate the ideal of the "new man." But Veronika reminded him that the new man had a brain and a heart, not two brains, and urged him to drop his habit of "masking your feelings and emotions": "You are lonely, lonely in your personal life. And that is because you want to get very much and give almost nothing in return . . . You are a hermit and, unfortunately, a skeptic on top of that. Why? I don't know." Stepan was alarmed by Veronika's letter. She seemed to have divined his secret. He immediately broke off contact with her. Years later he would wistfully recall his encounters with Veronika and mourn his failure to make the relationship last.[55]

A fellow komsomolist, Rishat Khaibulin, was less kind in his assessment of Stepan's personality. After an altercation between the two about a Komsomol assignment that Podlubny refused to take on, Rishat sent him a letter, pointing out that Stepan had acted wrongly, and suggesting that this resulted from his failure to mobilize his will against his "negative traits." The letter ended: "Take my statement not as a reproach but as an argument in favor of raising our cultural level. Rishat."[56] These letters not only shed light on the way people around Podlubny saw him; they also show that Podlubny's efforts to define himself as a progressive young man of his age were shared by his peers, who were engaged in similar practices of self-perfection, mutual observation, and correction.

Complaining in his diary that in his Moscow life he had no one to confide in, Podlubny maintained an active correspondence with childhood friends from Ukraine, despite the threat to the preservation of his false identity. Many of his old friends had left Ukraine; some had been dekulakized like his family, others had left on their own for the cities and industrial sites. In his letters to them, Podlubny invariably portrayed himself as an industrious and "cultured" worker and student, proudly mentioning his salary and boasting about life in Moscow compared with the living standards on the "periphery," where one correspondent, his cousin Kornei Krivoruka, lived. In turn, Kornei, who served in the Red Army and was stationed in the far east, underscored the civilizing work that the Red Army men conducted among the local population. Perhaps even more forcefully than Podlubny's diary itself, this correspondence between two sons of kulaks, who presented themselves to each other as model Soviet citizens, demonstrates the way the revolutionary mandate of self-transformation had been reworked into a private identity even by persons targeted by the regime as potential counterrevolutionaries.[57]

Podlubny made two holiday visits to his home village in Ukraine in 1934 and 1936. The reality he discovered there proved incompatible with his newly found aspirations as a "cultured" young man. He was appalled by the villagers' lack of education, the prevalent patriarchal culture, and the misery of kolkhoz life. In contrast he made a point of appearing as an educated and well-dressed Muscovite to gain respect in the village. During his 1936 visit, when he was already a student, he wore fake eyeglasses to impress the villagers. Their response was mixed: young girls adored him, but there were others who complained that the kulaks had not been dealt with sufficiently at the time of dekulakization. Eventually Podlubny had to cut his visit short and escape. Friends had informed him that local authorities wanted to arrest him.[58]

Podlubny's posturing reveals him as a beneficiary of the Soviet system, which gave him authority, culture, and the assurance that he had emancipated himself from the idiocy of rural life. In particular his contacts with relatives and friends from his former home in Ukraine underscored to him that there was no viable alternative to his life in Moscow, the country's cultural center—conditional and precarious as that life was.

Willpower

In the winter of 1933, with the passport campaign in full swing, Stepan Podlubny went to a graphologist for an assessment of his personal qualities. A scientific analysis of his handwriting should help him solve the question of questions—whether he fit into the Soviet order or not. He put all of his savings, seven rubles, into that analysis, but did not regret the expenditure because he knew the graphologist to be the greatest authority in the field, "Zuev-Insarov himself." Several weeks later he received his analysis in the mail. Quoted in full, it reads like a catalogue of publicly proclaimed values of the time, against which Podlubny's personality traits are assessed:

> A personality full of initiative, who easily grasps the essence of a matter. Materialistic worldview. Politically oriented. Escaped the

> ideological influence of his family at an early age. Has a gift for observation. Can distinguish lies from sincerity in the voice of another person. In the company of others is sociable and pleasant, gentle, even good-natured, but when decisive measures are called for, or when an obligation or a strong desire has to be fulfilled, neither the pleas of close friends nor any other temptations can distract him from the goal he has set himself. Does not let himself be coerced in any fashion. Persistent in the realization of his intentions, although his perseverance is occasionally unsystematic and lacks precision: greater concentration of will is indispensable. Able to do many things at once, but has a tendency to defer things already started. Lazy. Shows little trust and is suspicious, has developed professional caution. A tendency for formal and logical reasoning, shows talent for treating issues with a scientific methodology, suited for activities in law and administration, is also mechanically talented. Can command respect. Has a literary vein. By nature suited to all varieties of social work. Gravitates toward self-education, although in this regard he should strive for a deepening, rather than broadening, of his knowledge. A great experimenter in terms of his passions, occasionally displays more curiosity than passion, inconstancy in his passions. Able to control his emotions, but not after releasing them. Extravagant with money, and does not know how to economize. Does not lose his head in moments of danger, does not fear for himself, not because, of course, he stands above universal human weaknesses, but simply because he believes in his strength and maintains a presence of mind.[59]

The model citizen who provided the background to this characterization of Podlubny was a politically inclined individual with a materialistic worldview, who in his character displayed firmness and determination—"concentration of will"—who expressed interest in science and in furthering his education, but who was also a good manual worker. For the most part Podlubny lived up to the ideal, according to Zuev-Insarov's analysis. When he received the document, he was impressed with how accurately he had been characterized, but was also surprised that the graphologist had assigned to him many positive qualities. Specifically with respect to his willpower, "as far as willpower is concerned, I didn't even expect that I have strong willpower. But he says that I'm persistent." He concluded: "The letter was useful for me. I've begun to know myself, to trust myself, to trust my actions and my strength."[60]

Podlubny obsessed about his willpower. In his understanding, will and consciousness were interdependent; one could not be attained without the other. This link becomes evident in entries in which he blamed his "weak will" for setbacks in his work performance and for his "idiotic and nonpolitical mood." But willpower was not only to impart the developed political consciousness of a good Soviet citizen, it also helped him preserve the double secret of his social background and his innermost "black" thoughts. Only through "will," "determination," and "cold-bloodedness" could he seal off his private thoughts from his behavior in public. Quite paradoxically, a strong will helped him at one and the same time become a member of the Soviet order and adapt to it as a disguised member of an imperiled species.[61]

To live, Podlubny noted, meant to struggle, continuously and on multiple "fronts." He once likened himself to a lonely sailor on the ocean, facing the sudden outbreak of a terrible storm. The only way to survive in an environment whose overwhelming forces could destroy him at any moment was to listen to his "instincts" and develop a "plan of self-preservation." Repeatedly Podlubny reminded himself to be prepared for imminent blows from any direction. He was especially suspicious about calm periods, when nothing seemed to threaten him, neither at work nor from the GPU. They reminded him of the "calm before the storm." Struggle was an unavoidable fact of life, but it also contained moral value, for it was in struggle that one became tougher and stronger, in both a physical and an emotional sense. If there were no obstacles to overcome, the will regressed, corrupting the self and undermining its fitness in the "survival struggle" of daily life. "A life without struggle is monotonous and a bad omen for the future."[62]

If willpower was the key element necessary for self-development in socialist society, it was also what Podlubny thought distinguished the classes in Soviet society. He considered to be "proletarian" someone who possessed great willpower and therefore could cope with the conditions of Soviet life. Describing the resourcefulness of his mother, as she eluded the watchful gaze of the omnipresent police, Stepan praised her willpower and described her attitude as "purely proletarian" in spirit. It was a paradoxical understanding of proletarian behavior, since it connoted the ability to protect oneself against the proletarian state. By contrast his main charge against the father was that Filip, a "pathetic creature," was unable to stand up for himself and engage in the type of struggle that defined a proletarian and, indeed, a human being, in opposition to mere animal-like existence.

In an unnerving extension of this logic, Podlubny defined those groups in society who could not cope with the Soviet environment as "weak-willed" and unfit for life. In the winter of 1933 he and his mother received a letter from their former home. It was a desperate cry for help from the three small children of Stepan's aunt Lisaveta, his mother's older sister. A widow, Lisaveta was in prison for having picked grain from the collective farm to feed her starving family. She was sentenced under Stalin's "five wheat-ear law," which imposed harsh punishment for the "theft of socialist property." The children wrote: "Aunt Frosya and brother Styopa! We are bloated from hunger, help us, if you can. Do not if you can't, we will have to die sooner or later anyway. But we want to live a little longer, our lives have been so short." While his mother "cried bitter tears," Stepan emphasized his own "cool" behavior. "For some reason," he added, reading the letter made him smile. Podlubny articulated his attitude toward his starving brethren in Ukraine more fully in the summer of the same year. His mother had traveled to their home village of Beryozovka, and she returned with horrifying images of the famine:

> Half of the people have died of hunger. Now they are eating boiled beet tops. There are numerous cases of cannibalism . . . All in all, what's happening is awful. I don't know why, but I don't feel sympathy for this. It has to be this way, because then it will be easier to remake the peasants' smallholder psychology into the proletarian psychology that we need. And those who die of hunger, let them die. If they can't defend themselves against death from starvation, it means that they are weak-willed, and what can they give to society?[63]

The shockingly utilitarian philosophy propounded by Podlubny was related to the revolutionary morality preached by the Bolshevik state but differed from it in significant respects. Podlubny consistently invoked character traits and categories of the Bolshevik personality such as willpower and self-control, yet he did so not only to express himself but also merely to survive in the harsh Communist world, to protect himself as a class enemy in disguise. He took his cues from "real life" and the behavior of others, rarely invoking theory or history as a guide to his personal life. He was an avowed believer in fate, expressing a conviction, consistent with his life experience, that there were forces beyond his volition that could reshape his life at any moment. Podlubny knew that such belief in fate was more characteristic of the traditional peasantry than of an enlightened, modern citizen, but he relied on it nonetheless. Moreover, he listened to the voice of his "instincts," a stark difference from Communists, who looked down on the disorganized, prehuman unconscious and worshipped the powers of developed reason.[64] Fittingly Podlubny described his plight as that of a "small animal" with only its instincts and powers of mimicry to rely on for survival in a predatory world. In almost comical ways this self-conception came to the fore during Podlubny's unmasking by the NKVD. When the officers prodded him about why he had not confided his true origins to them before, all he said was: "The little chicken also wants to live." It was a line from a popular song coming out of Russian prison culture, in which a "boiled and fried chicken" walks on St. Petersburg's Nevsky Prospekt and is arrested by the police because it does not have a passport.[65]

Only class aliens like him, Podlubny believed, lived the precarious existence of the small chicken. This survivalist mode applied only for the duration of his illegal standing in society. As soon as he crossed the gap toward legality he would be able to orient himself unconditionally toward the ideal, propounded by Gorky and other writers of the age, of the strong and unfettered personality with an integrated worldview.

Personal Crisis, Political Crisis

On December 1, 1934, the Leningrad party secretary, Sergei Kirov, widely regarded as Stalin's first deputy, was murdered. The party leadership reacted with outrage, demanding relentless persecution of the murderers, who were suspected to come from the political opposition. The Kirov murder was a turning point in the history of the Bolshevik system: it redirected the purge campaign, which up to then had targeted class aliens, capitalist exploiters, and bourgeois nationalists, toward the party itself, culminating in the arrests and executions of hundreds of thousands of Communists in 1937 and 1938. The time of the murder also marked a turning point in Podlubny's life. His view of himself, as well as the style in which he kept his diary notes, underwent a notable and lasting change. This change was connected to his realization that he appeared unable to part with character traits that were alien to the goals of the Soviet regime.

Podlubny had already made this discovery in 1933, during a series of illicit political conversations with a friend at work, Mitya Gorenkov. Gorenkov had been reciting to him poems and other writings that bespoke his personal unhappiness and the hardships of life. The conversations left Podlubny profoundly ambivalent. Mitya's thoughts echoed some of his own feelings, and the ability to voice them satisfied his craving for a "soul mate" beyond the diary. Moreover, the conversations with Mitya gave him a glimpse of an "unorthodox," "deep" person who had an "own opinion" and was not afraid of voicing it—in contrast to the career-minded "state parrots," who were shallow and mindlessly echoed what was "dictated" to them. Yet at the same time, Stepan could not help characterizing Mitya's critique of the political order as "pessimist" and petit-bourgeois, given that it clashed with the cheerful confidence, optimism, and resolve that were at the core of the extolled socialist personality. Stepan found it "unpleasant" to hear that Mitya planned to write a novel on "pessimistic and progressive youth," and wanted to base the "pessimist" characters on himself and Stepan, while another friend was to serve as inspiration for the "progressive" type. Stepan clearly preferred to be counted among the optimists.[66]

Podlubny made sense of his inner conflict by stating that there were two people inside him: "One of them is a bureaucrat who reminds me every day: stay on your guard, observe the rules, be very careful, don't talk through your hat, watch yourself and what you're saying! He always gives me instructions. This person lives in me most of the time. The second person, he's someone who collects all sorts of dirt in my soul, all the leftover garbage, and he waits for the right moment to pour this stinking mess over someone else's head to relieve himself from the burden of this dirt. This person is less present in me, but he exists." The second person, he added, was an effect of the "old wound of my origins and memories." Podlubny believed that the ideal type of personality, endowed with a single, integrated worldview, would be within his reach as soon as he became a legal member of Soviet society.[67]

Yet his unmasking by the NVKD, only days after he diagnosed the two people within him, not only dashed his hope for legalization but essentialized the very identity as a class alien from which he had sought to absolve himself all along:

> In every conversation with me they [his contact officers] remind me of my past, forcing me, inculcating everything unnecessary in me. Previously I didn't think about my past, I was an ordinary rank-and-file member of society, I was even in the vanguard. But now they, they themselves, have forced me to think differently. Then they will beat me for this, and there's no doubt that when they find out, they'll beat me. It's so horrible, horrible what is happening. Instead of curing me, they are making a cripple of me.[68]

Podlubny specifically blamed the NKVD for instilling in him new and wholly "unnecessary" thoughts, in blatant violation of their vocation as spiritual doctors who were to rescue Soviet citizens in moral crisis. These new thoughts were remarkable: in January 1935, hearing of the death of another politician, Valerian Kuibyshev, who was said to have died of a heart attack, Podlubny suspected that Kuibyshev had been killed on the government's orders, perhaps because the speech he was scheduled to deliver at a government congress was too critical and "so they decided to get him out of the way." He distrusted the official death report, "just the way one distrusts a thief who had stolen before"—a reference to the "comedy of the Kirov murder" the previous month. Yet while voicing these stark opinions, Podlubny also leveled serious accusations against himself, chiding himself for his "too realistic" perspective. No longer was he a member of "progressive" Soviet youth; his "ideology" had become "rotten."[69]

In the long run, two possibilities were available to him to accommodate his "reactionary" stance. One was to rearrange the categories of self-definition, so that his illegitimate thoughts would appear legitimate. If he proved unable to remake the world for himself, he was bound to marginalize himself: to accept his individual thoughts as a deviation from the norm and to seek the reasons for the deviation in himself. Podlubny engaged in both processes. His diary illustrates the ways in which he managed to rearrange his political vocabulary. In an entry of February 1935 he described the widening hunt for Kirov's murderers and their henchmen: "A time of reaction and persecution has set in . . . You can't describe it in a few words. It only reminds me of studying the history of the party in 1907: a raging black reaction, going on right now. A raging reaction, and the persecution of free thought."[70] These sentences enabled Podlubny to rid himself of his "reactionary" thoughts by defining the regime as reactionary and, by implication, portraying himself as "progressive." Even more striking is Podlubny's reference to the source that inspired this new conceptualization, and that brought him to denounce the party state: the Bolshevik party's history textbook. It was as if he used the Bible against the Church in legitimizing his unbelief. He invoked official Soviet discourse to undermine the legitimacy of the existing political regime. But at the same time, this stance cemented the Soviet platform of revolutionary activism that he shared with the political regime.

Podlubny was aware of the deleterious impact of his criticism on himself as a subject of the Soviet realm. Since his subjectivity as a Soviet citizen was defined by parameters supplied by the revolution—activism, enthusiasm, subordination to the collective, loyalty toward the workers' state—he came to regard his criticism of state policies as a process of personal degeneration. He noted that his new view on life, bereft as it was of uplifting thoughts, "paralyzed" him "morally" and made him feel "sluggish," as if he suffered from a "grave inner disease." What distinguished this from previous situations in which he had lamented the weakness of his will was his greater uncertainty as to whether his "sickness" could be cured. Was he a good Soviet citizen who had only temporarily succumbed to a corrupting influence, or was he alien to Soviet values in his very essence?[71]

Repeatedly Podlubny referred to himself as a person beyond help, irreversibly shaped by his origins and upbringing. If an individual's consciousness determined his class position, it only made sense that Podlubny regarded his persistent proclivity toward heretical thought as an expression of an alien class essence.[72] In deducing his social class identity from the state of his soul, he followed a scheme practiced by countless others in the public sphere of the 1930s. By means of denunciations and trials, the biographies of politically suspect people were systematically rewritten. Thus the defendants at the Moscow show trials—for the most part staunch Old Bolsheviks—were reconfigured by the state prosecution into reactionary White Guardists, capitalist spies, or mercenaries of imperialist powers. Yet Podlubny staged a trial against himself, and did so in his secret diary.

Podlubny evaluated not only his own thoughts and behavior but also those of other people as expressions of sociological background. He once compared himself to another son of a kulak, noting that both shared the same "psychology," revealed in their unsteady love lives: "Since we both have the same origins, I concluded that this phenomenon exists with all people who had a similar education, with everybody who has traveled this path in life." He once secretly read the diary of a visiting friend, Oleg Vachnadze. What he read made him suspect that Vachnadze was the "son of a nobleman and not at all what he says . . . His father is alive and lives abroad. When I analyze his adventures, and recall his tempers and pranks, my suspicion is hardened further. These intelligentsia pranks of a philistine, his love of powder, the elegance of his manners and his polished speech, his total exhaustion and feeble willpower—all of these things I notice in myself when my past is weighing on me, when I'm not left in peace. I find all these traits in him."[73] A person's character and in particular the development of his or her willpower, Podlubny implied, was determined by social background, so much so that personal character acquired a degree of biological determinism. The Soviet regime's strong emphasis on social origins could, as in Podlubny's case, lead to an essentialization of individuals' origins at the expense of their deeds.

In early 1936 Podlubny's kulak origins were publicly revealed at a Komsomol meeting and he was expelled from the youth organization. To the diary he reported how stunned he had been by this event, but also how daringly he had comported himself at the meeting. He had looked everybody straight in the eyes and "even [forgotten] to repent for my sins in a major way." In particular he took issue with the official charge against him, contending that his father's household had not been the size of a kulak farm. It had rather been a "large middle-peasant's farm." This statement, Podlubny reported, earned him an official reprimand for anti-Soviet behavior: "From my words regarding the household they concluded that I was against my father's dekulakization, although I stated more than once that I had not said this." Podlubny concluded his speech by declaring: "Feel free to expel me from the Komsomol if you want. But as far as the institute is concerned I will fight for my rights." In invoking his "rights," Podlubny was referring to the recent government decree of December 1935 that had removed the restrictions on university admission for persons of class-alien background.[74]

To counteract the threat of being excluded from the Medical Institute, Podlubny resolved to draw up a family tree. Sooner or later, he believed, this document would prove useful in his conflict with the authorities. Together with his parents and a cousin who was also living in Moscow, Podlubny reconstructed his father's genealogy, starting in the eighteenth century with his great-great-grandfather Miron. The family tree was to help him demonstrate that many members of his father's family, including his father himself, had not been enterprising capitalists deserving the label "kulak."[75] But the very act of tracing his genealogy suggests how much Podlubny's earlier idealistic expectation that class membership was a matter of conscious choice had been qualified by a notion of biological determinism. His rehearsal of the socioeconomic fortunes of his family's past four generations illustrated a belief that an important key to his subjectivity lay in his family background and the way it had conditioned his "psychology," rather than in personal deeds and the ability to remake himself. This biological approach to defining class identity was widespread in the Stalinist system even after the mid-1930s, when socialism was declared to be built and all class antagonisms had allegedly been resolved in Soviet society. At the Eighteenth Party Conference in 1941, the Politburo member Georgy Malenkov attacked this genealogical understanding of individuals. It was inadmissible, he declared, for party and state officials to sift through a candidate's family tree and ask him about his "grandfather and his grandmother," yet to ignore his personal qualities.[76]

Podlubny was allowed to remain in the institute, but his performance in the first two semesters of his medical studies had been so poor that he applied for, and was granted, a year-long leave, after which he planned to enroll again as a first-year student. Meanwhile, his parents, who had repeatedly received citations from the militia in 1934 and 1935, were forced to surrender their documents and ordered to leave Moscow and the surrounding 100 kilometer radius. Podlubny's father moved to Yaroslavl on the Volga, while his mother traveled to the city of Mozhaisk, just outside the radius. Helped by her son, she wrote petitions pleading for the restoration of her full civic rights. She was allowed to return to Moscow in December 1936.[77]

Podlubny's diary breaks off in late December 1936, resuming only in December 1937. In the first entry of that year, he explained the hiatus: the past year had been so appalling that he wanted to cross it out, "like an unnecessary page" in the history of his life. He mentioned financial troubles stemming from the loss of his scholarship. His year-long leave had led to the loss of friends from the institute. Finally there was the fear that he might have to quit the institute because of his failing grades and the need to earn money. Podlubny's diary fell silent as soon as his project of self-transformation, material and moral, appeared no longer viable. In talking about his life in 1937, he referred to a puddle of blood congealing under a dead body, and to a noose that he felt tightening around his neck. These were certainly references to the political violence around him and the threat that he might become its target.[78]

While Stalin's Great Purges of 1936–1938 aimed at cleansing the state and party administration of suspected oppositionists, scores of people who were neither Communists nor top state managers fell victim to them as well. "Kulaks, bandits, and other anti-Soviet elements" were the target group of NKVD order no. 447, issued on July 31, 1937, which produced arrests and executions in the hundreds of thousands. The order set arrest quotas for each of the country's regions. In the Moscow region alone five thousand anti-Soviet elements were to be executed and another thirty thousand sentenced to labor camps for eight to ten years. Over the next months regional NKVD leaders petitioned the Politburo to raise the quotas, as more enemies had been identified;

their requests were granted.[79] These staggering quotas could be met and exceeded in the spirit of socialist competition through examination of the files of people with a record as class aliens or political counterrevolutionaries.

Podlubny, who was not informed of this secret operation, relied on his trusted instruments of intuition and practical experience to protect himself and his mother. The tightening noose he described referred to the approaching elections to the USSR's Supreme Soviet, to be held on December 12, 1937. From past experience Podlubny knew that the police habitually conducted raids on the eve of major holidays. Because arrests always happened at night, he and his mother considered staying with friends for a few nights, but in the end they did not do so.

Stepan Podlubny with his mother and a cousin, 1936.
© Marina Gavrilova, Moscow

Podlubny did take one precaution, however: he hid his diary in a trunk in the corridor of their communal apartment, outside the room where he and his mother lived. At 4 A.M. on December 9 they were awakened by the dreaded knock at their door. An armed officer of the criminal police, accompanied by a janitor, demanded entry to their room and searched it, apparently for weapons, Podlubny suspected. After making a note that the search had yielded nothing, the officer asked Stepan's mother to get dressed and accompany him to the police station "for just a minute." She did not return that night.

In his reaction to the arrest Stepan Podlubny's extraordinary attachment to his mother became evident. He spent the next days and weeks trying to find her. Long lines formed every morning at the information office of the Moscow militia. To make it to the information window before it closed at 4 P.M. he had to be there shortly after five in the morning. Standing in a line extending for half a kilometer, watching the hundreds of other Muscovites who were searching for arrested relatives and loved ones, he discovered a world of people who were oblivious to the imperatives and the clichés of the official world: they were "absorbed in their own private concerns, for them the world outside does not exist." Then it was his turn at the small square window: "An inexplicable terror came over me. My knees shook and buckled under me, my fingers trembled nervously. My heart raced . . . It was only after I got home that I fully realized the meaning of what had happened. A huge lump in my throat cut off my breath. I lost control of my muscles." The official at the window had been unable to tell where his mother was. It was a unique scene in the diary in that Podlubny did not keep his cool. The presence of mind to which even the graphologist had attested eluded him, as he lost control over his life and his own body. Podlubny ultimately managed to locate his mother in a Moscow prison. During his visit she told him tearfully that an NKVD tribunal had sentenced her to eight years in prison "for concealment of social origins." His reaction was desperate and indignant at once: "How horrible, eight years. It's so easy to pronounce, but so hard to live through. And for what?! . . . And they say there is justice in this world." The entry ended on a defiant note. It echoed the language of revolutionary freedom fighters familiar from Soviet literature, but Podlubny turned it against the Soviet state: "No, there will be justice. Many people have perished in the name of justice, and as long as society exists, people will be struggling for justice. Justice will come. The truth will come."[80]

After his mother's arrest, Podlubny's diary turned more political in character, as he denounced the policies of the Stalinist regime in acerbic terms. The grandiose reception of a returning team of polar explorers was, in his words, an "unprecedented hullabaloo" that served only the purpose of deflecting popular attention from the trial and execution of the party's chief theoretician, Nikolai Bukharin. After reading *Quo Vadis?* by Henryk Sienkiewicz, which was situated in Imperial Rome in the first century A.D., Podlubny characterized Stalin as "our Russian Nero," specifically addressing his personal cult: "It appears that the unjustified lavishing of praise and attribution of good deeds, as well as deification, are possible in our times too, if only in a more subtle form."[81]

Podlubny referred to his diary entries of this period as a "naturalist fixation of facts." Seen through the lens of socialist realism's historical confidence, the naturalist perspective was by definition pessimistic and degenerative. Podlubny defended his use of naturalism. His purpose, he wrote, was to cast reality in a different light and thus estrange people from the rhetoric they reflexively invoked to describe their lives. A visit to his father in the provincial town of Yaroslavl was eye-opening. Although his father now lived an urban life, he shared a room not only with other workers but also with a piglet and swarms of bugs and lice. On a tour through the outskirts of Yaroslavl Podlubny discovered with shock that such living conditions appeared to be the rule. Yet all the people he questioned replied that they were doing well. Only his "fresh perspective" as a visiting outsider, Podlubny wrote, allowed him to understand the "inhuman" nature of these living conditions. "We mustn't live like this," he declared.[82] Tellingly, Stepan no longer blamed his father's backward outlook and weak will for his squalid living conditions. Instead, this and other entries resonated with a sense that the regime had failed to provide for people who had sincerely worked for its interests. A photograph of father and son, taken during Stepan's visit, suggests that the two had made peace, and also presents a new view of Filip. Dressed in a suit and tie, he appears as a modern urban citizen, cast in the image of his son, who poses next to him. Both the photo and Podlubny's descriptions of his father during the visit strikingly depart from his earlier representations of Filip as a wretched creature.

Yet to engage with Soviet reality in a naturalist style came at a price. It was not just a question of the danger that these writings posed for

Stepan Podlubny with his father, 1938.

Podlubny's safety; they also undermined his self-image, which rested in large measure on socialist realist conceptions of the person. In his diary of the late 1930s Podlubny had to contend with the fact that he had become a "pessimist" at heart, plagued by a lack of willpower, and that his attempt to turn himself into a socialist personality had failed. Having been forced to give up his university studies, he pondered his aimless, "useless" existence: "Life without a goal is like an animal's life! What sort of life is that? There is nothing, nothing and nobody to give me moral support." This life, "without the feeling of progress," deepened his pessimism. The fact that he did not fight to resume his studies and regain a cheerful perspective was evidence of a diseased will: "My willpower has been completely shattered, gone are my toughness and endurance, my persistence, indeed, my stubbornness. I have lost control over myself." Finally, there was the issue of his personal life. Now that he was about to turn 25, it was time to get married, yet the few girls who seemed available were all from the less-cultured classes.[83]

From this lowly position he enviously observed the "milieu" of the university students in whose company he had once been. In the spring of 1938 a friend, Vladimir Vorontsov, who had been expelled from the Komsomol two years earlier because his father had been uncovered as a Trotskyist, was readmitted into the youth organization. He had plans to study philosophy and join the Communist party. Stepan criticized Vladimir for his decision to become a party apparatchik; Vladimir in turn chided Stepan for his "egoism," for only taking from life but not giving. To voice purely negative views on existing reality invited charges of egoism, putting Podlubny in company with the likes of Nikolai Anisin, his fellow apprentice at the *Pravda* printing plant, whom he had denounced to the GPU on the same charge. In some sense the very outspokenness of Podlubny's political diary thus kept undermining the ideal of the collectivist, optimistic, and always-striving personality against which he continued to measure himself when he contemplated the failure of his life.[84]

On his own without his mother, Podlubny continued to follow his trusted techniques for avoiding brushes with Soviet authorities. Especially on the nights before state holidays, he made sure to sleep away from home. But he was arrested in the end. Podlubny's diary stops abruptly in October 1939, shortly after the German and Soviet invasion of Poland, which he followed attentively in his journal. A few days later he was to assist his cousin Kornei Krivoruka in selling off spare parts from the watch factory in which Kornei worked. Podlubny knew a watchmaker and got him interested in the deal. Yet when the three met to complete the transaction, the watchmaker brought the police along. Kornei was charged with speculation and sentenced to five years in a labor camp. Stepan was sentenced to eighteen months in a labor camp for failing to denounce his cousin to the authorities. He was taken to a camp about six hundred miles east of Moscow. In April 1940 he was transferred with other physically fit men to Pechora in the far north. There they were to build a railway track to the Arctic city of Vorkuta. Many prisoners perished under the conditions of extreme work, severe cold, and malnutrition. Podlubny survived because he managed to secure a place for himself in the camp administration. He was freed from the camp in April 1941, shortly before the railway construction was completed.

In early June 1941, only days before Germany invaded the Soviet Union, Podlubny was called to military service. Because of his criminal record, he was not allowed to serve at the front. From October 1941 he worked as a medical orderly, accompanying reserve units from Siberia to the front. In 1944 he was promoted to the rank of lieutenant of medical service. Podlubny's promotion to officer rank was possible only because he claimed to have completed his medical studies and received a diploma.[85] After the end of the war, he settled in Moscow. There he met his future wife, Zoya, and they married in 1947. Podlubny's mother had obtained an early release from labor camp in 1940. Following the war she and Filip moved into their son's apartment. Filip Podlubny died in 1964, Yefrosinia Danilovna in 1974. Until his retirement, Stepan Podlubny worked in different Soviet ministries, most of the time as an administrator in the ministry of health.

When released from the labor camp, Podlubny resumed writing his diary; he continued to do so until his death in 1998, at the age of 84. Yet his diaries from the war and the postwar period lack the drama characterizing his journal from the 1930s. Notably, they no longer mention the conflict between origins and deeds. It appears that the question of Podlubny's standing in the Soviet order was resolved during and after the war, with the regime recognizing him as an army officer and allowing him to work in the state administration.[86] Reading Podlubny's postwar diaries only underscores the urgency of his diary project of the 1930s—the pressing concern for the state of his soul, the searching introspection, and the work on his self.

I had the good fortune to talk with Podlubny as well as several other surviving diarists from the 1930s. My initial encounters with him, in Moscow in the early 1990s, were complicated and fraught with misunderstandings. I was struck by the degree to which he disavowed the striving for self-transformation so amply documented in the diary of his youth. In our conversations he sought to convey the point that his diary was the document of a victim of Stalinism, and that its purpose had been to chronicle his and his family's suffering at the hands of an inhuman regime. This conviction had prompted him to deposit the diary in a historical archive, a step he described as his personal contribution to establishing the truth about Stalinism.[87] Podlubny reacted impatiently to questions I had derived from reading his diary in the archive. He found it pointless to discuss his tense relationship with his father or the views he expressed in the diary about backwardness, culture, and ideal forms of selfhood. As he insisted, his critical writings about his father expressed only "certain moods," but in fact he had never stopped venerating him.

As part of his effort to rewrite his experience, Podlubny spent several years during the 1980s producing an edited version of his diaries of the 1930s, adding "necessary" commentary on events, people, and thoughts described in the original text. He edited the language to give it a more literary quality, and he dropped passages that he deemed useless. Podlubny was so convinced of the "scientific" and "artistic" superiority of the edited version of his diary that he even considered destroying the original.

Podlubny's attitude toward his diary is remarkable in light of Zinaida Denisevskaya's diary and its fate. Both authors had lived under a regime that looked upon their social origins with hostility; both suffered anxieties and doubts while also expressing hopes of overcoming their inner conflicts. In 1977 Denisevskaya's diary was submitted to a state archive to add the voice of a socialist citizen to the Soviet memory house. A little more than a decade later Podlubny adapted his record to claim the status of a lifelong victim of the Soviet state. The span of time between these two opposite diaristic gestures measures the loss of legitimacy that the Soviet political system underwent in the interim. In writing himself out of the time of his youth, Podlubny acted in concert with countless other survivors of the Stalin period who came to view their past in self-victimizing terms. They were encouraged by institutions such as the newly established "People's archive" in Moscow, which in appealing to the population to submit memoirs of their experience also structured the shape this experience was to take. It was in this archive that Podlubny deposited his diary.[88]

6

The Diary of a New Man

LEONID POTEMKIN

The first thing Leonid Potemkin showed me when I visited his apartment in the Olympic Village, a compound in Moscow built for the 1980 Olympics and subsequently used to house privileged Soviet citizens, was his collection of minerals adorning the bookcase in the living room. A retired deputy minister of geology of the Russian Soviet Republic (RSFSR), Potemkin had received many gifts from geologists and mining collectives in his career. He pointed to an elaborate paperweight, a present from Leningrad geologists to honor his sixtieth birthday in 1974. On a heavy foundation of black granite stood three books, representing books Potemkin had written, sculpted from red marble. "Do you know this stone?" Potemkin asked, indicating the marble. "It is the same stone that was used to build the Lenin Mausoleum."[1]

Leonid Potemkin had turned 88 when I met him in Moscow in the spring of 2002. He was a frail man with delicate features who in spite of health problems appeared younger than his age. Over the previous years he had turned down my repeated requests to meet with him, citing his poor health. There was another issue as well. Passages from Potemkin's journal had appeared in a Western anthology of Stalin-era diaries, and he was disturbed by the book's reference to him as a "young unlettered careerist." He eventually agreed to a series of interviews and granted me access to his entire personal archive, but only on the condition that my account of his life remain "objective" and

проверка знаний и окончательное их закрепление.
С 4/XII у нас начались военные занятия в студенческой батарее УЗИ 1 взвод ПВО и 2 взвода ВВП. Казарменный распорядок дня и 7 часов теоретических занятий.

1934 год.

12 января мне исполнилось двадцать лет. Выходной день; я ездил к маме и [illegible]
20 лет — какой это всесторонне зрелый образ рисует в воображении.
И насколько я еще слаб, не развит и не оформился. Я тяготился сознанием в силе личности, быть выше мелких неприятностей и частных трудностей (когда даже моя жизнь сказочна успехами) быть активному, козырчать, с [illegible] отвечать на [illegible] спокойно [illegible] даже

воодушевленно, твердо и решительно проявлять свои способности. Просто, не застенчиво с надеждой смотреть на жизнь общества. Я считаю что препятствием этому служит моя слабая нервная система.
С каким детским захватывающим интересом я стараюсь распознать жизнь, постичь людей, перенять, воплотить в себе их качества, крупные совершенные черты характера окружающего общества и из истории прошедших обществ и международной жизни.
Только общественная деятельность, руководящая, ответственная роль в обществе дает ощущать мне действительную жизнь, зажигает меня жизнерадостностью. Это смысл, сущность жизни. А пассивное положение меня бьет по самолюбию с такой силой, что отравляет [illegible] своего бытия. Я положение мое в

not "distort" the "true meaning" of any of the "facts" mentioned in his texts.[2]

Potemkin's worries, and his insistence on defining the terms of our collaboration, illustrate the sensitivity of live autobiographical testimony, especially if it involves a period as contested as the Stalin era. Naturally, any self-narrative by a surviving author invites a clash between authorial recollection and detached textual interpretation, and this may be particularly so in this case because Potemkin's lyrically expressive record is at such odds with our customary understanding of the Stalin period as an age of terror and repression. The researcher's first inclination might be to brush aside the author's interference as a hindrance, as a case of memory invading and reformulating past testimony. But it is also possible to view this interference in productive terms, turning it into an object of reflection. Potemkin's very insistence on a coherent, single meaning of his life, to be derived from an "objective" reading of the facts recorded in his diary, should make us pause. Regardless of whether we accept the author's textual representation of his life as *being his life,* his claim suggests a considerable personal investment in the creation of what he regards as his book of life. If we keep this investment in mind when analyzing Potemkin's diary, it begins to talk to us differently, its pages disclosing layers of interpretation that a reading of a personal source in the absence of its author may easily miss. The diary as a whole appears in a new light, much like the paperweight in light of Potemkin's comment on it. A paperweight can be a decorative item but it can also be read as a symbolic substantiation of Lenin's body and Leninist ideology. The veneration with which Potemkin treated this artifact speaks for itself.

Potemkin's case is of exceptional interest. The surviving corpus of

---

A page from Leonid Potemkin's diary.

personal texts that he produced contains a diary stretching over six years, letters he exchanged with his family and a girlfriend, excerpts from his course readings as a university student, a handbook on dialectical materialism he wrote in 1935, a manual on self-training written in 1942, memoirs—both verse and prose—written in his old age, and several albums of period photographs. Beyond the sheer volume, the most remarkable aspect of these sources is their shared thematic focus. Even more than other personal texts from this time, Potemkin's writings revolve around the theme of the self. For Potemkin the development of the "personality" *(lichnost')* was the central theme of the age, and accordingly also of his personal development. More deliberately than other diarists, he situated the record of his personal life in the revolutionary narrative of the emerging socialist personality, and his writings thus provide insights into the experiential domain of the new man, a figure often invoked by Stalin-era propagandists but rarely described in more than schematic form.

Leonid Alekseevich Potemkin was born in 1914 in the village of Poisava, near the city of Naberezhnye Chelni in the southern Urals, an area that today is part of the Autonomous Republic of Tatarstan. Prior to 1861, his ancestors had been serfs, peasants in the case of his mother's family and artisans on his father's side. At the time of Leonid's birth his father, Alexei Alexandrovich, headed the postal bureau in the village, and his mother, Klavdia Antonovna, was a housewife who looked after the four children of whom Leonid was the youngest. In his memoirs Potemkin portrays his parents as having progressive intelligentsia views and being eager to broaden their cultural and political horizons, but also suffering from their educational limitations. Alexei Potemkin liked to paint, but as a young man he could not afford to enroll in the Kazan Academy of Fine Arts. Leonid's mother had only four years of elementary village schooling. A photograph of 1913 shows the father dressed in his postal uniform as he sits on the living room sofa, holding the magazine *Niva* (Grainfield). According to Leonid Potemkin, this popular illustrated weekly, which regarded its mission as spreading enlightenment beyond the thin ranks of Russian educated society, was the family's favorite journal, their "university of culture."[3]

The modest bourgeois comfort that this photograph evokes was swept away by the ensuing turmoil of war and revolution. Leonid's oldest brother, Anatoly, joined the army as a volunteer in 1916 and soon disappeared, officially reported missing in action. His dream had been to become a mining engineer, but enrollment in the mining academy

Alexei Potemkin, Leonid Potemkin's father, 1913.
© Leonid Potemkin, Moscow

was limited to offspring of the higher ranks of society. Alexei Potemkin died from tuberculosis in 1919, at age 45. Left with three young children and no savings, his wife was forced to move back to her parental village, where the house of her late parents was vacant. The village commune allotted her a small patch of land, which, given the lack of horsepower and working hands, did not feed the family. The family somehow survived the catastrophic years of civil war and famine, thanks in part to food supplied by the American Relief Association.[4] In the mid-1920s Leonid's sister Nina, five years his senior, left home to work and study, first in Sverdlovsk and later in Gorky. In Gorky she also met her husband, a doctor. She graduated from the city's Institute for Construction Engineering in 1938 and became an engineer. Potemkin's brother Vladimir, born in 1911, joined the Red Army and became a career officer.

Throughout his childhood, which he remembered as marked by abject poverty and constant hunger, Potemkin dreamed of obtaining a higher education. Nevertheless, he left the nine-year school a year early, in 1931, and hurried to get involved in the unfolding industrialization campaign. In 1933 he was accepted at the Ural Mining Institute in Sverdlovsk. Immediately after he graduated, with distinction, from the institute in 1939, he received orders from a Moscow ministry to head the exploratory bureau of the gigantic Balkhash copper works, which had just been built in the Kazakh steppe. His appointment, remarkable for a person his age lacking managerial experience, came in the wake of a purge of leading personnel. In August 1941, two months after the German Wehrmacht invaded the Soviet Union, Potemkin joined the Communist party, deliberately challenging the panic and doom that had gripped many Communists. He spent the war years on exploratory missions in the Caucasus, while his brother Vladimir, by now a decorated Red Army major, fought at the front. Like his older brother Anatoly in World War I, Vladimir vanished, and not until after the war ended was the family officially informed of his death, near Kharkov in the spring of 1942.[5]

The defining moment of Leonid Potemkin's career came shortly after the war, as he headed a geological expedition to the Nordic Pechenga region, which the Soviet Union had annexed from Finland in 1944. In 1947 he discovered an enormous deposit of nickel ores dispersed in a multitude of small mines. The mines, previously considered inferior because of their dispersed nature, were prospected according to an innovative method worked out by Potemkin, and the site gradually became the sprawling industrial city of Zapoliarny.[6] Potemkin rose in the party administration, becoming party secretary of the ministry of non-ferrous metallurgy in 1955, and party secretary of Moscow's Lenin district in 1956. His career was crowned by his appointment as deputy minister of geology of the RSFSR in 1965.

In his memoirs Potemkin played down his educational and professional achievements, explaining his biography in terms of the "massive rise of uneducated people" which he regarded as a "natural" outcome of the October Revolution. Far from being singular, he emphasized, his achievement had to be seen in the context of the so-called *vydvizhentsy* (workers promoted to administrative posts), a cohort of young people of modest social and educational backgrounds who in the late 1920s and the 1930s were actively promoted by the regime to fill its need for reliable, class-conscious cadres in the economy and the party and state administration.[7] Well-known members of this cohort included Nikita Khrushchev, Alexei Kosygin, and Leonid Brezhnev, who were slightly older than Potemkin but shared his biographical trajectory.

As the self-representation of a *vydvizhenets,* Potemkin's diary narrative enriches our understanding of the group of workers-turned-managers, whose subjective horizons have scarcely been mapped. Soviet historians confined themselves to hagiographic accounts of the workers and managers who selflessly and heroically built socialism, thereby contributing to the victory over the fascist invaders. Western historians became interested in the *vydvizhentsy* as they searched for "beneficiaries" of Stalinism, who would explain how a regime believed to be repressive in character could muster sufficient social stability to survive and thrive. More recent research has focused on the *vydvizhentsy* to study the civilizing effects of the Soviet system, its success in breeding not only loyal citizens but also cultured and self-disciplining subjects.[8] While the latter studies show the new managerial elite as an effect of the modernizing mission of the Soviet state, most Western scholars attribute the new cultural conservatism that took hold in the mid-1930s, when the regime revoked its iconoclastic agenda and advocated a "return to the classics," to the supposedly petit-bourgeois, "middle-class" instincts of the regime's chief constituency, who openly craved consumption, possession, and the pursuit of a good life.[9]

Such representations of the *vydvizhentsy* appear incomplete in light of Potemkin's self-narrative. To be sure, Potemkin's writings are filled with odes to "culturedness" and a life lived to the full, but his striving for culture was part and parcel of an overall commitment to the revolution. The central theme of his diary as well as his other writings of the period was the cultivation of his personality in the terms prescribed by the emerging socialist society. Potemkin's case makes the *vydvizhentsy* phenomenon appear as a large-scale program of personality formation, an agenda rooted in the revolution of 1917 and centering on the creation of the new man.

The Early Diary

Potemkin began to keep a diary in 1928, while still in school. Sensing the youth's literary and aesthetic proclivities, a village schoolteacher who was a friend of the family gave him a notebook and encouraged him to write in it regularly. From its inception the diary had two principal purposes: it functioned as a training ground for an aspiring writer; and at the same time it served as a tool of introspection and self-improvement. Potemkin bought booklets with titles such as *Technique of the Writer's Craft* and *Everything an Aspiring Writer Needs to Know.* He was also a frequent contributor to the wall newspaper at his school. Several passages in the diary are readily recognizable as attempts to master the genre of industrialization prose popular at the time. For instance, the sight of tractors in a remote village prompted him to rhapsodize about the noise of their engines, which evoked the "power of our state, the strength of the proletarian dictatorship. The tractor is created by workers, and in its engine can be heard the policies, resolve, and character of the working class. The tractor is the embodiment of the will of the proletariat." The first time he saw a tractor, Potemkin added, "I was ablaze with emotion and my cheeks tingled with excitement, but at that time I didn't happen to pour out my simmering feelings onto paper."[10]

One reason these passages are so easily identifiable as self-conscious literary efforts is that they do not harmonize with views of the collectivization process expressed elsewhere in the diary. Potemkin directly witnessed the furor of the collectivization campaign, and with evident compassion he described the "fear," "fatalism," and "apathy" of the peasants and townpeople in his native region who were being expropriated and arrested. Moreover some of his own relatives and friends, including his uncle and the teacher who had given him the diary, were victims of collectivization.[11]

While Potemkin maintained his literary ambitions through the years, the focus of his narrative became increasingly directed toward his self. His teacher had inserted an epigraph, by the ancient Greek poet Archilochus, in the empty notebook he gave his pupil: "Let there be attacks from all sides, stand firm, do not waver. If you vanquish—do not flaunt your victory. If you are vanquished, do not hide at home, weeping." The epigraph, Potemkin noted, "moved me deeply. . . . These words give me courage, compel me to be steadfast and insistent, lift me above the limits of everyday life."[12] The epigraph and Potemkin's reflections on it bear clear marks of *Bildung:* the formation of character through a series of internal and external obstacles, and the fixing of this story on paper.

The highest goal Potemkin set for himself from early on was to become a "leader and social activist." He was one of the best students in his school, and he also excelled as a tireless activist. At school he set up a brigade to introduce shock work standards in learning; with other activists he went to newly founded kolkhozes to support the spring planting; in addition he taught illiterate peasants and toured nearby villages seeking to interest the villagers in newspaper subscriptions (he won twenty subscribers). Yet beneath his outward successes Potemkin was plagued by "thoughts of an inner tragedy" that he confided only to his diary, "a scar on my soul." Both physically and psychologically he felt inadequate, lacking in the qualities required to command natural respect as a leader and an activist: "cheerful, strong, and beautiful." In tune with the materialist convictions dominating Soviet sociology and psychology at the time, he blamed his "weak organism," his uncoordinated nervous system, for his outbursts of "childish nervous agitation, anxiety, and dissatisfaction with myself resulting from it." The underlying cause for his personal deficiencies, however, he saw in his deficient environment. Recalling that until 1927 he had lived in a state of almost constant hunger, Potemkin concluded that "the dismal economic situation is what created the dismal state of the psyche." Furthermore, life in the countryside had reduced his "social education" to a minimum. His past life, spent in nature and outside the laboring collective, had made him soft, weak, lonely, and insufficiently prepared for contemporary life, which valued only collectivism, struggle, and the hardening of the self.[13]

It was this unbalanced state of his development that prompted Potemkin to leave school a year early, in 1931, and to reconstruct himself by joining the working class. He sought to transform both his inner and his outward life by coupling intensive self-analysis, in the service of "developing the psyche and creating a strong personality," with the pursuit of a new form of life as a proletarian worker. Combined,

Leonid Potemkin as a prospecting worker, 1932.

these two processes would lead to his "metamorphosis." He wrote that he wanted to become as precious and hard as a diamond. The power of his self-analysis was to generate the heat, and the proletarian environment would add the necessary "pressure," to turn "weakly, brittle, and somber" coal—his present self—into graphite, and from there into a diamond.[14] Potemkin used this geological metaphor years before he decided to become a geologist. This choice of language suggested the spread and familiarity of the mining trade in the southern Urals where he was growing up, and also how meaningful mining could become in his mind, as a symbol of forging the self.

Potemkin's actual encounters with the Soviet working class proved somewhat disillusioning. Most of the workers he encountered in Sverdlovsk and at the nearby prospecting site where he found employment as a driller fell short of his idealized image of them—they cursed, drank, wore rags, and were infested with lice. Potemkin's explanation was that these were not real proletarians, but "unskilled workers, migrants from the village." His comment illustrates the way this young author constructed his life experience, unwittingly reworking his immediate impressions according to ideological categories central to his self-understanding. Yet Potemkin also recorded with evident concern the political defeatism or outright oppositionism of "real" workers, peasants, and even a Communist activist with whom he discussed politics. Further challenges to the integrity of his worldview included dire living conditions, lack of decent food, and a miserable wage that did not allow him to buy much-needed warm clothes. An "inexhaustible reserve of strength" was required "to be inspired in the current stage of life." Also, his hopes for self-transformation in the company of the workers did not seem to be realized. He continued to complain about his weak body and his inability to cope with the challenges presented by life. More than six months into his new life he noted that he had "got stuck in passivity" and stopped working on himself. His new job was so physically taxing that he had not mustered the energy to enroll in the Komsomol or pursue social activism. His life had degenerated to the level of "gray, half-dead uneventfulness."[15]

On the face of it, Potemkin's fascination with the hardened, collectivist, class-conscious proletariat was no different from Stepan Podlubny's and Zinaida Denisevskaya's attraction to the working class. All three cases illustrate the profound biographical effects of the industrialization campaign. They show that beyond appealing to build a Soviet industrial foundation, the campaign contained a far-reaching injunction to all citizens to industrialize, rationalize, and harden their own souls. Yet what made Podlubny's and Denisevskaya's cases distinct from Potemkin's was that they were class aliens and for them acquiring attributes of a worker equaled salvation. Potemkin, by contrast, did not seek to merge with the working class, for the simple reason that he was not of a class-alien background. As soon as he had acquired proletarian toughness and imbued himself with a collectivist spirit, he hoped to accede to a higher stage and become a member of the Soviet intelligentsia. Exposure to the working class was a necessary step in the construction of his personality, but a transitory step nonetheless. To use Potemkin's own imagery, the proletariat was like graphite—an intermediate substance between raw coal and the polished diamond.

Self-Training for a Strong Personality

Development of the "personality" was the principal theme of Potemkin's diary. He systematically put the diary to use for an elaborate program of "self-training." Time and again, he compiled detailed exhortations, listing in paragraph form features of his self that he needed to work on. At key junctures, such as the New Year, his birthday, the anniversary of the October Revolution, or the end of a diary notebook, he took stock of results achieved. Here is an excerpt from one of his programmatic calls for self-change:

> I must retrain myself from one who is cold, morose, and inconspicuous in society into one who is quick in his wit and actions, healthy, an activist and leader with a strong character.
>
> §1
>
> I will be able to achieve happiness when I fit into society, when I am able to hold my own in company . . . I will play various kinds of sports, be agile, brave. I will sing, play musical instruments, at least to some extent.
>
> §2
>
> I will become acclimated, my mind and actions will achieve the proficiency demanded and made necessary by my stay in an industrial and cultured city.
>
> §3
>
> I will be strong from physical exercise and leading my life in a correct and sober manner.
>
> §4
>
> I will develop a strong character, surmounting all kinds of obstacles . . .
>
> §5
>
> I will become an activist when I merge with the masses, become of them—expressing their mood and desire. When I listen to the masses and understand them. I will be in step with the masses. I will treat every member of society as a comrade and an equal.

> §6
>
> I will be able to become a leader when I am a guide of the masses and take them with me. I will be mature politically, will speak my mind at meetings. Having devoted my efforts to production, I will strive to elevate productivity, will become a shock worker. Always, without interruption and abatement, I will be active. And then I will gain influence among the masses, and authority as a good worker, comrade, and organizer.[16]

These paragraphs show a clear dialectical progression. Work on the relaxation of body and senses was to be enhanced by a change of environment, the relocation to an industrial and cultured setting. Physical exercise was indispensable for the strengthening of will and character. Overall, the first four paragraphs figured as a necessary precondition for the next step, the finished subject's merging with the masses. Only on this basis could Potemkin legitimately claim a leadership position for himself, as he foresaw himself emerging from the masses by virtue of his advanced political consciousness. The program of action was to culminate in a heightened social activism which he hoped would never subside.

While pursuing this program, Potemkin showed dissatisfaction that there were no formal guidelines on the subject of "human personality and ethics" that would show him how to "correctly analyze oneself" and "scientifically" develop one's organism so as to become a "strong personality." Potemkin shared this disappointment with other diarists who complained that the Soviet regime failed to issue clear and binding guidelines on Communist ethics, or a scientifically "correct" model of self-development. Yet through their diaries these authors created the very parameters of identity formation that they hoped to find in public prescripts. For Potemkin the situation changed in the summer of 1932, when he triumphantly reported the discovery of exactly the type of book he had been looking for: Ivan Nazarov's *Culture of the Will*—a scientific treatise on psycho-physiological training that explicitly addressed "self-training into a strong, healthy personality." Nazarov's tract illustrates the obsession with physiology of the Soviet medical and psychological professions during the 1920s and early 1930s. According to the physiologists, the will resided not in some "abstract spirit" but in nerves and their reflexes. It was through training of the nerves and the establishment of a well-regulated central nervous system that a strong will could be developed. To reach this goal, Nazarov and others advocated the conscious regulation of impulses, deliberate muscle relaxation and breathing, gymnastics, a correct diet, and techniques of autosuggestion.[17]

Bolstered by Nazarov's scientific authority, Potemkin apprehended both his life and his diary in a new light. Previously he had considered his psychic life almost hopelessly rotten, and he even refrained from consulting his past diary entries for fear of being further contaminated by fatalist weakness. Now, however, Nazarov's scientific treatise helped him realize that his "bitter self-analysis" had from the very start served a transformative goal. The past no longer appeared severed from his dreams of the future, for the scientific diagnosis of his psychic sickness contained in itself the promise of restoration and health. Potemkin drew from this diagnosis a number of practical conclusions. After going through his old diaries and reviewing his "entire past life," he resolved to leave the geological prospecting site, for the diary had expressed a "longing for urban, factory, and culturally-socially active life." He also urged himself to join the trade union and Komsomol movements, to advance his political development, his oratorical abilities, and his "system of self-training." And finally, "to attain and perfect a strong personality and then enter the Institute of Dialectical Materialism."[18]

Less than two months after embarking on the Nazarov program, Potemkin entered the trade union movement, and shortly afterward he began to work as a social activist. He also asked a manager at the prospecting site for a private room, ostensibly in order to focus on his tasks as an activist, but in reality so he could "organize a useful life, engage in self-education and self-training according to Nazarov's system." To his surprise the request was granted, and he made a symbolically charged transition from the workers' barracks—home of the faceless masses—to an individual space where he could further cultivate his personality. He described furnishing his new dwelling: "I cleaned up and made the room comfortable. On the bare wall near the bed I hung a map; in the front, on the pier, a portrait of Maxim Gorky and a clock; and on the bulkhead a portrait of Lenin sitting in his office; and lower, over the desk, a calendar. On the desk are books, an inkwell, pen, pencil, and a notebook."[19]

The description lists core ingredients of Potemkin's projected work of personality formation: the writing and memory tools to chronicle and monitor his self-transformation; the scientific tools—clock and map—to situate the work in time and space; and two towering authorities in whose name he was to pursue his self-change: Lenin and Gorky. As he added: "I voraciously read the characterizations of Lenin, making his personality traits the standard to which I aspire." Reading his diary against the background of Lenin's biography, Potemkin deplored the social poverty and "absence of class self-consciousness" of his youth. But Lenin's life also inspired him, helping him discover meaning and, indeed, historical necessity in the deplorable fact that he had been sent to a prospecting site in a cultural backwater. His self-imposed exile was to serve as a "school, as prison had been for the revolutionaries."[20]

In the longer run, however, neither his experience as a worker nor his Nazarov-style training was able to tackle Potemkin's main problems: his underdeveloped "psycho-physical powers," his "weak character," and his "weak nerves." This catastrophic verdict stayed with him even after he stopped working at the prospecting site in the summer of 1933 and enrolled in the Sverdlovsk Mining Institute, a transition that he should have had every reason to celebrate as an extraordinary success. Potemkin chose to skip the preparatory year at the "workers' faculty" *(rabfak),* designed for workers without secondary education; he prepared for the entrance examinations on his own, relying in part on notes and excerpts produced by his sister when she had studied for admission to the Institute for Construction Engineering. Potemkin applied with about fifty other applicants, "some of them well dressed, with ties and briefcases, even a few old people." Most of the others were *rabfak* graduates, he noted, and only a few had had as little formal education as he had. He took exams in social sciences, Russian, chemistry, physics, and mathematics—and he passed.[21] Yet shortly afterward, when taking stock of his personal development, he listed not a single achievement, only the familiar deficiencies.

Potemkin drew up this balance sheet on the occasion of the revolutionary holiday and thus explicitly measured his individual time by the revolutionary calendar: "*November 8, 1933* I did not greet the sixteenth anniversary of the revolution as a shock worker, but with a sad heart, in a weakened state . . . How I dislike harsh reality, [and how I] like elegance, beauty—my very soul yearns for it." His psyche was too tender for an age that demanded of individuals to be collectivists at heart and prove themselves in labor and sport brigades. Potemkin saw himself as infected by a real "disease," a disease that also showed in his practice of keeping a diary: "The main deficiency is that the diary does not reveal a life that is woven into the social fabric, but an individual-subjective social life. There is no burning collectivism."

Time and again, when he dreamed of turning into a "strong personality," the "obstacle" to this projected self-transformation was his "weak nervous system." Potemkin was so despondent that he contemplated suicide. At one point he went to a neuropathologist, but he was less than convinced by the latter's therapy: to blame his parents for his weak nerves, exercise, and swallow "some kind of sour mixture."[22] Making things worse, in the spring of 1934 his scholarship support was suspended and an official inquiry was made into his social origins. The diary mentions the incident without elucidating it, but in later years Potemkin explained that his superior knowledge and his refined manners had given rise to suspicions that he was of intelligentsia background. Yet at the time he undoubtedly tied these suspicions to his own perceived weaknesses and surely wondered about what type of social essence his weak organism expressed.[23]

Yet such expressions of doubt also had an important function, as they called out to be challenged and negated. Potemkin's self-criticism was thus firmly embedded in a dialectical frame of struggle and transformation. Taken as a whole, his self-analysis evolved within the binaries of a weak and sensitive vs. a strong and hardened self, individual insufficiency vs. the promise of collectivist self-realization, lyrical and effusive nature vs. technological, machine-like precision. Riding home from work on the streetcar, he listened to the "stubbornness, insistence of the motor, its steadfast command, indifferent to everyone else. This kind of decisiveness—the hardness of a machine is what is necessary."[24]

The Emerging New Man

In late 1934 and early 1935 a striking break in Potemkin's self-narrative took place. The old binary of the (deficient) individual versus the (salutory) collective was displaced by the opposition between the poor and the rich personality, between a lowly, ordinary existence and an exalted, full-blooded life. The overall tonality of struggle receded as it was displaced by a new register of expression. In the course of this rearrangement, previously disdained features such as the contemplation of nature, lyricism, and sensitivity received new validation. Prerevolutionary readings made a proud comeback as "classics" in the diary. But the most important change was the unqualified celebration of the rich individual personality.

Arguably these changes could be attributed to Leonid Potemkin's personal development. He was growing steadily, both physically and intellectually; his standing and his grades at the institute were improving; and women were beginning to notice him, as can be gauged from the infatuations, previously missing from the diary, that he began to write about. Also, the inquiry into his social background was rescinded and he was able to join the Komsomol in the fall of 1934. But on their own, these developments cannot explain the major shift in tonality in the diary. Potemkin began to talk about himself in a new key, and the reasons are to be sought not in his personal development but in his cultural environment. Around 1933 and 1934 the Stalinist regime underwent a sweeping and far-reaching change in central values and styles of self-representation. Consistent with this change, Potemkin began to assume a more relaxed and rounded self-image, one that included topics such as exuberance and love, which had earlier been excluded from the lexicon of intense struggle that had marked his previous life as well as the life of the Soviet order.

The change that occurred during this time was based on a sense of historical progression, a sense that a new threshold of the revolution had been crossed. The First Five-Year Plan, the campaign of furious industrial construction along with the destruction of remnants of the old world, had ended and been proclaimed a success, and the foundations of a socialist society were declared to have been laid. In accordance with this diagnosis of the state of the revolution, the regime attempted to mold a distinctly socialist culture, an attempt most visibly expressed in its mandate to the disparate literary profession to merge into a single union of Soviet writers and produce only socialist realist works. The new socialist culture was chiefly defined through the new type of men and women that it created and represented.

In many respects this ideal figure served a legitimizing need. The material appearance of socialist men and women on Soviet soil was to furnish visible proof, particularly to all "left" and "right" oppositionists who had criticized Stalin's policies, that the revolution had remained on track and was now coming to fruition. The new man thus turned into a central emblem of the Stalinist state in the mid- and late 1930s. Revolutionary parades no longer featured marching workers in faceless rows; instead they showcased athletic young people arranged in human pyramids and stars, whose function was to represent the new man as an artifact of the utmost beauty and harmonious completion. The enormous potential for personal self-realization in socialist society was also a central theme of the Tenth Komsomol Congress, held in 1936. Speakers at the congress directly invoked the new man, who assumed plasticity and concreteness, distinct from the futurist and abstract tone that had characterized his portrayals in previous years and decades. "What does it mean to build the new man?" the writer Alexei Tolstoy asked at the congress. "It means to recognize all those conditions in which his personality, nourished by the collective and, in turn, nourishing the collective, develops in most free, splendid, and productive ways." Tolstoy added that the central defining feature of the new man was his well-rounded personality, to be attained in the study of technology and the sciences, the reading of literary classics, and interests in music and the arts.[25]

And yet, for all the specific instructions on how to work and study, Tolstoy and his contemporaries were reluctant to address members of the young generation as fully existing new men and women. It seemed preposterous to fill the very ideal of the revolution with living, and by definition tainted, human material. However pure and perfect exemplary members of Soviet society appeared, there remained a gap between the historical present and the utopian future that could not be bridged, no matter how much it seemed to narrow. It was a gap that also underlay the images of parading youth on Red Square. While these athletes represented the new men and women of the socialist era, they, like everybody else, were admonished to increase their work on themselves in order to further approximate the ideal. What is remarkable about Potemkin is that he sought to erase the modal gap between *is* and *ought* in the representation of the new man. He enacted in his life what in the portrayal of party leaders or members of the literary and artistic professions was a visionary figure or an ideological artifact. On the pages of his diary the new man turned into an acting individual subject, and a subject who squarely inhabited all spheres of his life—not only work and political activities but also the domains of culture, friendship, and love. At this turning point in the mid-1930s, Potemkin redefined his lifelong quest to remake himself into a developed, exemplary personality as the pursuit of the new man.

Potemkin began to clothe himself in the garb of the new man in late 1934, during the second year of his studies. His diary of this period contains extensive reports on so-called Universities of Culture that were being opened in Sverdlovsk, evening schools attached to various technical institutions of higher learning. Created to give science students a broader exposure to the arts and humanities, these schools conveyed the spirit of proletarian humanism and its call for the rounded, completed personality. Potemkin noted enthusiastically that his own Mining Institute was also planning to open a University of Culture, and he eagerly involved himself in the recruitment of students. The new school offered classes on an array of topics, from rhetoric to the sociology of art; Potemkin signed up for literature and art history, regretting that his schedule did not allow him to enroll in more classes. His diary records a passage from the university rector's inaugural speech: "What we need are people who will easily bear the enormous treasures of knowledge."[26]

As part of his newly discovered cultural pursuits, Potemkin also enrolled in a literary circle at the local Belinsky Library. The newspaper editor in charge of the writing class, to whom he read from his diary, was impressed with Potemkin's talent and suggested that he write about the life of a "typical student." The way Potemkin understood and translated this assignment is revealing. On his way home, he noted, he became engrossed in "the major, profound, original idea of depicting the new man with his extraordinarily rich inner world." Though the story was a one-time assignment, its overall theme preoccupied Potemkin for a much longer period. His diary and personal correspondence of the subsequent years turned into the ground for a grandiose project of incarnating the model socialist personality.[27]

It was no accident that the beginning of this project intersected with the opening of the Universities of Culture in Sverdlovsk. Mastery of culture was central to becoming a new man, as can be inferred from Potemkin's detailed descriptions of his manifold readings, visits to theater and opera performances, ice skating, and the ballroom dance classes and excursions to other cities that he organized for his fellow students. Yet while culturedness, subsuming formal education and civilized behavior, was a desired quality, it represented only an outward shell and did not convey the essence of what it meant to be a socialist personality. Potemkin was critical of those who mistook dressing up for true culture, and his criticism echoed the stance of Komsomol leaders who cautioned that wearing a foreign suit and reading books from the prestigious Academia publishing house did not suffice to make one a new man, a process that entailed true mastery of culture and also a program of self-change.[28] Rather, the essence of this human ideal resided in a harmonious "personality," for which the emerging socialist environment provided fertile soil, but which individuals nonetheless had to cultivate on their own.

This nexus shows very well in Potemkin's relationship with music. Confessing to his diary that he was afflicted with "hereditary musical deafness," he eagerly embraced the opportunities now offered to him to further his musical education—classes on music history and the sociology of art, organized at the University of Culture, as well as free admission to theater, concert, and opera performances that he received as a distinguished trade union activist. Potemkin's frequent commentaries on music in the diary, and especially his strenuous exegetical readings of the music he heard, can in part be explained by his desire to demonstrate the belated development of his musical sensibility. But more important for him was to tie music, as well as other cultural pursuits, to the cultivation of his personality, to stress the expressive and mobilizing effects that the appropriation of culture had for his self. This resonates in an account of his visit to the Sverdlovsk opera, where he sat in the "shock workers' box" and listened to Gounod's *Faust:*

> And Charles Gounod's music expresses my feelings . . . Because the composer's expression of his feelings and ideas is so rich, deep, and beautiful, my own feelings are ennobled, my personality develops. I dream about the ideal of my personality and I burn with a selfless, irrepressible passion for perfection for the "onward to the future!" that is so distant. I thirst, I demand gigantic capabilities of myself . . . I need to muster all my potentialities, all my abilities, so as not to smolder, but to blaze up, to inflame, illuminate, and warm people, this alone is the vindication, joy, and great happiness of life.[29]

For Potemkin, the depth of expression he sensed in Gounod's music (and, synonymously, in Gounod's personality) directed him to his own inner expressive potential and provided him with a standard of perfection for the further ennoblement of his personality. Yet in contrast to the Romantic notion of bringing the individual soul into communion with the cosmic spirit, the young Soviet geologist conceived of music as a medium of self-activation and social change. It was to coordinate the psyche, tune his nerves, elevate his will, and make him—as he once wrote after hearing music by Beethoven—"a victorious warrior on the battlefield of life." Beethoven created in him a "most delightful state, where there is no hardship, no self-doubt, where the whole organism is on alert, striving to act and able to act with lightning speed . . . I left Beethoven with life seething up inside me."[30]

One cannot help being struck by the contrast between these lines and Lenin's famous declaration, of about twenty-five years earlier, that there was no piece of music that he preferred over Beethoven's *Appassionata* and that he would readily listen to it every day. "But I can't listen to music often, it affects the nerves and you want to say stupid pleasantries and pat on the head the people who can create such beautiful things while living in hellish conditions. Today one must not pat people on the head—they will bite off your hand. One must beat them over the head, beat them mercilessly, even though ideally we object to any sort of violence against people."[31] The difference between Lenin's and Potemkin's reactions to music shows a temporal shift in their understanding of the Soviet revolutionary project. Lenin, referring to the initial stage of the revolution, called for aesthetic asceticism to temper the self for the bitter class struggle. The revolutionary deliberately sacrificed aesthetic pleasure for the sake of building a better future society that would yield unprecedented cultural richness and harmony. It was precisely from this imaginary future vantage point that Potemkin addressed the question of aesthetics. In socialist society, cultural expression and cultivation of the will went hand in hand, because aesthetic pursuits furthered the total expression of the liberated soul. Voracious consumption of culture, "drinking music," as Potemkin wrote, was a defining trait of the new man.

Far from irritating and softening the organism, as in Lenin's case, music replenished, strengthened, and harmonized Potemkin's psychophysical apparatus. Hearing Tchaikovsky's Sixth Symphony over a public loudspeaker, Potemkin wrote, "ignited in me an irrepressible surge of yearning" to aim for a superior grade in an upcoming exam. At his workplace, his "productivity rose noticeably, my mood was good, everything seemed possible and I felt a sense of fulfillment. At times I experienced fatigue, a clouded aching head, a semi-drowsy state and anxious dread, a nervous quiver, lack of faith in my own strength. From overwork." The last lines of this entry introduce us to a mode of exhaustion, insecurity, and depression that finds rare mention in a diary devoted to reaching a state of constant exaltation, rapture, and heightened political consciousness. But the lines are also remarkable for illustrating that to their author only two modes of being, fundamentally at odds with each other, seemed to exist: total elevation and total depression.[32]

It was not from music alone that Potemkin drew such self-mobilizing power. His summaries of films he saw, lectures he attended, and literature he read contain the same standard declarations as his reaction to Beethoven. A lecture on Heinrich Heine left him "overtaken by an irrepressible . . . urge to demand, exact from myself large-scale actions equal to those of the great people of the past." A film on Kirov filled him with "an irrepressible, surging desire to work with the commanding initiative and energy Kirov possessed." Potemkin read his notes on the film to his sister and she recommended that he submit them to the editors of *The Ural Worker.*[33] His sister's reaction suggests that she was impressed with Potemkin "correct" exegetical reading of the film's ideological message. Potemkin did not write these accounts in a calculating vein. He applied the exact same intensity to all spheres of his life, including personal entanglements. The mandate, so visible in his diary and letters of this period, was to decipher cultural forms for their ideological substance and voluntarist appeal. The ideological and psychophysical dimensions of this cultural engagement went far beyond an attempt to appear outwardly cultured.

And yet there was something specific about Potemkin's relationship toward music, something distinct from his reception of other art forms. This is suggested by the sheer number of references to music in his diary, whether beautiful and arousing tunes spilling from the loudspeaker in the institute's cafeteria, or the "marvelous, tender elegant melodies of the best music ever created by mankind and the charmingly beautiful sounds of the voices of Soviet singers" billowing in the air above a skating rink near his dormitory. While the sites and types of music varied greatly, most of these references shared a pattern in that they served as a background score against which he extolled the expressive richness of his life and the socialist system. At times he did not name the source of the sounds that charmed his ears, which suggests that he may have summoned them into being as an aesthetic device necessary to raise him to a higher, aestheticized plane from which he could rapturously contemplate the ideal.[34] Music, imagined or real, provided an aesthetic and sensual vocabulary that Potemkin employed to represent himself and the world in identical terms of beauty and harmonious unity. Adorning himself with the semantics of music, he could effortlessly fulfill the ideological mandate to cast himself as member of the most joyful and harmoniously configured country on earth. As the melodies formed in his head, he unlocked in himself an aesthetic register that allowed him to go beyond music, to the totality of his strivings in life.

There was another register that Potemkin frequently invoked, which contained an aesthetic and emotional potential similar to music. This was the language of love. In December 1934, only a few months after the University of Culture had opened, Potemkin reported that his busy schedule as a student and a trade union and Komsomol activist had forced him to drop the lectures at the University of Culture except for the literature classes. Without these classes he complained of feeling uninspired, and he looked for a female friend to "express his entire heart" *(dusha),* and to "ennoble" her with the "overflowing feelings of exquisite, tender love." It was as if the rich and refined personality that he was now acquiring required a kindred soul, always represented as a young woman, to whom he could reveal his rich inner world. It never occurred to Potemkin to look for a male friend who might fill this role of soul mate, because he invariably tied the expressive language of the soul to female sensibilities and the semantics of love. At the same time, however, he felt repelled by the girls around him, such as the employees of the university dorm, who responded to his flirtatious gestures. They were "plain, prosaic, and often rude and petty, and not endowed with a theatrical, gentle, sincere scent." He searched for an ideal partner: "In the tram, on the street, and in the reading room I observed people, looking for a friend among them—mainly based on appearance." Eventually, in the reading room of the Belinsky Library, he noticed a "brunette with exquisite facial features, in a blue dress that assumed the shape of her voluptuous but not fat figure of average height." He sat next to her and drew her into a conversation that allowed him to introduce himself. Later he invited her to the theater. When she consented he was so stirred up that he bought a new suit for 109 rubles.[35]

While thus trying to impress her as a cultured young man, he also wrote her a letter about his personality:

> My comrades have complained to me that my only values are refinement, purity, and beauty, but they notice only the external side, but in our socialist society we must demand this from each other too . . . as Marx says, the people's relations should be clear and transparent as rock crystal. This is the time of the socialist society. But there must and can be a special aura only around social roles, over the significance of work for society. All of this is the apogee of perfection. To attain perfection by serving society and succeeding at it, i.e., at socially useful labor, I experience expediency, happiness, and the joy of life . . . I realize I've bored you, but such is my cursory qualitative, and quantitative, too, if you will, analysis of personality.

In the end Potemkin decided not to send this letter, possibly because it portrayed him as overly self-engrossed and did not convey his social orientations and commitments. Instead he wrote her a different letter, which concentrated less on his personality as such than on the mobilizing and socially productive effects of his love: "Zina! Your image has kindled in me a mighty new flame of turbulent reveries and an irrepressible upsurge in my community life. This flame reflects as an aura around the immutable victories of a will destined for triumph." In closing his ardent missive, Potemkin wrote: "Forgive me for my inclination toward the engineering of men's souls, which was inborn to me. But I do not press upon you my canons, there is no need for you to talk to me in my own language. I value any progressive tendencies in a person. With miner's, comradely greetings, L.P."[36]

The type of expressive, activating love articulated by Potemkin was intrinsic to Stalin-era personality ideals. Love was legitimate and even mandated as an expressive conduit of the new man's unfettered soul, but only as long as this expression operated with an inbuilt socialized reflex and thus became sublimated love. Personal love, directed at a particular person, was in no way to eclipse or diminish the primacy of the citizen's social commitments, which demanded the highest tokens of enthusiastic dedication. Potemkin's feelings of love were generated by a particular woman, in this case the brunette from the Belinsky Library, but once he gave voice to these feelings, they transcended the girl and addressed society at large. When after a protracted courtship Potemkin realized that his efforts to woo Zina had failed, he indulged in the sublimating uses of this defeat: "Perhaps this unrequited love is mostly beneficial–it completes a person and, consequently, negates its unrequitedness." But even when a girl responded to his exalted feelings, he did not become totally engrossed in her, but sought to direct the emotional uplift generated by the relationship toward social purposes.[37]

As he did with music, Potemkin seemed to use love to generate an emotionally heightened devotion to the socialist cause. Expressions of personal love were like sparks that set ablaze his burning love for socialist society. In the following account, his description of love for a young woman, Lyudmilla, shifts to an ardent expression of love for the new man:

> Striving toward the greatest range of life, toward utmost fullness, purity, and brightness of life's spectrum, impassioned, I fixed upon Lyudmilla . . . My heart derived inexhaustible joy from her, blazing with an extraordinarily intense fire. It's as if life expressed all of its joy through her. I could not help rejoicing in her the way I cannot help rejoicing in everything truly wonderful–life itself, and happiness–which is life . . . Beauty is not extraordinary illusions, but that for which one strives and that which forges our society. It is the very best humanity has created, the sprouts of [everything] new in our country, beautiful people, and new, pure relations in our society. My heart burns with utmost passion.

In a letter to another girlfriend Potemkin confessed his "sincere and passionate love"—not for her, but for the collective of five hundred students entrusted to his leadership. His desire was to "ignite everyone with the enthusiastic warmth of [my] heart." Love, expressed in personal terms toward a woman, ultimately invoked socialism as the highest object of emotional affection and commitment, to such a degree that Potemkin represented the building of socialism as a labor of love.[38]

Thus Potemkin repeatedly fused images of idealized women with resolutions on work and odes to the socialist future. His ability to master the Stalinist economy of love shows in a passage describing his first date with a young woman: "*June 3 [1936]* Zoya and I went to Uralmash [the Ural Machine Tool Factory] wishing to see the movie *Circus* . . . The pleasant freshness of the evening after a very hot day, and the young and fragrant greenery of the public garden allowed me the joy of sitting with her until [the sounding of] the powerful yet soft, velvet midnight siren of Uralmash. I expressed to her my exalted views about love and life." There is a pronounced socialist sensibility to this picture of two lovers enjoying the fragrance of the square in front of the huge factory compound and exulting in the limitless prospects of their future to the sweet accompaniment of the midnight siren. Once again in need of a musical background for his rapturous odes to love and life, Potemkin imaginatively modulated the factory siren into the tender longing of a Romantic horn.

Potemkin's reveling in music and love as languages of the soul, and his urge to show himself and his environment in tune with the exalted state of his soul, reveals a Romantic disposition. Indeed, his case brings to mind the definition of "revolutionary romanticism" (Gorky), which for a time rivaled "socialist realism" as the official designation for the Stalinist aesthetic doctrine. Yet Potemkin himself used the term "romantic" only pejoratively. He rejected it as a lonely state of useless longing, a fantasy of completion on the part of an unfulfilled subject. In its place he advocated activist struggle as part of the laboring collective as a way to realize his ideals. After once looking in vain for Zina in the reading room of the library, he noted:

> So many touching and tender emotions and thoughts run through my experience. If I were a composer or a poet I would please the ears and inflame the hearts of people with them. Not seeing her, I experienced the loudspeaker's sad melodies with painful bitterness. I felt lonely. But I know that I simply ought to look at things enthusiastically, as a calm adult, and confidently. How often have I promised myself that I wouldn't ponder life, but live.[39]

Romantic brooding was a sad and isolating condition, cut off from life. Life, by contrast, generated optimism by providing a perspective, a purpose, and a role. An intriguing element in this entry is the loudspeaker, which for a change intones sad music, commensurate with the author's despondent mood.

The Making of a Leader

In the act of self-expression, be it through music, love, or work, Potemkin gave proof of his individuality, which he believed to be central to the definition of the new man. The new man was a self-created person; any Soviet citizen carried the potential total personality within himself, but whether this refined personality and its manifold talents and skills would develop was a matter of intense individual work and ultimately a question of will. This voluntarism that underpinned Potemkin's concept of the new man explained why he found it legitimate and important to highlight the unique essence of his personality and make it manifest through self-expression: "Life is irreversible. Life is fleeting. Am I not unique in this world? I grabbed on to life like a dying man . . . To give to society—to give myself the best possible opportunity . . . To make all opportunities blossom." His emphasis on self-created individuality was in tune with official views of the socialist person. Speakers at the Komsomol congress in 1936 emphasized that this was not a mass-produced, faceless resident of barracks socialism, as "bourgeois ideologists" would have it. "On the contrary, socialism means the highest development of individuality in people, it is a society in which every person can express his abilities and talents."[40]

The more one expressed one's personality, allowed its physical, intellectual, and artistic abilities to unfold, the more one received recognition as an exceptional individual in Stalinist culture. This situates the Stakhanovite movement in the logic of the emerging new man. Stakhanovite activists were venerated as iconic representations of the new man because they fully actualized and expressed their socialist selves. This also explains why Stakhanovites were not portrayed as *just* workers, as had been the case with the shockworker of the First Five-Year Plan, but as workers *and* cultured beings, and it was precisely the harmonious totality of their expressive lives that enabled them to accomplish their quasi-miraculous deeds. Stakhanovites were publicly portrayed as experiencing life differently from ordinary mortals: more fully, intensely, and authentically. Thanks to their extraordinarily developed personalities they were living the "full-blooded life of the Stalinist generation."[41] Similarly, Potemkin distinguished between two types of life, an inferior, gray existence that was *lived through* merely for the sake of its biological duration, and a vastly superior, heroic life, however brief, that *was actively lived* for the expressive capacities it offered: "I am contemptuous of those who are stingy in their lives. Those who shrink away from the hardships of life for the sake of preserving as much as possible their miserable, wasting life."[42]

Voluntarist and expressivist at heart, the new man logically had to excel as a hero or a social leader in order to be truly himself. Potemkin's diary of the mid-1930s is filled with claims that he occupied leadership roles—among others, trade union secretary, student organizer, military platoon commander, Communist agitator. When, in connection with the appearance of cultured activities in Sverdlovsk in 1934, he organized a class in ballroom dancing, his stated principal purpose was to practice leadership skills and master the choreography of "directing the masses," rather than to learn to dance.[43]

In describing his aspiration to be a leader, Potemkin often included observations on the development of his personality. To be a legitimate leader, to command other people and shape their personalities, he had to have full command over himself and be a fully formed personality. After being appointed a platoon commander in the Red Army summer camp, he commented: "How I longed to become a full-fledged commander. For to be a good commander means to be a full-fledged personality . . . Among our commanders here I have seen the most worthy people of our heroic time. They are heroic examples of the new men of socialist society. Men of the Bolshevik tribe." A full-fledged personality also possessed a collectivist consciousness. Potemkin described this consciousness as the critical agent that shielded him from any individualist abuses of his leadership role and ensured that he always served the interests of the collective. As a leader, he wrote, his desire was not to "excel but to do everything that is possible for the collective . . . the 'I' is embodied in principled, moral leadership, dissolves in the goals of the latter." And, Potemkin noted elsewhere, the role of leader was not static and stable, but was always defined in dynamic, dialectical terms vis-à-vis the collective. While he sought to mold the collective, the collective simultaneously furthered his own education.[44]

He anxiously monitored his performance as leader, his interactions with others, his authority. While at times he pointed to his "deficiencies," namely his "occasional lack of cheerfulness and self-confidence," at other times he felt that he had been fully transformed, that he was experiencing life fully for the first time. On a student geological mission in the spring of 1935 he quarreled with a brigade leader over working methods. In the end Potemkin was proven right. In his diary he wrote:

> Now, for the first time in my life, I have squared my shoulders freely, boldly, fervently, and maybe even audaciously and can look at people with triumphant self-confidence. I am in the front ranks of those who are mastering the technology of production. I am not only a member of a production brigade, I am an assistant brigade leader . . . With intense emotion and rapture I pronounce the words of S. M. Kirov: "Our working class has firmly taken into its own hands the population of our great country, 170 million strong." In this lies the invincible force of my will destined to triumph. This force is the great fairness, genius, and wisdom, the vital might of the class and its brain, the party, whose child I am being cultivated to become. We are free.[45]

His personal triumph did not stand on its own, but evolved from an individual ("I") to a collective subject ("we"). Stalin-era self-assertion, it seems, unfolded in a collectivist register, through the articulation of a personal voice that was embedded, both historically and socially, in the story of the lawful triumph of the Soviet working class, represented by its vanguard force, the Communist party.

In casting himself in such heroic terms, Potemkin did more than describe features of the socialist personality. His descriptions had the purpose of glorifying the healthy, optimistic, beautiful, and heroic life of the socialist era that made the appearance of this ideal human type possible. The recognition that, after the bitter struggles of the First

Five-Year Plan, life had become better and qualitatively different, not only was conveyed in Stalin's famous slogan "Life has become better, comrades, life has become merrier," but reverberated through other public statements as well, so much so that Stalinist ideology of the immediate prewar years might be summarized—somewhat paradoxically given the terror and repression that defined this age—as a call to live life to the full. Even a 65-year-old Leningrad worker who addressed the Tenth Komsomol Congress claimed that his life had only just begun now that the Soviet order gave him the opportunity to live freely and express himself fully.[46]

Life, invoked in such vitalist tones, was to be understood not empirically, in the sense of a person's daily life, but historically. It referred to a specific historical epoch, that of socialism, which was a priori defined in vitalist terms, as strong, optimistic, and full-bodied. When Potemkin and the old worker at the Komsomol Congress spoke of their "joyful life" they had in mind not a carefree state of being but a substantive existence with a historical duty to reorder life; it was in the execution of this mission that true happiness could be felt. As Potemkin wrote to a girlfriend: "Only the struggle to realize the aspirations of the mind is genuine life—its purpose and great joy. Our life and our youth are fortunate precisely because we have every opportunity not only to dream, but to realize our dreams." This glorification of "life" in terms of strength, health, beauty, optimism, and daring, in contrast to a lowly, philistine "existence," has an unmistakable Nietzschean flair. Several of the writers to whom Potemkin turned for inspiration—Maxim Gorky, Anatoly Lunacharsky, Nikolai Ostrovsky, Jack London, Upton Sinclair—were known to have been students of Nietzsche's. Yet important traits of Potemkin's new man were decidedly not Nietzschean. While Nietzsche's superman is a loner rising above the crowd, Potemkin advocated a collectivist subjectivity: the more the individual personality developed, the more it incorporated—in spirit and in deeds—

the life of the collective as a whole. The Soviet new man developed in line with history's progression, in contrast to the *Übermensch,* who was defined by his rebellion against historical and cultural constraints.[47]

Potemkin's view of his personal life was historicist through and through, reflecting an understanding that the laws of history shaped his individual life as much as they did the life of the revolutionary project. In his first diary entry for 1936 he wrote: "The new year finds me successful in my studies and in my community work. Set myself a new motto: more life! More ease in my work and deeds. I have to be able to take the joys of life, to embody them in myself and to be able to create them in others." If read outside their historicist context, these lines would bespeak a bizarre tension between the ease of life craved by Potemkin and the effort necessary to bring it about. But the "joys of life" were in fact ideological mandates, qualities that he had to embody to be in tune with history's progression, and mastering and effortlessly displaying them hence demanded a great deal of labor. Marking the beginning of a new year, these lines gave a sense of yet another threshold that the revolutionary project had crossed. The revolutionary calendar operated inside a dedicated Soviet citizen, structuring his personal life and lending it biographical shape.

Awareness of the historical time line operating in his life lent Potemkin's self-transformation urgency, impatience, and occasional dissatisfaction, given the lofty standards against which he measured his development. His, and Soviet youth's, historical mandate was nothing less than to rise above the towering cultural figures of the past. In a conversation with a fellow student Potemkin could not clearly state his goals in life. The other student remarked: "Goethe also did not know who he would become, but he believed that he would be a genius and studied philosophy, literature, art, and natural sciences. Consequently, a great poet with universal erudition was formed." Potemkin noted that this "resonated" with him, "inspired" him: "I cannot study—I am too preoccupied with the marvelous images of my fantasies." He was aware of how daunting a comparison this was, yet he believed that "in order not to drag yourself along in the footsteps of history, in order to go forth joyfully, worthy of our time and role in history, you have to be ahead of the leaders of the past, we need to be greater than the great people of the past."[48]

Potemkin's declaration unwittingly echoed the concluding section of Leon Trotsky's *Literature and Revolution,* written in the early 1920s, in which Trotsky predicted that, in the future socialist society, the "average human type" would rise to "the heights of an Aristotle, a Goethe, or a Marx. And above this ridge new peaks will rise." Trotsky meant that at the end point of a historical process of rationalization, actively pursued by the Communist regime, the human psyche would be so well ordered that it would release unheard-of creative energies. Trotsky located his vision in a far distant future, and he derided fellow revolutionaries who dreamed of creating the new man in the here and now.[49] Yet only a decade later this scenario was appropriated by a Sverdlovsk geology student who upon ordering his soul proceeded to express himself as a model new man, measuring himself against the most creative minds of the past. The dawning socialist age, Potemkin repeatedly pointed out, was beginning to produce people as beautiful as the Venus de Milo, people whose personal and social relations were "noble, bright, and clear as crystal." In the era of socialism, the purity of rock crystal and the grace of classical goddesses displaced the ideal of the diamond, symbol of the tough and virile proletarian worker.[50]

Given Potemkin's vocal commitment to a full-blooded and expressive life, it comes as no surprise that occasionally he was dissatisfied with his limited horizons as a scientist working on the Soviet periphery. He dreamed of transferring to the Moscow Institute of Philosophy, Literature, and History (IFLI), a recently founded elite university dedicated to humanist learning. In the midst of exalted musings on the dawning socialist age he paused: "Again, the thought of transferring to the Historical-Philosophical Institute has agitated me. The work of a geologist is a parody of my desires, strivings, and more than that, it is the death of my ideals." Yet in the end he remained at the Mining Institute—in part because his chances of being admitted to IFLI were very slight, but partly also because he came to find fulfillment elsewhere: in the Communist party.[51]

Early on, Potemkin had sought to become politically active. As a 16-year-old he gave improvised lectures in villages near his school to enlighten the peasantry. Throughout his diary, political education—the development of Communist theory as well as his practical skills as a political organizer and leader—emerges as his most important concern: "to tirelessly work on raising the level of my cultural-theoretical development, incorporating, absorbing into myself the ideal of a social activist and theoretician, a revolutionary, a party worker of the great school of Lenin." The recognition he received from lecturing to his peers filled him with relaxed and cheerful self-confidence—a quality of the ideal personality that he enviously perceived in other young people but felt mostly unable to experience himself, given his self-diagnosed psycho-physical underdevelopment.[52]

Potemkin applied for membership in the Komsomol in 1932, after arriving at the prospecting mine, but when the mine was disbanded and he enrolled in the Mining Institute his application fell through. The lingering suspicions about his social origins might explain why he did not join the youth organization in 1933, upon enrollment in the Mining Institute. In November 1934, on the eve of the revolutionary holiday, he finally became a komsomolist, and within a few weeks articles by him began to appear in the institute newspaper. For Potemkin the fall of 1934 marked a threshold in his development: "I celebrated the seventeenth anniversary of the October Revolution (at the age of 20), for the first time satisfied with a certain degree of personal worthiness." While augmenting his self-worth, the act of joining the Communist movement also flowed from Potemkin's conviction that a subjective existence on its own possessed no value unless it tied itself to a social movement with a universal purpose. But Potemkin cited yet another source of appeal. Communism was to him a supreme art that raised his own activity as a Communist to an artistic practice. His diary points to an important aesthetic attraction of the Communist project in its Stalinist guise.[53]

After serving as a trade union representative for several years, Potemkin was nominated to the responsible position of political agitator in 1936. For him a long-held "dream," the very essence of his "striving," had come true: "There is no role more meaningful or beautiful. I plunged rapturously into my study of this, the greatest of arts, at the feet of Lenin, Kirov, and other leaders of the party." After being reelected as trade union organizer he noted in similar terms: "My life was palpable to me: I felt that my personality was flourishing, and I was blooming with all my potential—as an artist with his talent."[54]

Potemkin described the agitator as artist in two ways. For one, he was engaged in the art of speech. Only a Communist who mastered speech was able to ignite and enrapture his listeners and thus connect to their souls. Potemkin wrote of the "oratorical art of the school of Lenin and Stalin" as "the most paramount, mighty, and delightful of all the arts." The evening classes he attended at the University of Culture included the subject "culture of speech," a discipline that also appeared as one of the desired qualities he listed in his New Year's resolution for 1935. He critically monitored his deficiencies as a public speaker, but also recorded his triumphant moments: "My pure, clear, resolute voice splendidly concentrates the attention of the platoon." On another occasion he wrote to his mother: "My voice not only commanded an auditorium with its power—it was bigger than that—it raised my spirit and self-confidence. My speech ended in applause." While the art of speech, when properly mastered, inflamed the audience, making it hot and malleable like melted iron, a second art was required of the activist to educate and mold the collective entrusted to him: the art of leadership. At the Tenth Komsomol congress in 1936 the "art of leadership," though repeatedly mentioned, was understood metaphorically. Potemkin, by contrast, endowed the term with a literal artistic meaning. The leader's task was to "take under [his] influence and leadership the personality of each student," to engineer their souls according to standards of aesthetic perfection, and ultimately, to forge a "cohesive collective." After "forcing them to correct their flaws, to overcome the residue of their former backward consciousness," Potemkin hoped to raise the students entrusted to his supervision to "full-fledged commanders" in their own right.[55]

Potemkin was satisfied to note that what he had previously sought to achieve in his own life, namely the cultivation of his personality, was now turning into a social task. The effects of his efforts to create model

Potemkin (center) and fellow aspiring geologists, 1935.
© Leonid Potemkin, Moscow

socialist personalities showed in the accounts *(kharakteristiki)* of the best shockworkers and activists, which he read to large audiences at the institute with "boundless delight." Presenting the biographies of his exemplary students, Potemkin assigned himself a life-creating role, and this demiurgic impetus underwrites the scenes in which he described himself "kindling the passion" of his comrades, or "igniting the flames of our shared joy."[56]

Leonid Potemkin in 1937.
© Leonid Potemkin, Moscow

The work of the Communist activist was an applied art that raised him from the role of an aspiring technical engineer to that of a human engineer cum artist. The Communist as artist could treat man and nature in their entirety as a huge canvas, to be worked on to realize his designs for a social order of utmost beauty and perfection.[57]

Potemkin's new self-representation as an unfettered socialist citizen was so much at odds with his extremely critical previous self-appraisals that one wonders how he could relate these views to each other and whether his claimed new identity contained credible biographical substance. As late as October 1934 he still moved within the old frame of self-definition as an underdeveloped, sickly youth. At that time he began a new diary notebook, which he entitled "The philosophical-lyrical sensations of an abnormal youth, i.e., a youth with a center of gravity not in the external world, but in the internal one."[58] And yet within only a few months this problematic youth began to represent himself as an emerging new man. An individual "pathology" suddenly acquired paradigmatic cultural value. How did Potemkin make sense of this stunning change in his self-representation?

Potemkin noticed—and appreciated—that he was changing outwardly. With evident satisfaction he reported that relatives and childhood friends whom he had not seen in a long time would exlaim that he had changed beyond recognition. Photographs of Potemkin during the years of his university studies show him changed as well: he appears dressed in a suit with tie and confidently faces the camera. Yet for all these external signs of change he stressed that the real locus and dynamic of his transformation were inward, in his mind and soul. And he insisted that his progression was lawful—that it corresponded to the Marxist laws of dialectical and historical materialism.

This becomes apparent in a diary entry recorded in the fall of 1935, which began with the words: "The primary source of my internal life was my experience of poverty and deprivations in childhood." Potemkin then described being sent by his mother and sister to beg "'in the name of Christ'": "Just seven years old, I'm showered with cruel ridicule and mocking insults . . . I don't go to school in the winter, I have nothing to wear . . . The usual carefree games of childhood passed me by." At this point Potemkin's retrospective frame widened, as the story of his subjective self was supplemented by a macrohistorical account: "The material violence committed against mental and moral freedom from generation to generation inculcated spiritual enslavement, feeblemindedness, and weakness of will in people doomed to material poverty. An inherited loss of a sense of one's own human virtues and of faith in one's own virtues and their free development. That is what troubled my consciousness and stirred my will to indignation and protest."[59] These and other autobiographical passages resonate with the Marxist history of the proletariat, subjugated by the capitalist system but then rising up against its oppressors. When Potemkin wrote about his own emerging consciousness and rebellious will, he inscribed himself into a universal narrative of the proletariat and the dialectic of suffering and rebellion, deprivation and fullness, being nothing and becoming everything that undergirded its mythical history.

The importance of the Marxist metanarrative of the proletariat for Potemkin's self-image can be gauged from his angry reaction when his aunt expressed surprise at seeing her nephew Lyonya transformed into an aspiring engineer dressed in suit and tie. Clearly in his youth she "had not seen through the shell of poverty" to recognize his potential. "No!" he exclaimed to his diary. "It is not by sheer chance that I am in the institute, it is the necessary consequence of the socialist revolution, which raised us up from below and elevated us above their heads . . . Our will is triumphant . . . Only we children of poverty and incredible hardship must and can create the new society . . . Only we are granted the mission of . . . giving mankind a chance to really bloom."[60]

Potemkin was deeply invested in Marxist-Leninist dialectics as a personal way of life. Dialectial materialism *(diamat)*—the Marxist science of the lawful development of nature, society, and consciousness in an ongoing process of struggle—to him signified more than a prescribed worldview learned from textbooks; it was the core of the Communist catechism and as such had tangible life-creating effects, unifying his past and present experiences, thoughts, and actions into a cohesive and purposeful biography. Dialectics was the red thread of his life, tying together and directing seemingly disjointed, accidental impulses and actions and unifying the various appearances of his self. The truth about his self was contained in its dialectical progression, and it was disclosed in the retrospective gaze, in the act of taking stock of his development and rereading past passages from his diary. In establishing the truth about himself, Potemkin made a point of distinguishing between psychology and history. Although at times he believed that he was propelled by "psychological motives," intense reflection helped him realize that the driving force in his life was his conscious will, which was historical and directed by the laws of Marxist dialectics. This explained the "sequential and purposeful" nature of his unfolding life.[61]

Besides being integral to Potemkin's conception of self, mastery of dialectics was also a key to his recognition and success in Stalinist society. In the diary he reported that the teacher of *diamat* was dissatisfied with the performance of the class. As student leader, Potemkin resolved to organize collective learning sessions for his peers in need of ideological training. For this purpose he even produced a handwritten textbook on *diamat*, numbering 186 pages.[62] At a subsequent oral exam in dialectical and historical materialism, Potemkin was called upon to compete against the best student of *diamat* in front of the class. The best student started first and received a good grade. Then it was Potemkin's turn. With clamorous support from the whole class (an important detail, given Potemkin's sensitivity to the collectivist underpinnings of selfhood), he displayed such an impressive knowledge of "the essence of Hegelian philosophy" that the instructor had to reconsider his earlier assertion that he would not give the highest grade to any ordinary human, or even to "God himself," but only to the one "who would grab stars from the sky"—a reference to Prometheus, the mythical forefather of the Marxist proletariat. In front of a faculty commission the instructor declared that Potemkin was a "leader in mastery of Marxism."

After one of his improvised lectures, Potemkin noted in his diary, he was "showered with attention": the girls seized him by the arms, him, whom "no one ever loved and in fact who had nothing to be loved for." He went on: "The love in me which was not accepted by a single girl flared up in the form of a love for society and the bright joy of a great love of society. Not only will I compel a girl who fascinates me to love me, but all society will love and respect me too." Even this commentary on *diamat* and its effects was dialectically informed. He who in the past had been ugly, insignificant, incapable of finding personal love, had embarked on a path of individual self-training, had embraced society, and now in turn was rewarded with a love from society that was infinitely superior to the love he had once felt for certain girls—superior to any notion of individual love. This pattern of thinking suggested that he now felt he had achieved a happy synthesis in his personal development, and indeed, in the margin next to one of the autobiographical diary entries he wrote in small letters: "triumph of development."[63]

Preserving Purity amid Filth

In the fall of 1934, when Leonid Potemkin met with the editor of the *Miner's Storm* and decided to represent himself as a model socialist personality, he stated programmatically: "I will recognize myself as an emerging writer. I know what to do. The plan is worked out. The only thing left to do is to execute it, . . . to completely realize the project." Almost exactly two years later, in September 1936, he decided to break off the project. While cruising the Volga on the steamship *Turgenev* and nearing the city of Gorky, he contemplated his "literary dreams." He realized that in comparison with the great Maxim Gorky, who had died earlier that year, his goals had been overly ambitious and he had failed at using the diary for the representation of his rich inner world. Instead he resolved to share his "psychic world and its achievements" in "written and oral" communications with other people.[64]

Looking back at his diary of the past five years, Potemkin tried to understand why it had come into being and what it had been about. When he was an adolescent, he explained, no one had paid attention to him or shown him respect. This had incited him to keep a diary and lock himself up in a "sphere of self-analysis." Diaries were surrogate companions for lonely or deformed people who lacked real-life comrades to help them carry out their work of self-analysis and self-transformation. Now that he was widely noticed as a leader, he could "confidently and with affection turn over to people the treasure of my inner world." Potemkin had in mind female friends in particular. A woman to him was a "comrade in spiritual and creative life." Intimate dialogue with a female friend best expressed the life of the soul and would stir him into the heightened aesthetic sensibility essential for his vocation as a Communist. But it was not easy to find a woman who shared his platonic vision—all his female friends thought about was how to get him to marry them.[65]

It is with these thoughts that Potemkin's diary notebook ends. There is, however, a source that sheds light on his personal life for the next two years, 1937 and 1938. It is his correspondence, 157 pages of it, with Ira Zhirkova, a young woman who was studying literature in Gorky. She seems to have come as close to his ideal of a female soul mate as he could possibly expect.[66] In his letters to Zhirkova, Potemkin remained committed to the agenda of personality formation and the ideal of the new man. In showing these issues in the interactive exchange between friends, the letters shed light on the meaning of friendship and the contours and significance of privacy as understood by two young Soviet citizens.

Potemkin met Zhirkova through his sister, who had left Sverdlovsk in 1932 to study at the Gorky Institute for Construction Engineering, and he initiated their correspondence after this encounter. While expressions of affection and longing in the letters could suggest that the two were lovers, Potemkin later insisted that the relationship was entirely platonic. The principal theme and purpose of the correspondence was spiritual communion. Both correspondents sought to exhibit their innermost, most tender emotions and their striving for moral purity. As Zhirkova put it, the letters were to aid in the education of their souls. Both emphasized how sincere they were in the display of their feelings. In response to Ira's accusation that in one letter he was hiding his true sentiments behind "official rhetoric," Leonid declared that he had never written anything other than what was in his consciousness and soul: "A letter is the most sincere expression of the emotions of my inner world."[67] To underscore their sincerity as well as their trust in each other, Potemkin and Zhirkova also gave each other their diaries to read.

Beyond the open display of the individual's rich inner world, the "anatomy of the soul" that Potemkin and Zhirkova performed in these letters was done for the purpose of monitoring and perfecting their spiritual progression. On the twentieth anniversary of the October Revolution, Leonid lauded the "splendid and majestic blossoming of the greenhouse of socialist culture," and in the same breath he wished Ira, who had been born the year of the revolution, "full and majestic blossoming of your spiritual capacity, to add even greater beauty to this greenhouse."[68] At times their exchange revealed ideological disagreements, which impelled Potemkin in particular to criticize the deviations of his erring partner. He read her letters sternly and analytically, as if grading a student's papers on historical materialism: "At last I have completed a detailed review of your letter. Now let me draw general conclusions." In one letter he listed ideologically questionable statements she had made, such as: "Nature in no way is created for human happiness and the human being is utterly incapable of forging happiness. Contemporary people cannot help wanting to run away from this unfortunate time." Following this incriminating evidence came his call to ideological reason:

> Ira, I am explaining this in a very tired state, late at night. You see, you cannot write from just any point of view. I do not want to give you my criticism of these glaring untruths because I hope that you yourself will refute them. I do not draw just any conclusions, but conclusions from the perspective of the society to which I belong, and I am displeased that you look at my reproofs, as you put it, with different eyes. And even more so if they do not force you to reconsider. I write this with pain in my heart.[69]

For her part, Zhirkova gently chided her friend as an "incorrigible dreamer": "You idealize everything. I completely agree with your arguments about life . . . But to your words one must add 'that's the way it ought to be,' and to mine 'that's the way it is, that's that.'" In response, Potemkin informed her that the idealism she attributed to him was a historically outdated position that progressive-minded people clung to as a way to "escape dreadful reality for a moment"; by contrast, the ideals he invoked were being realized in the construction of socialism, and his enthusiasm was founded on the knowledge that he himself would be among the first to "see the first incarnation of the ideal in real life."[70]

But Potemkin also confessed to weaknesses in his worldview and asked Zhirkova for advice: "Ira, my darling, please hear the confession of my worthless heart." He admitted to a "latest [bout of] depression" of sorts. Having attained everything—highest grades, recognition as a student leader, and "blind attraction to a woman"—he had no more goals to strive for, and the "blaze" of his "soul" was extinguished: "O, Mining Institute, nothing within your scope is capable of inflaming my soul anymore. I'm like a cat that ate the cream and gazes at what's left on the plate with an unhappy expression. No, I'm not an engineer, nor a geologist—my heart stands in the way."[71]

Potemkin's affliction might be diagnosed as a case of utopian melancholia. If his sense of self was defined historically, and if he thus realized himself in the act of becoming, attainment of the ideal could not provide lasting fulfillment. On the contrary, it undermined his sense of self and undercut his willpower, which was generated in the very striving toward higher goals. Utopian melancholia could not have afflicted Soviet citizens in the 1920s, when the utopian ideal of Communist society was so clearly distant from the impure present order. Once socialism was declared to have come into being, however, this form of melancholia became possible. Its outbreak was a sign that the Communist in question had slipped in willpower and surrendered to the temptations of his uncontrolled body. If he could not bring himself to fight his residual old self, it was the duty of his friend to help. Acting as Potemkin's confessor, Zhirkova chastised him for "pessimism" and a "lack of courage and confidence in your strength." Any depression reflexively unleashed self-accusation and thus was enjoined by a call for renewed action.[72]

For Potemkin these mutual confessions and corrections formed the essence of his relationship with Zhirkova: "I derive so much gratification from our friendship because it allows us to understand, share the life of the inner world, and help each other evaluate our strengths in order to use them intelligently. Friendship ought to help one correct flaws, develop the culture of personality, and live a conscious, aspiring life." The central purpose of Potemkin's correspondence with Zhirkova was to forge a Communist type of friendship. The spiritual affinity between friends was to be used for mutual personality formation and the pursuit of a rationalist, ideologically committed life. Sharing a "common language of the soul," friends could help each other detect and overcome personal deficiencies.[73]

The edifying and exemplary qualities of Potemkin's friendship with

Potemkin making a copy of one of his letters to Ira Zhirkova.

Zhirkova demanded to be put on display. While both correspondents stressed their total sincerity toward each other, they never conceived of their writings as private in the sense of a hidden, secret realm distinct from public values. A photograph of Potemkin sitting in the reading room of the Mining Institute is suggestive in this regard. As he later explained, after writing one of his first letters to Zhirkova, he read it to his friend Nikolai Aleinikov (also shown in the picture). Nikolai "noticed something interesting" in the letter and urged Leonid to make a copy to keep. As the photo illustrates, the correspondence with Zhirkova thrived on the semi-private stage Potemkin shared with his friends at the institute. The writing of the letter was monitored not only by fellow students (Nikolai and the photographer) but also by the young Lenin, whose statue adorned the reading room. The wall newspapers in the background underscore the link between the intimate letter and Communist ideology, suggesting that Leonid's letters to Ira elaborated on the newspaper's odes to socialist life.[74]

Potemkin's and Zhirkova's gestures of sincerity must be situated in the context of the suspicion, denunciations, and forced confessions that pervaded the time when they took up their correspondence. Seen through this lens, the sentimentalist mode they practiced can be read as a form of moral cleansing and absolution indispensable for their physical and spiritual self-preservation. Zhirkova frequently mentioned that she wrote the letters late at night, and they both alluded to being exhausted by their schedules of education, work, and social and cultural activities. As Ira noted in one letter:

> I'm up to my neck in work right now and have literally not a free minute for myself. The morning in the institute, errands during the day; at work starting at 4 P.M. and from there to foreign language courses at 7:30 P.M. I go to the theater, the movies, read lit-

> erature, and of course work on myself. Sometimes such a life is a bit exhausting, but all in all I'm satisfied . . . I'm writing [this] during the literature class.[75]

The exalted language of the soul in these thoughtful, crafted letters was produced in an environment of impatient learning, frenzied construction, and incessant political campaigning against double-dealers and hidden enemies of the people.

A background of political terror appears in oblique ways in Potemkin's diary and correspondence. His embrace of a healthy, strong, vitalist life carried a hidden shadow, a mostly implicit but at times direct and harsh condemnation of weak, outdated social phenomena. In early 1935 he mentioned a public presentation at the university devoted to the "low-life scum of the Zinoviev group." A rare direct reference to political repression came from Ira: "Leo, I'm so happy that you are one of those people I respect, before whom I bow down and on whom I look with wide eyes—because you are one of the few who, amid utter dirt, has preserved a purity within yourself." Both correspondents thus extolled their ideals of spiritual beauty and purity, and their vision of a bright future, against a largely unmentioned but looming background of present impurity, struggle, and death.[76]

In the context of political terror the friendship between Potemkin and Zhirkova had certain Romantic connotations. In ways similar to German Romanticism, which cultivated friendship as a refuge from the egoism of the bourgeois world, these young Soviet citizens engaged in their mutual projections of virtue and purity in part to shield themselves from the polluting incursions of the political realm. However, Potemkin did not cultivate friendship as a polar opposite to the social sphere; on the contrary, he always insisted that personal feelings remain subordinate to his overriding commitment to build the new order.

A Symbolic Life

In one letter to Zhirkova, Potemkin reminded her: "You see, the human being is born not for just any purpose, merely to live out his lifespan, but so that he can make the world better by his presence in it. And this is impossible without striving toward perfection, toward an ideal personality and [an ideal] society." Potemkin's attempt to realize himself as a model personality of his time fits Lydia Ginzburg's notion of symbolic behavior. Symbolic behavior occurs at the junction between a historical personality type and a given individual. The more an individual imbues himself with the features of the generalized ideal type of personality, the more symbolic his behavior becomes. Ginzburg adds: "Real-life symbolization is most clearly evident at historical turning points when 'new men' with new principles of behavior are born . . . when especially close attention is paid to individual personality. The most 'semiotic' and expressive people at such times are those whose individual features are best suited to the historical model in question." Ginzburg traced symbolic behavior in the lives of nineteenth-century Russian thinkers, including Alexander Herzen and Vissarion Belinsky, who had grown up in the spirit of German idealism but were disappointed with its political conservatism and groped toward a new, "realist" ethics that put greater emphasis on a critical engagement of the self with the world. In similar fashion, Potemkin lived through a turning point when the Soviet regime began to deploy a new ideal type of personality, and it was this model new man that he sought to embody. Like his Romantic forebears he used the medium of "documentary fiction," personal letters and the diary in particular, to represent himself in terms of this ideal personality. The chief purpose of the letters was not publication but the articulation of the new personality type.[77]

Of the Russian Romantics discussed by Ginzburg, the most persistent in incarnating a new, democratic personality type was the literary critic Belinsky. The acute desire to remake himself into an exemplary new man of the dawning realist age may have stemmed in part from Belinsky's attempt to transcend his modest social background, which separated him from the other, aristocratic members of his intellectual circle. In Potemkin's case, too, his lowly social background seems correlated with the intensity of the quest to remake himself. And in fact in his quest for self-perfection Potemkin explicitly and repeatedly cited Belinsky.

The correspondence with Zhirkova abounds with references to Belinsky's views on personality and personal fulfillment, and in addition, as part of his studies at the Ural Mining Institute, Potemkin filled two notebooks with excerpts from his readings of Belinsky. As a revolutionary democrat and humanist, and as a precursor of the socialist realist aesthetic, Belinsky was often cited in Soviet literary and pedagogical discussions of the mid- and late 1930s, a time that also witnessed a surge in the publication of books about him. The Sverdlovsk library in which Potemkin had attended the literary circle and met a girl of his dreams bore Belinsky's name. In his correspondence with Zhirkova, Potemkin referred to Belinsky's notion of "spiritual friendship" and "spiritual union" as the source of personal fulfillment and the essence of life. He once wrote to her: "My soul is alive and at peace only in those moments that I devote to Goethe, Belinsky, and others. Only they make my soul rise from the gloom of everyday interests, refresh the perception of life, and illuminate consciousness. My only wish now is to be in your embrace, read Belinsky with you, and think and write with you."[78]

Potemkin fully subscribed to Belinsky's ideal of an authentic life to be reached through the elevation of the subjective self to the level of objective reality, embodied in the general principles of "society," "humanity," and the "laws of history."[79] Most of all, the way Potemkin posed as a new man and connected this pose to a moral commitment echoed Belinsky's case. A moral absolutist, Belinsky held that moral ideas expounded in a literary text were valid only if they were fully embraced by their author in his personal life. It seems that in letters to his friends Belinsky deliberately put his moral personality on display, open for himself and others to judge. Potemkin likewise talked about his desire to live a historically paradigmatic life, and given the moral stakes of this project, he also felt the imperative to make it publicly visible. He once noted in his diary that he wanted to "live life beautifully so that others could learn from it," and added: "I feel that I will [one day] stand before the court of society, where the details of my life will be examined. I feel that I am under inspection."[80]

While Potemkin consciously modeled himself on Belinsky, Belinsky also projected himself onto Potemkin and the young Soviet generation. A monograph on Belinsky published in 1939 featured as epigraph a quotation from Belinsky: "We envy our grandchildren and great grandchildren, who are fated to see Russia in 1940—standing at the head of the educated world, providing laws to science and art, and receiving tributes of respect from all enlightened humanity." There was thus a dialogue on the new man connecting Potemkin and Belinsky across a century of revolutionary thought and practice, a dialogue that because of the historical consciousness they shared could be practiced in both chronological and reverse chronological order. The positions of the two differed only in that Belinsky perceived himself as a mere precursor of the new man. One hundred years later, and right on schedule according to Belinsky's timeline, Potemkin portrayed himself as a living new man who had approximated the ideal harmony between the personal and the social.[81]

Potemkin retained his interest in personality formation beyond the period documented in the diary and the correspondence with Zhirkova. In the summer of 1942, while he was on a geological mission in the Caucasus and at about the time when his brother Vladimir, a Red

Army officer, went missing in action, Potemkin wrote a manual entitled "Strategy of Life." The booklet was to provide direction for young Soviet men and women on "what personality and life ought to be in the epoch of socialism." That epoch was the first time in mankind's history when a whole society proceeded on the path of "conscious and lawful development." This demanded that each socialist citizen "become involved in solving the social problems of your time," and in so doing rise

Leonid Potemkin (right) with his mother, his sister Nina, and his brother Vladimir, 1940.

"ideologically and creatively to the heights of the epoch." At a moment when "streams of human blood" were being shed in the war and ever more of his peers were being killed, Potemkin felt the need to pass on to future generations the insights his generation had gained in the previous decade.[82]

The document makes it clear that the new man remained central to Potemkin's understanding of himself and his time. The first pages featured aphorisms from, among others, Pushkin, Belinsky, Heine, Gorky, Jack London, and Nikolai Ostrovsky, extolling an expressive or heroic life and summoning readers to fight for the realization of their ideals. Following the opening remark, "The socialist revolution raised the question of personality," a subsequent section listed quotations, mostly with references to a source (a newspaper or journal—*Pravda, Komsomolskaya Pravda, Molodaya gvardia,* or a Soviet leader—Lenin, Stalin, Zhdanov) on the features of the Soviet new man. Positive character traits, such as "an unwavering strength of Marxist convictions, iron willpower, inner concentration, decisiveness, precision, and great simplicity of people of action," were juxtaposed to outdated, bourgeois personality features: "subjectivism of the past," "philistinism," "jealousy," "arrogance," "obsequiousness," "decadence," "suffering." The remaining sections of the booklet listed recommended methods of self-perfection, including mastery of culture and science, techniques of labor rationalization (with suggestions on timekeeping and on how to divide work from rest), training of the will, daily gymnastics, and bodily self-control. All in all, Potemkin regarded his manual as a call for purposeful thought and behavior in the service of building a Communist society and advancing human progress, tasks of such magnitude that it was unacceptable to "live . . . 'as you wish.'"[83]

In this tract Potemkin defined himself as falling just short of the ideal of the new man: "I received a higher education, but I am still far from reaching that for which I strove. May the representative of the future live the way I dreamed of living." He explained his imperfections historically, saying that the time he was living through was only the dawn of the socialist age. Back in the mid-1930s he had asserted with aplomb that the Soviet present was producing people as beautiful as the Venus de Milo, but now this vision acquired a tangible futurist sense. This time of classical perfection, he now noted, was "not far; a time when people will be as wonderful as Venus de Milo, and human relations, in the words of Karl Marx, will be clear and transparent, like rock crystal."[84]

While Potemkin's subjectivity was historically determined, he re-evaluated his sense of the progression of history based on the diagnosis of his own personal development. If with increasing age he did not become steadily purer, this had to mean that history was not as developed as he had previously believed. His new sense of his imperfections, formulated in 1942, implied that the new man had in fact not yet been born. The figure of the new man, Potemkin's case suggests, was extremely difficult to fully incarnate. As an ideal he seemed most palpably present as one struggled to approximate him, but he could not be firmly and durably appropriated. Ultimately, the work-in-progress character of Communist subjectivity was more important than the claim to perfection, which bred melancholia and depression.

Potemkin's writings from the Stalin period provide insight into Communist subjectivity—the desired and valued characteristics of personal development during this period, and the way a young Communist engaged these values and sought to transform them into biographical substance. Keeping a diary from an early age, Potemkin complained about its "subjectivism," its myopic focus on his inner world, and its failure to represent "real life," which he identified with the laboring collective. His self-assessment changed dramatically in the mid-1930s: when the Soviet regime proclaimed its success in establishing the foundations of a socialist system and heralded the appearance of "new" socialist men and women, he began to present himself according to this new ideal. The shift in his picture of himself was facilitated by the fact that the socialist personality rehabilitated features, among them culture and sensitivity, that Potemkin recognized as his own but had previously felt compelled to disavow, but he explained the transition in terms of a dialectical progression of his self.

As Potemkin emphasized time and again, the essence of the new man for him lay not in behavior, nor in bodily appearance or dress, but within him, in his cultivated soul. This perspective enriches our understanding of the first generation of young Soviet citizens, notably the *vydvizhentsy,* whom historians have defined through their striving for outward culture and a civilized life. In Potemkin's account culturedness always took second place to the cultivation of personality, a category that subsumed education, moral striving, social and political activism, and aesthetic expression. Whereas the *vydvizhentsy* are usually portrayed as careerist, neo-bourgeois, and aloof to Soviet revolutionary values, Potemkin consistently fashioned himself in heroic and Romantic terms. In striving to transform and perfect his personality, he inscribed himself—in part consciously, in part unconsciously—in a genealogy of revolutionary life creation that reached back, via Gorky and Nietzsche, to Russian Romantics of the 1830s, who had been among the first to search for the new man.

Ideally, Potemkin believed, a Communist should make himself permanently at home in a heroic universe by means of uninterrupted, sustained ideological thinking and acting. His ideal of self-realization—tantamount to his notion of "happiness"—was a lasting state of transcendence, a higher reality towering over the grayness of daily life. Potemkin was more successful than many other Soviet diarists in inhabiting this heroic mode, but he was not spared failures and lapses. He interpreted these failings as personal deviations from a mandated norm. Instead of "burning with assured calm," with the "smooth fire of constant inspiration," attributes of the perfect Communist, he had to contend with his "passionate, sensitive nature" which subjected him to highly uneven emotional states: "At times I am set aflame by burning rapture, my heart completely blazing with emotion; at other times I am extinguished, as if my heart had burned out; my energy disappears."[85]

Like socialist realist art, Potemkin's writings cannot be properly decoded if they are measured against a standard of mimetic representation of existing reality. Socialist realism strove to capture a different reality, that of future socialist perfection as it emerged in the present, and more important, as a given artist felt it to be emerging. The reality Potemkin sought to represent in the first place was that of his unfolding revolutionary consciousness and its transformative powers for his life and his environment. For him the act of writing performed a mobilizing function. His intimate writings both laid out standards of the perfect personality and served as exhortations to implement those standards in his own life. He extended this interventionist and transformative function to literature at large, including novels and newspaper accounts: "Literature that does not incite a striving toward the better, toward becoming a better person, is not literature."[86]

Throughout his autobiographical writings Potemkin portrayed his life in a uniform manner, embedding the growth of his subjective self in the story of the October Revolution and the building of socialism, and highlighting the dialectical interaction between subjective and objective factors in the development of his personal life.[87] Many aspects of the Soviet Marxist myth, so central to Potemkin's biographical thinking—a myth of a poor, dark, and oppressed class that is liberated and gains material, intellectual, and aesthetic fulfillment—were empirically borne out in his and his sister's lives. As young, poor villagers who migrated to the city and obtained higher education, political consciousness, and professional validation as engineers, they were living embodiments of the Soviet dream. The existential fulfillment Potemkin found as a Soviet citizen cannot be denied.

During one of our meetings in his Moscow apartment, Potemkin showed me another stone that was on display in his book cabinet, next to the granite and marble paperweight. It was a rock of mineralized sea lilies, discovered in the Urals and suggesting that millions of years ago the region had been covered by ocean. Potemkin remarked that, like all other living organisms, human beings became mineralized after their death, and the medium of their mineralization was their writings. This striking image helped me understand why Potemkin had written so fervently throughout his life and why he had invested so much care in preserving his personal archive. Much of his life was shaped by the moral mandate to become an exemplary personality of his time, and writing was a way to give enduring substance to this model personality. And while he viewed his texts as a privileged domain of self-representation, he also insisted on their reality, historical truth, and existential purpose, thereby repeatedly crossing the boundaries between text and experiential life.

As we finished our last round of interviews, Leonid Potemkin declared that I must not leave without a gift. He handed me the rock of mineralized lilies, in memory of our conversations about his life.

7

Stalin's Inkwell

ALEXANDER AFINOGENOV

In a key scene of Alexander Afinogenov's popular play *Fear*, which premiered in 1931, Bobrov, a bourgeois professor of reflexology, clashes with the young Communist scientist Elena over who can claim legitimate authority to transform mankind and chart the course of history—bourgeois scientists or Communist politicians. Only scientists think in "the perspective of centuries," Bobrov argues; they possess cultural authority and, unlike politicians, are not encumbered by pressing questions of the day:

> *Bobrov:* Even the very best of politics compels one to waste time, like money, on details . . . You know that the State farm "The Giant" was the first to finish sowing . . . But you have forgotten who was the author of "Faust."
>
> *Elena:* I haven't seen that opera.
>
> *Bobrov:* May I inform you that "Faust" should be read, not heard? You cannot tell the difference between a piece of Sèvres china and a Saxon cup.
>
> *Elena:* I drink tea out of a glass.
>
> *Bobrov:* History has raised us from a herd of monkeys to select cultivated individuals, while you are crushing these facets in the mortar of collective politics.
>
> *Elena:* We are making history. Try for once to involve yourself in

real life, and you will understand that we are not just crushing facets.[1]

Fear established Afinogenov, up to then a promising young playwright, as a leading Soviet dramatist. The play premiered in Moscow and Leningrad and proved an instant sellout. Over the course of eigh-

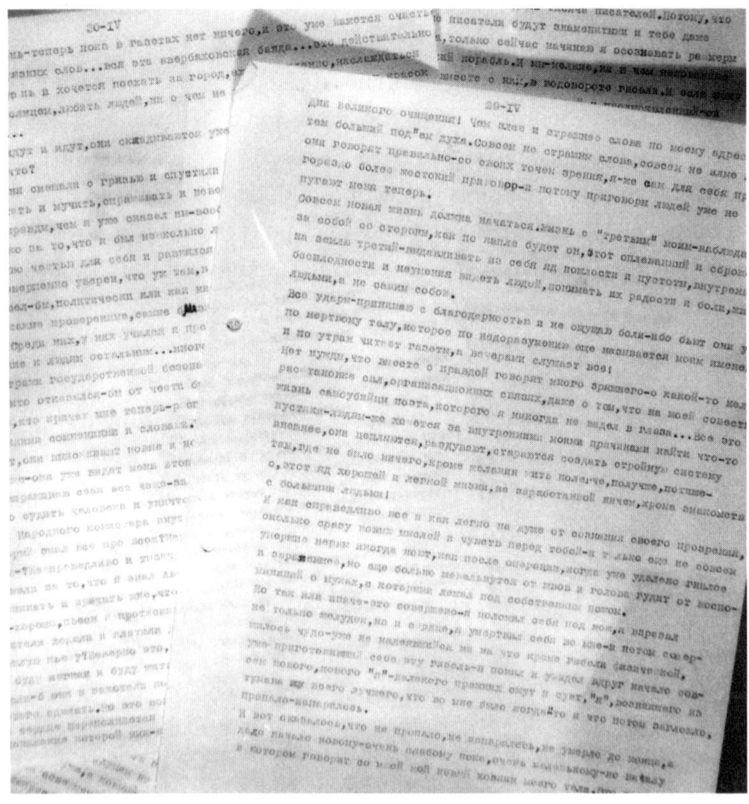

Pages from Alexander Afinogenov's 1937 diary.
© Russian State Archive of Literature and the Arts, Moscow

teen months, the Leningrad Drama Theater alone presented three hundred performances; by the mid-1930s the play was a staple of theater programs throughout the Soviet realm.[2]

Fear shows the difficult road traveled by the non-Soviet intelligentsia toward acceptance and embrace of the Soviet regime. The professors come to understand that in the past bourgeois prejudice distorted their research, leading them to believe that all human behavior was determined by basic physiological stimuli and that the overriding stimulus in the Soviet context was fear: of political deviations and purges, of arrest and deportation. This fear, they claimed, paralyzed Soviet citizens, much as the rabbits in their laboratory were paralyzed by the sight of a boa constrictor and submissively waited to be crushed in its deadly embrace. In the course of the play the professors are stunned by the enthusiastic energy of untrained young Communists like Elena, who burn with devotion to socialism. In the end they realize that the Soviet regime, as the creator of these exceptional people, furnishes the true "perspective of centuries," and they eagerly join the collective construction campaign. The happy synthesis of bourgeois science and Communist politics is sealed when Elena, meanwhile appointed institute director, tells Bobrov that she has read Goethe's *Faust* during a brief business trip. While this impatient, fast-learning young proletarian assimilates progressive elements of the bourgeois past, she discards everything deemed not of social use. Elena directs a symbolically fraught cleaning of her communal apartment, instructing Bobrov to remove the belongings of an aristocratic lady who refuses to abjure her outdated way of life.

The Communist state, the play signals, does not crush all individuals, as Bobrov had feared. It invites into its collective fold everyone who demonstrates a sincere desire to become involved in the construction effort. Moreover, it breeds a generation of fearless, optimistic people who will inhabit the socialist home. Fear is felt only by those who situate themselves against history, who obstruct the construction: together with their useless belongings, they are swept away in the housecleaning and crushed, like useless cups of Sèvres china.[3]

Afinogenov, when writing the play, did not foresee that in 1937 he himself would become the target of a purge as described in *Fear.* As the Stalinist Great Purge unfolded, engulfing the playwright along with thousands of others, he recorded his experience not in the form of a play, but in a personal diary—an intimate theater, as it were, in which he staged the drama of his life. Afinogenov, whose life during the 1930s is also richly documented by his plays, public appearances, and personal letters, viewed the purge that threatened him as a time of historical possibility. It was a moment when history breathed directly on him and when the drama of his life was elevated to a world-historical level. He saw the year 1937 as a critical juncture in both his personal development and the development of the Soviet system. For him, the policies of purification launched by Stalin illustrated the need to embark on a similar campaign of self-purification.

To some extent, the repeated blurring of the lines between life and text in Afinogenov's writings was the work of a professional playwright who could not help conceiving of his life in dramaturgical terms. More fundamentally, however, it expressed a Soviet Communist's attempts to align his "subjective" self with "objective" reality. Here Afinogenov's talent as a playwright only lent richer literary form to a striving he shared with other Communists of his time. Organized according to a literary-historical script, Afinogenov's self-narrative is reminiscent of Leonid Potemkin's, but the playwright's scenario vastly surpassed that of the geology student in symbolic behavior. Both men regarded themselves as "engineers of human souls" with great historical responsibilities, as a Communist agitator Potemkin worked with audiences of a few hundred students at best, while Afinogenov's plays reached millions of spectators. Rooted in a tradition dating back to the nineteenth-century critics Belinsky and Chernyshevsky, Afinogenov knew that his priestly status as an ideologue who preached new historical life forms to his mass audience would be effective and legitimate only if he personally exemplified the path toward the new life.

Unlike his prerevolutionary predecessors, however, who were free to fantasize about the perfect future and the type of people who would inhabit it, Afinogenov worked under the constraints of a Communist state whose leader claimed the authority to define the stages of historical development that the Soviet order was traversing. As a Communist playwright, Afinogenov had a responsibility to reveal the work of history toward the perfect future; yet the role of historical legislator claimed by Russian writers in the past now fell to Stalin. While showing how demanding a task it was, intellectually and aesthetically, to discern history under Stalin's watchful eye, Afinogenov's diary also shows that his vocation as Stalin's writer provided possibilities of self-realization unavailable to ordinary Soviet citizens.[4]

Engineer of Human Souls

Alexander Afinogenov was born in 1904 in a small town in Riazan province. His father, a railroad employee, left the family soon after the boy's birth to work in Siberia, where he started a writing career. Alexander was raised by his mother, a village schoolteacher and part-time editor of a local newspaper. After the outbreak of the revolution the 13-year-old Alexander was elected secretary of a local Union of Communist Students. Three years later he joined the Communist party, after which he worked for the Soviet regime in six different functions, including military censor and newspaper editor. As he remembered in an autobiography: "I came to school . . . and scared the teachers with my domineering appearance and the revolver attached to my belt."[5]

Afinogenov moved to Moscow in 1927 and joined the Russian Association of Proletarian Writers (RAPP), the most vocal and militant literary organization of the time; he was elected to its board of directors in 1929. His early plays, *The Eccentric* (1929) and *Fear,* followed the "proletarian realist" aesthetic advocated by RAPP, focusing on contradictions in Soviet society without seeking to embellish reality.[6] Faithful to this directive, Afinogenov did not refrain from exposing personal failures and administrative deficiencies within the Communist party. His plays were widely popular and received praise from Communist leaders. Joseph Stalin, after attending *The Eccentric* with other members of the Politburo, reportedly "prescribed" that members of the Central Committee go and see this "remarkable" and "necessary" play.[7] By the early 1930s Afinogenov was corresponding with Stalin, whom he regarded as his supreme literary mentor, and to whom he would later submit drafts of his plays for criticism. One of Afinogenov's plays, about the life of a Red Army commander, was read before its official premiere in the apartment of the people's commissar for defense, Kliment Voroshilov. Another chief mentor was Maxim Gorky. Afinogenov was a guest at Gorky's house in Italy for three weeks in the spring of 1932.

Afinogenov's rise to the apex of the Soviet literary establishment coincided with the effort, on the part of Communist leaders as well as Gorky, to make literature the foremost medium for the propagation of a distinctly "Soviet" culture commensurate with the dawning socialist age. In April 1932 a party decree abolished all existing literary organizations, including RAPP, and called for the establishment of a single association of Soviet writers. Soviet literature was henceforth to be produced in a unified "socialist realist" style, to chart and help bring about the emerging new world. Key to the socialist realist aesthetic was the artist's proper grasp of the direction in which history was traveling. Only artists with superior insight into this process could qualify as Communist artists. As Andrei Zhdanov, Central Committee spokesman on literary matters, formulated the task awaiting the writing profession: "Soviet literature must be able to . . . glimpse our tomorrow. This will not be a utopia, since our tomorrow is already being prepared today on the basis of planned and conscious work . . . The writer must not lag behind the events, he has to be among the first ranks of the people and show the people the path of its development."[8]

Stalin personally prescribed to Soviet writers the subject of their trade. In October 1932 he convened a group of writers, including Afinogenov, in the Moscow residence of Maxim Gorky, who had just returned from living in Italy. Stalin appealed to Soviet writers to join the industrialization campaign and become "engineers of human souls." While the industrialization campaign recast the social existence of millions of citizens at breakneck speed, writers were to help citizens organize their inner lives. It was according to their portrayals of the socialist hero's emotional-intellectual world that each Soviet reader or theatergoer was to mold himself. Stalin addressed the assembled playwrights in particular: "What should you write? Poetry is fine. Novels are even better. But plays are now best of all. Plays are easy to understand . . . Plays are the art form we need most of all. Workers can watch plays easily . . . It is no accident that the bourgeois class, at the outset, produced some of its greatest geniuses in drama: Shakespeare, Molière . . . We must make our own plays."[9]

Afinogenov, who after this meeting was appointed to the committee that organized the founding congress of the Union of Soviet Writers, followed Stalin's demand in literal fashion. His public statements of the period 1933–1936 called for portrayals of the new man's rich psychological world, as Afinogenov defined the term "soul."[10] Yet this approach remained controversial. Vsevolod Vishnevsky and Nikolai Pogodin, two fellow playwrights, attacked Afinogenov for his emphasis on characters' inner lives, which in their eyes smacked of "reactionary" traditionalism. Instead they advocated a monumental style saturated with dramatic action; they sought to foreground heroic masses, not isolated individuals. Essentially the two camps disagreed over what served Soviet readers and spectators better: literature that highlighted psychological conflicts within the new man while showing ways to resolve them; or epic scenarios that mobilized readers and viewers through the projection of the perfect future.[11] All participants in this debate defended their positions as the "correct" implementation of the party mandate to produce art commensurate with the emerging socialist age. They clung to prescriptive statements and signals issued by Stalin, Zhdanov, and other leaders as authorizations of their positions. But these authorizing gestures only masked the fact that at bottom there was no clear indication of what a socialist realist "method" amounted to—what kind of plot structure it foresaw, what relative

The playwright at work. A strategically placed issue of the journal *USSR under Construction* is visible beside his typewriter.
© Russian State Archive of Literature and the Arts, Moscow

weight was to be given to the imperfect present and the perfect future, and how much conflict and ambivalence a script could have in its depiction of the struggle toward the future. It remained for the participants in the debate to put into practice what they saw as the key principles of the new aesthetic sensibility. Theirs was an experimental and often quite risky pursuit.[12]

The controversial nature of Afinogenov's psychological approach came to the fore in the reception of his play *Lie,* which premiered in the fall of 1933. Written at the very juncture of the shift from "proletarian" to "socialist" realism, from accounts of present-day deficiencies to projections of the perfect future, the play had a more critical than optimistic bent. In the tradition of Afinogenov's previous work, it reveled in ambiguity, portraying the unsteady worldview of a young Communist, Nina. Nina is lured by an another party member, who unbeknownst to her is plotting a counterrevolution, into believing that the Soviet Union is a country of lies and deceit. In the end a mature Communist rescues the entangled heroine from her dangerous political liaison. Both Gorky and Stalin, to whom Afinogenov sent copies of the script, slammed it for distorting the Communist party. As Gorky observed, most of the Communist characters in the play were shallow and rendered in shades of gray, in contrast to the lively portrayal of their foes. Even though he, Gorky, was not a party member, he could recognize a Bolshevik's personality. "A Bolshevik is interesting not for his faults," he lectured Afinogenov, "but for his virtues. His faults are rooted in the past which he is tirelessly destroying. His virtues, however, are rooted in the present, in the work of building the future . . . We have to train ourselves to appraise the past and the present from the vantage point of our future goals."[13]

Afinogenov's supreme critic, Stalin, reacted even more negatively than Gorky. Why, he demanded, were there no committed Communists in the play, "sincere and unselfish, devoted heart and soul to the workers' cause"? "Open your eyes and you will see that we have such workers in the party." In the margin of a passage where Nina acknowledges that socialism is being built, but at the price of such indifference that when a streetcar runs over a woman the bystanders merely curse the traffic delay, Stalin noted a sarcastic "ha–ha–ha." He crossed out an entire section toward the end of the play where Nina confesses that she and other young Communists have lost their revolutionary commitment: "We don't know what the [party's] general line will be tomorrow. Today it is called the line, tomorrow a deviation. And the newspapers don't write the whole truth. I'm tired of living like this." "Who needs this dismal and tedious gibberish?" Stalin commented. In an accompanying note he endorsed Afinogenov's idea for the play but recommended major revisions. The playwright reworked *Lie,* which premiered in revised form at a theater in Kharkov and was received enthusiastically. Three hundred other Soviet theaters also contracted to produce the play, among them several leading Moscow houses. But a few days before the scheduled Moscow premiere, Stalin again voiced his disapproval. Immediately Afinogenov sent telegrams to the theaters ordering *Lie* to be withdrawn from the repertoire.[14]

In the eyes of his critics, Afinogenov had failed to meet the demands of socialist realism. Instead of showcasing the firm and developed Communist will that underpinned Soviet leaders' trust that the perfect future would be attained, his play sowed confusion and doubt. Given his skewed portrayal of Communist protagonists, Gorky and Stalin even doubted whether Afinogenov was a true Bolshevik at heart. This reproach that, despite his membership in the Communist party, Afinogenov's plays showed Soviet reality only "from the outside" and through a "distorted mirror," was repeated in official reviews over the next years.[15]

Gorky's and Stalin's criticisms of *Lie* were echoed in a private evaluation by a friend of Afinogenov's, the actor Boris Igritsky. Commenting in his diary on the failure of the play, Igritsky attributed it to Afinogenov's overly narrow life experience. "Alexander did not go through the school of the civil war and did not take part in the economic construction work, he did not become deeply absorbed in workers' culture, nor in village life. He was never organically infected with the passions of our party and never got carried away by the party's Sturm und Drang, nor was he drawn into them." Igritsky, too, doubted Afinogenov's Bolshevik credentials, implying that the shortcomings of his oeuvre expressed his lack of political consciousness. Expanding on this theme, Igritsky accused Afinogenov of not leading a life worthy of a Communist. A visit to Afinogenov's new Moscow apartment—which, the diarist noted, had cost twenty thousand rubles—underscored for Igritsky how little the playwright partook in either the deprivations or the enthusiasms of the Soviet collective: "A large, separate four-room apartment, lots of furniture, chandeliers, things. Everything new and expensive . . . How comfortable everything is, how cozy and empty! I felt sad being with him. A craftsman working alone, a piece broken off from the whole." Igritsky attributed Afinogenov's perceived artistic deficiencies to a defect in his moral personality. In his friend's eyes, Afinogenov was not sufficiently rooted in the Soviet cause.[16]

Afinogenov was indeed affluent, and not just by Soviet standards. He drew a monthly income of 14,000 rubles, whereas the average income for Soviet workers was a few hundred rubles. He had access to special shops reserved for the Communist elite and was allowed to travel abroad. After an extended trip to Europe in the spring and summer of 1932, Afinogenov returned to Russia in his new car, a Ford. Together with friends from the theater world he vacationed in ministerial dachas in the Crimea and on the Black Sea coast. The diary of the theater director Nikolai Petrov records the poker games he played with Afinogenov and others while on vacation. Hundreds of rubles crossed the table during these games, which included an unspecified variant of "wild Asian poker." Adding to Afinogenov's appeal was his marriage to an American ballerina—and Communist—whom he had met in Moscow in the late 1920s. Thanks also to his wife, Jenny, Afinogenov was a regular guest at receptions in Moscow given by the American ambassador. According to Boris Pasternak, another friend, Afinogenov was

Alexander and Jenny Afinogenov at a Black Sea resort, 1933.
© Russian State Archive of Literature and the Arts, Moscow

"surrounded by half of Moscow's art world."[17] The playwright was among the first residents of the writers' colony of Peredelkino, a village fifteen miles west of the capital. The colony consisted of expensive dachas set up by the state to create the best conditions for its outstanding writers to pursue their trade. It was in Peredelkino that the drama of Afinogenov's life would play itself out in 1937.[18]

Gymnastics of the Soul

Afinogenov's diary reveals that he, like his friend Igritsky, interpreted the failure of *Lie* as related to his failure as a person. Afinogenov began to keep a diary in 1926 and did so for the rest of his life. Except for the period from 1936 to 1938, his diary survives only in fragments—scraps of mostly undated typewritten sheets without a clear sequence. The originally cohesive diary was torn apart by Afinogenov himself: in preparing his plays, he repeatedly went through his diary with scissors, cutting out passages and arranging them thematically. This habit provides a clue to a principal function of the diary: to serve as a sketchbook for his literary work. For the most part, diary entries abound in observations of Afinogenov's daily life: conversations at home and with colleagues, street scenes, thoughts on nature, human psychology, and political life.[19]

A striking feature of this sketchbook is its self-reflective quality. Afinogenov's self-observation was tied to his calling as a Communist writer. He practiced a moral mandate dating back to the nineteenth-century critic Chernyshevsky, according to which a writer had to personally embody the revolutionary standards that he preached. For Afinogenov this meant that, to be a worthy engineer of souls, he must engineer his own soul. His portrayal of the new man's interior life could only succeed as a projection of a consciousness that he personally felt. The writer must "invest his soul in his works," he noted in his diary. Writing should be "writing about the self, the theme of the [writer's] own 'self.'"[20] Socialist realism required the artist to bring out the relationship of the object under investigation to the course of history. In Afinogenov's case, the object to be investigated was his own soul. Keeping the diary was to help him observe himself. When referring to himself in the diary, Afinogenov usually used the third person. He observed himself on the pages of his journal as if he was a character on a stage. Given the diary's function as a quarry for his works, this made sense: in the diary the autobiographical "he" and the characters of his plays moved on the same level and became interchangeable. This also meant that both the stage characters, conceived of in socialist realist fashion, and the diaristic "he" were subject to the same standard of an exemplary revolutionary life.

Afinogenov's diaristic self-analysis disclosed to him a corruption of his soul. The success of his early plays had brought him fame and encouraged him to indulge in the pleasures of life. As a result, he had turned lazy and complacent and stopped struggling. On New Year's Day 1935, looking back on the past year, he wrote: "Confusion, depression, . . . and the search for myself, in constant uncertainty . . . And only now has it suddenly become clear that I can't go on living like this." A year later, in late December 1935, he noted: "Nothing real has been done, the year was spent at the expense of what had been done the previous year . . . Isn't that parasitism?"[21] This emptiness and lack of movement signaled degeneration, for to be a Communist meant to be moving ahead in constant struggle, in tune with the inexorable march of history. An undated note by Afinogenov from this period, entitled "The Separation," suggests the extent of his crisis. It was about Jenny, who had just left him and returned to the United States after discovering his love letters to a young actress. In harshly self-accusatory terms Afinogenov recalled standing next to her the day she left, but feeling internally miles apart from her:

> He didn't feel anything except all sorts of rooting around and moaning concerning himself. A petty egoist and callous person. His dear, at one time intimate companion, who had done so much for him, nurturing his character and will, his wife often took pride in the fruits of her labor, here's the sort of man that she has reared from a weak-willed and low-spirited boy. But in two years' time—all this nurturing was blown away, like a dandelion, he drifted to the old ways, and she had to begin everything all over again.

Afinogenov's self-characterization echoed Boris Igritsky's judgment that his friend was careless and spoiled, a true "mama's boy." But Afinogenov's note also suggests how steeped he was in a culture of critical self-analysis, and that he viewed his wife, and also friends like Igritsky, as confessors who were to provide the steadfastness that he himself lacked. (Jenny later returned to her husband; it is unclear when.)[22]

In this context Afinogenov viewed his diary as a means to regain the discipline and dedication essential to his vocation as an engineer of souls. He conceived of writing the diary as a technology of the Communist self. Keeping the diary made possible a continuous process of baring and cleansing the self, which Afinogenov likened to the results of prayer: "The significance of prayer—the cleansing before the coming day. Cleansing the soul. This is not that stupid at all, of course, not in the form of a prayer learned by rote, but like this: to reflect on the day to come as well as on the past day . . . gymnastics for the soul." One of Afinogenov's many appeals for self-improvement was formulated as a prayer: "Well, make use of it . . . show yourself over the next ten years . . . in such a way that not a single day is wasted and not a single hour is spent on extravagance or revelry . . . Demand more of yourself! Learn to criticize yourself, so that others will criticize you less . . . Learn to hope and to believe in yourself . . . Amen."[23]

Afinogenov deliberately used the religious idiom to describe his work of self-transformation. As he noted repeatedly, the new socialist society, while possessing a language of the soul, lacked institutions and mechanisms that incited citizens to cultivate the purity of their souls, on which the strength of the Soviet system ultimately rested. Soviet politics simply did not cover the area of everyday ethics, and religion, rightly exposed as an instrument of oppression, was of course no alternative. It was the task of the writer to step in and provide spiritual guidance to help readers work through crises and restore their social commitments. Afinogenov likened the Soviet theater to a church: "One must go there to learn how to live and behave, and as you listen to the words on the stage, apply them to yourself and to your relations with friends both near and far away, enemies, strangers, and family."[24]

Yet there remained a fundamental problem: How could the playwright perform his priestly calling if he himself lacked spiritual fortitude? Afinogenov described his crisis in the outline of a novel that he sketched out in his diary in 1935. It was a novel he had "to write without any consideration of what might be crossed out on ethical or political grounds," a novel, in other words, that he knew would not pass the desk of his literary censor, Stalin:

> I must write a simple story about nothing, about the thoughts and the actions of a person who can't determine who he is . . . And write it in such a way that there won't be any numbers, nor any statistics about the Second Five-Year Plan, as simply as if this person were living on an island, reading the newspapers out of sheer habit, and by this same habit forgetting everything he's read. A story about life becoming a habit and the difficulty of making oneself over in a heroic fashion. This book will be about many people, moreover, people whom we all know . . . a novel without a theme, without a goal: he simply gets up, looks around, and un-

derstands that he is living poorly. But he can't explain to himself why he is living poorly.[25]

The protagonist, a writer, was not well because he could not feel the grandeur of his age. He read the newspaper mechanically, not with genuine dedication. His soul was empty, void of the fervent enthusiasm required to translate the directives and charts printed in Soviet newspapers into visions of an imminent perfect future. His crisis was a loss of faith, which Soviet Communists expressed as a loss of historical certainty. The hero's sickness resulted from his dissociation from the collective of which he had once been an organic part. While unable to feel the real "life" somewhere in the distance, he knew that it was "making gigantic strides." This literary antihero was patterned on Nina, the doubting Communist in *Lie.* By contrast, the ideal to which he was unable to connect was the strength of mind, revolutionary fervor, and youth embodied by Elena, the protagonist of *Fear.*[26]

Significantly, this prospective novel was about "many people . . . whom we all know." It addressed the crisis of the Soviet "creative intelligentsia" at large. Along with their enormous privileges, Afinogenov and his colleagues held the equally enormous responsibility of writing the history of the age. Stalin's engineers of souls were bombarded with calls in the Soviet media, such as this appeal by *Pravda:* "Millions of readers and viewers want the highest images of art; they avidly wait for their life and struggle, for the great ideas and deeds of our century to be shown in artistic works of great force and passion, in works that will enter the history of socialist culture, filling and organizing the thoughts and feelings not only of contemporaries but of future generations." So overwhelming were these expectations, Isaak Babel said in his address to the Writers' Congress, that they simply silenced him as a writer. It was a remark made only half in jest.[27]

Afinogenov responded differently. Whether at the Writers' Congress or in his diary, he kept urging himself as well as his colleagues to remake themselves into exemplars of the new man in order to live up to their calling. But their dilemma was that their comfortable lives of privilege estranged them from their task of recording and synthesizing the real, historical life that unfolded on Soviet construction sites and in coal mines, on ice floes in the polar sea, and in the stratosphere. The problem was in plain view. At the Tenth Komsomol Congress in 1936, which heralded the appearance of a new generation of untainted Soviet youth, speaker after speaker denounced "some" writers for "lagging behind" in their vocation as engineers of souls. The cause was identified as their "obesity . . . their abandonment of struggle."[28]

A profound sense of historical crisis is palpable in Afinogenov's diary, his correspondence with friends, and his public statements of the mid-1930s. He described it as an urge to accelerate work on himself so as to remain in step with history. History was moving ahead at a rapid pace; a new generation was about to enter political and cultural life, while he was growing older (he was only 30 in 1934), more complacent, and physically heavier. It was an anxiety that a gap had formed between his self and the course of history, and that it was becoming ever wider. This was happening to a writer whose task was to chart the road of history. Afinogenov confided this anxiety to Nikolai Petrov, and he also stated it in more muted tones at the Writers' Congress. Writers, he declared, should not focus on the conflict between the new man and an old past; the decisive conflict of the present played itself out within the new man. It was the new man's "dissatisfaction with himself in relationship to the tasks posed to him by the country, his dissatisfaction . . . with his growth in relation to the overall growth of the country."[29]

Afinogenov craved a sense of communion with history. His ability to reveal the laws of history and to align himself in its progressive march was the decisive measure of the purity of his Bolshevik spirit. Only with, and in, history could he realize himself as a Communist individual and writer. Hence his yearning to observe "historical epochs," "events," and "turns" around him; hence also his anxiety that the course of history might pass him by or, even worse, that he might lose the will to turn in his tracks and transform himself into a subject of history.

The Great Purge

It was with this historical disposition that the playwright entered the year 1937, which would devastate the lives of thousands of high-ranking Communists and an even larger number of less prominent Soviet citizens. Over the course of 1936 Afinogenov faced an increasing barrage of official criticism. He first received a reprimand in March in connection with the campaign against formalism. Later in the year his play *Hail, Spain!* premiered in Moscow. The immediate response was favorable. *Pravda* wrote approvingly that the performance elicited standing ovations, and emphasized the play's powerful effect on a delegation of visiting Spanish soldiers. Only a few days later, however, after Stalin and other Bolshevik leaders had seen a performance, *Hail, Spain!* as well as all other plays by Afinogenov were suddenly withdrawn from the repertoire of Soviet theaters. Afinogenov told a friend in early January 1937 that he had a premonition that the new year would bring a fundamental challenge to his existence: "for the first time" he was confronted "with fundamental questions of my life, my movement, and my fate." He could no longer ignore the unfavorable results of his life: "I have lived too long and achieved too little!"[30]

While decreeing a turn in his personal life, he noted in his diary that the entire Soviet system likewise stood at a crossroads. In November 1936 the Eighth Congress of Soviets ratified the new Soviet Constitution, which was officially praised as the most democratic in the world. Among other civic entitlements, the constitution foresaw a secret ballot in elections to all the state's representative bodies, including the newly established Supreme Soviet. The first election to the Supreme Soviet was scheduled to take place in late 1937. In the months following the ratification of the constitution, the Soviet press publicized several Central Committee resolutions that called for a more democratic process in the upcoming election campaign and exhorted rank-and-file party members to be more critical of the performance of their local leaders. As *Pravda* reported in March and April 1937, after the introduction of secret balloting in local elections, numerous officeholders had been voted out of office. Afinogenov was impressed by the quality of self-criticism suffusing a meeting of the Moscow party organization in early 1937. In concluding his entry about this meeting he wrote: "Life will take a sharp turn now. The Constitution is not just a scrap of paper! This is what many don't understand, oh so many!" And a few weeks later: "Oh, what a gigantic turn: genuine History is upon us, and we are granted the joy of witnessing these turns, when Stalin mercilessly chops off all and everything, all the unfit and weakened, the decaying and empty . . . Life has now taken a turn onto the new, the real; in this way and no other will we march forward to genuine Communism. Whoever says otherwise is lying!"[31]

For Afinogenov the campaign to purify the party's ranks amounted to a threshold moment in the life of the country as well as his personal life. It was the culmination of a revolutionary agenda of purification involving both the social realm and individual selves. The decisive question he faced was whether he was sufficiently pure to claim a rightful place in the socialist world. His diary reveals that he was deeply involved from the start in the purification campaign that was to peak in the Great Purge. In early 1937, before he was targeted by the terror, Afinogenov understood the purge as his last chance to redeem himself and to show everybody that he was a Bolshevik at heart.

At about the same time, Afinogenov's diary changed in character:

the introspective gaze became ever more prominent and nearly eclipsed the diary's other purpose as a writer's sketchbook. Afinogenov's increased urge to reflect on the state of his soul is also conveyed in his more frequent use of the first-person "I," rather than "he," to refer to himself. This switch suggests greater psychological immediacy, but it also expresses a sense that events unfolded so swiftly that he lacked time and analytical distance to reflect on himself as a literary character. He wrote in his diary more often in this period, and the entries were longer. Hardly a day passed without his writing at least one typewritten page, and often his entries for a given day spanned three or more pages. If members of Soviet society are thought to have ceased keeping diaries as the regime stepped up its repressive policies, Afinogenov's case points to a different dynamic: for him the terror induced a veritable explosion of autobiographical writing. The Stalinist purge emerges in his case not as an expression of absolute estrangement between state and citizens, but as an intense synergetic link between individuals and the state, in which the respective agendas of social purification and individual self-purification fused. The phenomenon of terror, Afinogenov's diary suggests, was far more than a policy threatening the integrity of the self from without; it had a profoundly constitutive effect on the self, which was expressed in torrents of confessional writing designed to cleanse and rework the self. As the Stalinist regime increased its demands for the unmasking of Trotskyist enemies, Afinogenov by means of his diary proceeded to scrutinize and cleanse his soul.

The official campaign of self-criticism reached a new stage with the publication, on March 29 and April 1, 1937, of two speeches Stalin had delivered to the Central Committee plenum in early March, in which he demanded the unmasking of thousands of enemies who had infiltrated the party. Throughout the Soviet Union, the publication of these speeches set off an avalanche of enemy-hunting, accusations, counter-accusations, and confessions. As a contemporary of the purge campaign later remembered, "large and crowded lecture halls were turned into public confessionals." Within only a few days of the publication of Stalin's first speech, a meeting of the Moscow Association of Playwrights (a division of the Soviet Writers' Union) was hurriedly convened to "discuss the decisions of the CC plenum."[32]

In keeping with the guidelines provided by the Central Committee, the meeting of playwrights was devoted primarily to the unmasking of enemies and the exposure of corrupt bureaucratic structures within their association. On April 4, while the meeting was under way, *Pravda* carried a short notice containing explosive news: Genrikh Yagoda, head of the NKVD until the fall of 1936, had been stripped of all his official functions and arrested on charges of criminal activities. For Afinogenov this information was alarming. He and another playwright, Vladimir Kirshon, had been in close contact with Yagoda and had been frequent guests at Yagoda's dacha outside Moscow. Afinogenov's ties to Yagoda were not addressed at the Moscow meeting, but he was criticized, together with many of his colleagues, for his record as a literary official and for failing to practice sufficient self-criticism, that is, to criticize the political mistakes of his plays. Furthermore, Afinogenov noted in his diary, a number of his colleagues believed he had already been arrested, and others tried to avoid him.[33]

Events took a dramatic turn for the worse two weeks later. *Pravda* reported the unmasking of a literary circle led by Leopold Averbakh, the former secretary of RAPP. The circle was said to have set up a "Trotskyist agency in literature" and plotted to undermine the Soviet system. Averbakh, who had been arrested earlier in April as a Trotskyist enemy of the people, was married to Yagoda's sister. Along with Averbakh, *Pravda* identified Afinogenov and Kirshon as leaders of the conspiracy. Against this background, another meeting of the Moscow Association of Playwrights was convened on April 27. The secretary, Vsevolod Vishnevsky, devoted his entire speech to Averbakh's crimes and the need to excise all members of his camp from the association. The gist of his accusations was directed against Kirshon. But Afinogenov was evidently another target of the gathering, being third in the assigned speaking order, following Vishnevsky and Kirshon.[34]

Kirshon emphatically denied Vishnevsky's accusation, insisting on his spiritual purity as a Communist. Like Kirshon, Afinogenov began by refuting the specific charges against him, namely that he had been involved in a conspiracy with Averbakh to undermine the Soviet system. But he then used the public forum to expose his own inner corruption and by cleansing himself reverse the process of degeneration. He admitted to "much more serious" errors than those with which he was charged, errors impossible to summarize in the fifteen minutes he was allowed to speak. After a week of sleepless nights he had realized clearly what kind of person he was. Through his contacts with Averbakh and other "literary prima donnas," he had "imperceptibly imbibed, drop by drop, the very poison of unprincipledness, and cultivated in my relationships with others an ignorant and boorish attitude of conceit and bureaucratism, which this literary prima donna [Averbakh] possessed in full measure." These qualities had "corrupted" Afinogenov. Under Averbakh's influence he had turned away from the party and produced pieces that were "absolutely not what the country demanded and wanted from me. I didn't understand why I forgot to listen to the country and why I forgot how to write." He summarized his confession: "As a person, as a writer and a party member, I began to degenerate."

Afinogenov affirmed, however, that his current situation constituted a turning point in his life. The charges against him had given him a final opportunity to "understand and appreciate" his past life "as a life which clearly destroyed me, gradually at first, but then with increasing speed." He declared that he had "realized, conclusively and absolutely, the essence of the poisonous disease that goes by the name of

'Averbakh leprosy'—a disease that requires surgical intervention." In concluding, he implored his colleagues to acknowledge that he had broken with his past once and for all and taken the first step on the difficult road of self-renewal.

The assembled playwrights ignored his plea. Several conceded that his confession had been sincere, unlike Kirshon's defense, which amounted in their eyes to a "crafty lawyer's speech." Yet in his very sincerity, Afinogenov had demonstrated to them just how alien he was to the spirit of the party. As one speaker remarked, this lack of understanding of "the real role of the party" was "one of the gravest sins of his dramaturgic work of the past years." In the course of the four-day meeting, more than thirty writers spoke out against the "henchmen of the Trotskyist Averbakh," Kirshon and Afinogenov. The association passed a motion to discuss their removal from the board of the Writers' Union.[35]

Both Afinogenov and Kirshon were expelled from the party in May 1937. Kirshon was arrested in August 1937 and executed in June 1938. Afinogenov remained free for the time being. Evicted by the NKVD from his Moscow apartment, he moved to his dacha in the writer's colony of Peredelkino, where he lived with his wife, their newborn daughter, and a housekeeper in nearly total seclusion. The telephone remained silent for days on end, and Afinogenov commented bitterly on former friends who had turned out to be as fearful as rabbits. Sitting on his porch, he watched as neighbors in the writers' colony deliberately looked the other way as they walked past his dacha, unwilling to extend even a cold greeting. The radio was his principal link to the outside world: "Voices from distant worlds, orchestras and laughter, speeches and operas—he listened to everything, thereby joining the world from which he had been excluded." That world appeared to be awaiting his annihilation. One day, on a suburban train, Afinogenov overheard a conversation between two military officers who expressed satisfaction that the "Japanese spy Averbakh" had finally been dealt with, and that "Averbakh's henchman Afinogenov" was now in jail awaiting trial.[36]

While waiting to learn his fate and observing the waves of arrests which engulfed the Communist elite both in Moscow and around him in Peredelkino, Afinogenov used his diary to grapple with questions of why he had become a target of the terror campaign and what motivated the purge policies as a whole. His personal record closely replicated his public self-accusation at the playwrights' meeting. Two days after the meeting, Afinogenov produced in his diary another full-fledged confession, expanding on his public narrative. Again, he confessed his sins as a step toward self-purification: "Days of great cleans-

Afinogenov and his wife in front of their dacha in Peredelkino, 1937.
© Russian State Archive of Literature and the Arts, Moscow

ing! The more evil and terrible the words addressed to me become, the more my spirits rise. These words aren't terrible at all, and the people are not a bit evil, they are speaking the truth from their point of view. And I have pronounced a much harsher verdict on myself, and therefore people's verdicts no longer frighten me." Afinogenov relished each accusation leveled against him, for the more severely he was criticized, the more he would be able to recognize and denounce his sins and the purer he could become.[37]

He then detailed the work he had already performed on his self-renewal. The diary makes clear that the public confession to the meeting of playwrights played a central role in this project. It was the act in which he had renounced, indeed killed, his former self; a necessary precondition for the type of "rebirth" Afinogenov aimed for. Harking back

Afinogenov in 1937.

to his speech at the meeting, where he had spoken of the need for "surgical intervention" to remove his Averbakhian disease, he now reported that he had successfully carried out an operation on himself, removing "not only the stomach, but the heart as well." It was not enough to cut out the stomach, which symbolized his life of complacent affluence; the purge targeted his very essence as a person:

> I killed the self inside me—and then a miracle happened: no longer hoping for anything and having already prepared myself for this death, I understood and suddenly saw the beginning of something altogether new, a new "self," far removed from previous troubles and vanity, a "self" that arose out of the mist of all the best that had ever been in me and that had faded, vanished, evaporated. And now it turns out that it hasn't faded or evaporated, it hasn't died completely but has laid the foundation of a new—if still very weak and small—beginning, in which the new master of my body speaks to me.[38]

In describing how he shed his former self and invited a new master into his body, Afinogenov employed a narrative of radical conversion akin to the Christian notion of rebirth. Rebirth in Christian theology is the act by which the believer reaches the stage of salvation, leaving behind his old sinful nature and attaining a new life in God's spirit. In the Soviet context, rebirth was frequently used to describe the inner transformation of a person who joined the Communist party. By joining the party, the initiate reached new insight and understanding; he was "born anew," "saw," "knew," and "spoke of" new things, for in that moment he left the world of profane reality and entered a realm of higher knowledge and vision.[39]

The notion of rebirth was essential to Afinogenov's subjectivity in the context of the purges, for it allowed him to accommodate his past sins while at the same time giving him the assurance that he would eventually be saved. Since rebirth presupposes the existence of a prior, sinful self, Afinogenov could identify this self as the "degenerate playwright Afinogenov," as he had been labeled by his accusers but as he also saw himself. By the same token, however, he was able to renounce this self through the act of confession. By undergoing a symbolic death prior to being reborn, he could claim that he had emerged as a new, pure being who no longer had anything in common with the old Afinogenov. In his diary he remarked that the attacks against him in the newspapers were being directed against a "dead body which by a misunderstanding is called by my name."[40]

Even after having shed his former self and been reborn as a new person, Afinogenov had to face questions about the credibility of his claim to self-renewal. His critics rejected the very premise on which he had based his claim, namely, that he had been a degenerate party member, an erring Bolshevik who had temporarily slid from full consciousness but was now firmly back on track. As *Literaturnaya gazeta* remarked on the occasion of his expulsion from the party: "All of Afinogenov's activities . . . show that the only reason he can't be called a degenerate [party member] is that he has always been a person who was fundamentally alien to the party." As if in response to this damning verdict, Afinogenov stated programmatically in his diary: "This new self is a person whose word the people will hear at some point, and they will understand that this word is the word of a Bolshevik, no matter what!" Given Afinogenov's exclusion from the collective, the diary was practically the only medium in which the Bolshevik he was determined to become could raise and train his voice.[41]

It would be misleading, however, to reduce Afinogenov's diary of 1937 to a narrative of self-fashioning in a Bolshevik vein. Rather, the diary speaks in several voices. It portrays an individual excluded from the collective, desperately trying to make sense of his personal existence in relationship to the political process engulfing him. In rapid succession, expectations are paired with doubts, hope with anguish. Only days after his confession and self-renewal, Afinogenov spoke of himself very differently in his diary, maintaining that he was innocent and suspecting that his denunciation was part of a "devilish" fascist conspiracy seeking to "annihilate talented Soviet artists." The clarity of mind that he seemed to attain during the day oscillated with moments of despair in the darker hours: "The evening sets in, and a renewed outburst of depression and pain . . . What for? What for? . . . Bela Illesh has poisoned himself. I'm still sturdier, but who knows, maybe I will soon run out of strength and make loud statements, with a voice that is not mine, about something absolutely horrible! Where are the people? Where is the voice of support and comfort? Where is salvation and life?"[42]

Similar vacillation characterized Afinogenov's reactions to the official decision to expel him from the Communist party on May 20, 1937. His entry of that day described the meeting of the party section of the Writers' Union during which party secretary Alexander Fadeev "with a stony face called me a vulgar and philistine person, a degenerate bourgeois, and a good-for-nothing artist." All members of the section then openly voted to expel him from the party. When the meeting turned to a different point on the agenda, Afinogenov got up and left the room "in deadly silence." As soon as he was outside, he regained his "calm, bordering on happiness," because he knew that he was "not guilty of anything." His mood was different later in the day, however, when a colleague, Ilya Selvinsky, visited him at home to "comfort him and cheer him up":

> We spoke about the entire life of a person, in which there cannot not be any mistakes. And then when you have to answer for a mistake, all of a sudden everybody forgets about all the good things

> that this person could have done in his life and which he probably had done. Like Gretchen, who lived her entire life in a chaste and pure, sinless and good way. But she had only to commit one sin, just one, with Faust, for all her previous piety and goodness, to go from the gates of heaven straight to hell.[43]

Likening himself to Gretchen, Afinogenov admitted to having sinned against the party, even if his discussion with Selvinsky also suggests that he believed his punishment to have been unduly harsh. Afinogenov's expulsion from the party, which stood for the public exposure of his sinful self, thus compelled him to accept his depravity even in a non-official setting such as a private conversation. Moreover, he recorded this conversation in his diary, thereby qualifying the proclamation of innocence he had just made. As he further noted, he spent the days and weeks following his expulsion researching the concepts of fall from grace, sacrifice, and redemption. In works by Cervantes, Bruno Frank, and Dostoevsky, he hoped to find models of spiritual guidance: "Yes, now, in solitude, he felt at last the urge to comprehend that which earlier had not been accomplished. He wanted to read works on the philosophy of life not for the sake of some kind of 'education,' but because he needed an immediate answer to the questions of how to live henceforth with people, how to relate to them, and how to conduct himself."[44]

In his attempt to become a new person, Afinogenov resolved to make drastic changes in his life. Shedding his former corrupted self entailed first and foremost an end to his oblivious and pleasure-seeking way of life. But it also meant leaving behind former friends and colleagues, exposure to whom had corrupted him. Afinogenov once observed in his diary that most of his former associates had turned out to be "enemies": they had been "either arrested or picked to pieces." Suspecting that many more acquaintances would soon be arrested as enemies of the people, Afinogenov went even further in search of self-purification. In his eyes the entire city of Moscow, where arrests were most frequent, became a site of pollution. He resolved to avoid this dangerous source of contamination and to pursue instead an isolated existence in Peredelkino: "On the whole, every trip to Moscow is a nervous shock. You mustn't go there anymore, you must live alone by yourself, you must rest and be glad that you are alive and can lie in the sun without thinking about anything except your small and simple life, which alone you understand."[45]

Afinogenov implicitly juxtaposed the pure, "small and simple life, which alone you understand" to a morally depraved, treacherous world filled with hidden enemies intent on betrayal. He dreamed of leaving behind his impure social environment and seeking refuge in a remote place:

> Become a hermit, settle either alone or with my child—and not depend on anybody, not be tied down by anybody. I'm afraid of people now, although I have this occasional urge to sit with them and talk, but I'm afraid. This was such a life lesson, when the people you trusted most of all turned out to be traitors and enemies. Now, except myself, I don't trust anybody. I can't vouch for anybody and I want to go far away and live in such a way that I don't have contact with anybody.[46]

Living like Robinson Crusoe in his self-imposed exile, and in the midst of continuous waves of arrests, which were also taking their toll among residents of the writers' colony, Afinogenov came to extol values wholly at odds with the Bolshevik notion of man as a collective being. Afinogenov not only discovered that a private "life for himself"—anathema for a dedicated Communist—was viable; he described it as a highest form of self-realization:

> They played cards, he had a streak of luck. Then they drank tea and ate sweet pierogi with cherry filling. He went home, it was a warm summer night. Strolling under the stars, he whistled and tenderly thanked life that it was now so clear and peaceful for him. He suddenly understood that he had always wanted a peaceful life like this, even at the price of such a terrible catastrophe. It didn't matter. Now he was not needed by anybody and what made him happy was that he could live for himself.[47]

It was only a small step from embracing the new ideal of a solitary life to condemning his former life in the service of the party:

> Strange things are happening to me. Since the age of 14 I haven't belonged to myself. First the Komsomol, then the party. I have always carried the consciousness of some sort of sacrifice on my shoulders. I was a soldier and honestly served in the ranks, I did everything that the party ordered me to do and had never had any bad thoughts about it . . . But now they suddenly begin to suspect something and have ignominiously removed me from the ranks. It is as if they had cut out my eye and said: We don't need you now, go where you want. And at first, ah, what terrible days of isolation and solitude these were . . . Oh well, I had to leave the ranks. I took my bag and left. And then, as I was leaving town and following my nose, I discovered for the first time since my distant childhood the happiness of a free step. You are not needed by anybody, yes, nobody needs you, go where you want and work for the benefit of the people and the country, but by yourself and inconspicuously, for you are not needed. How wonderful this is that

> nobody is pursuing you with calls to meetings, or with orders to write an article or to give a speech and say something boring . . . Oh, how wonderful—to go and work where you deem necessary.[48]

Afinogenov no longer viewed his expulsion from the party in terms of an absolute loss or a fall from grace. On the contrary, he described his former life as an act of self-sacrifice. Now that he was no longer a soldier in the ranks, executing party orders, he discovered a new sense of freedom and purpose: a small but peaceful and stable existence. His expulsion from the party was like a mutilation of his eye: it entailed a loss of the superior vision he had previously possessed as a Communist and a writer. This vision had imposed on him particular social responsibilities as an engineer of human souls, and it was precisely the loss of this burden of responsibility that Afinogenov had in mind when hailing his new existence as someone who was "not needed by anybody."

Just as urgently as Afinogenov embraced the ideal of an individual existence, however, he began to repudiate it within a few weeks. His diary of July and August 1937 is filled with passages hailing his arrival at a new stage of consciousness. The first of these entries, written only three days after his dream of becoming a hermit, began: "This chapter might be entitled 'The Return to Life' . . . This is a day on which I suddenly felt that life is bustling around me . . . Once again the lines of the newspapers are bringing to life my former attitude." Afinogenov continued: "This feeling of being close to life fills you with joy, you listen once again to the words of the 'Latest News,' you read about the record harvest, about the flight of the Chkalov team and the reception for them in the Kremlin, and all this makes you happy and excited. And once again you awake from a lethargic sleep. The knockout is over, and the person begins to live."

Afinogenov now referred to his earlier dreams of an autonomous life as moments of "lethargic sleep," as a "knockout" phase, implying that he had lacked any consciousness when recording those thoughts. By contrast, the "return to life" subsumed his reintegration into the Soviet system and his renewed participation in the heroic life of the collective and in the course of history. As long as his personal existence evolved away from the collective body of the Soviet people, it remained small and insignificant. Only in aligning himself with the Soviet system could he realize himself as a person.[49]

He described a similar turning point a few days later, referring to it as an "awakening." As he now disclosed, he had spent the past nights waiting to be arrested. But now he knew that his fears were unfounded: "Over there, at the Lubianka, the people are intelligent. Despite their busy schedules and the insane amount of work, they see down to the roots of everything . . . and no wave will force them to arrest an innocent person." The following day Afinogenov once more celebrated his "fundamental and unusual break," namely, his newfound certainty that he would not be arrested. He felt embarrassed that he had confided his earlier fears to the diary. To underscore how different he now felt, he even questioned the authorship of those despairing thoughts: "Where did these thoughts spring from? Who wrote them?"[50]

Afinogenov seemed to be implying that there were two different persons living inside him, who assessed the political situation in opposite terms and therefore also pursued contrasting means of self-realization. One lived in permanent fear of arrest and dreamed of a solitary existence which would shelter him from the corrupt social environment. The other disclaimed the likelihood of arrest and, indeed, the impurity of the social order, calling for the individual's integration into the Soviet system. It would be tempting to view these diverging notions of individual autonomy and social self-integration as expressions of Afinogenov's private and public selves, with Afinogenov privately yearning for personal independence and freedom, while maintaining in public an image of himself that would conform to official Soviet norms. The fact that these contrasting identities were played out in Afinogenov's private diary would seem to suggest how much his official self-image interfered with his own self-definition and how difficult it was for him to retain a private sense of himself in distinction from the social identity prescribed by the regime.[51] Yet this interpretation, which emphasizes the disparity between private and official self-definitions and proceeds from a belief in the primacy of the private domain, obscures the links between Afinogenov's diverging assessments of himself. If we stop treating individual entries in isolation, and view them instead as elements of a larger narrative structure, the diary emerges as a form of spiritual writing, organized in such a way as to enact the experience of conversion. Afinogenov described this conversion variously as a return to life, a new birth, and the attainment of a higher consciousness and purity. The diary thus served as a means of furthering his personal salvation.

Conversion was the founding experience for a Communist. Communists could make no credible claim to party membership without proving that they had experienced conversion. For all their variations, Communist autobiographies from the early Soviet period, which were written as part of the application process for party membership, described a conversion experience dividing the lives of candidates into two phases: an early phase marked by backwardness, passivity, and a lack of consciousness; and a mature, active, and conscious phase induced by exposure to the teachings of the Communist party. It was on the strength of a Communist's insight into the historical role of the party and his ensuing conversion that he acquired his vanguard status as a leader of progressive mankind.[52]

Afinogenov realized that conversion could not be reduced to a single experience of rebirth, such as the one he had described after his self-critical speech at the meeting of Moscow playwrights. As with a Christian believer, his conversion was rather a lifelong process, to be reenacted and reaffirmed time and again. The initial occasion of seeing the light and turning in one's tracks, however dramatic, constituted only a prelude to an extended spiritual life. As a scholar of Christian conversion has written, after the "initial startled awakening," the convert had to remain "steadily alert to signs of saving grace and backsliding, always questioning the genuineness of the former and fearing false security . . . Assurance, like joy, grief, or fatigue, generates its own other set of dangers such as pride, despair, or complacency. Each achievement can thus spark another cycle of guilt and self-testing."[53]

In the period following his expulsion from the party, Afinogenov through his diary writings consistently tried to turn in his tracks and reach a purer form of consciousness, which he sometimes referred to as a "second stage" of comprehension. For example, on hearing that a number of colleagues, among them a former friend, the writer Vsevolod Ivanov, were spreading a rumor that he was under arrest, Afinogenov wrote: "How can one live among such double-dealers, cowards and fainthearted types!" The next day, however, he took a different stance: "Yesterday I didn't succeed at all in reaching the second stage . . . Today I did, and I'm happy about it." Now, he wrote, he understood the all too human motivations of Ivanov's behavior; no longer indignant, he reacted with understanding and compassion. The diary also recorded instances when Afinogenov was unable to sustain a conversion and reverted to his old self. On October 2, 1937, he noted his enthusiasm for a speech in which Stalin had declared that enemies were frequently those who showed excessive zeal. In striking contrast, the entry of the following day resounded with despair: "Depression, what leaden depression! . . . Now that I've retreated from my confidence and fallen back into my ordinary state, I'm suddenly afraid that I won't be able to hold out, again I began to fear that I might lose my mind." A few weeks later, again noting that he kept returning to his customary doubts and fears, he reprimanded himself: "Why did you become weak?"[54]

This dialectical pattern of certainty and self-assurance giving way to doubts which in turn are dispelled in the name of a higher consciousness can be observed not only in the sequence of diary entries but within single entries as well. Many entries of the period of his exclusion from the party begin with doubts, despair, and complaints that he cannot comprehend his position. Typically these entries end on a confident and optimistic note, with Afinogenov hailing his rediscovered sense of belonging and purpose. The function of the diary was to dispel doubts and dissonance so as to allow him to achieve a higher form of consciousness and unity. Afinogenov likened the emergence of a new "insight" to an "almost mystical miracle through which I was reborn."[55]

In fact, a conversion motif underlies the entire structure of Afinogenov's diary from the onset of the purge campaign. It is a narrative of a gradual coming to the light, a progression that at the outset is tortuous and marked by frequent backslidings, but that becomes increasingly steady and determined. In May 1937, on the day of his expulsion, Afinogenov confided to his diary that he could make little sense of this act. No longer an active participant in the unfolding of history, he felt brutally pushed about by an external force and therefore uncertain about his fate.[56] In late summer of that year, though, he looked back on months following his loss of party membership as a "knockout" phase, a time filled with doubts, fears, and escapist dreams. As much as he condemned this phase, it had served an important purpose: the narrative of conversion and rebirth could not function without a previous degeneration and death. It was as such, as a period of backsliding and weakness of mind, that Afinogenov integrated his doubts and his incipient criticism of party policies into the overall conversion narrative of his diary.

Beginning in the late summer of 1937, Afinogenov showed himself increasingly convinced that he had gained profound insight into the political processes at work around him. He understood better than before that the purge policies paved the way toward the Communist paradise and that it was ludicrous for an individual to oppose this world-historical process. With this insight, Afinogenov also saw himself as justified in reclaiming his position as a leading Communist dramatist, for he had now attained precisely the type of deeper understanding of reality in its revolutionary development that was essential to a Soviet artist. His previous lack of this vision had been at the core of all attacks and criticism against him in previous years. He now repudiated his occasional fantasy of leaving the writing profession and becoming a simple member of the Soviet collective, a tractor driver somewhere in the provinces.[57] Afinogenov condemned what may be termed a "small deeds" ethos typical of the late nineteenth-century Russian intelligentsia in favor of what he now considered an infinitely more meaningful, life-transforming mission as a Soviet writer serving the Communist regime. In his capacity as an engineer of human souls, he would have unique opportunities to contribute directly to the creation of the new man.

Inkwell on the Master's Desk

Afinogenov scripted these conversion scenarios against a background of intense existential uncertainty. His proclamations of reintegration into the Soviet universe were belied by his pariah-like standing in society. His position worsened on September 1, 1937, when the presidium of the Writers' Union expelled him from the union's ranks. It was a shattering event, a public ostracism on a par with his expulsion from the party, or perhaps even worse, because he had now lost all institutional connection with Soviet society and was not even recognized as a writer.

He had every reason to see his removal from the Writers' Union as a prelude to his arrest.[58]

One of the very few people who stood by Afinogenov in this period of utmost duress was Boris Pasternak. The two writers had known each other since 1936, when they were awarded neighboring dachas in Peredelkino. In the summer and fall of 1937 Pasternak, who at the time was working on sketches that he would later extend into the novel *Doctor Zhivago,* was not afraid to talk with the ostracized playwright, to take long walks with him through the village, or to visit him at his dacha. Their conversations allowed Afinogenov to share his despair and his fears with a trusted person who comforted and helped him retain his sanity. Beyond lending such vital support, Pasternak also embodied a model of personal comportment that fascinated Afinogenov. He admired Pasternak's literary passion, which rendered him oblivious to the world: the buzz of the Moscow literary scene, the intrigues in the Writers' Union, the feats of heroic Soviet citizens lauded by the media. Afinogenov was particularly impressed by Pasternak's fearlessness, an attitude that was rooted in his self-mastery. He was a "living model of this vital sort of stoicism." In the presence of people like Pasternak, "you learn the most important thing—the ability to live independently under any circumstances whatsoever." But while he admired Pasternak's "crystalline transparency" and exclusive dedication to his art, Afinogenov was unable and unwilling to adopt this behavioral model for himself. That Pasternak did not read newspapers or listen to the radio amazed him: "This is strange to me, who can't live through a single day without the news." It was imperative for Afinogenov to reside in the world, and not to situate himself outside it in a mode of stoic indifference. This world was the universe of the emerging socialist society. Even if that society barred him from recognition as a cultural leader, he could not help following its construction, as it was relayed through the lines of the newspapers and the voices of the radio.[59]

While Afinogenov documented his encounters with the poet in his diary, he also used the diary to engage in several other conversations, to come to terms with the question of his fate. On September 4, 1937, three days after his expulsion from the Writers' Union, he wrote an imagined interrogation scene. The long entry reveals how feverishly his thoughts revolved around his imminent arrest, the accusations he would face, and the ways he could respond to them. The "minutes of an interrogation," written as a dialogue between an "interrogator" and a first-person narrator (whom I will call Afinogenov), also makes clear that Afinogenov could not help thinking about his personal fate in dramaturgical terms. On the world-historical stage, the life of the Communist writer was entering the decisive act. He knew it to be a turning point, but the form of its resolution remained unclear.

Time and again in this transcript, the NKVD interrogator prodded Afinogenov to admit to his "counterrevolutionary work" with "base enemies of the people" and to confess his "enormous guilt." Afinogenov in turn professed ignorance about the reasons for his arrest. He had not committed a single crime against the Soviet order and was free of any "social guilt." His exclusion from society was "unjust," all the more so because he had changed since the spring of 1937. He no longer had anything in common with his previous self, who, he implied, had not been entirely guiltless. What was chiefly at stake in this interrogation, he and the interrogator agreed, was the purity of Afinogenov's Communist conscience. Like Pasternak, Afinogenov was committed to an ideal of inner purity, but his was not the purity of the artist communing with his work. Afinogenov conceived of himself first and foremost as a builder of the new world. Purity of his soul was a vital precondition for membership in the new world, and it could only be attested by the guardians of that world—the NKVD. Afinogenov asked his interrogator for an in-depth "political-moral evaluation" of his case. Once his purity was attested he would be readmitted into society and its vanguard formation, the Communist party. This test could take as long as three years, Afinogenov suggested. "Or perhaps five," the interrogator interjected, referring to the time Afinogenov would have to spend in prison or exile before becoming eligible for rehabilitation. The protocol ended as the interrogator readied himself to take notes: "Let us now begin, point by point."

This conversation with the NKVD did not, of course, take place in reality. The understanding Afinogenov reached with the interrogator was imaginary. It remained to be seen whether Afinogenov could sustain the confidence that his narrator showed under interrogation, given the pressure of waiting, night after night, for the dreaded black limousine that on several occasions had stopped near his dacha to collect one of his neighbors.[60] A long diary entry written a few days after the protocol revealed a despair that the description of the interrogation lacked, but it also showed how Afinogenov believed he could overcome his crisis. Although highly personal in tone, the entry incorporated elements of Afinogenov's plays. It reads as an outline of the way he believed the drama of his future life would unfold.

He began by describing his sadness and saying he was haunted by a perennial question: "Why? Why do I, a person and a writer who is completely innocent, now have to live like an individual cut off from the world? Why don't I have the right to rejoice with everybody else? Why am I instead excluded, lonely, and looked upon with suspicion . . . why?" Yet in the next sentence Afinogenov scolded himself for being so weak-spirited and selfish: "You again think that everything has to do with yourself. You still can't grasp the thought that you will understand everything only when the purpose of all that is taking place has become clear to you. That purpose now is the general purge of our Soviet house of all impurity. During this purge, which will allow the whole country to breathe freely and happily, inevitably a few will get hurt and for no reason." It could happen, for example, that a cup would be thrown away by accident even though it was still in good condition. If he were an object like the cup, Afinogenov reasoned, he would be able to do nothing but deplore his fate:

> But after all you are a human being. And you must understand with all your heart that, even if you are destroyed, there is no reason to cry. You have to be happy that the time of such a purge has come and that you have been swept away not because of somebody's evil intentions but by pure chance. And would this be a reason for you to request a halt to the removal of garbage? Of course not . . . When the zealous master, while sweeping out the garbage, finds behind the window the inkwell that had been thrown out by mistake, he will give orders to have it washed and put back on the table. The inkwell—that is you! And you will have a place on the master's table for a long time yet, and who knows, perhaps he will even use you to write some new remarkable thoughts? In any event, is the purpose of what's currently going on now clear to you? Yes. Do you want to be a participant in this purpose or an inanimate object? A participant, of course![61]

The scenario is familiar from Afinogenov's *Fear.* The purge proceeds as an act of housecleaning. A particular object resurfaces, too: it is the Sèvres cup, an artifact of a faded aristocratic culture that has no place in a socialist home. Afinogenov invoked it in his diary to represent a dead and passive object, against which he situated himself as a conscious and active revolutionary subject. The juxtaposition of object and subject makes clear that Afinogenov understood his role as a Communist writer as the highest form of active participation in the unfolding of history. As a playwright standing next to Stalin, he was endowed with a demiurgic capacity to mold social relations and partake in the creation of the perfect world of the future.

And yet this highest stage of self-realization as a Communist and a writer entailed Afinogenov's displacement from a subject to an object: to the inkwell on Stalin's desk. The highest level of subjectivity for a mortal Communist was to become an object in the hands of the immortal Soviet god and leader, Stalin. As Afinogenov clearly stated, it was *through him* that Stalin wrote his own thoughts. He was a tool by means of which history—embodied by Joseph Stalin—wrote itself. The most creative writer in the Stalinist system was thus one whose work was directly animated by Stalin. Stalin personified history's revolutionary development, playing a role comparable to Hegel's world spirit, and for this reason the highest aspiration for Afinogenov—and other Soviet artists, as well—was to occupy a place near Stalin in order to share in his prophetic vision and transformative powers.

As Afinogenov's description suggests, self-realization had different gradations according to an individual's place in the Soviet system. In the lowest echelon were those who did not belong to the party; lacking in consciousness, they possessed at most only dim insight into historical progress and thus were largely its objects rather than its subjects. Party members could attain a much more profound understanding of the laws of history, and it was this higher epistemological status that legitimized their endeavor to transform and perfect the world. Yet even a party member's insight was only partial, as Stalin alone possessed a total vision.

In his diary Afinogenov once likened himself to a "bricklayer who stands on the scaffolding and has trouble understanding the meaning of what he is building and its architectural form."[62] As a construction worker, he was actively taking part in the raising of the Communist edifice. What is more, his workplace on the scaffolding elevated him to great heights and thus granted him a scope of vision unavailable to ordinary earthbound beings. Still, he lacked the full conceptual grasp of the project that only the architect, Stalin, possessed. Working on the scaffolding was also perilous, as any careless move, any slip in historical interpretation, could cause a deadly fall. Even so, the bricklayer's vocation, at once limitless, circumscribed, and dangerous, was what animated Afinogenov throughout the 1930s.

These passages of the diary offer a glimpse into the self-destructive dynamic of the Communist project that was particularly apparent during the Great Terror. It was not that Afinogenov was forced to submit to laws of history decreed by Soviet leaders. He himself actively worked to create a historical existence for himself as a highest form of self-realization. And yet even the ideal subjectivity in the Soviet order, for which Afinogenov strove, could not transcend an object relation toward Stalin, who was the ultimate subject of history. This explains why Afinogenov (and other Communists as well) accepted the prospect of being crushed by the party and thrown into the dustbin of history: this apparent act of self-destruction contributed to history's eventual consummation and thereby satisfied the central purpose to which he, as subject, had devoted his life.

In the fall of 1937 Afinogenov became increasingly convinced that he would soon be readmitted to the Soviet collective. In his eyes, the celebration of the twentieth anniversary of the revolution on November 7 and the elections to the Supreme Soviet in early December represented the threshold of the new socialist society. He expected the purges to reach their logical end at the close of 1937, when the new political order would have come into being, staffed by a new generation of pure Soviet citizens and freed from the impurities of the past. He, too, he believed, could belong to this new order, thanks to his efforts to purify his self. Yet, ultimately, only "honest [literary] work" for the country would ensure his reintegration into society, "not letters, protests, complaints. None of this will do; there have been too many of these complaints and letters." To qualify as legitimate, useful labor, writing had to leave the descriptive mode and become transformative. This was not the case with the petitions and protests he had composed in the wake of his expulsion from the party, which had harped on the injustices or errors committed in his case and thus merely invoked a static sense of himself. The only acceptable way to write about the self was by means of a narrative of transformation and renewal.[63]

The specific project through which Afinogenov hoped to redeem himself as a Soviet writer was a novel—the same novel he had sketched out in his diary in 1935. In late 1937 he began to work on the project in earnest. Entitled *Three Years,* the novel was to span the period from December 1934 to the end of 1937. It was to trace the development of its protagonist, Viktor, through the stages of personal degeneration, crisis, and subsequent recovery. By means of the novel, Afinogenov sought to convey how the Soviet population had experienced the Stalinist purge campaign. Back in 1935 his idea had been to address the loss of faith he felt in himself and in his environment. Now, almost three years later, the story was teleologically reworked into a dialectical cycle of crisis, dissociation, and higher synthesis. At the same time, the personal story of the autobiographical hero described a historical narrative. The three years of his crisis and recovery matched the three years of a larger Soviet crisis and its resolution: from the first appearance of counterrevolutionary action in connection with the murder of Kirov in December 1934 to the victorious autumn of 1937, when the new socialist society would have freed itself of its enemies.[64]

In a diary entry Afinogenov sketched out a central scene of the projected work. A character, possibly the protagonist, returns to Moscow after serving his term of exile and meets an old friend who had written him off. "It's as if he had arrived from the world beyond the grave, and he is in a hurry to express everything: that he has returned a completely different person, that now he has changed as much as this remarkable city."[65] A central theme of the planned novel was thus the self-transformative labor brought about by the Stalinist purge policies.

Afinogenov sought to portray an individual who, responding to the call of the purge campaign to transform himself, worked on himself and ultimately emerged as a new person. Obviously one of the goals for Afinogenov in writing the novel was to underscore his own self-transformative work and thus to support his claim for readmission into the circle of Communist writers. Yet his autobiographical exercise also revealed the extent to which he sought to write himself into history. Looked upon in retrospect, after his successful regeneration, his expulsion from the Communist party and subsequent work on himself appeared as the very course of history working through his body and spirit.

Afinogenov's diary bore a close and complex relationship to his work on the novel. Notwithstanding its highly personal character, the diary retained a distinct literary purpose throughout the entire purge period. While attempting to resolve personal uncertainties and fears, Afinogenov plotted them in such a way as to make them fit the structure of his novel. (To be sure, a comparison between the two works has to remain speculative, since the novel was never finished, and only a few chapters exist, along with outlines and scattered scenes recorded in the diary.) The diary and the novel concerned the same themes of personal degeneration, work on the self, and renewal. In this respect, the diary served Afinogenov as an autobiographical construction site. It was a laboratory of the self, revealing the inner workings of the soul, including its darker aspects: doubts, weaknesses, sins. Most important, the diary narrative was open-ended; it referred to an unfinished, ever expanding self-project. The novel, by contrast, even though it also addressed impurities of the soul, would have presented a finished, harmonious picture of the human psyche. Its narrative would have spanned a full—and, from the beginning, preordained—cycle of degeneration and regeneration, culminating in the hero's salvation. This distinction suggests that Afinogenov never intended to publish the diary itself.

Rather, it was a literary quarry from which to carve material for his novelistic self-presentation. Thus it made sense for him to cut his diary into pieces, integrating the segments he deemed most worthwhile into his published works.

While accumulating in the diary raw material for his novel, Afinogenov admonished himself to practice utter sincerity. Only if his writings captured the essence of his inner struggle could his twofold project of restoration as a writer and self-renewal as a Soviet citizen succeed. He was aware of the questions that such professions of sincerity raised in the context of the purges and his possible arrest. A section of the invented interrogation protocol addressed this problem. To prove how dedicated he was to self-renewal, the narrator told the interrogator that he kept a diary in which he made notes on his "personal growth and development."

Interrogator: I don't believe your notes.

I: I knew that as well.

Interrogator: Why?

I: Because once a person is waiting to be arrested and starts keeping notes, it's clear, I should think, that he's keeping them for the future reader, the interrogator, and that means that he's embellishing everything as much as he can, in order to prove his innocence. And the notes from the past, from past years, how shall I put it, are "edited"—he makes corrections, makes cuts, crosses things out . . . That's what you thought, isn't it?

Interrogator: Yes.

The narrator confided that he, too, had thought about this, and had wondered whether he should stop writing. The problem he voiced was the problem of sincerity in an age of intense surveillance and mandated openness. How could Afinogenov credibly state his genuine devotion to the revolution when he had nothing but words with which to do so, and when the truth of these words, as judged by a suspicious state reader, would determine whether he lived or died? Awareness of this future reader would undermine the whole enterprise of writing sincerely. But the need to write, so as to remember his inner experience of the purge, proved stronger than these doubts. In making this decision he was also helped by the realization that the NKVD would not believe his account. As his narrator explained:

> That you don't believe these notes, well, that's natural, so be it; of course, if you had found pernicious thoughts or even anecdotes, then you would have believed them, that is, you would view them differently, you would view them as proof of my guilt. But that's understandable as well. But you don't believe what I have written for myself, I knew that, I thought about that, and this immediately made it easier for me to decide the issue—yes, I must continue to write. Because, if I had thought that you would believe my notes, then it would have been as if I were writing for a stranger, and there goes my ability to be candid with myself—all the same I would have felt your eye on these pages in the future. But once I had already understood that you wouldn't believe anything in any case and would only scoff as you read what I had recorded, then I immediately was relieved of your presence during my work on my diary and once again began to write freely and simply, as I had done before, in years past.[66]

This is not to say that Afinogenov wrote his diary without the NKVD in mind. The day after he composed the interrogation scene he pondered what had been more strongly at work in it: "sincerity or the desire to pour out onto paper everything I'd wanted to talk about with the interrogator for a long time. It's probably both things at once. But that's not what is important. What is important is the understanding that Dostoevsky, when describing Myshkin's epileptic fits, was writing about himself and his own feelings, and that this is not only an artist's right, it is his primary obligation."[67] Afinogenov had trouble disentangling the political, moral, and literary pressures at work in him. The question of whether he wrote his diaristic confession for the NKVD or for himself could not be clearly answered. Expelled from the party and under threat of arrest, he was under intense political pressure to perform Bolshevik self-criticism, but at the same time he embraced this voice of the contrite Communist as his true, moral self. What is more, both political and moral pressures fused with his task as a Soviet writer to produce literature that was socially and morally exemplary and possessed a kernel of subjective truth. Afinogenov knew that the literary worth of his projected novel would depend on whether it expressed his inner truth. To be able to write morally exemplary literature thus required raising oneself to the heights of moral thinking.

It was with all of these political, moral, and literary aims in mind that Afinogenov wrote his diary. The diary played a crucial role in his quest for self-renewal as a Soviet citizen, a Communist, and a writer. In the fall of 1937, looking back at the previous months, he wrote: "The notes have saved me. Every night I would sit down and write about everything that I had given so much thought to during the night and carried in me, all my agonizing and oppressive thoughts. And as soon as these thoughts spilled onto the paper, I felt better. My mind and heart were relieved of the pressure; it was as if another person had assumed the burden of my somber thoughts and given me respite." Freeing him from the burden of his "black thoughts," the diary figured as a rubbish heap of sorts. Like Stepan Podlubny, who discharged onto the pages of his diary all the refuse accumulating in his soul, Afinogenov sought to unburden himself in his diary of all that was illegitimate in the Communist world and all that he regarded as evidence of his impurity. Yet at the same time the diary provided him with a perspective on his self-renewal. The sequence of entries constituted, in his own words, road marks on the path from darkness to light, along which he was traveling. One of Afinogenov's principal goals in keeping his diary throughout the period of terror was thus the production of a visible record of self-development.[68]

Self-constitution in the Bolshevik vein was for Afinogenov an unending process of struggle and transformation, which he accomplished through writing. To stop on this road would mean to retreat into one's present, and hence imperfect, self. And stasis was tantamount to degeneration: "Right now, today, for example, I got up with the desire to move forward somehow . . . Not to stop reflecting, and to accumulate what I've already begun to accumulate; to look back continually and examine myself, and not allow myself to become my former self, not even a tiny bit." Conversely, purity could be experienced only in the act of purification, in the very struggle against lingering impurities within. Writing was a tool by which to discard impurities and also to excavate a pure inner essence, which Afinogenov understood as the Communist essence in his soul. Tellingly, he discovered this pure essence, "the best" that was in him, just before the revolutionary holiday of November 7, 1937. The holiday, which was to summon a new generation of young leaders into existence, also marked the day of Afinogenov's own rejuvenation:

> Today . . . I looked through my notes of the past two years. Carefully, every single day. My impression: an enormous amount of time wasted, an inability to make use of circumstances for work; a lot of futile meetings, of grudges at every turn, of vain expectations for something better, and it seemed to me that this "something better" would inevitably come from someone else, but that I myself should just sit there, with my arms folded, and wait for

> this person. Only now do I understand that the best is within me. This summer, these feverish thoughts of mine, my notes—they are the best that is in me . . . Ahead of me lie arduous work and new tasks that are so different and more difficult than anything I have done in the past. The more difficult the life ahead, the more fruitful will it be.[69]

Afinogenov welcomed the obstacles that marked the distance he had already traveled and the road still ahead of him. The more challenges, weaknesses, and doubts he encountered, the more effort he would expend to overcome them and the purer he would emerge as a result. This mode of self-constitution and self-perfection, defined as an unending process of work and self-transcendence, was most clearly present in Afinogenov's diary of the terror period, and this was the chief reason he considered this period to be the most precious in his entire life.

Reinstatement

Convinced that by now he had reached the level of inner purity expected of a Communist, Afinogenov petitioned for his rehabilitation in December 1937. In his diary he concluded the fateful year 1937, which had nearly destroyed him, with exclamations of gratitude for having had the opportunity to regain himself as a person and be reborn. Calling 1937 the "year of my birth," Afinogenov undoubtedly had in mind many other party members and fellow writers for whom the year had brought destruction and death.[70]

On January 18, 1938, the Central Committee issued a resolution admitting that many Communists had been unjustly expelled from the party in the preceding months. They had been the victims of enemies within the party and the state administration who concealed their true faces behind the appearance of zealous vigilance. In the following weeks, thousands of party members were reinstated, Afinogenov among them. His diary describes his readmission in detail. He was called to a meeting in the local district committee, where the party secretary declared that Afinogenov's expulsion and his suffering were the work of enemies still hiding in the Soviet literary administration. But she also asserted that the playwright bore a personal responsibility for his entanglements with the enemy:

> "Of course, if Afinogenov had found in himself enough steadfastness to break with Averbakh and Kirshon back then [in 1932], after the Central Committee's resolution on RAPP, he wouldn't have gone so far in his ties to them. But I think that what he went through in these nine months is enough of a school for him. This should enable him to still write something." Everybody agreed. My eyes became misty with tears. I muttered something, that they would not regret their decision, that I would justify their trust through all my life and work—and I was dismissed.[71]

In the diary Afinogenov fully accepted his personal responsibility for his tribulations. While the party had indicated that many of the arrests of 1937 had been prompted by enemies masquerading as zealous Communists, he had been too weak and complacent to notice this and intervene. His weakness, he wrote, was in fact an "illness" that he had carried long before the outbreak of the purges. Harmless at first, like a body ache or a cold, it was recurrent and became more serious over time. Enemies in the Writers' Organization noticed his vulnerability and took advantage of it, using him to demonstrate their vigilance against subversive elements. While he thus characterized his expulsion from the party as a move by his enemies, Afinogenov did not question the inquisitorial mechanism of the purge as such. On the contrary: he owed his life to the party's insistence on testing the purity of its followers. On his own he would not have found the strength to free himself from his near-fatal corruption. Looking back he realized that not only had he withstood the pressure, he had emerged from the nine-month purgatory as a better and purer person: "Now I am . . . proven and tested in the hottest fire . . . Now I am not just a Stalinist artist but also a Bolshevik of Stalinist steel!"[72]

Afinogenov reserved his highest gratitude for Stalin. In waiting, not acting precipitously on the denunciatory appeals against Afinogenov, the Soviet leader had expressed his trust in his literary disciple: "Long live He, to whom all my thoughts are now directed. Long may he live and rule over us with his genius, the genius of Georgian passion, Russian reason, American sweep, Leninist revolutionary principledness, and Human humaneness!" At its core, Afinogenov implied, the Soviet system was defined by Stalin's "human sensitiveness"—the fostering care he extended to each individual who was willing to work on himself and demonstrate his usefulness for society and history. Apart from Stalin, Afinogenov also felt obliged to the NKVD: "And thanks also from the bottom of my heart to those, up there at the Lubianka, engaged in their furious work rooting out the enemy riffraff, who didn't heed the deafening howls of scribblers hiding behind their newspaper pseudonyms; who conduct their work without blunders, who don't tolerate errors, but strike into the enemy's very heart." The playwright also gratefully remembered the friends and colleagues who had stood by him throughout the most difficult time of his life.[73]

Even after his rehabilitation Afinogenov supported the purge campaign, which now targeted overzealous opportunists who had furthered their careers by denouncing "honest" Communists. He longed for the unmasking of the literary officials who in his eyes had instigated the mass expulsion of writers like himself. He leveled against them the same accusations that had been made against him, condemning them for their lack of commitment to the Bolshevik government and for their distortion of Soviet reality. Reading a recent novel by Veniamin Kaverin, Afinogenov felt a "wave of fury toward these insipid, cold books, written with an indifference for life, a life that [these authors] are called upon to justify but that, in the depths of their souls, they don't like." He denounced the novel as "harmful and poisonous like Yagoda's quicksilver fumes," which "slowly engulfed the soul, causing degeneration and emptiness." His impulse was to "smash the author's face" and "drag to the NKVD all those who had the audacity to waste so much paper for this vile little novel."[74]

In the wake of his reinstatement to the party, Afinogenov turned to his diary again, intending to follow his usual practice of cutting out segments of it and transferring them to the outline of the novel. But he made an exception for the entries from the terror period: "Yesterday, as I was working on the novel, I took scissors to the 'reserve fund'—the diary of 1937. It grieved me to destroy the pages. So much is associated with them. But I didn't get as far as the fateful dates and notes. They must be left intact; after all, I remember my New Year's resolution to read these notes more often!" In his eyes, the diary of 1937 stood out as material evidence of the process of his renewal and of his new identity as a true Bolshevik. In this respect the diary of this period was no less important than his party membership booklet, which he kept looking at with unceasing wonder in the days after his reinstatement. Afinogenov had to preserve the diary entries of the most critical period in his life in order to know that he was truly one of the new Soviet men. It is only for this reason that his diary from the terror period has survived to the present day.[75]

In late 1938 Afinogenov sent a draft of a new play, *Moscow, Kremlin,* to Stalin for his evaluation. Around New Year's of 1939 he received a brief note from Stalin, addressed to "Comrade Afinogenov," apologizing for being too busy to read the script. Although Afinogenov was delighted that "*His* hand is writing to me again," Stalin's note indicated in a nutshell the playwright's weak standing in Soviet society. Stalin recognized him as a comrade, but had no time to read his work. Afinogenov was formally rehabilitated, but his career did not pick up, at least not immediately. As he noted in his diary, there was a cloud of suspicion hanging above him; colleagues would praise his work, "but with a reservation"; they would promise to present his plays, but not follow through; "meanwhile, time marches on and the plays are not staged." His salary for January 1939 consisted of 6 rubles; for February, of 20 rubles. When in the same month 170 Soviet writers received awards for achievement, he was not among them. Afinogenov was unable to get another play, *Her Children's Mother,* produced. This was his fifth piece that was not accepted for the Soviet stage. Earlier in his career, he mused, such rejections might have been tolerable. But in his present situation they were "sometimes exhausting." He was haunted by a feeling that his work would never be allowed back onto the stage.[76]

As before, Afinogenov situated his personal ruminations on recognition and failure in a historical frame. His situation as an outcast from the theater world confirmed his earlier fears that he would be swept away by the historical changes occurring in Soviet society. The young generation whose rise he had been observing since the mid-1930s had by now entered political and cultural life, assuming the positions of an older generation of officeholders. The specter of these young people made Afinogenov acutely aware of his own age. Yes, he had been reborn in the purge, but that period had also taken a toll: his rebound was "slow," and he again felt "tired and sick." He, once the youngest playwright who ever conversed with Stalin, now had to recognize that a new generation had passed him by. Afinogenov's diary of this period is filled with anxious reflections about his advancing age and his waning achievements.

Consistent with his belief that only youth imparted strength, vigor, and historical optimism, Afinogenov adopted a logical, if radical, solution. He sought to realize himself in an early death. Hailing his discovery of "indifference toward my personal life," he invoked a theme familiar from the 1937 diary; this time, however, it did not initiate his return into the life of the Soviet collective. Rather, it was to prepare him for his death which, he was certain, would occur soon. He conceived of his death not as a suicide, a self-willed expulsion from Soviet society, but as the culminating point of a historically defined life, and as a way to remain young forever. His diary of 1939 concluded with a series of aphorisms, the last of which read: "He who dies as a young man cannot age. For us his face remains wonderful and young for all time."[77]

These thoughts developed in ways characteristic of Afinogenov, in his diary as well as in his works for the stage. In 1940 he started working on a new play, *On the Eve*—a play documenting the eve and the first days of the great war that, he was sure, was imminent. The play, he wrote in a note to the defense committee of the Writers' Union in February 1941, was to be set "on the eve of those events that we are currently approaching. It is about how people in light of these events reconsider norms governing their personal lives and their mutual relations." Just like Afinogenov in his diary, the protagonists of *On the Eve* learned to cope with their fear of death and to understand the relative value of a personal life in a moment of world-historical proportions. The play was officially commissioned within days after Germany's invasion of the Soviet Union. Afinogenov had only to endow the abstract enemy forces of his first draft with the faces of the invading Nazi forces.

Afinogenov outlined both his play and the historical plot for his personal life before the outbreak of the German-Soviet war. Both came to life after June 1941. Ten days into the war, on July 1, 1941, he began a new diary. He wrote it by hand in a notebook, outwardly distinct from the loose sheets of paper on which he had typed his diary in preceding years. He entitled it "Diary of the Last War." The title referred to the apocalyptic battle between the forces of socialism and imperialism that Soviet Communists had been anticipating for at least a decade, but it also had a personal meaning: "I'm speaking of myself. For me this is the last step in life. I don't know on what day my life will end or how I will die, but I will die. I know that, and I am prepared." Millions of Soviet citizens would live on, Afinogenov wrote, but he would not be among them, and he would not live to see the perfect future. It was not that he sought death in war "as an atonement or a sacrifice"; rather, he embraced it as a "natural end to a life lived in a fateful period of world history."[78]

The playwright found his fate. He remained in Moscow in the summer and fall of 1941. In mid-October his family was evacuated to Tashkent; meanwhile, he was sent on mission to Kuibyshev, where parts of the Soviet government had been relocated. In late October he returned to the beleaguered capital to obtain clearance to travel to England and the United States and give lectures on the heroic struggle of the Soviet people against the invaders. He died on October 29, 1941, struck by a German bomb, when he was in the Central Committee building, the institutional heart of the Soviet Communist party.[79]

Postmortem

While describing in his war diary how he mastered his fear of death, Afinogenov voiced one worry: Would his diary survive? "You, my future accidental reader, where will you find this notebook? As you wander the highways of this great country, with a sack on your shoulders, will you stop to pick up this dust-covered little book from the ground, or will you, like others, tread on it, tired from the long journey, and keep walking?"[80] For Afinogenov, who remained uncertain about the extent of his rehabilitation as a Soviet playwright, these questions referred to more than his diary. The decisive question was how his life as a whole would be remembered. Would he be recognized by posterity as a genuine Bolshevik, or would the Soviet people trample his plays, which had been discarded in the Stalinist purges, underfoot as they lay in the dust?

Afinogenov's insistent orientation toward his death and afterlife in Soviet collective memory was consistent with Communist self-realization, which reached its highest point with the Communist entering the pantheon of history. A Communist's biological life span was brief and inferior compared with his life as a historical subject, which could extend long after his death, but which depended on whether historically more advanced posterity granted him a "historical" existence.[81]

Eulogies by friends and colleagues in the years after his death vindicated Afinogenov as a Communist who communed with history. In a memoir prepared for the third anniversary of Afinogenov's death, Boris Pasternak described him in terms uncannily similar to the mold of youthful immortality that Afinogenov had sought to preserve for himself: "There was something ideal . . . about him. He was tall and slender, and he moved gracefully; his highly held head had features of classical regularity, somehow corresponding to the beauty of his inner character, which united purity and strength. Such was also his talent: it exuded the freshness of youth, a light, transparent, classical mold." Pasternak did not directly refer to history, but in casting Afinogenov as a classical hero he aligned him with the Stalinist system's self-representation as a neoclassical age standing at the apogee of developed humanity. Writing in 1946, Boris Igritsky addressed the historical quality of Afinogenov's life more directly. The playwright had "searched for many things, . . . experimented a lot . . . but he never shunned or hid from life, from his epoch, its storms and tempests, its passions, and its difficulties. He grew with the party and the people, he boldly marched forward, forward." Images like this one, of "boldly marching forward with the party," were standard Soviet laudatory formulas and were equally applied to honor other dead writers. But set against the background of Afinogenov's intimate writings these rhetorical clichés disclose an intense transfer of meaning between Soviet ideological language and the Communist's subjective experience.[82]

On October 29, 1946, the fifth anniversary of Afinogenov's death, an "evening of remembrance" took place at the Moscow House of Writers. A range of writers paid tribute to their late colleague; presiding over the meeting was Vsevolod Vishnevsky, the same Vishnevsky who had formulated the public accusation against Afinogenov at the fateful meeting of April 1937. The most remarkable speech of the evening came from the writer Viktor Fink. He had studied Afinogenov's diary and wanted to share his impressions about the document with his audience:

> Before you lies a voluminous stack of paper, in which a person lives just with himself and onto which he has poured his soul. It presents a new, hidden world, invisible to the people around him, a set of ideas and deeds that nobody has known about . . . [The diaries] do not just present interesting biographical and literary material, they are interesting material for the study of a progressive person of our time: what he wrote about and how he wrote, how he lived. In reading through hundreds of pages, I did not see anything but themes of fundamental social, literary, and political interest. This was a man who embraced the highest ideals. The wholehearted nature and spiritual purity of this person filled me with envy and delight.

In light of the spiritual integrity of this journal, Fink went on, a thought had occurred to him. In analogy to the science of archaeology, which was able to restore past civilizations to life, "perhaps the human sciences will advance to the point that people will learn how to reconstruct the moral and physical features of a person based on his writings." In such fashion a future scientist would be able to "reconstruct . . . Afinogenov, a person who was physically handsome, tall, endowed with the round head of a young Greek demigod; a person who lived with a calm confidence in the justice of life, and confidence in his own creative powers."[83]

What Fink laid out was a literal application of Nikolai Fedorov's philosophy of resurrection. Believing that personal writings formed the core of a person, the nineteenth-century philosopher had advocated a state order that would preserve these writings until scientific progress would make possible a person's physical resurrection from the spiritual extract of his texts. Fink shared an assumption with Fedorov and generations of the Russian intelligentsia that the core of a person resided in his or her writings. A text was not simply a reflection of reality; it was the very heart of consciousness. For Fink, Afinogenov's diary formed the essence of a fully lived, extraordinary life.[84] Any reader of the diary, Fink said, would take away a powerful sense that only "great people and a great epoch" could have given birth to someone like Afinogenov. His remark revealed that the historical consciousness that had animated Afinogenov's life lived on after his death. Just like Afinogenov, Fink and others searched for historical markers that would affirm the reality of socialist society. Now Afinogenov, through his early death, had become one such historical road mark. The unassailable integrity and beauty of his life was seen by his surviving contemporaries as evidence that the new socialist man did in fact exist. It was an interpretation that belied Afinogenov's own sense of his incompleteness.

None of those who eulogized Afinogenov at the anniversaries of his death mentioned his family: what had happened to his wife and daughters or how his aged mother had coped with the loss of her only son. Afinogenov's diary, too, had been largely silent about this side of his life. Both the diarist and the writers who remembered him focused insistently on history. They stressed those aspects of a person's life which they believed to carry historical value. Despite its introspective and reclusive tone, Afinogenov's diary of 1937 was not a record of his personal life. For instance, he hardly mentioned the birth of his second daughter. The deeply personal quality of that year's diary stems in the first place from Afinogenov's recognition that his life had suddenly acquired historical meaning: history, in the form of Stalin's purges, was passing directly through him. He seized on the drama of his own life as a drama of historical proportions. In addition, the vocation of playwright was inextricably connected to his life as a Communist, a life defined by a striving for a historical existence. This craving for historical significance explains why Afinogenov sought to realize his life to the fullest in a time of utmost struggle, coercion, and destruction.[85]

8

The Urge to Struggle On

The years of Stalin's rule stand out as one of the most violent chapters of the twentieth century. The Communist regime shattered countless lives and caused suffering on a scale that has still not been fully revealed. Personal diaries from the Stalin era, unearthed in great numbers after the opening of the Soviet archives, document in poignant detail how the regime's violent practices entered the lives of Soviet citizens, often with catastrophic effects. Yet many of the same diaries resonate with a striking urge for expression and self-realization amid conditions of massive repression. They reverberate with their authors' desire to be involved in the very revolutionary currents of thinking and acting that carried such destructive power for others and for some of the diarists themselves. The association of self-expression and terror in the making of these personal records is jarring to the contemporary Western reader, and it requires explanation.

An investigation of Stalin-era diaries reveals the appeal of Communist ideology to the self. Bolshevik activists called upon all members of the Soviet population to adopt the agenda of revolutionary transformation and become personally transformed in the process. To belong to the revolutionary community and to help carry out the laws of history promised intellectual, moral, and aesthetic fulfillment. Many diarists aligned themselves with revolutionary politics as a way to acquire a personal voice, which they alternatively referred to as their "personality," "biography," or "worldview." This voice took shape in critical engagement with an individual's previous disorganized, "passive," or selfish existence, for the purpose of sculpting a more socially valuable, less selfish, and enlarged self. Joining the revolution could thus spring from a self-expressive urge and not, as some commentators have claimed, from an impulse toward self-effacement.[1]

While a large number of diarists evinced a preoccupation with self-cultivation and self-transformation, the ideological language of self was highly variegated. Yet many of these records can be grouped according to shared themes and particular moments during the period of the 1920s and 1930s, when the desire for self-expression seemed to be particularly pronounced. Diaries in a first group were written by "class aliens" or "class enemies," most of them of intelligentsia pedigree, who sought to dismantle their "bourgeois personalities" in the context of the Communist campaign to bring down the "old world," which was in full swing in the late 1920s and early 1930s. Another set of diaries described processes of learning, acquisition of culture, and personality formation. Kept mostly by young people of lower-class origins, these began to appear in the early 1930s and were written against the background of an emerging "socialist civilization." Finally there was the Communist diary, which revealed a dramatic rise in self-expression in connection with internal party purge campaigns, culminating in the years of the Great Purges.

"If you think about it, how many lives are being lived around you," the young teacher Vera Pavlova noted in her diary in 1932, "lives long and short, full and barren, bright and dull, happy and unhappy. How many different people—creative and destructive, those who build, those who struggle alone and those who do so with the collective, people who in one way or another become part of the common edifice of the life of society, people like grains of sand, whom history invisibly inscribes on its pages." Pavlova was struck by the variations in the attitudes of the people around her; yet more striking are the categories she employed to make sense of life. These were the Manichean categories of construction and destruction, collectivism and individualism, bright expression and dull existence, which characterized the emerging socialist age.[2]

Pavlova believed that all these different, indeed contrasting, lives unfolded in historically lawful fashion. This idea—that history furnished the ultimate standard of a person's life and that the more a person's life served the needs of society and the more expressive it therefore was, the more historically valuable it was—goes beyond Pavlova's personal case. It was constitutive of self-definition more generally in the Stalin years, particularly during the prewar phase of "socialist construction." It is this orientation toward self-expression within a larger collective and in the service of historical action that constituted socialist subjectivity. On account of its communal strength and historical significance, this life promised authenticity and profound meaning, and it was intensely desired. It was contrasted to a life lived outside the collective or the flow of history. As much as diarists longed to partake in the life of the collective, they feared the void of meaning that expulsion from this universe entailed. Some spoke of their fear of turning into a "superfluous person," not needed by society; others compared themselves to the helpless characters of Chekhov's plays, who passively watched as life and history progressed beyond their waning personal horizons. They struggled not to be superfluous in an age when both their public worth and their self-esteem were determined above all by the extent of their "usefulness to society." In this struggle, diarists framed their hopes for belonging as well as their fears of not belonging in highly corporeal terms. They described the collective as a living organism, adherence to which imparted personal power, meaning, and vitality. In turn an inability or unwillingness to march in step with the collective could have crippling or paralyzing effects, as diarists felt cut off from the pulsating, enthusiastic, forever young revolutionary body.

A recurrent image in several diaries is that of the radio providing a surrogate connection to society for lonely individuals bypassed by the "general stream of life." As a transmitter of the festive sounds of Soviet holiday parades, or of the evening news with its proclamations of the Soviet people's most recent exploits, the radio became an embodiment of the collective. The more its broadcasts infused solitary listeners with enthusiasm, the more they described a sense of belonging in the Soviet historical universe. Yet the very picture of the lonely diarist, unable to create a feeling of connection other than through the crackling sounds of the radio or the recording of his thoughts in a diary, evokes isolation and despair, the unstated obverse to intensely described scenarios of belonging.

Socialist subjectivity is best understood not as a fixed entity, something one could possess once and for all, but as a state of mind that was attained in the very act of raising the self above its petty, parochial concerns onto the higher plane of historical engagement and action. To be lasting, this disposition required an ongoing effort to situate oneself in the world. Not every diary from this age shows the workings of socialist subjectivity in equal measure, and even fewer reveal the sum of its defining traits. But this disposition with its triple valuation of self-expression, collective action, and historical purpose mapped the default position for self-definition in the Soviet realm. This ideal form of personhood was markedly illiberal in the sense that it lacked a positive evaluation of autonomy and private values. Significantly, not only Communist ideologues but also critically minded Soviet intellectuals expressed disdain for "bourgeois" claims to individualist creativity and exceptionalism.

Bolshevik activists were successful in propagating the urgency of individual growth through adherence to the revolution because such thinking was rooted in Russia's historical past. The moral duties of self-improvement, social activism, and self-expression in concert with history were a staple of Russian intellectual and political life for almost a century before the revolution of 1917. As Stalin-era diarists worked to align themselves with history and to achieve a historically grounded notion of selfhood, they acted in striking consistency with generations of educated Russians since the early nineteenth century. To behave in such ways was what distinguished a member of the Russian intelligentsia.

The founding generation of the intelligentsia, a small group of highly educated young Russians, convened in literary-philosophical salons in Moscow and St. Petersburg, united by a profound disaffection with Russia's "backward" social and political conditions and a moral commitment to changing them. They found an instrument of swift and certain transformation in German idealism, notably Hegel's philosophy of consciousness unfolding through history, which they studied not just as a set of ideas, but as a guide to personal, social, and political life. Hegel's teachings imparted to them a belief in the existence of universal laws of history, which also applied to Russia and provided hope amid a bleak present. Though Russia was currently lagging behind the more advanced West, it could catch up by means of the concentrated efforts of "conscious" individuals, who knew the laws of history and devoted their lives to applying them for the country's benefit.

The fact that most of these young people had been born into positions of privilege translated for them into a moral obligation to raise their countrymen, the benighted peasant—and, later, worker—masses, from slavelike creatures to the stature of true human beings, who would then rise up against oppression and help move Russia forward. The primary duty for the *intelligent*, however, was self-reflective: to cultivate in oneself a disposition toward social and political change; to remain obligated to the idea that one's life had to serve history. It was this disposition that members of the intelligentsia had in mind when they spoke of the ideal of "personality" *(lichnost')*, which they defined as an ethical ideal with a transpersonal essence—a historical orientation and an investment in collective rather than individualistic aims, in the service of reaching the better future.

These responsibilities, while demanding, also carried significant rewards. The belief that one's thoughts and actions had historical relevance provided meaning where none was to be found in the official structures of tsarist Russia, from which these "superfluous people" saw themselves barred on account of their critical opinions. History offered an escape from the unbearable present, and a rich future expanse in which they could make themselves at home. To some of them, that future looked most auspicious. With an eye to the West, which dictated the pace of historical development, they sensed that intense cultivation of personality in Russia would one day propel this "young" nation past the "old" West, which they saw as weighed down by degenerative, self-seeking "bourgeois" values.

The main arena in which the intelligentsia developed its ideas about historical change was literature. Given the conditions of political censorship under autocratic rule, it was in the ostensibly nonpolitical literary sphere, in novels, critical essays, and literary autobiographies, that the properties of the "new man" were sketched out and discussed. By the same token, the reading of these works provided members of the intelligentsia with a mirror into which to gaze so as to be transformed. Thus a relationship of intense reciprocity between life and art took hold, where the intellectual's exemplary life served as a model for a literary character on whom readers in turn patterned themselves. These highly porous boundaries, linking, rather than separating, life and text, would persist through much of the twentieth century, and they are a remarkable feature of Stalin-era diaries.[3]

Lenin and other Bolsheviks lived by the mandate, relayed through literature, to lead a model life in the service of history. They patterned their attitudes on seminal readings about the new man, and in turn they preached models of behavior in correspondence with their evolving convictions about necessary historical action. Lenin's treatise on a new type of political party of professional revolutionaries, *What Is to Be Done?* (1902), also reads as a manual of personality cultivation. A tightly knit party milieu was to rear comrades of the utmost dedication and steadfastness, men and women who commanded such consciousness and iron willpower that they were capable of ushering backward Russia into the whirlwind of world revolution.

After coming to power, the Bolsheviks systematically suppressed competing scenarios of historical change propounded by non-Bolshevik members of the intelligentsia. Inside the party, a parallel process went on, of shutting off "oppositional" voices and imposing a "General Line" that increasingly became identified with Stalin's personal will. The spirit of the radical intelligentsia was at work within the Communist party, but it found even broader application in institutions and campaigns set up by the Soviet state. From the first days of its existence the Soviet government engaged in comprehensive literacy and education campaigns, which proved astoundingly successful.[4]

As it was Sovietized, the intelligentsia ethos became transformed. From affecting a small layer of Russia's educated society, it spread to become a universal ideal that was propounded through the institutional apparatus of the Soviet state. While the ideal became narrower in interpretation and more authoritarian in character, its contours remained distinctly present: in the form of a mandate, now extended to every Soviet citizen, to lead an ideologically integrated, "conscious" life, devoted to the needs of "society," and ultimately to the progression of history. The intricate ways in which commitments carried over from before 1917 into the Soviet period are illustrated in the diary of Zinaida Denisevskaya, who identified with the enlightening mission of the intelligentsia throughout her life. But intelligentsia values also shaped the self-conceptions of peasant workers who grew up in the 1920s and

1930s. Leonid Potemkin used his diary to systematize his efforts to remake himself into a socialist personality. Stepan Podlubny's efforts were hampered by the burden of his suppressed past, but his road to *Bildung* revealed a similar aspiration.

The question remains how to situate these narratives of intense introspection and striving in relation to the political pressures, psychological and physical, applied by the Soviet regime. In view of the Communist state's demands for enthusiastic participation in the "building of socialism," its determination to police the thought of its citizens, and its persecution of even the slightest indications of oppositional behavior, it may be suspected that diarists wrote primarily for the eyes of the NKVD and worked hard to present an image of themselves as ardent supporters of Soviet power, in departure from their actual convictions and beliefs.

Zinaida Denisevskaya kept her diary for more than thirty years, across the double threshold of 1917 and Stalin's industrial revolution a decade later. Throughout this period her self-understanding kept evolving, but without sudden breaks or shifts in tonality; it unfolded with consistency, and according to its own logic. Nowhere did Denisevskaya turn in her tracks, shifting from a style of sincerity and self-disclosure to a more calculated form of self-presentation intended for an outside reader. The other diaries cover shorter time spans, but their beginnings extend back to the period preceding Stalin's repressions. They, too, are consistent in thematic focus and self-expressive style. Alexander Afinogenov addressed his artistic and personal crisis as early as in 1932, but it was only in 1937, under intense pressure from the regime, that he earnestly engaged with his "degeneration." When Leonid Potemkin began to keep his diary, he devoted it to his self-education, a project that he pursued systematically in the following years. He gave up writing in the diary in 1936 because it no longer aided him in his quest for a better self. Instead, he turned to direct interchange with his peers, including his extensive correspondence with Ira Zhirkova. Stepan Podlubny's case is more complicated in that he consciously led a double life, pretending to be a worker while knowing that he was from a different class. Yet his diaristic voice was consistent; his diary unfolded as a critical commentary and a search for a solution to his double life, not as its extension. In each of the four chapters about particular diarists, I have drawn on other sources in addition to the diary—private letters, poems, memoirs, photographs, published writings, and interviews. Studied in concert, they reveal a more complex notion of individual subjectivity than a diary alone can impart; yet they do not invalidate or contradict the diaristic account. What is evident both in the diaries and beyond them is a pervasive agenda of social surveillance, self-intervention, and self-perfection.

Podlubny's, Denisevskaya's, and Afinogenov's diaries are rich in expressions of personal doubt and political opinion, especially pronounced at times when political pressures were intensifying. Recall Podlubny, who addressed his diary as a repository of his "reactionary" thoughts; or Afinogenov's attempt to escape from his Communist life into a private existence; or Denisevskaya's doubts about the validity of the party's General Line. Had the diaries been confiscated and read with the distrustful eyes of a state prosecutor, these trains of thought would doubtless have given rise to charges of "degeneration," "oppositionist moods," or "counterrevolutionary intent." Thus the presence of such passages effectively invalidates the suspicion that these diaries were produced primarily for the eyes and ears of the Stalinist security apparatus. Still, some might hypothesize that even these statements of doubt and despair were aimed at the NKVD, to evoke a picture of struggling believers who deserved to be trusted precisely because they did not conceal their doubts. Yet to read page after page of a diary as expression of a calculated pose, maintained for years on end, does injustice to these documents and their authors. Such a reading cannot account for the myriad autobiographical documents from the Stalin era which indicate that introspection and self-education were established cultural practices. Authors went to great lengths to procure paper and notebooks, which were in scarce supply; this and their prolonged attachment to their records suggest that they were strongly motivated to confront, work through, and resolve pressing questions about themselves.

Seen in this light, the diaries I have discussed are more than textual artifacts and a form of passive testimony. They are also a material residue of sustained efforts at self-searching and self-change, efforts encouraged by a culture that defined its members in terms of revolutionary selves. Diaristic accounts of struggle and self-becoming point to a sphere beyond the diary, and beyond the social profile of a given diarist. In expressing their strivings, diarists longed to realize themselves in a mode of historical action outside their diaries, in practical and ongoing work. The diary, steeped in thought alone, described at best a form of surrogate historical action. Many self-reflective diaries were written by people who were excluded from the collective and turned to their journals to create a substitute sense of belonging. Diaristic reflection could further the project of reworking the self, but the principal arena of this project was elsewhere, in the spheres of work and active social engagement. Thus these self-reflective diary narratives direct our view to a much wider field of self-construction and reconstruction that permeated the Soviet social, political, and economic landscapes.[5]

As is true for any other historical period, we gain a deep understanding of Stalin-era subjects only by situating them in their cultural environment, which supplied the very categories of speech, thought, and action that went into the production of their diaries. If Soviet citizens insisted on a paramount need for self-cultivation; if they claimed they kept diaristic laboratories for working on their selves and exchanged letters with friends for the purpose of monitoring each other's souls, we have no reason not to take them at their word, even if we judge their agenda to have been deluded or misguided. The imperative of self-change and the ideal of a socialized self in tune with history, which held defining importance for these authors, need to be acknowledged in analytical appraisals of the Stalin period as well. Such historical understanding in no way implies sympathizing with, or endorsing, historical actors' choices. The goal is, on the contrary, to separate the self-understandings of our historical subjects from our contemporary conceptions of self. Sympathy has the opposite effect: it breaks down analytical distance by projecting onto historical actors our own values and notions of self. We remake those actors in our image, shaped by liberal ideals of individualism and autonomy, and we relativize or discard aspects that do not fit that image.

The plight of the engineer Julia Piatnitskaya, discarded from Soviet society after her husband was arrested, invites sympathy. Yet it is difficult to identify with her condemnation of Nikolai Bukharin as a traitor and spy in 1938. A year earlier Piatnitskaya's husband had defended Bukharin against his accusers in the Communist party, and this stance had probably led to Piatnitsky's own arrest. Reading Bukharin's confession, at the Moscow show trial, that he had orchestrated terrorist plots (which in fact had been invented by his NKVD interrogators), Piatnitskaya came to the conclusion, disturbing to us today, that her husband had erred in defending a spiteful enemy in disguise.[6] We may equally sympathize with Zinaida Denisevskaya, particularly in light of the many calamities that punctuated her short life. Yet there is no place in this reading for Denisevskaya's insistence on embracing every new political turn as historically unavoidable and desirable, even the Soviet politics of class war that ultimately killed her. Stepan Podlubny's psychological drama as a stigmatized son of a "class enemy" is sure to invite sympathy. Yet his comments about the starving peasants in Ukraine are chilling ("Let them die. If they can't defend themselves against death from starvation, it means that they are weak-willed, and what can they give to society?"). And then there is Leonid Potemkin, who worshipped the building of socialism in aesthetic terms, but whose vision of the new world of beauty and expression was premised on scenarios of violent struggle, degeneration, and decay, which he understood in more than just metaphorical ways.

What renders these modes of thought so challenging to contemporary Western readers is their acceptance of violence in the service of self-realization. While the Stalinist regime practiced extreme forms of violence toward its citizens, their own self-understanding was suffused with symbolic violence as well. Struggle, campaigns against external and internal enemies, and the destruction of the Old Man in order to build the New Man were all core components of Soviet subjectivity. Promethean celebrations of strength, health, and beauty went along with open disdain for those who were considered weak, sick, and unfit for life. Individual subjects and state actors were aligned on parallel trajectories of revolutionary purification of social space and individual souls, and both regarded violence as a necessary tool to mold society and the self. Viewed diachronically across the thresholds of war, revolution, and Stalinist industrialization, diaries reveal that individual forms of self-engagement depended on an environment of violence to reach fulfillment. Entries written in daily succession suggest an increased urgency in thinking about oneself, while lapses and gaps in the record point to a reduced incentive to turn the gaze inward. The war against the "old world" launched by the regime in the late 1920s engendered much reflection on the part of individuals who identified with the "bourgeois intelligentsia"; the Communist inquisition of the 1930s sent Bolsheviks caught in the line of fire on journeys of introspection. Individual diarists thus turned the political violence applied against them into a catalyst for introspection. In the process many reworked external pressure into internal reflection, administrative coercion into psychological desire. Yet in so doing they kept elaborating views of themselves that had existed before a particular purge or campaign. While reflecting on the pressures they faced, diarists retained authorship of their narratives, and we have no reason to classify their densely textured records as instances of mere "singing along"—reciting incantations prescribed by the Soviet regime.[7]

To further their self-transformation, diarists sought to excise and discard unnecessary or harmful thoughts. To call this "self-censorship" is not entirely appropriate. In these instances, diarists confronted and worked on the voice of their not fully conscious mind and body to enable their true moral "self" to emerge. Self-cultivation was predominantly a moral pursuit, applied for the purposes of self-improvement and existential validation. By contrast, "self-censorship" should be used only for acts of individual self-repression motivated by diarists' fear that their thoughts or actions would be politically sanctioned. Both aspects, moral shaping and political self-censorship, figured in Stalin-era diaries, and they often overlapped and fused, with diarists making no distinction between fear of external repression and existential self-loss. This fusion is poignantly expressed in the plight of Soviet diarists who, in times of spiritual crisis, addressed the NKVD—the chief agency of Stalinist political violence—as the ultimate moral authority over their lives, pleading that it intervene and correct their errant thoughts.[8]

For many Stalin-era diarists, history provided the impetus to align their selves with the political present, however repressive that present appeared to them. To know where history was headed and to join its revolutionary current was the condition of possessing a developed self and being a legitimate member of Soviet society. The present could be bleak, but if it offered a path toward the future, it became livable or even eminently worthwhile. No one expressed this link between suffering and salvation more poignantly than Julia Piatnitskaya, who had lost husband and son in Stalin's purges and yet could not conceive of giving up her efforts in the service of the Stalinist state: "Your nearest and dearest perish, you're tormented, you see on all sides suffering and death, but you walk on, standing tall, you look straight ahead to the future of society—your life will be brighter and richer, and more useful to others. You must live in action, not in contemplation, and if it becomes impossible not to see the old, dark life, then rise above it, sever yourself from it, and seek the joyful and radiant path."[9] Other diarists as well described stark tensions between personally observed reality and the "revolutionary truth" propagated by the regime, but they proceeded to resolve these tensions through intense historical reflection. They tended to register achievements of socialist construction as historical markers indicating that history was on track and marching along.

Their interpretation had some justification: the physiognomy of Soviet Russia was rapidly changing; millions of people from the lower classes were receiving education; the modern values of rationalization, discipline, and science, relentlessly preached by the regime, seemed to be superseding ingrained Russian notions of submission and apathy. The sense that the country was soaring to new heights received further confirmation by comparison with a capitalist West mired in economic depression and political crisis. History, thus understood, acted as a powerful narcotic. It could impart intoxicating meaning and sweep to a person's life, and in so doing it could mitigate the pain of observed reality as it clashed with the mandated truth. While Alexander Afinogenov and other members of the artistic intelligentsia sometimes deplored the conditions of creative constraint in which they worked, their role as engineers of the new world rewarded them with opportunities to participate in history that dwarfed the role of the artist in the nonsocialist world.[10]

Visions of a lawful progression of history also informed those who criticized the Soviet regime and refused to accept its historical claims.

In devoting themselves to an alternative future, these critics clung to an identical notion of a self that realized itself in the revolutionary flow of history.[11] Yet to engage the regime in such terms required not only great courage but also an ability to conceptualize oneself through categories, such as "history," "the revolution," or "the people," which the regime sought to monopolize. Judging from the diaries I have discussed, the Stalinist regime was successful in silencing many of its critics not only through direct repressive means or the threat thereof, but indirectly, through social ostracism and control over the semantics of socialist selfhood. Under intense pressure from the regime, which practiced ritual expulsion scenarios, graphically severing individuals from the collective body before discarding them onto the "dustbin of history" (Trotsky), many "superfluous people" turned into lonely and self-doubting subjects, "not needed by anyone"—a terrible fate given their striving for a life of social usefulness and historical purpose.[12]

The longing to be part of a movement that promised an all-embracing worldview, certainty, meaning, and fulfillment was not specific to the Soviet Union. It was integral to European cultural and political life in the first half of the twentieth century, when emerging mass politics and technological experimentation militated against traditional bourgeois values. Intellectuals across Europe, including Georges Sorel, Ernst Jünger, and Walter Benjamin, extolled the morally redemptive and aesthetically purifying energy of political violence. The artistic landscapes of interwar Europe were suffused with experiments in aesthetic violence, ranging from formalist style to futurist poetry and avant-garde filmmaking. New and immediately popular radical parties on the left and the right vied with one another for the realization of aestheticized visions of society, cleansed of polluting or degenerating agents. All these activists, whatever their backgrounds and political orientations, shared a determination to break with antiquated, "academic" or "bourgeois" habits, and an insistence on violence as necessary for their project of re-creating the world. And they all heralded the superior power, beauty, and moral standing of organized masses, in contrast to the "weak" and "outdated" age of "bourgeois individualism."[13] The cynical practices and the sheer destructive power of these movements have since discredited them in the eyes of many, but the image of a unified social body that they invoked carries relevance to this day. The image speaks to us as modern subjects, freed from bonds of tradition and yet cast adrift in our individual lives.

Although these cultures of violence characterized Europe as a whole in this period, only in the Soviet Union did an inquisitorial culture develop that sought to identify and expose the polluting Other *within* the revolutionary movement. Communist ideology did not conceive of a fixed—racialized or sociologically static—image of an enemy against whom the struggle for moral and aesthetic perfection was to be waged. Membership in the future Communist world depended on the purity of one's consciousness, and thus every individual became subject and object of purification at the same time. The malleability of the self posited by Communist ideology could pose a major threat, but at first it emanated promise and fascination. The extraordinary appeal to the self was specific to the Soviet Communist state. Neither of the other twentieth-century regimes of mass mobilization, Fascist Italy and Nazi Germany, issued such a far-reaching call to individuals to transform themselves in the act of joining the revolution. And neither of those regimes produced an autobiographical literature that rivaled the Soviet record in volume and reflective depth.

The subjectivizing thrust of Soviet ideology sprang in part from Marxism and its Romantic roots, but also in part from the mandate to be socially useful that had been a staple of Russian culture long before the revolution. To truly live meant to rise above selfish pursuits and devote one's life to society and history, so as to remake accursed, backward Russia through the power of personal example and an unflinching orientation toward the future. This disposition was at work, in extreme but recognizable form, throughout the years of Soviet rule, and it found particularly strong expression in Stalin's time. In the post-Stalin period its intensity waned. Writing in 1936, the brooding young Moscow worker and komsomolist Alexander Ulianov resolved his feeling of being torn between two girls by proclaiming his devotion to the real love of his life—the "dear" Communist party. "The party is my family . . . She is close, so close to me, and every day I sense her presence, I work for her. And I need her as much as she needs me." In 1955, two years after Stalin's death, the poet Yevgeny Yevtushenko took up the same theme, but with revealing modulations. In a poem addressed to a woman, he wrote: "I have two loves in the world: the revolution and you." His was a divided love, no longer an exclusive commitment to society and history. Moreover, the poet asked both his lovers to forgive him for occasional infidelities.[14]

Notes

My transliterations of Russian words follow the Library of Congress system, simplified in the text for general readers, except when a proper name is already familiar in a standard English form (hence *Potemkin*, for example, rather than *Potyomkin*).

The following abbreviations are used in the notes:

AVMBR	Arkhiv vserossiiskoi Memuarnoi Biblioteki Russkogo Obshchestvennogo Fonda Aleksandra Solzhenitsyna, Moscow
GAKO	Gosudarstvennyi arkhiv Kalininskoi oblasti, Tver'
GARF	Gosudarstvennyi arkhiv Rossiiskoi Federatsii, Moscow
GASO	Gosudarstvennyi arkhiv Sverdlovskoi oblasti, Ekaterinburg
OR RGB	Otdel rukopisei Rossiiskoi gosudarstvennoi biblioteki, Moscow
RGAE	Rossiiskii gosudarstvennyi arkhiv ekonomiki, Moscow
RGALI	Rossiiskii gosudarstvennyi arkhiv literatury i iskusstva, Moscow
TsDNA	Tsentr Dokumentatsii "Narodnyi Arkhiv," Moscow

Prologue: Forging the Revolutionary Self

1. *Golgofa: po materialam arkhivno-sledstvennogo dela No. 603 na Sokolovu-Piatnitskuiu Iu. I.,* ed. V. I. Piatnitskii (St. Petersburg, 1993), 41 (2/15/1938).

2. Ibid., 76, 79, 100 (3/26/1938, 4/9/1938, 5/27/1938).
3. When speaking of liberal subjects, I refer to a theoretical construct grounding Western conceptions of self. The private-public distinction is essential for the liberal democratic conception of a community based on the consent of individual subjects. See Michael Halberstam, *Totalitarianism and the Modern Conception of Politics* (New Haven: Yale University Press, 1999), 46–49, 113–117.
4. George Orwell, *1984* (San Diego: Harcourt Brace Jovanovich, 1984), 7–8.
5. N. A. Bogomolov, "Dnevniki v russkoi kul'ture nachala XX veka," in *Tynianovskii sbornik. Chetvertye tynianovskie chteniia* (Riga: "Zinatne," 1990), 148–158. After 1917, Georges Nivat observes, "the diary as a genre of intimate writing disappears. Neither the revolution nor the terror is favorable to it . . . The new man has no more interiority. A private diary? He does not even know what that means." George Nivat, "Le journal intime en Russie," in Nivat, *Russie-Europe: la fin du schisme. Etudes littéraires et politiques* (Lausanne: L'age d'homme, 1993), 146.
6. Bulgakov then urged his wife to keep a diary, and she did: Elena Bulgakova, *Dnevnik Eleny Bulgakovoi* (Moscow: Izd-vo "Knizhnaia palata," 1990). Large portions of Bulgakov's diary survived in the form of a typewritten copy produced by the secret police.
7. Lydia Chukovskaya, *The Akhmatova Journals,* vol. 1: *1938–1941* (New York: Farrar, Straus and Giroux, 1994), 5. In fact, however, Chukovskaia kept several diaries throughout the years of Stalin's terror. See Lidiia Chukovskaia, *Po etu storonu smerti: iz dnevnika 1936–1976* (Paris: YMCA-Press, 1978). V. Kaverin, *Epilog: memuary* (Moscow: Agraf, 1997), 233.
8. Stefan Plaggenborg, *Revolutionskultur. Menschenbilder und kulturelle Praxis in Sowjetrussland zwischen Oktoberrevolution und Stalinismus* (Cologne: Böhlau, 1996). In Russian the term "new man" *(novyi chelovek),* while grammatically masculine, refers to humanity in a generic sense, and it represented an ideal toward which both Russian men and

women strove. Nevertheless, the "new man" had distinctly male features.

9. Igal Halfin, *Terror in My Soul* (Cambridge, Mass.: Harvard University Press, 2003); Oleg Kharkhordin, *The Collective and the Individual in Russia: A Study of Practices* (Berkeley: University of California Press, 1999), 57–60.
10. N. I. Bukharin, *Tiuremnye rukopisi N. I. Bukharina,* vol. 1: *Sotsializm i ego kul'tura* (Moscow: "Airo-XX," 1996), 66. Bukharin formulated these ideas in 1934. N. Bukharin, "Krizis kapitalisticheskoi kul'tury i problemy kul'tury v SSSR," *Izvestiia,* 3/6, 3/18, and 3/30/1934.
11. Michael S. Gorham, *Speaking in Soviet Tongues: Language Culture and the Politics of Voice in Revolutionary Russia* (DeKalb: Northern Illinois University Press, 2003); Evgeny Dobrenko, *The Making of the State Writer: Social and Aesthetic Origins of Soviet Literary Culture* (Stanford: Stanford University Press, 2001).
12. See esp. Susan Morrissey, *Heralds of Revolution: Russian Students and the Mythologies of Radicalism* (New York: Oxford University Press, 1998); Mark Steinberg, *Proletarian Imagination: Self, Modernity, and the Sacred in Russia* (Ithaca: Cornell University Press, 2002); Marina Mogil'ner, *Mif o podpol'nom cheloveke. Radikal'nyi mikrokosm v Rossii nachala XX veka kak predmet semioticheskogo analiza* (Moscow: Novoe literaturnoe obozrenie, 1999). The term "ecosystem" is inspired by Katerina Clark's notion of an "ecology of revolution"; Katerina Clark, *Petersburg: Crucible of Revolution* (Cambridge, Mass.: Harvard University Press, 1995), 1–29; see also Michael David-Fox, *Revolution of the Mind: Higher Learning among the Bolsheviks, 1918–1929* (Ithaca: Cornell University Press, 1997), 190–191.
13. Michel Foucault, "What Is Enlightenment?" in *The Foucault Reader,* ed. Paul Rabinow (New York: Pantheon, 1984), 41. Iurii Lotman advocates reading modern autobiographical literature as a "culture of program of behavior"; Iu. M. Lotman, "Literaturnaia biografiia v istoriko-kul'turnom kontekste. (K tipologicheskomu sootnosheniiu teksta i

lichnosti avtora)," in Lotman, *Izbrannye stat'i,* vol. 1 (Tallinn: "Aleksandra," 1992), 372.

14. While inspired by the work of Foucault, this understanding of subjectivity does not build on Foucault's notion of *assujetissement.* He devised this term to emphasize the illusion of individual autonomy, and thus to critique liberal modernity; it poses problems when applied to the illiberal Soviet state. See Laura Engelstein, "Combined Underdevelopment: Discipline and the Law in Imperial and Soviet Russia," in *Foucault and the Writing of History,* ed. Jan Goldstein (Cambridge: Blackwell, 1994); Jan Plamper, "Foucault's *Gulag,*" *Kritika* 3, no. 2 (2002); Jochen Hellbeck, "The Analysis of Soviet Subjectivity Practices: Interview with the Editors of *Ab Imperio,*" *Ab Imperio,* 2002, no. 3, 217–260, 397–402. For Foucault and subjectivity, see *The Foucault Reader;* Hubert L. Dreyfus and Paul Rabinow, *Michel Foucault: Beyond Structuralism and Hermeneutics* (Chicago: Chicago University Press, 1983). See also Nick Mansfield, *Subjectivity: Theories of the Self from Freud to Haraway* (New York: New York University Press, 2001).
15. See Stephen Kotkin, *Magnetic Mountain: Stalinism as a Civilization* (Berkeley: University of California Press, 1995); Martin Malia, *The Soviet Tragedy: a History of Socialism in Russia, 1917–1991* (New York: Free Press, 1994); *Russian Modernity: Politics, Knowledge, Practices,* ed. David L. Hoffmann and Yanni Kotsonis (New York: St. Martin's, 2000); David L. Hoffmann, *Stalinist Values: the Cultural Norms of Soviet Modernity, 1917–1941* (Ithaca: Cornell University Press, 2003).
16. *Golgofa,* 76 (3/26/1938).
17. Hannah Arendt, "On the Nature of Totalitarianism: An Essay in Understanding," in Arendt, *Essays in Understanding, 1930–1954* (New York: New York: Harcourt, Brace, 1994), 338–339.
18. See esp. Sheila Fitzpatrick, *Education and Social Mobility in the Soviet Union, 1921–1934* (Cambridge: Cambridge University Press, 1979); J. Arch Getty, *The Origins of the Great Purges: The Soviet Communist Party Reconsidered, 1933–1937* (Cambridge: Cambridge University Press, 1985).
19. An exception is *Magnetic Mountain,* Stephen Kotkin's superb micro-

history of the city of Magnitogorsk, which has inspired my own work. I differ with Arendt on the relationship between ideology and subjectivity. Arendt is not interested in the individual as an active subject. For her, ideology itself is the driving force: "independent of all experience," ideology eliminates subjectivity in its encounter with the individual. This view underrates individuals' active and creative participation in the appropriation of ideology, a process which asked them to rework, rather than abandon, subjective experience. See Hannah Arendt, *The Origins of Totalitarianism* (New York: Harcourt, Brace, Jovanovich, 1979), 470. See also Eric Naiman, *Sex in Public: The Incarnation of Early Soviet Ideology* (Princeton: Princeton University Press, 1997).

20. "Aligned life" *(ausgerichtetes Leben)* was a term coined by a German: Siegfried Kracauer, *Schriften, I: Der Detektiv-Roman. Ein philosophischer Traktat (1922–25)* (Frankfurt/Main: Suhrkamp, 1971), 109, 111, 118, 129. For conceptions of illiberal selfhood across Europe, see Robert Wohl, *The Generation of 1914* (Cambridge, Mass.: Harvard University Press, 1981); Peter Fritzsche, *Germans Into Nazis* (Cambridge, Mass.: Harvard University Press, 1998); Jeffrey Herf, *Reactionary Modernism* (New York: Cambridge University Press, 1984).

1. Rearing Conscious Citizens

1. Dm. Furmanov, *Sobranie sochinenii v chetyrekh tomakh,* vol. 4: *Dnevniki, literaturnye zapisi, pis'ma* (Moscow: Gos. izd-vo khudozh. lit-ry, 1961), 92–93 (3/26/1917).
2. Ibid., 100, 216, 224 (8/18/1917, 12/29/1919, 3/1/1920).
3. On the "new life" and the "new man" see Boris Kolonitskii, *Simvoly vlasti i bor'ba za vlast': k izucheniiu politicheskoi kul'tury Rossiiskoi revoliutsii 1917 goda* (St. Petersburg: D. Bulanin, 2001), 326–335. Maxim Gorky, *Untimely Thoughts* (New York: S. Eriksson, 1968), 7.
4. N. G. Chernyshevskii, *Chto delat'? Iz rasskazov o novykh liudei* (Leningrad: Nauka, 1975), 148–149, 215.
5. Nikolay Valentinov, *Encounters with Lenin* (New York: Oxford Univer-

sity Press, 1968); Georgi Dimitroff, "Die revolutionäre Literatur im Kampfe gegen den Faschismus," *Internationale Literatur* 1935, no. 5, 10. Irina Paperno, *Chernyshevsky and the Age of Realism: A Study in the Semiotics of Behavior* (Stanford: Stanford University Press, 1988), 38.

6. A. V. Peshekhonov, "Materialy dlia kharakteristiki russkoi intelligentsii" (1900), in Peshekhonov, *K voprosu ob intelligentsii* (St. Petersburg: Tipografiia N. N. Klobukova, 1906), 62, 65.

7. Furmanov, *Sobranie sochinenii,* vol. 4, 214–215 (entries for 12/26/1919, 8/12/1921). This novel understanding emerged most clearly in retrospect, but Furmanov was already working toward an ideal of completion before the revolution. The revolution, his case suggests, was built into the biographical script of the radical *intelligent;* it was anticipated as a threshold of self-realization (see 23–25, 2/8/1911 and 3/13/1911); see also Pavel V. Kupriianovskii, *Neizvestnyi Furmanov* (Ivanovo: Ivanovskii gos. universitet, 1996).

8. L. Trotskii, *Voprosy byta. Epokha kul'turnichestva i ee zadachi* (Moscow: Krasnaia nov', 1923), 71; Clark, *Petersburg,* 201–223.

9. A. Vedenov, "K voprosu o predmete psikhologii," *Psikhologiia* 1932, no. 3, 43–58 (p. 55). I thank Peter Holquist for bringing this and other sources on Soviet military-psychological research to my attention.

10. Leon Trotsky, *Literature and Revolution* (Ann Arbor: University of Michigan Press, 1971), 255.

11. Ibid., 256. On Enlightenment imagery, see Kotkin, *Magnetic Mountain;* Katerina Clark, "The 'History of the Factories' as a Factory of History," in *Autobiographical Practices in Russia,* ed. Jochen Hellbeck and Klaus Heller (Göttingen: Vandenhoeck & Ruprecht, 2004).

12. The writing of *Chapaev* was thus an autobiographical practice for Furmanov; see Jochen Hellbeck, "Russian Autobiographical Practice," in *Autobiographical Practices in Russia,* ed. Hellbeck and Heller. On *Chapaev* see Ronald Vroon, "Dmitrii Furmanov's *Chapaev* and the Aesthetics of the Russian Avant-Garde," in *Laboratory of Dreams: The Russian Avant-Garde and Cultural Experiment,* ed. John E. Bowlt and Olga Matich (Stanford: Stanford University Press, 1996).

13. Furmanov, *Sobranie sochinenii,* vol. 1, 277. A section of Furmanov's diary of the civil war period bore the title "The Power of the Word": *Sobranie sochinenii,* vol. 4, 271.
14. Podvoiskii and White officer cited in Mark Von Hagen, *Soldiers in the Proletarian Dictatorship: The Red Army and the Soviet Socialist State, 1917–1930* (Ithaca: Cornell University Press, 1990), 98, 113.
15. Peter Kenez, *The Birth of the Propaganda State: Soviet Methods of Mass Mobilization, 1917–1929* (Cambridge: Cambridge University Press, 1985), 72–73, 77, 72.
16. A. Vedenov, "Psikhologiia i politprosvetrabota," *Psikhologiia,* t. IV, vyp. 2 (1931), 188–213. Gorky in *Izvestiia,* 1/5/1930, 5.
17. I. Kuznetsov, "Razvitie ustnoi rechi v sisteme kompleksnogo prepodavaniia," *Sputnik Politrabotnika,* 1924, no. 3, 69–70. B. Tal', "Voprosy metodiki partprosveshcheniia," ibid., 19. *Pedagogicheskaia entsiklopediia,* vol. 1 (Moscow: Rabotnik prosveshcheniia, 1927), 587.
18. Sheila Fitzpatrick, "The Problem of Class Identity in NEP Society," in *Russia in the Era of NEP: Explorations in Soviet Society and Culture,* ed. Sheila Fitzpatrick (Bloomington: Indiana University Press, 1991); Naiman, *Sex in Public.*
19. "Instructions for carrying out verification of party documents and purging the party membership" (6/15/1921), in *Revelations from the Russian Archives: Documents in English Translation,* ed. Diane Koenker and Ronald Bachman (Washington: Library of Congress, 1997), 58–61; *Partiinaia etika. Dokumenty i materialy diskussii 20-kh godov* (Moscow: Izd-vo politicheskoi literatury, 1989), 310, 326–327.
20. Igal Halfin, *Terror in My Soul: Communist Autobiographies on Trial* (Cambridge, Mass.: Harvard University Press, 2003), 43–95.
21. From "The New Man" (1922), in *Kino-Eye: The Writings of Dziga Vertov,* ed. Annette Michelson (Berkeley: University of California Press, 1984), 7–8.
22. Frederick Corney, *Telling October: Memory and the Making of the Bolshevik Revolution* (Ithaca: Cornell University Press, 2004).
23. *Pravda,* 6/13/1928, 5.

24. Hans Günther, *Der sozialistische Übermensch: M. Gor'kij und der sowjetische Heldenmythos* (Stuttgart: Metzler, 1993).
25. *Pervyi vsesoiuznyi s''ezd sovetskikh pisatelei. Stenograficheskii otchet* (Moscow: Sovetskii pisatel', 1934), 549.
26. Clark, "History of the Factories"; Gorky in *Pravda,* 6/13/1928, 5.
27. Bukharin, *Tiuremnye rukopisi,* vol. 1, 61.
28. RGALI, f. 2172, op. 3, ed. 5 (12/8/1937).
29. A. K. Gastev, "O tendentsiiakh proletarskoi kul'tury," in *Proletarskaia Kul'tura,* 1919, no. 9/10; *Problems of Soviet Literature: Reports and Speeches at the First Soviet Writers' Congress* (New York: International Publishers, 1935), 11.
30. E. Krenkel', *Chetyre tovarishcha. Dnevnik* (Moscow: Izd. Glavsevmorputi, 1940), 311. Stalin made this toast to life three days after directing the execution of his rival Nikolai Bukharin.
31. *Pervyi vsesoiuznyi s''ezd sovetskikh pisatelei,* 501. See also Leonard P. Wessell Jr., *Karl Marx, Romantic Irony, and the Proletariat: The Mythopoetic Origins of Marxism* (Baton Rouge: Louisiana State University Press, 1979).
32. *Pravda,* 1/29/1935, 1–5. Stalin's metaphor brings to mind Zygmunt Bauman's notion of totalitarian government as "gardening"; Bauman, *Modernity and the Holocaust* (Ithaca: Cornell University Press, 1989).
33. Citations from Raymond Bauer, *The New Man in Soviet Psychology* (Cambridge, Mass.: Harvard University Press, 1952), 147, 149. Boris Grois, *The Total Art of Stalinism: Avant-Garde, Aesthetic Dictatorship, and Beyond* (Princeton: Princeton University Press, 1992), 61; Halfin, *Terror in My Soul,* 256–262.
34. Bauer, *New Man in Soviet Psychology,* 47. Halfin, *Terror in My Soul,* 33–38. When referring to the core of a person's convictions, Bolsheviks in the 1930s frequently used the term "soul." The soul was a psychological aggregate of the person's character and disposition. This essentialist understanding of the person differed markedly from interpretations of the 1920s, which viewed the individual as a composite of

physiological reflexes responding to stimuli in the social and physical environment.

35. Peter Holquist, "State Violence as Technique: The Logic of Violence in Soviet Totalitarianism," in *Landscaping the Human Garden: Twentieth-Century Population Management in a Comparative Framework*, ed. Amir Weiner (Stanford: Stanford University Press, 2003).
36. Robert Thurston, *Life and Terror in Stalin's Russia, 1934–1941* (New Haven: Yale University Press, 1996), 113–115.

2. *Bolshevik Views of the Diary*

1. Kharkhordin, *The Collective and the Individual in Russia*, 55, 228.
2. Michael Walzer, *The Revolution of the Saints: A Study in the Origins of Radical Politics* (Cambridge, Mass.: Harvard University Press, 1965), 143; Charles E. Hambrick-Stowe, *The Practice of Piety: Puritan Devotional Disciplines in Seventeenth-Century New England* (Chapel Hill: University of North Carolina Press, 1982).
3. *Knizhka krasnoarmeitsa* (Ekaterinoslav: Tipografiia gubernskogo voennogo komissariata, 1919).
4. Aron Zalkind, "Kul'turnaia revoliutsiia i voprosy pedologii. (K itogam pervogo Vsesoiuznogo pedologicheskogo s"ezda)," *Revoliutsiia i kul'tura*, 1928, no. 1, 27–32. Quotation from N. A. Rybnikov, "Iunosheskie dnevniki i ikh izuchenie," *Psikhologiia*, t. 1 (1928), vyp. 2, 85–87. L. Zagorovskii, "O nekotorykh voprosakh metodiki izucheniia povedeniia starshego shkol'nogo vozrasta," *Psikhologiia*, 1930, t. 3, vyp. 1, 39–40.
5. *Dnevnik podrostka (predislovie Professora Voenno-meditsinskoi Akademii V. P. Osipova)* (Leningrad: Vremia, 1925), 4: translation of *Tagebuch eines halbwüchsigen Mädchens* (Vienna: Internat. psychoanalyt. Verl., 1919). See also M. M. Rubinshtein, *Iunost' po dnevnikam i avtobiograficheskim zapisiam* (Moscow: Vyssh. pedagogich. kursy pri Mosk. vyssh. tekhnich. uch-shche, 1928); Alexander Etkind, *Eros of the Impossible: The History of Psychoanalysis in Russia* (Boulder: Westview, 1997).
6. Gorham, *Speaking in Soviet Tongues*, 89–95. N. Ognev, *The Diary of a*

Communist Schoolboy (New York: Payson & Clarke, 1928); idem, *The Diary of a Communist Undergraduate* (New York: Payson & Clarke, 1929). Private archive of Leonid Potemkin (Moscow), diary, t. 4, l. 50ob, 51ob (8/22/1933, 8/29/1933).

7. Aleksandr Etkind, "Biograficheskii institut: Neosushchestvlennyi zamysel N. A. Rybnikova," in *Litsa. Biograficheskii al'manakh,* vol. 7 (Moscow: Feniks-Atheneum, 1996), 420. Zagorovskii, "O nekotorykh voprosakh," 40. Quotation from Rybnikov, "Iunosheskie dnevniki," 88. Etkind believes that Rybnikov's initiative was inspired by Nikolai Fedorov's philosophy of resurrection. Resurrection, according to Fedorov, could be "scientifically" managed through the writing and conservation of individuals' autobiographical writings, which described the essence of a person. This essence would bring the person back to life in a future age, once technologies were sufficiently developed to achieve this. Meanwhile society had to turn into a "psychocracy": all citizens were to keep "psycho-physiological diaries" and gather in rituals of mutual confession to record all "biographical-psychological" details necessary for resurrection. Rybnikov's agenda overlapped with Bolshevik designs to spread consciousness through the biographical medium. In the late 1920s he proposed to study the biographies of the *vydvizhentsy,* upwardly mobile workers who were being trained for service in the state apparatus. Such studies would contribute to the creation of "outstanding personalities" on a mass scale. Rybnikov, "Opyt psikhologicheskogo analiza biografii vydvizhentsev"; see idem, *Avtobiografii rabochikh i ikh izuchenie* (n.p.: Gosudarstvennoe izdatel'stvo, 1930).

8. *Vecherniaia Moskva,* 1/8/1997, 3; I thank David Brandenberger for bringing this publication to my attention. A pedagogical handbook published in 1927 recommended that teachers encourage the writing of diaries as a means of developing "students' individuality," but it also cautioned against the chaotic structure, the discordance that the diary was unable to overcome. *Pedagogicheskaia entsiklopediia,* vol. 1, 582. Exursions were systematically organized by the Soviet state as a

means of civic and political education: see Plaggenborg, *Revolutionskultur,* 223–228.

9. *Literatura Fakta* (1929), ed. N. F. Chuzhak (Munich: W. Fink, 1972), 31–33.
10. Ibid., 60.
11. Josette Bouvard, "Le moi au miroir de la société nouvelle: les formes autobiographiques de l'histoire" (manuscript), 61–62; see also Josette Bouvard, "Une fabrique d'écriture, le projet de Gorki *L'Histoire des fabriques et des usines* (1931–1936)," in *Autobiographies, autocritiques, aveux dans le monde communiste,* ed. Claude Pennetier and Bernard Pudal (Paris: Belin, 2002), 63–83. S. V. Zhuravlev, *Fenomen "Istorii fabrik i zavodov": Gor'kovskoe nachinanie v kontekste epokhi 1930-kh godov* (Moscow: In-tut rossiiskoi istoriii RAN, 1997).
12. Bouvard, "Le moi au miroir," 64–65, 68, 89.
13. Ibid., 62.
14. Ibid., 59, 64, 67.
15. Ibid., 64–67.
16. Ibid., 68–69, 84.
17. *Rasskazy stroitelei metro* (Moscow, 1935); *Kak my stroili metro* (Moscow: "Istoriia fabrik i zavodov," 1935).
18. Bouvard, "Le moi au miroir," 85. An encyclopedia article of the period praised the memoir's ability to organize an author's life "through the prism of a specific ideological concept" and disdainfully characterized the diary as the "most primitive form of memoir literature," a chain of "molecular link[s] between individual entries," held together only by the "narrator's unity." "Memuarnaia literatura," in *Literaturnaia entsiklopediia,* vol. 7 (Moscow: Izd-vo Kommunisticheskoi akademii, 1934), col. 131–139.
19. Diary-writing appears to have been widely practiced in the prerevolutionary socialist movement. The critics and writers Chernyshevskii and Nikolai Dobroliubov, in whose image many revolutionaries molded themselves, kept diaristic records of introspection and self-improvement. See Paperno, *Chernyshevsky and the Age of Realism;* O. G.

Egorov, *Dnevniki russkikh pisatelei XIX veka. Issledovanie* (Moscow: Flinta, 2002). The social-democratic hero of a novel from the 1910s kept a diary for which he designed a cover featuring a Greek trireme floating beneath the caption "MY HOPES." Each oar "was inscribed with the word LABOR. In the center of the mast with a quadrangular sail appeared the inscription LIBERTY. At the top of the mast was a flag with the motto IDEAL. On the stern the name of the trireme could be discerned: LIFE; and two wide plaques set into the flanks of the ship read SCIENCE and BATTLE. The helm of the ship was called WILL-POWER." Mogil'ner, *Mif o podpol'nom cheloveke,* 101.

20. Furmanov, *Sobranie sochinenii,* vol. 4, 214 (12/29/1919). The diary of Nicholas II was published in *Krasnyi arkhiv,* 1927, no. 1–3; 1928, no. 2.
21. Cited in Kharkhordin, *Collective and Individual in Russia,* 254–255.
22. See Oleg Kharkhordin, "Reveal and Dissimulate: A Genealogy of Private Life in Soviet Russia," in *Public and Private in Thought and Practice,* ed. Jeff Weintraub and Krishan Kumar (Chicago: University of Chicago Press, 1994); Vadim Volkov, "The Concept of Kul'turnost': Notes on the Stalinist Civilizing Process," in *Stalinism: New Directions,* ed. Sheila Fitzpatrick (London: Routledge, 1999).
23. This transition can be traced in Il'ia Erenburg's novel *Second Day,* first published in 1933. Erenburg breaks with other Soviet novelists (notably Furmanov and Fedor Gladkov) who featured Communist heroes as diarists. In Erenburg's novel a villain, Vasia Safonov, a morbid loner, keeps a secret diary to which he confides his counter-revolutionary thoughts; Il'ia Erenburg, *Den' vtoroi. Roman* (Paris: Pascal, 1933); Fedor Gladkov, *Energiia* (Moscow: Sovetskaia literatura, 1933).
24. See the diary of Ol'ga Berggol'ts, discussed in Chapter 3.
25. "'Nachalo razgroma profdvizheniia.' Dnevnik B. G. Kozeleva. 1927–1930 gg.," in *Istoricheskii arkhiv,* 1996, no. 5–6; 1997, no. 1. In an afterword to the diary (written in 1991), Kozelev's daughter notes that the Central Committee commissioned her father to go to Magnitogorsk. In view of his earlier decision to become a factory worker—a classical

way Communists responded to charges of degeneration—it is likely that he himself applied to join the battle for socialism.

26. N. Petukhov and V. Khomchik, "Delo o 'Leningradskom tsentre'," *Vestnik Verkhovnogo Suda SSSR*, 1991, no. 5, 15–18; Alla Kirilina, *Neizvestnyi Kirov* (St. Petersburg: "Neva," 2001).

3. Laboratories of the Soul

1. Shilling: GARF, f. 883, op. 1, d. 104 (1/12/1893); I thank Susanne Schattenberg for directing me to this diary. Paper shortage: Stepan Podlubnyi, TsDNA, f. 30, op. 1, dd. 15, 17 (1/1/1935, 1/18/1939); Private archive of Leonid Potemkin, diary, t. 2, l. 4, (1/9/1930); Evgeniia Rudneva, *Poka stuchit serdtse: Dnevniki i pis'ma Geroia Sovetskogo Soiuza Evgenii Rudnevoi* (Moscow: "Molodaia gvardiia", 1958), 62 (8/3/1938); *Pravda*, 12/22/1934, 3. Vladimir Biriukov and Aleksandr Afinogenov kept typewritten diaries: GASO, f. 2266, d. 1385–88; RGALI, f. 2172, op. 3, ed. 5–6.
2. GARF, f. 7900, op. 1, d. 7, 11–12. Accounting and bookkeeping were central pursuits for diarists from different cultures and epochs; see *Marginal Voices, Marginal Forms: Diaries in European Literature and History*, ed. Rachael Langford and Russell West (Amsterdam: Rodopi, 1999). Vladimir Biriukov's diary was kept on pre- and postrevolutionary letterhead.
3. See, e.g., the diaries of Fedor Shirnov, Zinaida Denis'evskaia, and Dmitrii Furmanov. Shirnov wrote his entire diary, from 1888 to 1938, in a single volume; see *Intimacy and Terror: Soviet Diaries of the 1930s*, ed. Véronique Garros, Natalya Korenevskaya, and Thomas Lahusen (New York: New Press, 1995), 67–97. Denis'evskaia kept her diary in a series of bound volumes until 1919, after which she used notebooks (see Chapter 4). After the revolution Furmanov wrote in account books; Furmanov, *Sobranie sochinenii*, vol. 4, 6.
4. Diary of Stepan Podlubnyi, TsDNA, f. 30, op. 1, d. 11 (9/2/1932). This intense historical consciousness is reminiscent of the Napoleonic period, which also saw an outburst of autobiographical writing with

a historical slant. See Peter Fritzsche, *Stranded in the Present: Modern Time and the Melancholy of History* (Cambridge, Mass.: Harvard University Press, 2004); A. G. Tartakovskii, *Russkaia memuaristika i istoricheskoe soznanie XIX veka* (Moscow: "Arkheograficheskii tsentr," 1997).

5. "1933–1936 gg. v griazovetskoi derevne (Dnevnik A. I. Zhelezniakova)," in *Vologda. Istoriko-kraevedcheskii al'manakh* vyp. 1 (Vologda: Izd-vo "Rus'," 1994), 455 (5/30/1933).

6. John Scott, *Behind the Urals: An American Worker in Russia's City of Steel* (1942), ed. Stephen Kotkin (Bloomington: Indiana University Press, 1989), 118–119.

7. Vsevolod Vishnevskii, *Sobranie sochinenii v 5 tomakh,* vol. 6, *(Dopolnitel'nyi): Vystupleniia i radiorechi. Zapisnye knizhki. Pis'ma* (Moscow: Gos. izd-vo khudozh. lit., 1961), 411 (1/22/1942).

8. Diary of Nikolai V. Zhuravlev, GAKO, f. r-652, op. 1, ed. khr. 2 (1/6/1936, 1/7/1936). Despite Zhuravlev's intention to focus on "facts" and not on the "turns of my heart," his diary did turn largely into a confessional genre, recording intrigues at the workplace and problems with his adulterous wife. On Soviet designs to revolutionize everyday life, see Naiman, *Sex in Public,* 185–188; Clark, *Petersburg,* 242–260; David-Fox, *Revolution of the Mind.*

9. OR RGB, f. 442, op. 1, ed. khr. 4–5 (2/18/1930, 3/1/1930, 4/12/1933, 5/7/1933).

10. RGALI, f. 2211, op. 3, ed. khr. 18 (4/8/1961). Peregudov's diary notes of the 1930s are indeed shallow, consisting largely of weather reports and minute descriptions of his activities ("I slept . . . got up . . . drank two cups of tea . . .").

11. TsDNA, f. 336, op. 1, ed. khr. 32 (10/15/1931, 7/8/1932).

12. See Stuart Sherman, *Telling Time: Clocks, Diaries, and English Diurnal Form, 1660–1785* (Chicago: University of Chicago Press, 1996), 58–68.

13. GASO, f. 2266, d. 1388 (4/23/1938, 4/24/1938). Private archive of Viacheslav Ul'rikh (Heidelberg), entry for 4/12/1931; see also Malte Rolf, "Constructing a Soviet Time: Bolshevik Festivals and Their Ri-

vals during the First Five-Year Plan," in *Kritika: Explorations in Russian and Eurasian History,* 1, no. 3 (2000), 447–473. Pavlova: TsDNA, f. 336, op. 1, ed. khr. 32 (7/16/1933). The novel in question was *The Precipice (Obryv).*

14. *The Diary of a Soviet Schoolgirl (1932–1937)* (Moscow: Glas, 2003), 8, 42–43 (3/24/1933).
15. A. G. Man'kov, *Dnevniki 30-kh godov* (St. Petersburg: Evropeiskii dom, 2001), 16, 42 (3/30/1933, 4/23/1933). I have consulted the original manuscript of the diary, in Man'kov's private archive in St. Petersburg, and compared it with the published version. Man'kov later became a well-known historian of pre-Petrine Russia.
16. V. I. Vernadskii, "Dnevnik 1938 goda," *Druzhba narodov* 1991, no. 2 (1/4/1938, 3/1/1938); see also V. P. Volkov, "Kadet Vernadskii," *Neva* 1992, no. 11–12; *Minuvshee* 7 (Paris, 1989), 447.
17. Private archive of Man'kov (7/6/1933); naming the uncle after a Chekhov character underscored his inability to adapt to the demands of the day. M. M. Prishvin, "1930 god," *Oktiabr',* 1989, no. 7 (5/6/1930); idem, *Dnevniki* (Moscow: Izd-vo "Pravda," 1990), 365 (2/24/1946). Throughout the 1930s Prishvin grappled with the conflict between desire and necessity (*khochetsia/nado*), a moral formulation that resonated with the Bolshevik dichotomy of spontaneity and consciousness. Prishvin's diaries, kept from 1905 until his death in 1954, are his major literary-philosophical work. See personal collection of L. Riazanova and V. Krugleeva, Moscow. Riazanova and Krugleeva are in the process of publishing a critical edition of the full diary.
18. "'Ischez chelovek i net ego, kuda devalsia—Nikto ne znaet.' Iz konfiskovannogo dnevnika," *Istochnik* 1993, no. 4, 51, 52, 58 (5/1/1931, 2/17/1937).
19. *Intimacy and Terror,* 111–165; see also *Na razlome zhizni: dnevnik Ivana Glotova, pezhemskogo krest´ianina Vel´skogo raiona Arkhangel´skoi oblasti 1915–1931 gody* (Moscow: Rossiiskaia akademiia nauk, 1997); *"Dnevnye zapiski" Ust'-Kulomskogo krest'ianina I. S. Rassykhaeva: 1902–1953 god* (Moscow: Institut, 1997).

20. *Intimacy and Terror,* 114 (10/30/1936). Like Nina Lugovskaia's father, Arzhilovskii prodded his children to write diaries (ibid., 137, 1/12/1937).
21. M. M. Prishvin, "'Zhizn' stala veselei . . .' Iz dnevnika 1936 goda," *Oktiabr',* 1993, no. 10 (3/12/1936); Nadezhda Mandelstam, *Hope against Hope: A Memoir* (New York: Atheneum, 1971), 126.
22. N. Ustrialov, *Pod znakom revoliutsii* (Kharbin: Tipografiia "Poligraf", 1927), 87; "'Sluzhit' rodine prikhoditsia kostiami . . .' Dnevnik N. V. Ustrialova 1935–1937 gg.," *Istochnik* 1998, no. 5–6 (9/3/1935, 7/5/1936, 2/18/1937).
23. OR RGB, f. 543, k. 32, ed. khr. 15 (7/14/1935, 9/17/1935); see also Tat'iana Leshchenko-Sukhomlina, *Dolgoe budushchee* (Moscow: Sovetskii pisatel', 1991), 5–7.
24. OR RGB, f. 543, k. 32, ed. khr. 15 (7/13/1936).
25. Ibid., (7/24/1936, 7/29/1936, 9/29/1936); her arrest and sentencing are described in Leshchenko-Sukhomlina, *Dolgoe budushchee,* 302–309.
26. TsDNA, f. 336, op. 1, ed. khr. 32 (7/31/1930, 8/14/1930, 5/5/1931, 7/9/1931).
27. OR RGB, f. 442, op. 1, ed. khr. 4–5 (3/23/1930, 7/1/1932); Vera Inber, *Stranitsy dnei perebiraia . . . : Iz dnevnikov i zapisnykh knizhek,* rev. ed. (Moscow: Sovetskii pisatel', 1977), 24 (7/9/1933); RGALI, f. 1072, op. 4, ed. khr. 4 (3/7/1936).
28. *Chelovek sredi liudei: rasskazy, dnevniki, ocherki* (Moscow: Sovetskii pisatel', 1964), 171, 174 (11/17/1930, 11/29/1930).
29. TsDNA, f. 30, op. 1, ed. 11 (9/13/1932); RGALI, f. 1072, op. 4, ed. khr. 4 (12/31/1934).
30. *Chelovek sredi liudei,* 175 (12/3/1930). TsDNA, f. 336, op. 1, ed. khr. 32 (4/10/1932).
31. Denis'evskaia: OR RGB, f. 752, op. 2, ed. khr. 7 (11/6/1930). Lev Deich, "Zapisnye knizhki L. G. Deicha," *Voprosy istorii* 1996, no. 3, 28 (2/28/1935). Vishnevskii: RGALI, f. 1038, op. 1, ed. 2074 (5/28/1937).
32. OR RGB, f. 442, op. 1, ed. khr. 5–6 (12/24/1932, 1/12/1934).
33. *Chelovek sredi liudei,* 174 (11/29/1930).
34. TsDNA, f. 30, op. 1, ed. 12, 15 (12/30/1933, 10/31/1935).

35. *Chelovek sredi liudei,* 175 (12/1/1930); "1933–1936 gg. v griazovetskoi derevne," 514 (10/12/1935).
36. Nikolai Ostrovskii, "Mysli o samovospitanii," *Iunost',* 1955, no. 3, 71. Vishnevskii, *Sobranie sochinenii v 5 tomakh,* vol. 6 *(Dopolnitel'nyi),* 354, 377 (11/7/1938, 4/16–17/1940).
37. "Nakanune 1934 goda," *Pravda,* 12/30/1933, 1. Balance sheets figure in the diaries of Leonid Potemkin, Aleksandr Afinogenov, Nikolai Zhuravlev, Anatolii Ul'ianov, and Galina Shtange (for Shtange, see *Intimacy and Terror,* 167–217). "The urge for a permanent account of accomplished deeds," a dictionary of the language of the Soviet revolution notes, "is expressed in the frequent use of the terms 'sum,' 'results,' and especially 'summing up.'" A. M. Selishev, *Iazyk revoliutsionnoi epokhi. Iz nabliudenii nad russkim iazykom poslednikh let, 1917–1926* (Moscow: Rabotnik prosveshcheniia, 1928), 108.
38. OR RGB, f. 442, op. 1, ed. khr. 5 (12/9/1932); TsDNA, f. 336, op. 1, ed. khr. 32 (5/7/1932).
39. Private archive of Potemkin, diary, t. 5, l. 55 (undated, after 7/31/1935).
40. "1933–1936 gg. v griazovetskoi derevne," 493 (11/10/1933).
41. *Poka stuchit serdtse,* 48 (11/25/1937).
42. J. R. Becher, *Der gespaltene Dichter: Gedichte, Briefe, Dokumente* (Berlin: Aufbau, 1991), 14.
43. RGB, f. 801, op. 1, ed. khr. 3 (3/9/1932, 3/10/1932). See also the diaries of Vera Inber and of Fedor Kaverin: Inber, *Stranitsy dnei perebiraia,* 23–24, 7/9/1933; Muzei Bakhrushina, f. 454, d. 447; 9/3/1928, 12/7/1928.
44. Iurii Olesha, *Kniga proshchaniia* (Moscow: Vagrius, 1999), 35–36, 45 (5/5/1930, 5/7/1930).
45. Ibid., 37, 45 (5/7/1930); for a different interpretation, see Boris Wolfson, "Escape from Literature: Constructing the Soviet Self in Yuri Olesha's Diary of the 1930s," *Russian Review* 63 (10/ 2004).
46. TsDNA, f. 336, op. 1, ed. khr. 32 (12/21/1932). By the "three letters" Pavlova meant the Soviet Communist party (VKP).
47. Ibid. (12/9/1932).
48. Ibid. (3/9/1933).

49. Ibid. (1/29/1932, 4/25/1933).
50. "Fragments du journal inédit d'Ivan Ivanovic Sitc," *Cahiers du monde russe et soviétique* 28 (1987), no. 1, 91–92 ("First days of June [1930]"). *Pravda*, 6/26/1930, quoted in the diary of Lev Deich, "Zapisnye knizhki L. G. Deicha," 22 (6/27/1930).
51. RGALI, f. 1072, op. 4, ed. khr. 4 (*9/27/1937*).
52. TsDNA, f. 336, op. 1, ed. khr. 32 (letter to Ol'ga Kozlovskaia, 10/15/1930; letter to her mother and her sister Liza, 9/24/1930; entries for 2/21/1932, 4/15/1933); see also Inber, *Stranitsy dnei perebiraia*, 28 (8/24/1933); RGALI, f. 1072, op. 4, ed. khr. 4 (2/16/1938); Chukovskii, *Dnevnik 1930–1969*, 65 (7/4/1932).
53. See Jeff Weintraub, "The Theory and Politics of the Public/Private Distinction," in *Public and Private in Thought and Practice*, ed. Weintraub and Kumar.
54. Karl Marx, *Economic and Philosophic Manuscripts of 1844* (Moscow: Foreign Languages Publishing House, 1959), 104.
55. *Komsomol'skaia Pravda*, 12/15/1938, cited in Kharkhordin: "Reveal and Dissimulate," 357; Krupskaia (1924) cited in Naiman, *Sex in Public*, 92.
56. Podlubnyi: TsDNA, f. 30, op. 1, ed. 11–12 (6/7/1932, 6/1/1933). Ul'ianov: OR RGB, f. 442, op. 1, ed. khr. 4–5, 7 (undated, before 2/18/1930; 2/18/1930, 3/1/1930, 7/1/1932, 1/26/1935).
57. OR RGB, f. 442, op. 1, ed. 7 (2/6/1935).
58. Vladimir Paperny, *Architecture in the Age of Stalin: Culture Two* (Cambridge: Cambridge University Press, 2002); Volkov, "The Concept of Kul'turnost'."
59. RGAE, f. 525, op. 1, ed. 70 (5/5/1935, 12/13/1935, 3/6/1937).
60. *Tolkovyi slovar' russkogo iazyka*, ed. D. N. Ushakov, t. 1 (Moscow: Gos. in-t "Sovetskaia entsiklopediia," 1935), 613. "Zapisnye knizhki L. G. Deicha," 26 (11/20/1933).
61. AVMBR, f. R-242 (1/13/1940). Antonina Koptiaeva, a university student who later became a writer, kept a diary in 1937 that began with entries listing only headlines from *Pravda*. These passages are abruptly fol-

lowed by a series of entries, dated 1939, recording intimate fantasies and dreams. RGALI, f. 2537, op. 1, ed. khr. 127.

62. AVMBR, f. R-242 (1/27/1940, 2/5/1941).

63. Zhelezniakov: "1933–1936 gg. v griazovetskoi derevne," 468, 520–1 (6/11/1933, 12/13/1936). GASO, f. 2266, d. 1387 (1/15/1937).

64. Mankov also commented that society and state no longer made up a unified whole in the Soviet Union, with the state interests eroding and atomizing broader social ties. In effect he was diagnosing a dual life not just of the individual but of the social order as a whole. Man'kov, *Dnevniki 30-kh godov,* 285 (11/4/1940).

65. Ustrialov: "'Sluzhit' rodine prikhoditsia kostiami . . .', 13 (9/3/1935). Kirillov: "V seredine tridtsatykh. Dnevniki ssyl'nogo redaktora," *Nash sovremennik,* 1988, no. 11, pp. 111, 121 (2/21/1935, 5/20/1935); Kirillov's appeals for reinstatement were denied; he committed suicide in 1936. O. A. Aroseva, *Bez grima* (Moscow 2003), 51 (1/15/1934).

66. Man'kov, *Dnevniki 30kh godov,* 197 (10/25/1938); TsDNA, f. 30, op. 1, ed. 12 (1/23/1933).

67. AVMBR, f. R-242 (5/17/1940). For a different view see Kharkhordin, *The Collective and the Individual in Russia,* 271.

68. See, e.g., Aleksandr Afinonenov's diary: RGALI, f. 2172, op. 3, ed. 5 (7/29/1937).

69. OR RGB, f. 442, op. 1, ed. khr. 10 (11/9/1936). In Russian, "party" *(partiia)* is a feminine noun.

70. Piatnitskii was shot in July 1938, after at least 220 hours of interrogation, which included physical torture. He never signed the protocol listing his alleged crimes. See Boris Starkov, "The Trial That Was Not Held," *Europe-Asia Studies* 46, no. 8 (1994), 1307; *Golgofa,* 29, 46, (7/18/1937, 2/25/1938).

71. Radek: *Pervyi vsesoiuznyi s"ezd sovetskikh pisatelei,* 317. Ioganson cited in Grois, *The Total Art of Stalinism,* 53–54.

72. Ervin Sinkó, *Roman eines Romans. Moskauer Tagebuch* (Cologne: Verlag Wissenschaft und Politik, 1962), 196–197 (7/15/1935).

73. Chukovskii, *Dnevnik 1930–1969*, 64 (7/4/1932).

74. Private archive of Arkadii Man'kov (4/7/1933). This and several other self-critical passages are missing in the published version of Man'kov's diary. After a conversation with someone who defended the legitimacy of Soviet power, Man'kov wrote in his diary: "My close friend, my steady partner—the all-negating, hating, destructive spirit. This is my demon who has filled all my blood vessels and is running through my fibers." Man'kov, *Dnevniki 30-kh godov*, 95 (9/27/1933).

75. RGALI, f. 1072, op. 4, ed. khr. 4 (8/7/1933); TsDNA, f. 336, op. 1, ed. khr. 32 (1/29/1932); f. 30, op. 1, ed. 15 (10/31/1935); GAKO, f. r-652, op. 1, ed. khr. 2 (2/9/1936).

76. GASO, f. 2266, d. 1388 (3/10/1938, 3/12/1938). The reference is to Lion Feuchtwanger, *Moscow, 1937* (New York: Viking, 1937).

77. Sinkó, *Roman eines Romans*, 138, 197 (6/20–21/1935, 7/15/1935). For other cases of self-censorship, see TsDNA, f. 30, op. 1, ed. 16 (12/6/1937); RGAE, f. 525, op. 1, ed. 70 (9/18/1937); Lugovskaya, *Diary of a Soviet Schoolgirl*, 8; Chukovskii, *Dnevnik 1930–1969*, 3. Aside from visible gaps in the diary narrative, indicated by a break in the daily rhythm of the diary, or by erasures and torn pages, it is difficult to pinpoint instances of self-censorship. Elliptical style in writing about the purges is not in itself sufficient evidence of an unwillingness to speak out, especially if this style characterizes diary entries from earlier years. Witness the diary of Vsevolod Vishnevskii. Consider also the following entry from the diary of Galina Shtange: "*3/2/1938* Today the first day of the [trial of the] right Trotskyist bloc. I won't write about it since I'm saving the papers and it all can be read there." To infer from this passage that Shtange was afraid to voice her true attitude toward the trial is problematic, given that she expressed herself in identical terms in a different, more cheerful setting: "*6/12/1936* Last night Stalin's new Constitution was adopted. I won't say anything about it; I feel the same way as the rest of the country, i.e., absolute, infinite delight." What Shtange appears to be saying in both entries is that the Soviet

press or the public were in a much better position to express her subjective feelings than she herself. For a different interpretation, see *Intimacy and Terror*, xvii.

78. AVMBR, f. R-242 (2/2/1940).
79. Ibid. (11/13/1940).
80. Ibid. (7/2/1940, 10/12/1940, 12/12/1940).
81. "Bezumstvo predannosti. Iz dnevnikov Ol'gi Berggol'ts," *Vremia i my* 57 (1980), 277–287 (12/14/1939, 12/23/1939, 12/25/1939). See also the diaries of Aleksei Kirillov, Ivan Litvinov, and Aleksandr Solov'ev: Kirillov, "V seredine tridtsatykh"; I. I. Litvinov, "Dnevnik," in *Neizvestnaia Rossiia. XX vek*, no. 4 (1992), 81–139; A. G. Solov'ev, "Dnevnik krasnogo professora (1912–1940)," in *Neizvestnaia Rossiia. XX vek*, no. 4 (1992), 140–228.
82. Podlubnyi: TsDNA, f. 30, op. 1, ed. 12 (1/23/1933). Private archive of Arkadii Man'kov (6/12/1933, 12/5/1933). Sinkó, *Roman eines Romans*, 266 (8/31/1935). Lugovskaya, *Diary of a Soviet Schoolgirl* (9/5/1933, 9/22/1933, 11/8/1933, 11/9/1933, 3/18/1934, 2/10/1935, 11/6/1936).
83. *Golgofa*, 32–33, 46–48 (7/18/1937, 7/20/1937, 3/1/1938, 3/13/1938).
84. Keith Baker speaks of "transparison" as a new style of politics created by the French Revolution; Baker, "A Foucauldian French Revolution?" in *Foucault and the Writing of History*.
85. *Golgofa*, 97, 103 (5/25/1938, 5/28/1938). The avant-garde artist Gustav Klutsis similarly acted as confessor for his wife, Valentina Kulagina; excerpts from her diary are published in Margarita Tupitsyn, *Gustav Klutsis and Valentina Kulagina: Photography and Montage after Constructivism* (New York: International Center of Photography, 2004), see esp. 196–1977 (4/14/1930, 4/27/1930). The gender relationship could also be reversed. The Communist Mil'da Draule counseled her husband, Leonid Nikolaev, after his expulsion from the Communist party, but her mentoring did not prevent him from killing Sergei Kirov several months later. Petukhov and Khomchik, "Delo o 'Leningradskom tsentre'," 18; Kirilina, *Neizvestnyi Kirov*, 253–254.

86. Inber: RGALI, f. 1072, op. 4, ed. khr. 4 (1/29/1933, 1/11/1934). Vishnevskii, *Sobranie sochinenii v 5 tomakh,* vol. 6, *(Dopolnitel'nyi),* 370. "Bezumstvo predannosti," 282 (3/1/1940).
87. *Report of Court Proceedings in the Case of the Anti-Soviet Trotskyite Center Heard before the Military Collegium of the Supreme Court of the USSR, Moscow, January 23–30, 1937* (Moscow: People's Commissariat of Justice, 1937), 488.
88. *Golgofa,* 61, 75, 97, 103 (3/13/1938, 3/22/1938, 5/25/1938, 5/28/1938); TsDNA, f. 30, op. 1, ed. 13 (10/26/1934), 15 (1/5/1935).
89. *Golgofa,* 75, 101–103 (3/22/1938, 5/28/1938); see 114–116 for Piatnitskaya's imprisonment and death.
90. *Partiinaia etika,* 308; see also Naiman, *Sex in Public,* 93.
91. Metaphors of amputation and bodily pain in early Soviet culture are discussed in Lilya Kaganovsky, "How the Soviet Man Was (Un)Made," *Slavic Review* 63, no. 3 (Fall 2004).
92. Siegfried Kracauer, "The Mass Ornament," in *The Weimar Republic Sourcebook,* ed. Anton Kaes, Martin Jay, and Edward Dimendberg (Berkeley: University of California Press, 1994), 404–407.

4. Intelligentsia on Trial: Zinaida Denisevskaya

1. OR RGB, f. 752, op. 2, ed. khr. 2 (11/4/1917); ed. khr. 6 (3/29/1929); ed. khr. 7 (1/13/1932); op. 3, ed. khr. 17 (letter to A. S. Dankov, 1/1930). Zinaida Antonovna Denis'evskaia's diaries are preserved at the Russian State Library in Moscow.
2. Ibid., op. 1, ed. khr. 1 (11/3/1901); ed. khr. 4 (11/26/1911); op. 2, ed. khr. 6 (2/20/1930).
3. Ibid., op. 1, ed. khr. 1 (1/18/1906); ed. khr. 2 (9/3/1908); op. 2, ed. khr. 2 (12/5/1920).
4. OR RGB, f. 752, op. 1, ed. khr. 1 (3/21/1905); T. B. Kotlova, "Gimazistki na rubezhe vekov: dukhovnye tsennosti i idealy," *www.ivanovo.ac.ru/win1251/jornal/jornal2/kot.html.*
5. See Hellbeck, "Russian Autobiographical Practice."

6. OR RGB, f. 752, op. 1, ed. khr. 1 (11/19/1904, 7/23/1905, 7/25/1905); ed. khr. 4 (11/7/1910).
7. Ibid., op. 1, ed. 1 (11/23/1904, 2/5/1905, 7/10/1905, 11/11/1905); ed. khr. 2 (10/17/1906).
8. Ibid., ed. khr. 2 (2/15/1907).
9. Laura Engelstein, *The Keys to Happiness: Sex and the Search for Modernity in Fin-de-siècle Russia* (Ithaca: Cornell University Press, 1992), 383–388, 405–406; Mogil'ner, *Mifologiia "podpol´nogo cheloveka,"* 121–123.
10. OR RGB, f. 752, op. 1, ed. khr. 2 (10/24/1907, 10/15/1908, 10/23/1908, 10/24/1908); Bianca Pietrow-Ennker, *Russlands "neue Menschen": die Entwicklung der Frauenbewegung von den Anfängen bis zur Oktoberrevolution* (Frankfurt: Campus, 1999).
11. OR RGB, f. 752, op. 1, ed. khr. 2 (2/17/1907, 6/22/1907, 11/6/1908, 11/12/1908). Sexuality in her understanding was not the exclusive property of "women." She once described her father as a slave to his "sensuality," adding that her affliction might have been inherited from him. "His sensuality throws him into the embraces of various women, it has made him coarse, vulgar, petty, despotic, and cruel. His spiritual beauty has faded and become extinguished." Ibid., op. 2, ed. khr. 1 (12/19/1913).
12. Aleksandra Kollontai, "Novaia zhenshchina," in *Marksistskii feminizm. Kollektsiia tekstov A. M. Kollontai* (Tver': Feminist Press, 2003), 154–191.
13. OR RGB, f. 752, op. 2, ed. khr. 1 (9/9/1913); Kollontai, "Novaia zhenshchina," 159, 162.
14. OR RGB, f. 752, op. 2, ed. khr. 1 (6/20/1915); ed. khr. 2 (11/13/1916, 3/6/1917).
15. Ibid., ed. khr. 2 (3/9[22]/1918, 4/2/1918, 7/5[18]/1918, 8/16/1918, 9/8/1918).
16. Ibid. (4/2/1918, 4/21[5/4]/1918, 8/16/1918, 9/8/1918, 1/5/1919, 4/25/1919).
17. Ibid., op. 1, ed. khr. 2 (6/22/1907); op. 2, ed. khr. 1 (12/29/1914, 6/20/1915); ed. khr. 2 (3/13/1918, 6/21/1918).
18. Ibid., op. 2, ed. khr. 3 (8/6/1920, 4/17/1921); op. 3, ed. khr. 9 (letter to

Varvara Malakhieva, 12/9/1921); op. 3, ed. khr. 4 (letter to Ol'ga Bessarabova, 3/15/1922).

19. Ibid., op. 2, ed. khr. 4 (10/16/1926, 3/29/1927).
20. Ibid. (12/31/1926, 2/14/1927).
21. N. Sakulin, in *Sud'by russkoi intelligentsii: materialy diskussy 1923–1925 gg.* (Novosibirsk: "Nauka," 1991) 19.
22. Bukharin, ibid., 35–36, 39.
23. OR RGB, f. 752, op. 2, ed. khr. 4 (10/7/1926, 10/16/1926); ed. khr. 5 (4/7/1928); op. 3, ed. khr. 4 (letter to Ol'ga Bessarabova, 4/23/1925).
24. Ibid., op. 2, ed. khr. 5 (1/11/1927, 12/16/1928, 12/18/1928).
25. The young generation first appears in the guise of Zinaida's younger cousin Veronika, a co-worker on the experimental farm. Zinaida admired her cousin's resilience and cheerfulness, but criticized her eagerness to reduce complex social and political phenomena to a single ideological truth. Ibid. (6/3/1927); ed. khr. 6 (10/24/1929).
26. Ibid., ed. khr. 5 (9/8/1928, 12/31/1928); ed. khr. 6 (4/18/1929, 4/25/1929).
27. Ibid., op. 3, ed. khr. 4 (letters to Ol'ga Bessarabova, 4/23/1925, New Year 1926, 9/23/1926); ed. khr. 17 (letter to Dankov, 1/10/1930).
28. Ibid., ed. khr. 4 (letter to Bessarabova, New Year 1926); op. 2, ed. khr. 4 (9/23/1926).
29. Ibid., op. 2, ed. khr. 6 (9/21/1929).
30. Ibid., op. 3, ed. khr. 17 (letter to Dankov, 9/28–30/1929); ed. khr. 18 (letter from Dankov; 7/13/1932).
31. Ibid., op. 2, ed. khr. 6 (10/24/1929, 10/28/1929, 4/20/1930). Soviet marriage practices at the time were regulated by the lax marriage code of 1926, which legalized de facto marriages of partners living together. In *Bed and Sofa,* a film produced in 1927 which explored social and moral problems ensuing from the code, the visiting guest Volodia, after sleeping with his host's wife, concludes his marriage with her with a simple handshake. At the same time she remains married to her first husband.
32. OR RGB, f. 752, op. 2, ed. khr. 6 (1/6/1930); 1933 speech by Anatolii Lunacharskii, cited in Lars T. Lih, "Melodrama and the Myth of the

Soviet Union," in *Imitations of Life: Two Centuries of Melodrama in Russia,* ed. Louise McReynolds and Joan Neuberger (Durham: Duke University Press, 2002), 182.

33. OR RGB, f. 752, op. 2, ed. khr. 6 (10/28/1929).
34. Ibid., op. 3, ed. khr. 17 (letter to Dankov, 11/27–29/1929). A single postcard from him is preserved in the archive; it is addressed, "Zinaida Antonovna!" and confirms her description of his style. Possibly she discarded Alyosha's postcards because they did not reveal his psychology and were thus worthless for her autobiographical project. Ibid., ed. khr. 18, letter from Dankov (7/13/1932).
35. Ibid., op. 2, ed. khr. 6 (2/11/1930, 3/10/1930); op. 3, ed. khr. 17 (letters to Dankov, 11/27–29/1929, 12/4/1929, 2/12/1930).
36. Ibid., op. 3, ed. khr. 17 (letter to Dankov, 12/16/1929); op. 2, ed. khr. 6 (3/10/1930, 3/30/1930).
37. Ibid., op. 2, ed. khr. 6 (1/28/1930, 3/17/1930).
38. Ibid. (12/16/1929); op. 3, ed. khr. 17 (letter to Dankov, 1/28/1930).
39. Derek Müller, *Der Topos des neuen Menschen in der russischen und sowjetrussischen Geistesgeschichte* (Bern: P. Lang, 1998), 123; Andreas Guski, *Literatur und Arbeit: Produktionsskizze und Produktionsroman im Russland des 1. Fünfjahrplans (1928–1932),* (Wiesbaden: Harrassowitz, 1995), 300–302. In Fedor Gladkov's novel *Cement* (1926) no protagonist is without a severe personal defect, and all fall short of intimate, emotional love. See Eliot Borenstein, *Men without Women: Masculinity and Revolution in Russian Fiction, 1917–1929* (Durham: Duke University Press, 2000).
40. Kollontai, "Novaia zhenshchina," 187.
41. OR RGB, f. 752, op. 2, ed. khr. 6 (3/30/1930); ed. khr. 7 (7/16/1930, 7/22/1930); op. 3, ed. khr. 17 (letter to Dankov, 6/28/1930).
42. V. A. Dobrynin, *Kondrat'ev N. D. i Chaianov A. V. o reshenii agrarnogo voprosa v Rossii. Lektsiia* (Moscow: Izd-vo MSKhA, 1994); V. N. Baliazin, *Professor Aleksandr Chaianov 1888–1937* (Moscow: Agropromizdat, 1990), 240–245. Bukharin had been expelled from the Politburo in November 1929, but he was a still a member of the party's Central Committee.
43. OR RGB, f. 752, op. 2, ed. khr. 6 (2/28/1930, 3/13/1930, 3/19/1930).

44. P. V. Zagorovskii, *Sotsial'no-politicheskaia istoriia tsentral'no-chernozemnoi oblasti, 1928–1934* (Voronezh: Izd-vo Voronezhskogo universiteta, 1995), 62. OR RGB, f. 752, op. 2, ed. khr. 7 (8/12/1930, 11/20/1930).
45. *Pravda,* Sept. 22, 1930; OR RGB, f. 752, op. 2, ed. khr. 7 (9/27/1930).
46. OR RGB, f. 752, ed. 2, ed. khr. 7 (8/27/1930, 10/16/1930).
47. Ibid. (10/27/1930, 10/28/1930, 11/21/1930, 1/23/1931).
48. Ibid. (11/20/1930).
49. Ibid.; on Pistsov's fate see V. Bazilevskaia, "Vspomnim ikh . . . ," in *Iz nebytiia: Voronezhtsy v tiskakh stalinshchiny* (Voronezh: Tsentral´no-Chernozemnoe knizhnoe izd-vo, 1992), 32.
50. OR RGB, f. 752, op. 2, ed. 7 (4/12/1931).
51. Ibid., op. 1, ed. khr. 1 (10/12/1901); op. 2, ed. khr. 3 (2/25/1921); ed. khr. 7 (10/13/1931); op. 3, ed. khr. 6 (letter to Evgeniia Birukova, 2/24/1928).
52. Ibid., op. 2, ed. khr. 6 (1/6/1930). *"Intelligentka-odinochka,"* a clichéd expression of the times, fully expressed Denisevskaia's plight.
53. Ibid., ed. khr. 3 (2/25/1921). For parades in Voronezh, see Malte Rolf, *Sovetskii massovyi prazdnik v Voronezhe i Tsentral´no-chernozemnoi oblasti Rossii: 1927–1932* (Voronezh: Izdatel'stvo Voronezhskogo gosudarstvennogo universiteta, 2000).
54. OR RGB, f. 752, op. 3, ed. khr. 9 (letter to Varvara Malakhieva, 11/12/1928); see also op. 2, ed. khr. 5 (11/7/1928).
55. Ibid., op. 2, ed. khr. 6 (2/20/1930, 2/23/1930, 5/1/1930).
56. Ibid., ed. khr. 7 (7/17/1930).
57. Ibid., ed. khr. 8 (12/26/1932).
58. Ibid., ed. khr. 7 (10/28/1930, 1/23/1931).
59. Ibid. (11/7/1930; see also 11/24/1930, 11/26/1930).
60. Ibid., ed. khr. 6 (5/1/1930); ed. khr. 7 (8/10/1931); ed. khr. 8 (1/20/1933). Visiting Moscow during the October holidays in 1932, she commented: "So festively did Moscow shine with light . . . the whole Tverskaya [street] looked like the corridor of a big home." Ibid., ed. khr. 8 (11/6/1932).
61. Ibid., ed. khr. 8 (12/27/1932, 1/17/1933).

62. Zagorovskii, *Sotsial'no-politicheskaia istoriia tsentral'no-chernozemnoi oblasti,* 85–88. OR RGB, f. 752, op. 2, ed. 8 (1/17/1933).
63. OR RGB, f. 752, op. 2, ed. khr. 8 (2/19/1933); op. 3, ed. khr. 16, l. 1.
64. Ibid., ed. khr. 16, l. 6.
65. Ibid., op. 1, ed. khr. (1/2/1907); op. 2, ed. khr. 2 (4/6/1917); ed. khr. 8 (1/20/1933); op. 3, ed. khr. 4 (letter to Ol'ga Bessarabova, 4/23/1925).

5. Secrets of a Class Enemy: Stepan Podlubny

1. For autobiographical accounts see Ivan Gudov, *Sud'ba rabochego* (Moscow: Politizdat, 1970); David Hoffmann, *Peasant Metropolis: Social Identities in Moscow, 1929–1941* (Ithaca: Cornell University Press, 1994). See also N. N. Kozlova, "Krest'ianskii syn," *Sotsiologicheskie issledovaniia,* 1994, no. 6; idem, "Zalozhniki slova?" *Sotsiologicheskie issledovaniia* 1995, nos. 9–10.
2. On the wolf metaphor see Fitzpatrick, "The Problem of Class Identity in NEP Society," 20; idem, *Stalin's Peasants: Resistance and Survival in the Russian Village after Collectivization* (New York: Oxford University Press, 1994), 124.
3. Podlubnyi's diary for 1931–1939, along with other personal documents from that period, is in TsDNA, f. 30, op. 1, d. 11–18. Large sections have been published in German: *Tagebuch aus Moskau 1931–1939,* ed. Jochen Hellbeck (Munich: Deutscher Taschenbuch Verlag, 1996). Podlubnyi's diary notes for 1936–1938 are in *Intimacy and Terror,* 293–331. Countless other kulak dependents shared his predicament as a wolf in disguise. Podlubnyi told me about three of his cousins who metamorphosed into Soviet citizens, never revealing their social background; one became a Red Army officer and a member of the Communist party. The poet Aleksandr Tvardovskii was also from a kulak family. The theme of redemption from impure social origins figures in his work; A. T. Tvardovskii, "Pravo po pamiati," *Znamia,* 1987, no. 2; see also his brother's memoirs: I. T. Tvardovskii, "Vospominaniia," *Iunost',* 1988, no. 3; 1989, nos. 10–11; and see *Memories of the Dispossessed: Descendants of Kulak Families Tell Their Stories,* ed. James Riordan (Nottingham: Bramcote, 1998).

4. Interviews with Podlubnyi, 6/22/1994, 6/28/1994.
5. The document is from the private archive of Marina S. Gavrilova, Stepan Podlubnyi's daughter, in Moscow.
6. *Pravda,* 4/3/1930.
7. See Podlubnyi's "autobiography," written in the 1980s; TsDNA, f. 30, op. 1, ed. 4; see also ed. 14 (8/10/1934).
8. The article was later published in the newspaper of the *Pravda* plant: *Pravdist,* 7/19/1931, 3; TsDNA, f. 30, op. 1, ed. 11 (6/27, 6/30, 7/10, 7/21, 7/23, 8/2/, 8/10, 8/11, 8/12/1931).
9. On normalization in the Stalin-era workplace, see Kotkin, *Magnetic Mountain,* 198–237.
10. TsDNA, f. 30, op. 1, ed. 11 (5/5/1932, 10/27/1932); ed. 12 (11/1/1932, 7/9/1933); Katerina Clark, "Little Heroes and Big Deeds," in *Cultural Revolution in Russia, 1928–1931,* ed. Sheila Fitzpatrick (Bloomington: Indiana University Press, 1978).
11. TsDNA, f. 30, op. 1, ed. 11 (5/10/1932, 9/2/1932, 9/9/1932, 10/10/1932); ed. 13 (9/25/1934); ed. 15 (9/18/1935).
12. Ibid., ed. 12 (11/3/1932, 1/23/1933).
13. Golfo Alexopoulos, *Stalin's Outcasts: Aliens, Citizens, and the Soviet State, 1926–1936* (Ithaca: Cornell University Press, 2003), 13–43; Elise Kimerling, "Civil Rights and Social Policy in Soviet Russia, 1918–1936," *Russian Review* 41 (1982), 24–46.
14. The largest contingent was deported to the Northern Region, which included Arkhangel'sk. See Lynne Viola, "The Other Archipelago: Kulak Deportations to the North in 1930," *Slavic Review* 60/4 (Winter 2001), 734.
15. Sheila Fitzpatrick, "Ascribing Class: The Construction of Social Identity in Soviet Russia," *Journal of Modern History* 65 (12/1993), 757, 756; Alexopoulos, *Stalin's Outcasts,* 31–34. TsDNA, f. 30, op. 1, ed. 12 (11/17/1933).
16. Alexopoulos, *Stalin's Outcasts;* Fitzpatrick, "Ascribing Class," 752–755, 757–759; Bauer, *New Man in Soviet Psychology,* 47. See also Tat'iana

Smirnova, *"Byvshie liudi" Sovetskoi Rossii: Strategii vyzhivaniia i puti integratsii. 1917–1936 gody* (Moscow: "Mir istorii," 2003).

17. On Soviet officials' fear of bourgeois cunning and deception, see Alexopoulos, *Stalin's Outcasts,* 40.
18. *Chelovek sredi liudei,* 175, 178 (12/3/1930, 12/13/1930).
19. TsDNA, f. 30, op. 1, ed. 12 (8/25/1933).
20. Ibid., ed. 11 (8/22/1932, 10/18/1932); ed. 12 (11/6/1932, 12/6/1933); ed. 13 (10/5/1934).
21. Ibid., ed. 11 (8/22/1932); ed. 12 (4/1/1933, 1/25/1934).
22. Ibid., ed. 11 (9/13/1932).
23. Ibid., ed. 13 (9/25/1934).
24. Ibid., ed. 11 (8/2/1932). Podlubnyi copied excerpts from *Das Kapital:* TsDNA, f. 30, op. 1, ed. 33. Nadezhda Krupskaia, in *Organization of Self-Education* (1922), compares Communists' autodidactic attempts to master *Das Kapital* to trying to kill a bear with one's bare hands; she proposes several stages of learning before setting off on the hunt. Kharkhordin, *Collective and Individual in Russia,* 232. Stalin called *Das Kapital* an "examination of human thinking" and recommended reading it as a means to becoming a good Communist. *The Diary of Georgi Dimitrov, 1933–1949,* ed. Ivo Banac (New Haven: Yale University Press, 2003), 19 (5/2/1934).
25. TsDNA, f. 30, op. 1, ed. 11 (10/6/1932); ed. 15 (1/29/1935); ed. 12 (2/6/1933, 1/1/1934); ed. 13 (2/18/1934, 10/15/1934). Children of class-alien background petitioned Gorky to intervene on their behalf: *Kem khotiat byt' nashi deti: Sbornik detskikh pisem dlia ottsov* (Moscow and Leningrad, Gosud. izd-vo, 1929), 5–6.
26. TsDNA, f. 30, op. 1, ed. 11 (8/26/1932, 10/6/1932).
27. Ibid., ed. 12 (12/21/1933).
28. Ibid., ed. 11 (8/18/1932).
29. Ibid. (10/1/1932).
30. Ibid., ed. 12 (11/15/1932, 11/17/1932).
31. Ibid. (12/8/1932).
32. Ibid., ed. 11 (10/1/1932); ed. 12 (12/18/1932).

33. Ibid. (11/27/1932); ed. 13 (7/23/1934, 8/1/1934) ed. 6.
34. See *Rapports secrets soviétiques. La société russe dans les documents confidentiels 1921–1991,* ed. Nicolas Werth and Gaël Moullec (Paris: Gallimard, 1994), 44–46; Hoffmann, *Peasant Metropolis,* 52–53; Kotkin, *Magnetic Mountain,* 99–101.
35. TsDNA, f. 30, op. 1, ed. 12 (1/23/1933).
36. Ibid. (1/15/1933, 2/4/1933).
37. Ibid. (2/4/1933, 2/30/1933). The actual numbers were lower, though still extraordinary: according to an internal government report of August 1934, the passport campaign had reduced Moscow's population by 578,000 persons, who either were denied passports or fled the city in anticipation of reprisals. *Rapports secrets soviétiques,* 46.
38. TsDNA, f. 30, op. 1, ed. 12 (3/10/1933).
39. Ibid. (6/1/1933).
40. The boa may have been a reference to Aleksandr Afinogenov's popular play *Fear* (1931); see Chapter 7.
41. TsDNA, f. 30, op. 1, ed. 28 (1/16/1934).
42. Ibid., ed. 13 (6/18/1934, 10/5/1934).
43. Ibid. (10/5/1934, 10/15/1934, 10/26/1934).
44. Ibid., ed. 15 (3/2/1935).
45. Ibid. (9/18/1935). Podlubnyi owed his admission to the Medical Institute largely to his fictitious worker origins. Upon failing a preparatory math exam he went to the dean and asked to be reexamined. The request was granted because of his claim to be a proletarian. At his second exam, the teacher handed Podlubnyi a written assignment and then, without looking at the results, gave him a satisfactory grade (interview with Podlubnyi, 6/23/1992). Until 1935 admission to Soviet higher education was regulated by social quotas that heavily favored candidates of proletarian background. The purpose was to facilitate the creation of a working-class intelligentsia. In 1928 one-quarter of all Soviet students were of proletarian background; by 1935 their share had risen to 45 percent. *Kulturpolitik der Sowjetunion,* ed. Oskar Anweiler and Karl-Heinz Ruffmann (Stuttgart: Kröner, 1973), 62–63.

In December 1935 a government decree proclaimed the right of all Soviet citizens, regardless of origins, to study at institutes of higher education. This new policy, however, did not put an end to discrimination against class aliens. Fitzpatrick, "Ascribing Class," 757–758.

46. TsDNA, f. 30, op. 1, ed. 11 (8/13/1932).
47. Ibid., ed. 12 (7/9/1933, 1/24/1934); ed. 13 (3/28/1934, 5/9/1934).
48. See Yuri Druzhnikov, *Informer 001: The Myth of Pavlik Morozov* (New Brunswick, N.J.: Transaction, 1997).
49. TsDNA, f. 30, op. 1, ed. 11 (9/2/1932).
50. On such in-migration and particularly the use of village networks, see Hoffmann, *Peasant Metropolis,* 54–72.
51. TsDNA, f. 30, op. 1, ed. 12 (2/12/1933).
52. Ibid. (10/24/1933).
53. Ibid. (6/18/1933); ed. 15 (12/7/1935); ed. 16 (1/1/1936); ed. 55 (Podlubnyi, letter to Tat'iana Silaeva); ed. 102 (Tat'iana Silaeva, letter to Podlubnyi).
54. Ibid., ed. 16 (1/30/1936).
55. Ibid., ed. 12 (10/10/1933); ed. 16 (12/20/1937); ed. 75, ll. 1–4 (letter from Veronika E. Ivanova, 10/1933).
56. Ibid., ed. 105 (letter from Rishat Khaibulin, 2/1935).
57. Ibid., ed. 46 (letters to Kornei P. Krivoruka); ed. 82 (letters from Krivoruka).
58. Interview with Podlubnyi, 3/28/1995; TsDNA, f. 30, op. 1, ed. 16 (12/20/1937); for a similar case see Hoffmann, *Peasant Metropolis,* 71.
59. TsDNA, f. 30, op. 1, ed. 12 (3/16/1933). The analysis is preserved in Marina Gavrilova's private archive.
60. TsDNA, f. 30, op. 1, ed. 12 (4/1/1933).
61. Ibid., ed. 11 (6/7/1932); ed. 12 (12/6/1933, 12/30/1933).
62. Ibid., ed. 12 (10/10/1933, 11/3/1933); ed. 13 (2/18/1934, 3/23/1934, 12/27/1934); ed. 15 (12/8/1935).
63. Ibid., ed. 13 (2/4/1933, 8/14/1933).
64. Ibid. (2/4/1933, 2/7/1933).
65. Podlubnyi's behavior matches Golfo Alexopoulos's notion of the "rit-

ual lament," practiced by many class aliens, who in petitions to the Soviet regime underscored their own helplessness in order to solicit the authorities' care. Alexopoulos, *Stalin's Outcasts.* Yet his case also shows this self-representation extending beyond official interaction with the regime, impinging on Podlubnyi's sense of self.

66. TsDNA, f. 30, op. 1, ed. 12 (12/23/1933); ed. 13 (9/25/1934).
67. Ibid., ed. 13 (9/25/1934).
68. Ibid., ed. 15 (1/5/1935).
69. Ibid. (1/5/1935, 1/26/1935). Many historians believe that Stalin masterminded Kirov's murder: Robert Conquest, *Stalin and the Kirov Murder* (New York: Oxford University Press, 1989); Robert Tucker, *Stalin in Power: The Revolution from Above, 1928–1941* (New York: Norton, 1990), 288–302. For more skeptical assessments see Kirilina, *Neizvestnyi Kirov;* J. Arch Getty, "The Politics of Repression Revisited," in *Stalinist Terror: New Perspectives,* ed. J. Arch Getty and Roberta Manning (Cambridge: Cambridge University Press, 1993). There is no doubt, however, that Stalin used the murder as a pretext to launch a terror campaign against his foes.
70. TsDNA, f. 30, op. 1, ed. 15 (2/12/1935).
71. Ibid. (10/28/1935, 10/31/1935); ed. 16 (2/17/1936).
72. Ibid., ed. 15 (10/31/1935); ed. 16 (3/5/1936).
73. Ibid., ed. 15 (10/31/1935).
74. Ibid., ed. 16 (2/13/1936).
75. Ibid. (2/22/1936).
76. *Pravda,* 2/16/1941, 4, cited in Fitzpatrick, "Ascribing Class," 764. Another indication of the strength of Podlubnyi's sense of class determinism is that his diary contains no reference to Stalin's widely circulating phrase, formulated in December 1935, that "a son does not answer for his father," which meant that the offspring of class aliens or political counterrevolutionaries would not be held responsible for their parents' misdeeds. Fitzpatrick, "Ascribing Class."
77. TsDNA, f. 30, op. 1, ed. 16 (5/30/1936, 10/8/1936, 12/31/1936).
78. Ibid. (12/6/1937, 12/18/1937).

79. Order no. 447 is reprinted in *Tragediia sovetskoi derevni: Kollektivizatsiia i raskulachivanie. Dokumenty i materialy. 1927–1939. Tom 5: 1937–1939, Kniga 1: 1937* (Moscow: Rosspen, 2004), 330–337; for the implementation, see 372–390.
80. TsDNA, f. 30, op. 1, ed. 16 (12/18/1937, 12/25/1937, 1/7/1938, 1/11/1938), English translation from *Intimacy and Terror;* interview with Podlubnyi, 6/21/1994.
81. TsDNA, f. 30, op. 1, ed. 17 (3/18/1938, 4/15/1938).
82. Ibid. (3/18/1938, 4/3/1938, 4/5/1938, 4/9/1938). "We must not live like this" is a famous phrase from Gorky's *Lower Depths.*
83. Ibid., ed. 16 (1/11/1938); ed. 17 (6/21/1938, 12/10/1938, 12/10/1938).
84. Ibid. (5/12/1938); ed. 18 (1/18/1939).
85. Interview with Podlubnyi, 6/28/1994.
86. The war constituted a new founding moment for Soviet society, in that one's performance during the war overshadowed previous parameters of social identity. Amir Weiner, *Making Sense of War: The Second World War and the Fate of the Bolshevik Revolution* (Princeton: Princeton University Press, 2001).
87. Interview with Podlubnyi, 3/28/1995.
88. On the goals of the "People's archive," see *Tsentr dokumentatsii "Narodnyi arkhiv": spravochnik po fondam* (Moscow: Narodnyi arkhiv, 1998); on the memories of kulak's children, see *Memories of the Dispossessed,* ed. Riordan. On memory and archival practices after the fall of the Soviet regime, see Jan Plamper, "Archival Revolution or Illusion? Historicizing the Russian Archives and Our Work in Them"; Peter Holquist, "A Tocquevillian Archival Revolution? Archival Change in the Longue Durée," both in *Jahrbücher für Geschichte Osteuropas* 51 (2003), no. 1; and Irina Paperno, "Personal Accounts of the Soviet Experience," *Kritika* 3:4 (Fall 2002).

6. The Diary of a New Man: Leonid Potemkin

1. Interview with Leonid Potemkin, 3/24/2002. Potemkin's three books are *U severnoi granitsy. Pechenga sovetskaia* (Murmansk: Murmanskoe

kn. izd-vo, 1965), *Lenin i razvitie mineral'noi syr'evoi bazy* (Moscow: "Znanie," 1969), and *Okhrana nedr i okruzhaiushchei prirody* (Moscow: "Nedra," 1977).

2. The anthology is *Intimacy and Terror.* Potemkin lodged a formal complaint about it in *Moskovskii zhurnal mezhdunarodnogo prava* 1997, no. 4; see also the carefully worded response by a contributor to the anthology: Véronique Garros, "Traduction: trahison? ou comment faire place aux conflits d'interprétation?" *La lettre du CEMS, centre d'étude des mouvements sociaux* no. 4 (4/30/1999), 2–3. When citing passages from Potemkin's diary that appear in *Intimacy and Terror,* I follow, with few exceptions, Carol Flath's translation. Potemkin's diaries, letters, and memoirs are in his private archive in Moscow.
3. L. A. Potemkin, "Rodnye istoki (istoriko-biograficheskie ocherki)," manuscript (1995), 56–75, 108, 118b, 128, 157.
4. Ibid., 135. In an interview (4/23/2002) Potemkin recalled the bean and meat soup and bread he received at school and took home to share with the family. He specifically requested that his gratitude to the ARA and the people of the United States be publicly expressed.
5. L. A. Potemkin, "Balkhashskoe kreshchenie" (manuscript); Potemkin, "Rodnye istoki," 153.
6. Potemkin, *U severnoi granitsy;* for life histories of Soviet engineers, see Susanne Schattenberg, *Stalins Ingenieure: Lebenswelten zwischen Technik und Terror in den 1930er Jahren* (Munich: Oldenbourg, 2002).
7. Potemkin, "Rodnye istoki," 160; interview with Potemkin, 4/27/2002.
8. See *Sovetskaia intelligentsiia. Istoriia formirovaniia i rosta 1917–1965 gg.* (Moscow: "Mysl'," 1968). The classic study of Soviet *vydvizhentsy* is Fitzpatrick, *Education and Social Mobility;* on the regime's civilizing mission, see Volkov, "The Concept of 'Kul'turnost'."
9. See Vera Dunham, *In Stalin's Time: Middle-Class Values in Soviet Fiction* (Cambridge: Cambridge University Press, 1976), esp. 13–18.
10. Potemkin, diary, t. 2, l. 23 (5/31/1930), l. 28ob (8/3/1930), l. 46, ll. 125ob–126ob (8/14/1931). Potemkin recorded his diary notes (1/1/1930–9/23/1936) in four notebooks, which he designated "volumes 2–5." The di-

ary is sparsely dated. My citations therefore include the manuscript page number in addition to the nearest date.

11. Ibid., t. 2, l. 6ob. His uncle was arrested, and the teacher exiled. Ibid., ll. 6ob, 49–50ob. Potemkin later erased the word "uncle," replacing it with "neighbor" (1/24/1930). This is one of few passages in the diary where he made later editorial changes. Judging from the handwriting, the editorial changes were made at young age.
12. Ibid., ll. 49–50ob (1/11/1931), 58ob–59 (1/17/1931).
13. Ibid., ll. 4ob, 10ob, 40ob, 90ob–91, ll. 48–48ob, ll. 35–35ob (10/1/1930), 43ob–44ob (11/10/1930), 72ob (3/28/1931), 86 (4/30/1931); t. 4, ll. 61ob–62 (1/23/1934); t. 2, l. 54 (1/12/1931); t. 4, l. 58–58ob (10/18/1933).
14. Ibid., ll. 128ob–129 (8/17/1931).
15. Ibid., t. 3, ll. 3–3ob, l. 60–60ob; t. 4, ll. 9ob–10 (10/25/1932); t. 3, l. 11–11ob, ll. 17, 28ob–29 (3/9/1932).
16. Ibid., l. 130ob–132ob (8/17/1931).
17. Ibid., t. 2, ll. 113ob–114 (6/17/1931). I. T. Nazarov, *Kul'tura voli. Sistema samovospitaniia zdorovoi lichnosti.* 2nd, expanded ed. (Leningrad: O-vo razr. metoda dost. koord. organizma, 1929); Potemkin, diary, t. 3, l. 75ob (8/1/1932). Potemkin found the book while browsing the library of his sister's husband, the doctor (interview, 4/23/2002).
18. Potemkin, diary, t. 3, ll. 76–77ob (8/1/1932).
19. Ibid., t. 4, l. 13 (10/25/1932), l. 15 (10/17/1932).
20. Ibid., t. 3, ll. 77–77ob (8/1/1932); t. 4, l. 16ob (11/1/1932).
21. Ibid., l. 29 (2/8/1933), 61 (1/12/1934), 70 (5/12/1934), ll. 47–49 (8/21/1933).
22. Ibid., t. 4, ll. 60ob–61 (1/12/1934, Potemkin's 20th birthday), ll. 58ob–60 (11/8/1933), l. 72 (5/12/1934). On Soviet neuropathological diagnoses and treatments of the 1930s, see Eric Naiman, "Discourse Made Flesh: Healing and Terror in the Construction of Soviet Subjectivity," in *Language and Modern Revolution: The Making of Modern Political Identities,* ed. Igal Halfin (London: F. Cass, 2002).
23. Potemkin, diary, t. 4, l. 65–65ob (3/1/1934). In an interview (12/18/2004) Potemkin revealed, with some pride, that his grandmother had been the illegitimate daughter of an aristocrat.

24. Potemkin, diary, t. 4, l. 67 (3/24/1934).
25. *Desiatyi s"ezd Vsesoiuznogo Leninskogo Kommunisticheskogo soiuza molodezhi 11–21 aprelia 1936 g. Stenograficheskii otchet* (Moscow: Molodaia gvardiia, 1936), t. 1: *1–11-e zasedanie,* 11, 23–24, 186; *Molodaia gvardiia* 1936, no. 5, 19.
26. Potemkin, diary, t. 5, ll. 2ob–4 (10/1/1934).
27. Ibid., l. 5ob (10/1/1934).
28. *Desiatyi s"ezd,* t. 1, 42; Potemkin, diary, t. 5, ll. 73ob–74 (after 6/1936).
29. Potemkin, diary, t. 5, ll. 13–13ob (1/8/1935), l. 34ob (4/4/1935).
30. Ibid., l. 27 (3/6/1935).
31. Maksim Gorkii, "V. I. Lenin," in Gorkii, *Sobranie sochinenii v tridtsati tomakh,* t. 17 (Moscow: Gos. izd.-vo khudozh. lit-ry, 1952), 39–40.
32. Potemkin, diary, t. 5, l. 15 (after 1/12/1935).
33. Ibid., ll. 9 ob (12/6/1934), 15ob (1/25/1935).
34. Ibid., ll. 3ob (10/1/1934), 15 (1/12/1935), 17ob (1/30/1935), 53ob (after 9/28/1935), 65 (5/1936), l. 62 (after 1/1936).
35. Ibid., ll. 7 (12/19/1934), 17ob (1/30/1935), 19 (after 2/ 4/1935).
36. Ibid., ll. 41–42 (4 or 5/1935), ll. 42–42ob.
37. Ibid., l. 31ob (3/24/1935); on Communist sublimation, see Halfin, *Terror in My Soul,* 166–175.
38. Potemkin, diary, t. 5, l. 81–81ob (summer or fall 1936); correspondence, l. 8 (letter to Ira Zhirkova, 11/1937); diary, t. 5, l. 69ob (6/1936). While the Soviet hierarchy of love ascended from the individual to the collective or to depersonalized forms (enthusiasm for labor, Soviet patriotism), socialism as the highest object of love could be addressed in a personalized mode in the form of love for the leader and father, Stalin. See Jeffrey Brooks, *Thank You, Comrade Stalin: Soviet Public Culture from Revolution to Cold War* (Princeton: Princeton University Press, 2000).
39. Potemkin, diary, t. 5, l. 26 (3/1935).
40. Ibid., l. 39 (after 4/4/1935). *Desiatyi s"ezd,* t. 2: *12–19-e zasedanie,* 33.
41. *Desiatyi s"ezd,* t. 1, 186; see also Lewis Siegelbaum, *Stakhanovism and the Politics of Productivity in the USSR, 1935–1941* (Cambridge: Cambridge University Press, 1988).

42. Potemkin, diary, t. 5, l. 39 (4/4/1935).
43. Ibid., ll. 32ob–33 (3/24/1935).
44. Ibid., ll. 45ob–46 (7/10/1935); Potemkin, correspondence, l. 11 (letter to Zhirkova, 11/1937); diary, t. 4, l. 24 (1/11/1933).
45. Potemkin, diary, t. 5, ll. 48–48ob (7/10/1935), 39ob–40ob (5/1935).
46. *Desiatyi s"ezd,* t. 1, 130–131.
47. Potemkin, correspondence, ll. 73–74 (letter to Zhirkova). See Bernice Glatzer Rosenthal, *New Myth, New World: From Nietzsche to Stalinism* (University Park: Pennsylvania State University Press, 2002).
48. Potemkin, diary, t. 5, l. 26ob (3/5/1935), l. 9ob (12/1934).
49. Trotsky, *Literature and Revolution,* 185–186. Addressing the First Congress of Soviet Writers in 1934, Bukharin referred to Pushkin, who at age 14 had had a breathtaking command of languages and literature, and called for the creation of a literature that would rise up as a "towering ridge in the history of humanity and the history of art." *Pervyi vsesoiuznyi s"ezd sovetskikh pisatelei,* 503.
50. Potemkin, diary, t. 5, ll. 17 (1/30/1935), ll. 41–42 (4 or 5/1935); L. A. Potemkin "Strategiia zhizni" (manuscript), l. 7ob.
51. Potemkin, diary, t. 5, l. 16ob (1/26/1935).
52. Potemkin, diary, t. 5, l. 10; t. 4, l. 25–25ob (1/11/1933).
53. Ibid., t. 5, l. 8ob (12/20/1934), l. 6ob (11/7/1934). On the aesthetic appeal of communism see Grois, *Total Art of Stalinism.*
54. Potemkin, diary, t. 5, l. 23ob (after 2/4/1935). He often used the terms "meaning" and "beauty" in the same breath, implying that the intellectual power of Communism was synonymous with its aesthetic attraction. The total meaning afforded by Communist ideology equaled total beauty.
55. Ibid., l. 10–10ob (New Year's resolution, 1935), ll. 15 (1/23/1935), 47 (after 7/10/1935), 61, 62 (1/1936); correspondence, ll. 177–179 (letter to his mother, 11/22/1936); *Desiatyi s"ezd,* t. 1, 58–59.
56. Potemkin, diary, t. 5, ll. 47 (after 7/10/1935), 55 (after 9/28/1935).
57. In fashioning himself as an engineer of human souls Potemkin did not seem to think about his background as a technical engineer.

While professional writers occupied a privileged role in Stalinist society as engineers of human souls, technical engineers and architects created the most memorable aesthetic monuments of the age, opulent high-rises, grandiose artificial waterways (the Belomor, Moskva-Volga, and Fergana canals), and subterranean palaces (the Moscow metro). In the words of an engineer involved in the building of the Fergana Canal: "The joy of the sculptor is understandable, who has turned a block of marble into a work of art which for centuries fills the viewer with joy. But how much more majestic is the joy of a man who has turned dead land into flowering gardens, and destitute regions into happy, fragrant oases"; N. Dmitrieva, "Esteticheskaia kategoriia prekrasnogo," *Iskusstvo* 1952, no. 1, 78. See also Thomas Lahusen, *How Life Writes the Book: Real Socialism and Socialist Realism in Stalin's Russia* (Ithaca: Cornell University Press, 1997); Schattenberg, *Stalins Ingenieure.*

58. Potemkin, diary, t. 5, l. 1 (10/1/1934).
59. Ibid., l. 51–51ob (after 9/28/1935).
60. Ibid., ll. 59ob–60 (1/1936).
61. Ibid., t. 4, l. 25ob (1/11/1933).
62. Leonid Potemkin, "Dialekticheskii i istoricheskii materializm (st[udent] III kursa RGI, L. Potemkin)," undated manuscript (the notebook bears a stamp showing that it was produced in 1935).
63. Potemkin, diary, t. 5, ll. 52, 57–58ob (after 9/28/1935).
64. Ibid., ll. 5ob–6 (10/1/1934), ll. 97ob–98 (9/23/1936).
65. Ibid., l. 98.
66. The correspondence with Ira Zhirkova went on for more than thirty years; interview with Potemkin, 4/20/2002.
67. Potemkin, correspondence, l. 76 (letter from Zhirkova, 1/14/1938), ll. 23 (to Zhirkova, after 11/11/1937), 62 (from Zhirkova, 11/21/1937).
68. Ibid., ll. 15, 134 (to Zhirkova, 11/1937 and 3/27/1938). Potemkin's reference to the greenhouses of socialist culture was not entirely metaphorical. The culture of the Stalin era represented itself in terms of warmth and lushness, to underscore its vitalist aspirations. In the

1930s Moscow was dotted with kiosks selling cold drinks and ice cream, which were intended to make the wintry city resemble a summer resort. In the same spirit many government offices were decorated with potted palm trees. See Vladimir Papernyi, *Architecture in the Age of Stalin: Culture Two* (Cambridge: Cambridge University Press, 2002), 132–134.

69. Potemkin, correspondence, l. 61 (to Zhirkova, after 11/24/1937).
70. Ibid., ll. 18 (from Zhirkova, 11/11/1937), 22–27 (to Zhirkova, 11/1937).
71. Ibid., ll. 129–130, 132 (to Zhirkova, 3/9/1938, 3/27/1938).
72. Ibid., ll. 85, 112–113 (from Zhirkova, 2/2/1938, 3/2/1938). I thank Jan Plamper for suggesting the term "utopian melancholia."
73. Ibid., l. 139 (to Zhirkova, 4/13/1938), l. 128 (to Zhirkova, 3/9/1938); Potemkin, "Strategiia zhizni," l. 8.
74. Potemkin, correspondence, title page.
75. Ibid., ll. 100–101 (to Zhirkova, 3/20/1938).
76. Potemkin, diary, t. 5, l. 11 (1/1935); correspondence, l. 52 (from Zhirkova, 11/24/1937).
77. Potemkin, correspondence, l. 123 (to Zhirkova, 2/23/1938). Lydia Ginzburg, *On Psychological Prose* (Princeton: Princeton University Press, 1991), 16, 60.
78. Potemkin, correspondence, ll. 8, 73–74, 130 (to Zhirkova, 11/1937, 1/1938, 3/9/1938). On Belinskii see, e.g., A. Malinkin, "Neistovyi Vissarion," *Molodaia gvardiia,* 1936, no. 6; G. Brovman, "O Belinskom i Pushkine," ibid.; A. Bubnov, "O V. G. Belinskom," *Ogonek,* 16 (6/30/1936); A. Lavretskii, "Realizm Belinskogo," *Oktiabr',* 1936, no. 6; G. Brovman, "Velikii kritik," *Novyi mir,* 1938, no. 6; I. G. Avtukhov, "Pedagogicheskie vzgliady V. G. Belinskogo," *Sovetskaia pedagogika,* 1938, no. 6. None of these publications, and none of the speakers who cited Belinskii at the Tenth Komsomol congress, invoked him directly as an ideal for Soviet personality formation. This was Potemkin's own contribution.
79. Potemkin's copious excerpts from Belinskii are contained in two notebooks: "V. G. Belinskii," and "V. G. Belinskii. Tom 2 (1840–1842)."

80. In this entry Potemkin confided his physical desire for a woman he did not love. He was relieved that he had not become involved with her and had preserved his "spiritual purity," and he added: "Perhaps she will have to tell the people *(obshchestvu)* about me." Potemkin, diary, t. 5, ll. 84ob–85 (summer or fall 1936). This is a telling indication of the way surveillance structures—the danger of being denounced as immoral, and hence also as politically unreliable—fed into his desire to live a moral existence.
81. M. Iovchuk, *Belinskii: ego filosofskie i sotsial'no-politicheskie vzgliady* (Moscow: Sotsekgiz, 1939), 3. Belinskii referred to himself as a member of "an unlucky generation weighed down by the curse of its time, an evil time! . . . The new generation gladdens me: it is full of life and devoid of the rotten habit of introspection." Ginzburg, *On Psychological Prose,* 79–81.
82. Potemkin, "Strategiia zhizni," ll. 6–6ob, 3. Scattered notes stuck inside the booklet indicate that Potemkin wanted to use the text and his correspondence with Zhirkova for a larger publication in the form of a correspondence or a discussion on current ideals of personal life and the new forms of humanity. Ibid., l. 2ob.
83. Ibid., ll. 4, 10–11ob, 3, 5ob, 6ob. Potemkin cited books from which his self-training instructions were presumably borrowed: Mendel'son, *Vospitanie voli;* Nechaev, *Sila voli i sr. ee vosp-ia* [*sic*]; Andreev, *Dnevnik samokontrolia.* Ibid., ll. 27ob, 31ob, 39.
84. Ibid., ll. 3ob, 7ob.
85. Ibid., l. 6ob; Potemkin, diary, t. 5, ll. 76–76ob (8/1936).
86. Grois, *Total Art of Stalinism,* 55–56. Interview with Potemkin, 4/11/2004.
87. He cast the biographies of his family members in much the same light; Potemkin, "Rodnye istoki," 129, 141, 155.

7. Stalin's Inkwell: Alexander Afinogenov

1. Alexander Afinogenov, "Fear," in *Six Soviet Plays,* ed. Eugene Lyons (Boston: Houghton Mifflin, 1934), 410–411.
2. A. N. Afinogenov, *Izbrannoe v dvukh tomakh,* t. 1: *P'esy, stat'i, vystupleniia*

(Moscow: Iskusstvo, 1977), 548; see also Boris Wolfson, "Staging the Soviet Self: Literature, Theater, and Stalinist Culture, 1929–1939" (Ph.D. diss., University of California, Berkeley, 2004), 140–182.

3. Afinogenov wrote *Fear* in 1930 against the background of the trial of the Industrial party, which also figures in the diary of Zinaida Denis'evskaia. He wanted to explore the conflicted inner world of the bourgeois specialists and thus explain how they could commit the monstrous deeds of which they were accused. See Julie A. Cassiday, *The Enemy on Trial: Early Soviet Courts on Stage and Screen* (DeKalb: Northern Illinois University Press, 2000), 176–181.
4. On Stalin as literary critic, see K. M. Simonov, *Glazami cheloveka moego pokoleniia. Razmyshleniia o I. V. Staline* (Moscow: Izd-vo Agentsva pechati Novosti, 1988).
5. A. V. Karaganov, *Zhizn' dramaturga: Tvorcheskii put' Aleksandra Afinogenova* (Moscow: Sovetskii pisatel', 1964), 8–9; Afinogenov's 1933 autobiography is cited from Nikolai Afanas'ev, "Ia i On. Aleksandr Afinogenov," in *Paradoks o drame. Perechityvaia p''esy 1920–1930kh godov* (Moscow: Nauka, 1993), 358–359. Aleksandr's father, Nikolai, published under the pseudonym N. Stepnoi.
6. See Edward J. Brown, *The Proletarian Episode in Russian Literature, 1928–1932* (New York: Columbia University Press, 1953).
7. RGALI, f. 2172, op. 2, ed. 49, l. 2.
8. *Pervyi vsesoiuznyi s''ezd sovetskikh pisatelei*, 5.
9. A. Kemp-Welch, *Stalin and the Literary Intelligentsia, 1928–39* (New York: St. Martin's, 1991), 129–130. According to Nikolai Afanas'ev, Afinogenov was the "generally acknowledged leader" of Soviet playwrights of the period; Afanas'ev, "Ia i On," 346; see also Wolfson, "Staging the Soviet Self," 14–51.
10. In his address to the Congress of Soviet Writers, Afinogenov defended the "new" Soviet usage of "soul" against an orthodox Marxist view that he cited from an encyclopedia: "Marxist psychology has done away with the notion of the soul, proving it to be immaterial and unscientific." *Pervyi vsesoiuznyi s''ezd sovetskikh pisatelei*, 429.

11. Karaganov, *Zhizn' dramaturga,* 221–224, 241; A. O. Boguslavskii and V. A. Diev, *Russkaia sovetskaia dramaturgiia. Osnovnye problemy razvitiia, 1917–1935* (Moscow: Izdatel'stvo Akademii nauk SSSR, 1963), 301–375.
12. See Katerina Clark, *The Soviet Novel: History as Ritual,* rev. ed. (Bloomington: Indiana University Press, 2000), 6–15.
13. *Gor'kii i sovetskie pisateli: Neizdannaia perepiska* (Moscow, 1963), 34. As Wolfson shows in "Staging the Soviet Self," the characters of *Lie* had to be cast in ambiguous terms to ground the play's dynamic of progressive psychological clarification.
14. RGALI, f. 2172, op. 3, ed. 10, ll. 118–119; f. 2358, op. 1, ed. 413, l. 13; Karaganov, *Zhizn' dramaturga,* 297; Afanas'ev, "Ia i On." The reworked *Lie* was not published until 1982: *Sovremennaia dramaturgiia,* 1982, no. 1. As Afinogenov later recalled, he had an hour-long conversation with Stalin in late 1933, during which they discussed the play's shortcomings (see diary entry of 9/11/1937; all quotations from Afinogenov's 1937 diary are from RGALI, f. 2172, op. 3, ed. khr. 5).
15. See, e.g., B. Polianskii, "Krivoe zerkalo (O p'esakh Afinogenova)," *Sovetskoe iskusstvo,* 12/11/1936.
16. RGALI, f. 2172, op. 2, ed. khr. 82, l. 13–14.
17. Afinogenov's earnings are mentioned in the diary of Kornei Chukovskii, who was told by a fellow writer, Il'ia Il'f. K. I. Chukovskii, *Dnevnik 1930–1969* (Moscow, 1994), 78. See also Afinogenov, *Izbrannoe,* t. 2, 76 (letter to a friend from an NKVD health spa on the Black Sea, summer 1935); idem, "Dnevnik 1937 goda," *Sovremennaia dramaturgiia* 1993, no. 2, 234 (photo of Afinogenov in his Ford); RGALI, f. 2358, op. 3, ed. 63, ll. 23ob–24; f. 2358, op. 1, ed. 413, l. 19. Pasternak: RGALI, f. 2565, ed. 55, ll. 1–3. Jenny (Evgeniia Bernardovna, 1905–1948), née Schwartz, had met Afinogenov while touring the Soviet Union with a modern dance ensemble. She was his second wife. The couple had two daughters, Dzhoia (Joy, born 1937) and Aleksandra (born 1942). Marriages and liaisons between Russian Communist men and Western women were not uncommon in the Soviet art world.
18. The dachas belonged to the Union of Writers and were leased to care-

fully chosen residents. In turn, the Union of Writers was entitled to the rights of all literary works produced at the colony. Alexis Berelowitch, "Peredelkino: le village des écrivains," in *Moscou 1918–1941,* 199–212; Stephen Lovell, *Summerfolk: A History of the Dacha, 1710–2000* (Ithaca: Cornell University Press, 2003).

19. Afinogenov's diary notes from before 1937 are preserved in two parts: (1) the rump diary of each year, and (2) folders of clippings from the diary arranged by themes, such as "mode of life" *(byt),* "things," "celebrating the New Year," "children," "thoughts and feelings," "theater," "music." RGALI, f. 2172, op. 1, ed. khr. 124.
20. Afinogenov, *Izbrannoe,* t. 2, 330, 336.
21. Ibid., 273, 336.
22. A. N. Afinogenov, "Rasstavanie," undated, in personal archive of A. A. Afinogenova, Moscow; the context suggests that the note was written in 1934. Igritskii: RGALI, f. 2172, op. 2, ed. 82, l. 13.
23. Afinogenov, *Izbrannoe,* t. 2, 338 (undated, 1935), 226 (undated, 1934).
24. RGALI, f. 2358, op. 1, ed. 413, l. 23 (letter to Nikolai Petrov, 12/10/1934). Afinogenov first invoked the role of theater as a church in his speech at the Congress of Soviet Writers, referring to a remark by Lenin. *Pervyi vsesoiuznyi s"ezd sovetskikh pisatelei,* 431.
25. RGALI, f. 2172, op. 1, ed. khr. 119 (8/14/1936). See also *Izbrannoe,* t. 2, 401 (undated, 1936).
26. Gigantic strides: RGALI, f. 2172, op. 3, ed. 5 (1/30/1937).
27. *Pravda,* 8/17/1934, quoted in Jeffrey Brooks, *Thank You, Comrade Stalin! Soviet Public Culture from Revolution to Cold War* (Princeton: Princeton University Press, 1999), 116. *Pervyi vsesoiuznyi s"ezd sovetskikh pisatelei,* 279.
28. *Pervyi vsesoiuznyi s"ezd sovetskikh pisatelei,* 279, 429–431. *Molodaia gvardiia,* 1936, no. 5, 18.
29. RGALI, f. 2358, op. 1, ed. 413, l. 23; *Pervyi vsesoiuznyi s"ezd sovetskikh pisatelei,* 430.
30. *Pravda,* 11/28/1936, 8. RGALI, f. 2172, op. 1, ed. 119 (11/29/1936, 12/2/1936). *Izbrannoe,* t. 2, 80 (letter to B. V. Shchukin, 1/7/1937)

31. On the campaign for inner-party democracy, see Getty, *Origins of the Great Purges,* 137–163. RGALI, f. 2172, op. 3, ed. 5 (3/17/1937, 4/5/1937). Very few passages from Afinogenov's voluminous 1937 and 1938 diary were published in the 1977 edition (*Izbrannoe,* t. 2). Scholars were granted access to the original diary only after 1991. Selections have since appeared in A. Afinogenov, "Dnevnik 1937 goda," *Sovremennaia dramaturgiia* 1993, no. 1, 239–253; no. 2, 223–241; no. 3, 217–230.
32. *Pravda,* 3/29 and 4/1/1937. Eugenia Ginzburg, *Journey into the Whirlwind* (New York: Harcourt Brace Jovanovich, 1975); O. V. Khlevniuk, *1937-i: Stalin, NKVD i sovetskoe obshchestvo* (Moscow: Respublika, 1992), 137–138. *Literaturnaia gazeta,* 3/30/1937, 5.
33. *Pravda,* 4/4/1937, 1. RGALI, f. 2172, op. 3, ed. 5 (4/5/1937). In 1936 Afinogenov had severed his friendship with Kirshon, who had been his connection to Iagoda, so he was no longer invited to Iagoda's home. Other writers, including Gorky, Isaak Babel', and Vsevolod Ivanov, were known for seeking the company of NKVD leaders. See Vitaly Shentalinsky, *Arrested Voices: Resurrecting the Disappeared Writers of the Soviet Regime* (New York: Free Press, 1996); RGALI, f. 2172, op. 3, ed. 5 (1/1/1937, 9/10/1937).
34. *Pravda,* 4/23/1937, 1–3; *Literaturnaia gazeta,* 4/26/1937, 2. RGALI, f. 631, op. 2, ed. khr. 220 (minutes of the meeting).
35. *Komsomol'skaia Pravda,* 4/29/1937, 4; 4/30/1937, 4.
36. *Literaturnaia gazeta,* 5/15/1937, 1; see also RGALI, f. 2172, op. 3, ed. 5 (5/20/1937). RGALI, f. 2172, op. 3, ed. 5 (4/3/1937, 5/18/1937, 7/7/1937). It possible that Afinogenov escaped arrest because of his complete confession, while Kirshon's denials may have hardened the suspicion that he was concealing his anti-Soviet essence, and thus led to his arrest. Between April 20 and May 6, 1937, Kirshon wrote four letters to Stalin in which he stressed the purity of his Bolshevik conscience. He also complained that a press report had named "Afinogenov's slanderous and anti-Soviet play, *Lie*" on a par with his own works. Only in the last lines of the fourth letter did Kirshon embark on self-criticism: through his involvement with the "criminal, Iagoda" he had

"become corrupted, both as a Communist and as a person." "Ia okazalsia politicheskim sleptsom. Pis'ma V. M. Kirshona I. V. Stalinu," *Istochnik,* 2000, no. 1, 83, 89.

37. RGALI, f. 2172, op. 3, ed. 5 (4/29/1937). Residents of Peredelkino who became victims of the purge included Isaak Babel', Bruno Iasenskii, Boris Pil'niak, Artem Veselyi, and Vladimir Zazubrin. Berelowitch, "Peredelkino."
38. RGALI, f. 2172, op. 3, ed. 5 (4/29/1937).
39. "Rebirth," *New Catholic Encyclopedia,* vol. 12 (New York: McGraw-Hill, 1967), 123–125; Clark, *The Soviet Novel,* 174.
40. RGALI, f. 2172, op. 3, ed. 5 (4/29/1937).
41. *Literaturnaia gazeta,* 5/20/1937, 1. RGALI, f. 2172, op. 3, ed. 5 (5/2/1937).
42. RGALI, f. 2172, op. 3, ed. 5 (4/30/1937, 5/2/1937). If, as Afinogenov wrote, the Hungarian writer and Communist Béla Illés poisoned himself, he survived. Illés (1895–1974) lived in the Soviet Union between 1923 and 1945 and was a leading official of RAPP until the organization was disbanded in 1932. This affiliation probably spelled trouble in 1937, although what exactly happened to him during the purges is unclear. See *A magyar irodalom története,* vol. 6 (Budapest: Akadémiai kiadó, 1966), 412–413; *Kratkaia literaturnaia entsiklopediia,* vol. 3 (Moscow: Izdatel'stvo "Sovetskaia entsiklopediia", 1966), col. 85.
43. RGALI, f. 2172, op. 3, ed. 5 (5/20/1937).
44. Ibid. (5/25/1937; see also 6/2/1937).
45. Ibid. (6/8/1937, 7/26/1937).
46. Ibid. (7/26/1937).
47. Ibid. (7/19/1937). Afinogenov likened himself to Robinson Crusoe a number of times during this period. The story of Crusoe has long been recognized as a "laicized transposition" of the Puritan autobiography. On the island, Crusoe reaches a point of conversion through intense study of the Bible. He recognizes that his exile is God's punishment for his sin of not heeding his father's wish that he not go to sea. See George A. Starr, *Defoe and Spiritual Autobiography* (Princeton: Princeton University Press, 1965); RGALI, f. 2172, op. 3, ed. 5 (5/1/1937).

48. RGALI, f. 2172, op. 3, ed. 5 (7/7/1937).
49. Ibid. (7/29/1937).
50. Ibid. (8/4/1937, 8/9/1937).
51. Russians who lived under Stalin's regime often refer to this phenomenon as a split consciousness or a "dual soul" *(dvoedushie)*. See L. A. Gordon and E. V. Klopov, *Chto eto bylo? Razmyshleniia o predposylkakh i itogakh togo, chto sluchilos' s nami v 30–40e gody* (Moscow: Izd-vo polit. lit-ry, 1989), 221–242; Kotkin, *Magnetic Mountain*, 225–230.
52. Halfin, *Terror in My Soul.*
53. Kathleen M. Swaim, *Pilgrim's Progress, Puritan Progress: Discourses and Contexts* (Urbana: University of Illinois Press, 1993), 139.
54. RGALI, f. 2172, op. 3, ed. 5 (9/10/1937, 9/11/1937, 10/2/1937, 10/3/1937, 10/25/1937).
55. Ibid. (9/24/1937); from May to October 1937 alone, this pattern can be identified in 21 entries.
56. Ibid. (5/20/1937).
57. Ibid. (8/16/1937).
58. Afinogenov's daughter confirms that in the late summer of 1937 her father was sitting, literally, on a packed suitcase. Interview with Aleksandra Afinogenova, 12/19/2004.
59. RGALI, f. 2172, op. 3, ed. 5 (6/26/1937, 9/21/1937, 9/23/1937, 11/3/1937, 11/17/1937). See also E. B. Pasternak, *Boris Pasternak: biografiia* (Moscow: Izd-vo "Tsitadel'," 1997).
60. See his description of the arrest of his neighbor Valerian Pravdukhin: RGALI, f. 2172, op. 3, ed. 5; 8/17/1937.
61. Ibid. (9/9/1937).
62. Ibid. (9/1/1937).
63. Ibid. (9/12/1937).
64. Ibid., ed. 5 (12/18/1937, 12/22/1937). The novel was never completed. The first nine chapters appeared in 1958: A. N. Afinogenov, "Tri goda," *Teatr,* 1958, no. 3.
65. RGALI, f. 2172, op. 3, ed. 5 (10/11/1937; see also 12/18/1937).
66. Ibid. (9/4/1937).

67. Ibid. (9/5/1937).
68. Ibid. (10/7/1937).
69. Ibid. (11/4/1937, 11/16/1937).
70. Ibid. (12/30/1937).
71. RGALI, f. 2172, op. 3, ed. 6 (2/3/1938).
72. Ibid.
73. Ibid. (2/3/1938, 2/4/1938); Afinogenov, *Izbrannoe,* t. 2, 83 (letter to N. V. Petrov, 12/2/1938).
74. RGALI, f. 2172, op. 3, ed. 6 (3/16/1938). The novel was *The Fulfillment of Desires (Ispolnenie zhelanii),* 1934–35.
75. RGALI, f. 2172, op. 3, ed. 6 (2/7/1938, 2/8/1938, 2/9/1938, 2/10/1938).
76. RGALI, f. 2172, op. 2, ed. 43, ll. 195, 198 (2/15/1939, 2/27/1939); Afanas'ev, "Ia i On," 348. *Her Children's Mother* premiered in late 1939. In March 1941 the Moscow Mossovet theater staged another new play by Afinogenov, *Mashen'ka.* It proved a sellout and continued to be performed widely after the war. To the extent that Afinogenov is remembered today, he is chiefly remembered as the author of *Mashen'ka;* Afinogenov, *Izbrannoe,* t. 1, 551–552.
77. RGALI, f. 2172, op. 2, ed. 43, l. 201 (no date, 1939); ed. 44, l. 4.
78. Ibid., ed. 44, l. 3-3ob (7/1/1941).
79. Karaganov, *Zhizn' dramaturga,* 515. On the fifth anniversary of Afinogenov's death the writer Boris Gorbatov remarked: "He died a very good death. . . . There is something symbolic about this death. It is the death of a Bolshevik, a Communist, such as we all knew Afinogenov." RGALI, f. 1614, op. 1, ed. 255, l. 13. On Soviet Communist notions of death, see Halfin, *Terror in My Soul.*
80. RGALI, f. 2172, op. 2, ed. 44 (7/1/1941).
81. This self-conception as a historical subject prompted Nikolai Bukharin to write a letter "To a Future Generation of Party Leaders." He composed it on the eve of his arrest and urged his wife to learn it by heart so that its message would survive beyond his death. Bukharin addressed his last plea at his trial to "world history" as a "world court of judgment." See Anna Larina, *This I Cannot Forget: The Memoirs of*

Nikolai Bukharin's Widow (New York: Norton, 1993), 343–345; *The Great Purge Trial,* ed. Robert Tucker and Stephen Cohen (New York: Grosset & Dunlap, 1965), 667.

82. Pasternak: RGALI, f. 2565, ed. 55, ll. 1–2. Igritskii: RGALI, f. 2172, op. 1, ed. 256, ll. 12–13.
83. RGALI, f. 1614, op. 1, ed. 255, ll. 22–24.
84. On Fedorov see Chapter 2, and Irene Masing-Delic, *Abolishing Death: A Salvation Myth of Russian Twentieth-Century Literature* (Stanford: Stanford University Press, 1992).
85. Afinogenov's life keeps being rewritten. The 1977 Soviet edition of his diary censored his individualist moods of 1937 and portrayed him as a steadfast Communist, but a more recent publication privileges precisely these sections and casts him as a subject who resisted the Stalinist regime. Afinogenov, *Izbrannoe,* t. 2; idem, "Dnevnik 1937 goda."

8. The Urge to Struggle On

1. See, notably, Arthur Koestler, *Darkness at Noon* (New York: Bantam, 1968).
2. TsDNA, f. 336, op. 1, ed. khr. 32 (7/28/1932).
3. Irina Paperno, "Sovetskii opyt, avtobiograficheskoe pis'mo i istoricheskoe soznanie: Ginzburg, Gertsen, Gegel'," *Novoe literaturnoe obozrenie,* 68 (2004); idem, *Chernyshevsky and the Age of Realism.*
4. Dobrenko, *The Making of the State Writer;* Fitzpatrick, *Education and Social Mobility.*
5. See Yves Cohen, "La co-construction de la personne et de la bureaucratie: de la subjectivité de Staline et des cadres industriels soviétiques à travers de nouveaux usages des sources (années 30)," in *The Relations between Individual and System under Stalinism,* ed. Heiko Haumann and Brigitte Studer (Munich: Chronos, 2005).
6. *Golgofa,* 51 (3/1/1938).
7. For this criticism, see Eric Naiman, "On Soviet Subjects and the Scholars Who Make Them," *Russian Review* 60/3 (July 2001), 307–315; see also the forum entitled "Analysis of Soviet Subjectivity Practices,"

Ab Imperio 2002, no. 3, 217–402. The relationship between coercion and desire is brilliantly discussed in Lahusen, *How Life Writes the Book*, 41–61.

8. The dimension of moral self-cultivation is not discussed in scholarly accounts of Soviet censorship. See A. V. Blium, *Sovetskaia tsenzura v epokhu total´nogo terrora: 1929–1953* (St. Petersburg: Akademicheskii proekt, 2000); Herman Ermolaev, *Censorship in Soviet Literature, 1917–1991* (Lanham, Md.: Rowman and Littlefield, 1997).
9. *Golgofa*, 62 (3/19/1938).
10. See Grois, *The Total Art of Stalinism.*
11. See, apart from the diaries of Arkadii Man'kov and Ol'ga Berggol'ts, Nikolai Bukharin's final words at his trial, quoted on p. 411n81.
12. See Nikolai Ustrialov's, Arkadii Man'kov's and Zhenia Rudneva's diaries ("'Sluzhit' rodine prikhoditsia kostiami . . .'," 71 (2/18/1937); Man'kov, *Dnevniki 30-kh godov*, 75–78 (7/31/1933); Rudneva, *Poka stuchit serdtse*, 52 (1/11/1938); see also Régine Robin, *Socialist Realism: An Impossible Aesthetic* (Stanford: Stanford University Press), 114–148.
13. Georges Sorel, *Reflections on Violence*, ed. Jeremy Jennings (Cambridge: Cambridge University Press, 1999); Ernst Jünger, *Storm of Steel* (London: Allen Lane, 2003); Walter Benjamin, "Critique of Violence," in Benjamin, *Reflections: Essays, Aphorisms, Autobiographical Writings* (New York: Harcourt Brace Jovanovich, 1978); Clark, *Petersburg.*
14. OR RGB, f. 442, op. 1, ed. khr. 10 (11/9/1936); "Dve liubimykh," in Evgenii Evtushenko, *Vzmakh ruki. Stikhi* (Moscow: Molodaia gvardiia, 1962), 126–127; see also Svetlana Boym, *Common Places: Mythologies of Everyday Life in Russia* (Cambridge, Mass.: Harvard University Press, 1994), 65.

Note on Sources

Most of the diaries analyzed in this book became available to scholars with the opening of the Soviet archives during perestroika and after the implosion of the Soviet Union in 1991. Some of them are from former Soviet state and party archives. Though composed by political activists, writers, and artists loyal to the Soviet regime, they remained classified until the end of that regime for fear of their incendiary content. Others had been accessible in state archives for a long time. Still others come from "social archives," which were founded during the collapse of the regime to house documentary collections of persecuted individuals and political groups, or to collect personal documents from ordinary Soviet citizens. These unofficial institutions quickly built a sizeable inventory of autobiographical records that provide a counterpoint to the administrative and institutional perspectives that tend to predominate in state repositories. Yet other personal records have been made available by surviving diarists themselves or their families. Several of the diaries discussed at length in this book are from private archives, and in a number of cases I was also fortunate enough to meet the diarists. Our conversations were invariably rich and fascinating, though not always free of clashes in opinion and interpretation. The active involvement of these diarists served as a vocal reminder of the ethical challenges involved in treating as historical sources documents which form an intimate part of their authors' lives.

NOTE ON SOURCES

Impressive in number, the known personal records from the Stalin era appear to form only the tip of an iceberg. The greatest untapped repositories are the central and regional archives of the former NKVD, the Stalinist secret police, to which foreign researchers still have virtually no access. The few diaries that have been unearthed from these archives bear underlinings and remarks made by state prosecutors that offer insights into how the diarists' recordings were received and interpreted. Innumerable other diaries are scattered in private households across the post-Soviet realm. There is reason to fear that many of these records may never become available to scholars, because their current owners are unaware of their historical significance and consider them intensely personal records, awkward exercises in prose, or ephemeral texts, unfit for the historian's eye.

A sustained initiative to collect and inventory the autobiographical record of the Soviet past would surely yield great riches—scores of personal documents, not just from the early Stalin period but from the war years and the postwar decades as well. Some efforts are being made to create such inventories, but what they will achieve remains to be seen. Organizations like "Memorial" and the "People's Archive" are chronically underfunded and survive largely thanks to the enthusiasm and dogged persistence of their small staffs. They must contend with a social environment that is painfully adapting to the market economy and has lost much of its former interest in questions of social and cultural identity. Compounding this drop in historical awareness is the reluctance of Russia's current political leaders to come to terms with the legacy of the Communist regime and confront fundamental issues of political continuity and moral responsibility. To confront such issues would stir debate and risk social divisions, but the very terms of the debate would also foster the type of civic culture on which a political democracy can thrive.

Critical scholarship engaging autobiographical voices from the Soviet past cannot avoid their present-day reverberations. In analyzing Stalin-era diaries, it is crucial to reflect on the changing political conjunctures that account for why, at a particular time, particular documents are deemed to be of historical value and therefore are preserved in archives or showcased in published form. Such a critical perspective also helps us register the invisible personal sources that do not conform to the historical and political interests of their day and therefore do not make their way into an archive or a publication. Whereas diaries and memoirs published at the height of the Stalinist regime invariably portrayed their authors as enthusiastic Soviet citizens, during the post-Stalin thaw the diaristic hero acquired more complexity. Witness the publication of Nina Kosterina's diary in 1962. Kosterina, a Moscow schoolgirl and komsomolist who died as a partisan in the Second World War, wrote in her diary of her difficulty in coming to terms with her father's arrest in 1937 as an "enemy of the people." Kosterina's heroism consisted in her continued devotion to Communist values despite the distress and injustice she suffered in her personal life. Invoking the spirit of Khrushchev's reforms, diaries published in the early perestroika period featured devoted Communist diarists who suffered under Stalinism but nevertheless defended the values of the party. As perestroika failed, diaries more critical of the Soviet order appeared in print, and scholars began to study diaries as sites of resistance to Stalinism.

Diaries have played and continue to play an active role in the writing and rewriting of the experience of the Stalin period. Present-day politics of historical representation also affect the work of historians who consult personal testimonies as historical evidence. Still, historians are able to adopt a critical stance, by reflecting on the political and epistemological shifts that explain why a given diary is deemed to be of interest at a given time and why it is hence retained in an archive or published. Such a perspective helps us appraise an archive or a documentary publication, not as a transparent window into the past, but as an instituted site of memory construction, heavily implicated in the political and moral questions of the present.

NOTE ON SOURCES

Archives Consulted

Russian State Archive for Literature and the Arts, Moscow

Manuscript Division of the Russian State Library, Moscow

State Archive of the Russian Federation, Moscow

Russian State Archive of the Economy, Moscow

Russian State Archive for Social-Political History, Moscow

Documentary Center "People's Archive", Moscow

"Memorial" Society archive, Moscow

Solzhenitsyn Fund archive, Moscow

Bakhrushin Museum archive, Moscow

State Archive of the Kalinin region, Tver'

State Archive of the Sverdlovsk region, Ekaterinburg

Private archives of Aleksandra A. Afinogenova, Marina S. Gavrilova (née Podlubnaia), Leonid A. Potemkin, Liliia Riazanova, and Valentina Krugleeva (Moscow); Arkadii G. Man'kov (St. Petersburg); and Viacheslav Ul'rikh (Heidelberg)

Guidebooks and Bibliographies

Dokumenty lichnogo proiskhozhdeniia v arkhivnykh uchrezhdeniiakh severo-zapadnogo federal'nogo okruga Rossiiskoi Federatsii. Spravochnik (St. Petersburg, 2002)

Istoriia dorevoliutsionnoi Rossii v dnevnikakh i vospominaniiakh. Annotirovannyi ukazatel' knig i publikatsii v zhurnalakh, ed. P. A. Zaionchkovskii, 5 vols (Moscow: Kniga, 1976–1989)

Lichnye arkhivnye fondy v khranilishchakh SSSR. Ukazatel' (Moscow, 1963–1980)

Otkrytyi arkhiv. Spravochnik opublikovannykh dokumentov po istorii Rossii XX-go veka iz gosudarstvennykh i semeinykh arkhivov (po otechestvennoi periodike 1985–1995 gg.), ed. I. A. Kondakova, 2nd rev. ed. (Moscow: ROSSPEN, 1999)

Putevoditel' po fondam i kollektsiiam lichnogo proiskhozhdeniia (Moscow: Rossiiskii tsentr khraneniia i izucheniia dokumentov noveishei istorii, 1996)

Sovetskoe obshchestvo v vospominaniiakh i dnevnikakh: annotirovannyi bibliograficheskii ukazatel' knig, publikatsii v sbornikakh i zhurnalakh, ed. V. Z. Drobizhev, 4 vols. (Moscow: Kniga, 1987–2000)

Tsentral'nye arkhivy Moskvy. Putevoditel' po fondam lichnogo proiskhozhdeniia, ed. A. A. Kats (Moscow: "Mosgorarkhiv", 1998)

Vospominaniia i dnevniki XVIII-XX vekov. Ukazatel' rukopisei (Moscow: Biblioteka im. Lenina, 1976)

See also the "Personal Archives" sections in the multivolume series of guidebooks to state archives throughout the Russian Federation, published under the general title *Arkhivy Rossii* (Moscow: Zven'ia, 1999–)

Acknowledgments

This book would not exist without the support that I have received from many people and institutions, and I want to express my deep appreciation to them. Ben Eklof kindled in me a passion for Russian history. The fascination with the worlds of the peasantry that I developed in his seminars took me to the doorsteps of the People's Archive in Moscow where the story of this book began. I thank the staff members of the People's Archive, the Russian State Archive for Literature and the Arts, the Manuscript Division of the Lenin Library, the State Archive of the Russian Federation, the Russian State Archive of the Economy, the Solzhenitsyn Fund, the Bakhrushin Museum, and the State Archive for Social-Political History for their expertise and hospitality. They offered help whenever I was lost in a diarist's handwriting or in passages that appeared to make no sense. I am particularly indebted to Galina Popova and Galina Akimova at the People's Archive, and to the archivists at the State Archive for Literature and the Arts, for their selfless support over many years. I thank Leonid Potemkin, Stepan Podlubnyi, Tat'iana Leshchenko-Sukhomlina, and Arkadii Man'kov, all surviving diarists from the Stalin era, for their trust and patience. Our conversations about their diaries were intense and unforgettable. Marina Gavrilova (née Podlubnaia) and Aleksandra Afinogenova provided valuable information about their diary-writing fathers and kindly invited me to their homes. Véronique Garros, Natalya Korenevskaya, and Thomas Lahusen generously shared with me dozens of diaries they had located in a large number of Russian archives. I am grateful to Oleg Gorelov, Valentina Krugleevskaia, Liliia Riazanova, Semen Vilenskii, and Viacheslav Ul'rikh for directing me to yet further diaries. In Moscow, Al'bert Nenarokov, Arsenii Roginskii, and Larisa Zakharova supported my research in important ways. Because of Andrei Belizov, every visit to Moscow feels like a homecoming.

At Columbia University, Leopold Haimson taught me to approach historical actors with open eyes and ears. He immediately saw the significance of the documents I showed him, and he guided my research with analytical acuity and fatherly care. The unfailing support, critical engagement, and encouragement I received from Mark von Hagen and Richard Wortman were crucial for the writing and completion of the book. Stephen Kotkin provided revelatory insights. Frances Bernstein, Frederick Corney, Andrew Day, Anna Fishzon, Igal Halfin, Peter Holquist, Nadieszda Kizenko, Nathaniel Knight, Yanni Kotsonis, Laurie Manchester, Kenneth Pinnow, Charles Steinwedel, and Amir Weiner generated a wonderful sense of camaraderie and shaped my thinking in decisive ways. Igal Halfin, Peter Holquist, and Jan Plamper invited me on a prolonged journey of intellectual discovery and self-discovery. Many ideas expressed in this book originated in discussions with them, in the rooms and hallways of the Harriman Institute, the Indian restaurant around the corner, and beyond. I treasure their friendship. Other friends and colleagues read the manuscript, in portions or in its entirety, and generously shared comments and criticisms. I thank in particular Irina Paperno, Bill Rosenberg, Laura Engelstein, Boris Gasparov, Eric Naiman, Boris Wolfson, Gabor Rittersporn, Susanne Schattenberg, and Stefan Plaggenborg for detailed and helpful suggestions. Discussions with Jörg Baberowski, Yves Cohen, Michael David-Fox, Malte Rolf, Martin Sabrow, Karl Schlögel, Stefan Troebst, and Albrecht Wiesener helped me situate my research in broader contexts. The book was completed at Rutgers, where the breadth and depth of my colleagues' historical imagination has proven infectious. I am especially indebted to Belinda Davis, Ziva Galili, Paul Hanebrink, Catherine Howey, Jackson Lears, Phyllis Mack, and Bonnie Smith. I also thank the participants at conferences and seminars in the United States, Europe, and Russia where I presented my work in progress. It has been a privilege to work with Joyce Seltzer, my editor at Harvard University Press. Joyce believed in the project from the day she heard about it, and her unfailing advice has benefited the book tremendously. As manuscript editor for the Press, Camille Smith performed incisive interventions that were instrumental in bringing the narrative into shape. Special thanks to Alfonso Rutigliano, who helped me coin the title.

Research and writing were supported by grants from the Studienstiftung des Deutschen Volkes, Columbia University, the Michigan Society of Fellows, the Fritz Thyssen Stiftung, the Rutgers Center for Historical Analysis, and the Zentrum für Zeithistorische Forschung in Potsdam. Portions of this book are adapted from work published elsewhere and used here by permission: parts of Chapters 3, 5, and 7, respectively, from "Working, Struggling, Becoming: Stalin-Era Autobiographical Texts," *Russian Review* 60/3 (July 2001): 340–359; "Fashioning the Stalinist Soul: The Diary of Stepan Podlubnyi (1931–1939)," in *Jahrbücher für Geschichte Osteuropas 1996,* 3: 344–373; and "Writing the Self in the Time of Terror: Alexander Afinogenov's Diary of 1937," in *Self and Story in Russian History,* edited by Laura Engelstein and Stephanie Sandler, copyright © 2000 by Cornell University, used by permission of the publisher, Cornell University Press.

I am profoundly indebted to my parents. Their steady support and encouragement is the foundation on which I stand. And Katinka fills my life with joy. I dedicate this book to her, with love.

Index

The names of diarists whose writings are discussed in the book appear in bold.